ARCHITECTURE AND RETRENCHMENT

ARCHITECTURE AND RETRENCHMENT

NEOLIBERALIZATION OF THE SWEDISH MODEL ACROSS AESTHETICS AND SPACE, 1968–1994

Helena Mattsson

BLOOMSBURY VISUAL ARTS
LONDON • NEW YORK • OXFORD • NEW DELHI • SYDNEY

BLOOMSBURY VISUAL ARTS
Bloomsbury Publishing Plc
50 Bedford Square, London, WC1B 3DP, UK
1385 Broadway, New York, NY 10018, USA
29 Earlsfort Terrace, Dublin 2, Ireland

BLOOMSBURY, BLOOMSBURY VISUAL ARTS and the Diana logo are trademarks of Bloomsbury Publishing Plc

First published in Great Britain 2023
Paperback edition published 2024

Copyright © Helena Mattsson, 2024

Helena Mattsson has asserted her right under the Copyright, Designs and Patents Act, 1988, to be identified as Author of this work.

Cover design: Karolina Eriksson
Cover image: A concrete element to be used in "Bofill's Arc," Södra Station, Stockholm. Photographer unkown © Maud Livén

All rights reserved. No part of this publication may be reproduced or transmitted in any form or by any means, electronic or mechanical, including photocopying, recording, or any information storage or retrieval system, without prior permission in writing from the publishers.

Bloomsbury Publishing Plc does not have any control over, or responsibility for, any third-party websites referred to or in this book. All internet addresses given in this book were correct at the time of going to press. The author and publisher regret any inconvenience caused if addresses have changed or sites have ceased to exist, but can accept no responsibility for any such changes.

A catalogue record for this book is available from the British Library.

Library of Congress Cataloging-in-Publication Data
Names: Mattsson, Helena, 1965- author.
Title: Architecture and retrenchment : aesthetics, spatial practices and the neoliberalisation of the 1980s welfare state / Helena Mattsson.
Identifiers: LCCN 2022035435 (print) | LCCN 2022035436 (ebook) | ISBN 9781350148222 (hardback) | ISBN 9781350365681 (paperback) | ISBN 9781350148239 (pdf) | ISBN 9781350148246 (epub) | ISBN 9781350148253
Subjects: LCSH: Architecture and society–History–20th century. | Architecture–Political aspects–History–20th century. | Welfare state.
Classification: LCC NA2543.S6 M3823 2023 (print) | LCC NA2543.S6 (ebook) | DDC 720.1/03–dc23/eng/20220729
LC record available at https://lccn.loc.gov/2022035435
LC ebook record available at https://lccn.loc.gov/2022035436

ISBN:	HB:	978-1-3501-4822-2
	PB:	978-1-3503-6568-1
	ePDF:	978-1-3501-4823-9
	eBook:	978-1-3501-4824-6

Typeset by Integra Software Services Pvt. Ltd.

To find out more about our authors and books visit www.bloomsbury.com and sign up for our newsletters.

To my mother

CONTENTS

Preface	viii
Introduction: Constructing the Supermodel	1
Site 1: The Model (1968)	19
Site 2: The Suburb (1968)	45
Corporatism	57
Site 3: The Collective House (1935–94)	63
Human Capital	97
Site 4: The Globe (1982–9)	103
The Code	123
Site 5: The Postmodern Housing Area (1981–7)	131
Emancipation	151
Site 6: The Renewal (1985–94)	157
Epilogue: Elephant & Castle	179
Notes	185
References	233
Index	251

PREFACE

In the face of the polarized positions and violent confrontations of the present moment—including clashes on matters of climate crisis, migration, housing shortage, and escalating economic and social inequality—the call for a politically and socially engaged architecture is pressing. But the role of architecture in societal change is far from obvious. While architecture clearly does not stand outside politics, its political complicity and contribution to societal change is not easy to pinpoint. This book results from my engagement with questions pertaining to architecture's changing social contract and the discipline's decreasing involvement in the creation of the common good. For many years, I have tried to think through the architecture-politics-society-complex together with colleagues, friends, and students within architecture and in fields such as history, anthropology, economic history, media studies, philosophy, and art. My ambition to understand how the discipline branches out and materializes ideas in relation to a physical reality has led me to view architecture in an expanded sense.

In returning to a number of late-twentieth-century sites within architecture—places and moments where alternatives were in fact put forward, debated, and superimposed—it is my hope that this book might contribute to knowledge about how architecture acts upon the world. The book does not shy away from describing the tangled character of these realities by deferring to more utopian accounts (even if such dreams were often present). In each example discussed, we witness a tug-of-war between different interests; the forces of change vary radically between the different cases. Instead of showcasing "good examples"—which tend to exclude the more complicated aspects of a project's realization—I rather attempt to locate points where a range of different actors and intentions became enmeshed, interacting in such a way as to *intervene in* and *shift* the processes that are already at work in the situation.

Architecture is central to a society's aesthetic sensibility, living environment, and systems of cultural representation; it motivates political decisions and takes part in processes of state formation through its interactions with laws, decision-making processes, and representation. The architects who were embedded within the developments discussed in this book did not have the possibility to stand outside that which transpired around them—as such, this account of their work offers a timely reminder that even today, the architecture discipline must be understood as always performing some form of "social support function." *Architecture and Retrenchment* is thus a book for those who find themselves operating outside of the comfortable interior of the architecture discipline or those who are curious to explore the battlegrounds that surround that disciplinary interior.

Preface

The present publication stands in relation to *Swedish Modernism: Architecture, Consumption and the Welfare State* (the anthology that I edited in collaboration with Sven-Olov Wallenstein, 2010), which in part stemmed from a frustration with the limitations and path dependencies that dominated Swedish architectural history at that time. That book focused on one of the most mythologized and "heroic" events in the country's architectural history: the advent of early modernism and the formation of the welfare state through the *Stockholmsutställningen* exhibition in 1930 and the manifesto *acceptera* from 1931. If the idealization of the Swedish model that occurred in the opening years of the twenty-first century demanded critical interrogation at that time, today we rather confront a situation whereby that model has, as the result of its restructuring, become unrecognizable: the neoliberal struggle for freedom turns out to have been accompanied by a neoconservative, populist, and authoritarian movement, which acts as its afterimage.

Architecture and Retrenchment is written from within this changed ideological landscape and its primary task is not to ask whether or not the Swedish model existed but, rather, to identify the various models (Swedish or otherwise) that were in operation in the field of architecture in the twentieth century. What was architecture's role in the neoliberalization of Sweden? The transformations that occurred at the end of the twentieth century were as radical, in their own way, as those that occurred in the 1930s, and they form a history that Sweden shares with many other Western countries. How, the book asks, were the spatial and aesthetic articulations of a series of new social models respectively interwoven, resisted, or constructed? How did some models come to dominate and how did others become marginalized? I understand the historical processes described here as conflictual and replete with battles. As such, that which we now view as a process of neoliberalization may in fact in the future be understood to have led to something entirely different.

*

This book would not have been possible without collaborations. Most of the material has been presented and discussed in so many different contexts that it is impossible to trace all the important input I have received over the years. Together with Catharina Gabrielsson, I ran the research project Architecture of Deregulations, which has been an invaluable opportunity to develop ideas elaborated on in this book; I am grateful to Catharina for the countless stimulating discussions. Another cornerstone is my ongoing collaboration with Meike Schalk and Sara Brolund de Carvalho in Action Archive. Without their vision of architecture and participation, which encouraged me to reflect on the historiography, many silenced witnesses would never have started to speak. I also want to thank my colleague Jennifer Mack for her extraordinary capacity to see the big picture in the details. This book draws on first-hand experiences, and I would like to thank, among others, Gunilla Lundahl, Kerstin Kärnekull, and all the other members of BiG, and the architects Svante Berg and Ylva Larsson for their generous contributions.

Preface

I am grateful to everyone in the collaboration Exploring Nordic Models of Architecture and Welfare for the vivid perspectives on welfare far beyond the Nordic context, and especially I want to thank Thordis Arrhenius and Guttorm Ruud. Discussions with my Danish colleagues Heidi Svenningsen Kajita and Svava Riesto in our impromptu "solidarity group" have shed special light on the Nordic welfare model, and as a member of the advisory board for Spaces of Danish Welfare run by Kirsten Marie Raahauge I have been able to take part in a rewarding research environment.

Innumerable conversations and seminars with colleagues, students, and PhD students at KTH, Stockholm, have inspired me to take steps in directions not earlier explored. My special thanks go to Anders Bergström, Bojan Boric, Brady Burroughs, Hélène Frichot, Katja Grillner, Christina Pech, Helen Runting, and Erik Sigge for providing a rich intellectual climate. Ongoing conversations over many years have had an important impact on my thinking and especially I want to thank Sven-Olov Wallenstein, Reinhold Martin, Mary McLeod and Joan Ockman.

Many important conversations have been held in conjunction with lectures and presentations, and I wish to thank Tom Avermaete, Pier Vittorio Aureli, Petra Brouwer, Salomon Fausto, Janina Gosseye, Maros Krivy, Andres Kurg, Hilde Heynen, Mari Lending, and Tim Verlaan for providing such opportunities. I am grateful for a fellowship in 2018 at Architecture Criticism History (ATCH), University of Queensland, and the conversations with John Macarthur, Janina Gosseye, and Deborah van der Plaat. I also wish to thank Eeva-Liisa Pelkonen for her generosity in inviting me to a visiting fellowship at Yale in 2022, and Jenny Andersson and Orsi Husz for inviting me to join in the invaluable discussions in the network Neoliberalism in the Nordics. My warmest thanks go to friends and colleagues who have commented on parts of this book and provided important feedback: Irina Davidovici, Isabelle Doucet, Janina Gosseye, Jennifer Mack, Kristina Riegert, and Meike Schalk. I am thankful to Riksbankens Jubileumsfond, whose generous sabbatical grant made it possible to finish the book. I also wish to thank the publishers, Bloomsbury, and the anonymous reviewers for their insightful comments, and Charlotte Merton and Helen Runting for being protectors of the English language in any and every situation.

Finally, my thanks are for Mattias Tydén, who has been my greatest inspiration, toughest critic, sharpest reader, and most loving partner.

INTRODUCTION: CONSTRUCTING THE SUPERMODEL

When the "the next supermodel" appeared on the cover of *The Economist* in February 2013, he was armed with a Viking helmet and a face ready for war, the message "Why the world should look at the Nordic countries" printed across his breast.[1] This cover story followed up on "The New Model: A Bit More Unequal, a Lot More Efficient," a piece published in the magazine the year before.[2] Both articles conveyed the same message: the restructuring of the Nordic model of welfare had been, in comparison to other countries, *extraordinary* in terms of the speed and efficiency with which market mechanisms had been introduced. The narrative was clear: thanks to "an extensive overhaul of the welfare state, Sweden's economy has been transformed in the two decades since its banking crisis." The new model was thus presented as an example of "how to reform the public sector, making the state far more efficient and responsive"—to such an extent that, with reference to the standard market-based reform-package of the 1989 Washington Consensus, "Milton Friedman would be more at home in Stockholm than in Washington, DC."[3]

Architecture played a pivotal role in the formation of the "supermodel" described above; entangled with market deregulations, the discipline helped to drive the emerging logics of financial speculation forward. The new model first reached full operating capacity following the bank crisis in the early 1990s, when Sweden's overheated property market imploded, resulting in a slew of bankruptcies and shutdowns; architecture and building's realpolitik had thereby ushered in a deep economic crisis that left Swedish society and welfare in flux.[4] Once the cornerstone of the welfare state, architecture now played a decisive part in its demolition. How could architecture's role have changed so dramatically? From a form of public investment under Keynesian politics (acting on the labor market and constituting a form of capital for the state), architecture became an asset for public and private investors. Today, we live in the aftermath of this shift: not only has architectural production almost entirely disassociated itself from social welfare, but the built environment itself has become deeply inscribed in the derivative market and is now to a large extent determined by acts of speculation performed in relation to the future value of a given "asset."

Despite the radical nature of the sociopolitical changes witnessed in the early 1990s, which were as important as those that occurred in Sweden in the 1930s, this shift was not instantaneous: it was the result of processes that gradually transformed the welfare state from within, over a much longer period of time. Various state institutions, administrations, and bureaucratic systems all took part in these changes, which engaged most societal functions, including the discipline of architecture. This uneven process of gradual transformation not only affected policy making, economics, and forms of governing within the Swedish welfare state, it also—and perhaps more importantly—affected ways of thinking and what can be termed "a neoliberal reason."[5] In turn, this reorganization of notions of value and the common good established the grounds for the emergence of a new cultural and aesthetic landscape. This book investigates the redefinition of the relationship between architecture and society that occurred through this slow and gradual transformation of all sectors of society.

Thomas Piketty has demonstrated that, by the end of the twentieth century, inequality again began to drastically increase, a development he describes in terms of a "return" to the societal conditions of the period preceding the welfare state.[6] In *The Asset Economy*, Lisa Adkins, Melinda Cooper, and Martjin Konings build on Piketty's work in order to show that what we are experiencing today is not simply a return to the inequalities of the early 1930s, but the effects of a systemic change that has permeated the very fabric of social life.[7] Today, the authors show, as a result of policy changes and institutional reconfigurations pursued since the 1980s, the ownership of assets generates more income than salaries. Furthermore, the "democratized asset ownership" (e.g., housing and real estate) that is made possible through loans and debt has ensured that buy-in to this system is not only a possibility for the richest but a reality for all citizens.[8] With these developments in mind, this book contributes to existing knowledge about architecture's role in the long and slow shift into neoliberalization, whereby resources and commodities became assets for future profits through processes of democratization, participation, and emancipation.

This is not, however, a book about architecture as an asset, viewed through the logics of today's finance capitalism. Rather, it is an examination of how architecture was comprehended and used as a *resource* for neoliberalization—and deployed as such in acts of state retrenchment, privatization, and marketization. Through it, I revisit a conflictual landscape, which is redolent with contradictions and opposing forces, at a point when things were still in formation.[9] This was a moment when movements and countermovements interacted with, and worked through, architecture; architecture was thus mobilized in the service of contradictory goals. This is a blurry and murky path to walk. The entanglements of architecture and neoliberalization, often embedded in phenomena associated with other ideological agendas, are not always easy to detect and have tended to attract less critical attention from scholars of these processes.[10] Today, however, it is impossible to maintain that architecture stands outside the neoliberalization of the welfare state. Similarly, it must be acknowledged that the new welfare model which came to the fore in Sweden relied on state-led retrenchments and renewals, and a state-led neoliberalization of the built environment. As a result, this book dissects the reconstruction of the Swedish model of welfare from the perspective of architecture's engagement in state affairs, showing that this engagement brought about wide-reaching effects that affected individuals, market actors, and civil society as a whole.

A growing body of literature exists which addresses questions of welfare in architectural history of the recent past,[11] and a number of works by younger scholars have examined

Introduction: Constructing the Supermodel

such histories in relation to the Swedish context.[12] Despite the increasing volume of research on the relation between architecture and neoliberalism, a gap still remains in the architectural historiography of the discipline's role in the neoliberalization of the welfare state and thus its capacity to change society.[13] One reason for this gap might lie in the dominance that theories of architectural autonomy, often with a basis in art history, have exerted in defining canonical thinking about architectural history.[14] A challenge thus lies in locating intertwined understandings of aesthetic and spatial practices and the architectural object, and particularly ways to refigure the latter in terms of a constellation of multiple, material, and immaterial forces. Therefore, the contemporary history outlined in *Architecture and Retrenchment* tries to expand the notion of "architecture" in order to understand, on the one hand, how the discipline became a resource (and potential asset) for several actors in steering the transformation of the welfare model, and, on the other, the ways in which architecture itself was affected by the shift. In this task, the book draws on earlier work such as *Architecture and the Welfare State* by Mark Swenarton, Tom Avermaete, and Dirk van den Heuvel, and employs concepts not only from architectural history and theory but also from welfare studies, economic history, and other related subject fields.[15]

Despite the fact that I address events that played out in Sweden (and particularly in Stockholm), the local context is treated as an inseparable part of broader international political, economic, and social geographies. What may seem unique about a given situation is, after all, often shared with sites far beyond the edges of a national context; as such, I chose to focus on the role that such situations play in materializing forces that are understood as being simultaneously local and global. Today, it is not possible to talk about the nation state as a determining factor without acknowledging its intersectional character, as something inextricably crossed by lines of class, gender, race, geography, climate, politics, materials, and social conditions. While the example I discuss *situate* the often abstract and generalized discourse of neoliberalism in particular spaces, they also hold a geographic relevance that extends beyond Sweden's borders. The structure of the book is, as a result, deliberately designed to combine detailed readings of local situations with both more theoretical and more general thematic discussions. Empirically rooted *sites* are interleaved with more discursive *themes*, which elaborate on concepts that I see as crucial to architecture's role in the societal transformations that are the focus of this book.

Mapping the Borderland

Architecture and Retrenchment can be read as an incomplete map of the borderlands where architecture and neoliberalism came together, structured around six particular sites of "tension and restructuring" between 1968 and 1994. The narrative takes its point of departure in the critique of the Swedish model in the late 1960s, exploring two perspectives—those of the activists and the private enterprise—in order to demonstrate how notions of exclusion and inequality became foundations for a critique of modern architecture and of the welfare state. Through a series of empirical inquiries into the domestic sphere (housing) and spaces for leisure (a multi-arena and cityscapes), domains central to the welfare model's regulation of private and common space, I show how architecture was understood as a tool for societal transformations through state retrenchments and concomitant reorganizations. Unfolding over time and in space, the sites that I engage with emerged from the midst of moments when concepts changed in their meaning and means and ends switched places. As such, it is only by means of a local excavation that one can reach the deep lines that connect these sites, at their most intimate microscale, with the national and even global macroscale shifts which gave rise to their formation.

By considering architecture in terms of a landscape containing diverse networks of things and affects, I hope to reveal perspectives that lie outside of the world of architects. Rather than sole protagonists, in this book architects instead form one category of agents among many, acting within a complex diagram of interests, agendas, regulations, and power structures. Here, my historiographical walks follow in the footsteps of Mary McLeod and her seminal 1989 text "Architecture and Politics in the Reagan Era," which elaborates on the notion that architecture's intersection with politics is twofold: as a production process, architecture is obviously tied into economy and politics, and as a cultural object, it is inseparable from its formal aspects.[16] These dimensions of architecture are at times so deeply connected that they are impossible to distinguish, but at other times they are highly differentiated, independently activating very different worlds. Importantly, this book adds a third point of intersection between architecture and politics, expanding McLeod's twofold scheme to advance a view of architecture as not only a production process or cultural object, but also as a *discourse*.

This way of working requires shifting not only between different disciplinary networks but also between radically different scales. The book therefore drifts between the macroscale of economics and politics (regulations, policies, forms of governance) and the microscale of the subject and everyday life. This perspective also aligns with methods advanced by scholars of neoliberalism and the built environment who, like Jamie Peck, stress the value of connecting large-scale, abstract readings with "on the ground" specific situations—what Peck calls a "relational neoliberalization."[17]

Over the course of the 1980s and early 1990s, citizens were confronted with not only a series of societal transitions but also an administrative apparatus that had taken on a radically new form. Architecture was one of the infrastructures that supported these changes. To give an example, a 1993 memorandum from a meeting between inhabitants, the architects, and the Stockholm public housing company Familjebostäder (Family Housing) shifts the perspective from the macroscale of the "supermodel" to the very concrete effects of the same policy on a micro level. The document describes the final phase of an initially ambitious renovation project whereby architects, in line with the newly instigated Planning and Building Act, worked in close collaboration with the residents:

The basements storage is carelesely built [...] nothing is painted. All concrete and rubble remain. It can't be that we are supposed to clean ourselves. In the basement, the pile of faeces that was discovered in April was still there [in October] [...] Is there really no money for cockroach extermination in the one-room apartment? The rebuilding work is at a standstill due to this. [...] A few years ago the balconies fell down in Flemingsberg, were they on similar consoles as ours? The County Council has abandoned the project.[18]

This short report presciently identifies a number of the effects that followed in the wake of the crisis, including: inadequately realized and poorly built architectural projects; the abdication of cleaning responsibilities, which were instead devolved to the inhabitants themselves; internal divisions within public institutions and companies; and the withdrawal of those institutions and indeed the state itself. This was part of an active policy, advanced by the municipality together with the public housing companies, to transfer responsibility from the top to the bottom and thereby prepare inhabitants to take on the role of "property owners" in the coming sale of public housing (which was to turn some into millionaires and plunge others into lifelong debt).

I came across this memorandum in an archive of unsorted documents which had once belonged to the local district committee for the Stockholm suburb of Tensta, an institution that was dissolved during a subsequent period of restructuring. This discovery is rather indicative of the way in which the neoliberalization of the 1980s tended to erase its own tracks by moving things around: papers changed files and files were packed into boxes and then moved to new archives, where they were stacked on new shelves and catalogued differently. Archives constitute memory's infrastructure: the difficulty in locating the microhistories of Swedish neoliberalism indicate that a dilution of our collective memory occurred during this period. Perhaps unsurprisingly, this erasure has tended to affect society's most vulnerable groups (those who, for instance, received benefits)—and these groups were deprived parts of their own histories as a result.

By returning to the sites where architecture became a locus of conflict and moments where overlapping ideologies, needs, and wishes met, this book attempts to retrieve a history that is, at the present moment, largely missing in action.[19] In addressing material that lies outside of the established archives of architectural history, architectural references and art history perspectives have at times been required to take a back seat in this inquiry. This does not mean that architecture has been allocated a secondary role: to the contrary, architecture is my focus, even if I understand the discipline as operating within an "expanded field" wherein overlaps and connections can be traced between the aesthetic, spatial, and linguistic qualities of architecture and the categories of the social, the economic, and the political. The category "architecture" is impossible to define; it is under continuous transformations and takes on a variety of cultural meanings. Architecture is here addressed as an *assemblage* that is made up of material and immaterial components (e.g., discourses, drawings, models, bricks, concrete, architects, building workers, politicians, and planners),[20] and each site that I address is treated as a rich source of not only material but also narrative accounts—as a result, witness seminars and other oral history methods have also been employed in the task of constructing particular archives.[21]

If we understand these sites as the battlegrounds that they once were, the word "retrenchment"—a word, foregrounded in the title of the present work, generally understood as a synonym for austerity, layoff, or downsizing—takes on new meanings and associations. My decision to use "retrenchment" also consciously alludes to the military meaning of the term, which describes the creation of defensible structures inside, or behind, a fortification. Through the architecture discipline's engagements in neoliberalization, new assemblages (movements and countermovements) and retrenchments emerged, whereby space and material were articulated anew—and as the Swedish Model was "remodeled," architecture itself was also re-constructed. *Architecture and Retrenchment* thus plays upon the conceptual ambiguity of the term "retrenchment" to invoke the multifarious ways that architecture has actively constructed (and perhaps even fortified) new worlds and new subjectivities that have both collaborated in and resisted neoliberalization. Beyond engaging in acts that *defended* architecture through expressions of resistance, some of the architectural protagonists addressed in this book also created new constructions that managed to traverse and at times even offer lines of escape beyond existing disciplinary fortifications.

Postmodernism can be understood as one such "retrenchment" in the battleground that is architecture's disciplinary interior. The term "postmodernism" does not, however, play a prominent role in this book; while I do not avoid the concept, it is discussed only when invoked in the material that is being examined; such occasions are, however, rare—other concepts turn out to be more active in the debates and archives addressed here. There is another reason for my reluctance to make postmodernism a dominant perspective. In favoring other spaces, sources, and archives in the writing of this work, I found that the void created by postmodernism's absence left room for other interpretations. As Reinhold Martin argues, to critically speak of a neoliberal architecture, we need to "denaturalize" categorized periods, such as "modern architecture," and move away from architecture as a "timeless invariant." Instead, we must study how neoliberalism reshapes architecture as a regime of cultural significance.[22] In line with this thinking, this book foregrounds four alternative themes where concepts and techniques take on new meanings: corporatism, the code, human capital, and emancipation. Corporatism and the (building) code were, for example, systemic and legally instigated infrastructures that played crucial roles in the creation of a democratic, universalist society and were deeply involved with the architecture. Whilst only two of many infrastructures that were part of the neoliberalizations of the 1980s, in the material discussed in this book these stand out as areas where radical shifts took place. The themes of human capital and emancipation, in contrast, demonstrate two of the shifts in mentality that accompanied neoliberalization.

Introduction: Constructing the Supermodel

The Welfare Model: The Middle Way

To speak of existing social and political structures in terms of "models" is to enter a fraught territory from the outset—this terminology brings with it a range of problems. Whether it takes the form of a physical architecture model, a scientific description, or a mathematical model, a "model" generally constitutes an abstract image of an existing reality or a clear set of instructions regarding how a given operation shall be undertaken. Similarly, the idea of a Nordic, Scandinavian, or Swedish model (the nomenclature changes) implies the existence of a static model of governance that is not subject to change. This is, of course, not the reality of the matter. The idea of a singular Swedish model has created a highly simplified understanding of how Swedish society has functioned and been governed, which in turn has led to idealization on one hand and demonization on the other. Acknowledging this issue, recent scholarship has sought to problematize and dissolve existing static understandings of the Swedish model.[23] The aim of writing a more complex and open history has, further, sought to challenge the tendency to focus on the dominant influence exerted by the Social Democrat Party in order to make room for other actors (and conflicts) to take the stage.

In historical accounts of the twentieth-century Swedish model of welfare—often referred to as *Folkhemmet* (The People's Home)[24]—a standard reference has been the North American journalist Marquis Childs's book *Sweden: The Middle Way*, which noted the strength of a system capable of balancing tensions between different interests.[25] The book was written after a visit to the 1930 *Stockholmsutställningen* (The Stockholm Exhibition, an event which introduced modern architecture and design in a Swedish context) and a period of study of the Swedish housing and consumer cooperative movements. Childs's description of Sweden as pursuing a "middle way" between extreme individualism and collectivism, and between communism and capitalism, was widely disseminated and came to form the characteristic image of Sweden already in the 1930s. The formation of the model can, however, also be understood as part of a broader formation of a Nordic modernity and a response to the Great Depression. In the Nordic countries (with the exception of Iceland), the Social Democratic and Farmers' parties (of which the Social Democrats were the largest party) formed coalitions in order to deal with the economic crises of the 1930s.

This "politics of crisis" had its basis in broad political agreements and negotiations between the trade unions and private corporations, and emerging social reforms such as *bostadsociala utredningen* (The Report on the Social Condition of Housing), which lay the groundwork for the coming post-war housing policy.[26] In this, Thomas Piketty argues, Sweden offers an "astonishing example" of the importance of mass mobilization and sociopolitical processes in the transformation of inequality regimes—as he puts it, "Once the most restrictive of ownership societies, Sweden became easily the most egalitarian of social democracies."[27] Architecture was from the start deeply involved in this transformation of inequality. The four pillars of the welfare state—education, healthcare, housing, and social security—relied on qualitative architectural organizations of material and social reality. To deliver this, after the Second World War large-scale state institutions constructed an infrastructure of architectural design and production that included *Bostadsstyrelsen* (The Swedish Housing Board), *Svensk Byggnorm* (Swedish Building Codes), *Byggnadsstyrelsen* (The National Board of Public Building), *Statens Planverk* (Swedish National Board of Urban Planning), and *Bostadsdepartementet* (The Ministry of Housing).[28]

The "first" Swedish welfare state model was, however, short-lived, taking form in the 1930s, only being implemented after the war, and coming to an end in the 1980s. Traditionally, this model has been described as comprising of three elements.[29] The first was a "well-functioning" labor market, characterized by a rare use of strikes and salary levels that were decided by way of collective bargaining, through negotiations between the employer and the union (in the spirit of *Saltsjöbadsavtalet*—the Saltsjöbaden agreement).[30] The second was a large, tax-funded, universal welfare system, the technologies of which were directed at the population as a whole and not selected groups. This system came to characterize housing politics and construction for the entire postwar period. The third element was a corporatist political system (to which an entire chapter of the present volume is dedicated), which is often referred to in terms of *Harpsunddemokratin*, after the name of the large State-owned manor where industrialists, the union movement, and the organizations of civil society met at least once a year.

Danish sociologist Gøsta Esping-Andersen's oft-cited analysis of different welfare regimes stresses "decommodification" as a distinguishing feature of the Scandinavian welfare model, whereby decommodification is defined as "the degree to which [the regimes] permit people to make their standards independent of pure market forces," and in this way "social rights diminish citizens' status as "commodities."[31] It is, however, possible to question the degree to which Sweden has been characterized by "decommodification." When the Social Democrats came to power in 1932, the (then) finance minister Ernst Wigforss introduced a crisis-oriented policy platform which maintained strong similarities to that advanced by John Maynard Keynes in its emphasis on controlling the economy through central planning via "counter-cyclical" policies.[32] In this way, social democracy developed a way to balance socialist and liberal politics, whereby private consumption and entrepreneurialism were supported. Elsewhere, I have outlined how already in the 1930s, in line with the introduction of functionalism, architecture and design were clearly addressed as strategies for producing the consumer: the citizen should be a consumer aligned with a market and in this way they were made governable.[33] The central role that the individual was allocated as a consumer in fact contradicts the decommodification thesis.[34]

Notions of exclusion and inequality were not only starting points for the critique of the welfare state model and its architecture in the 1960s: these concepts were also part of the model's construction and were present from the start. The empowerment of the labor movement was accompanied by a host of exclusions predicated on the basis of gender, ethnicity, race, or other categorizations.[35] The strong housing and consumer cooperative movements, together with the corporatist system, opened up for voices otherwise not represented in the political democratic system; however, the actual effects of these movements can be debated—as we will see, it is, for instance, quite obvious that they did not give voice to important initiatives occurring within the field of architecture. The welfare model that aspired to be universal—to account for *everyone*—was, as it turned out, neither equal nor equitable. Instead, it was plagued by a "gender conflict" which stemmed from the contradictions of a double movement whereby on one hand, democratization and industrialization in the postwar period pushed women into the workplace and the public sphere, and on the other hand, the segregation that was built into the existing gender order held back these tendencies.[36]

This inherent tension, which limited the development of society and architecture, forms a red thread that links many of the sites addressed in this book. It is, however, important to acknowledge that the social contract of the welfare state, which managed to contain and incorporate labor movements in various stages of revolt, segregated not only on the basis of gender but also of race and ethnicity (Site 6).[37] Although conceived in the 1930s, the prerequisite for the construction of the Swedish model in the postwar period lay in the high volume of migrant workers arriving in Sweden: men who worked primarily in factories, and women who worked in factories, healthcare, cleaning, and domestic services. These workers kept an ethnically divided labor market afloat. During the 1970s, though, labor immigration became increasingly regulated and another group entered the workforce in the form of non-immigrant women (Site 3: The Collective House).

Neoliberalization and Retrenchments: The Third Way

The processes of deregulation, privatization, and neoliberalism are not possible to understand in terms of the position of political parties on a traditional left-right spectrum, even though most of the dramatic transformations in Sweden were made under a Conservative government in the early 1990s. Unlike most countries in the Western world, Sweden pursued an expansive Keynesian economic policy during the crisis of the 1970s. When the Social Democrat government lost power in 1976, the same support policy was continued under the Conservative government. It was first when the Social Democrats came back into power in 1982 and introduced a "Third Way" policy characterized by deregulation and neoliberalization that the political strategy radically changed. The Minister of Finance Kjell-Olof Feldt started the "politics of crisis" with a devaluation of Swedish currency that triggered a financial recession. After the devaluation, the high foreign debt level increased costs for the state and increased liquidity for businesses through exports; this transfer of capital to the private sector was the beginning of a more expansive transformation of Sweden.

After a long period of resistance from politicians, the deregulation of the Swedish credit market finally happened on November 21, 1985. Echoing the experience of most other Western countries, this may well be the most important monetary policy decision made in Sweden during the postwar period. It meant that the collateral requirements placed on banks were reduced, which in turn led to real estate and other assets such as shares being mortgaged at a higher value than previously. The Swedish Central Bank's (Riksbanken) control mechanisms had been removed, and individual banks could lend large sums to financial institutions, companies, and households. Speculation and borrowing hysteria ensued. In 1986, Sweden had left the crisis years behind—as a result, Feldt received much praise for his Third Way. Unemployment was low, purchasing power was high, and Swedish society seemed to flourish again, even if this prosperity turned out to be short-lived. The deregulation of the credit market was, however, also heavily criticized both at the time that it occurred and afterward; Ingvar Carlsson, deputy prime minister in the period 1982-6, has called the deregulations a "revolution" that was staged behind his back.[38] Mortgages and property prices increased rapidly during these years; commercial properties could be mortgaged for up to 100 percent of their value. The large amount of capital on the market created extreme growth in the value of real estate. The deepest recession since the interwar years was abruptly triggered when investors canceled payments on loans in the early 1990s and the Swedish Central Bank increased the interest rate to 500 percent for a short period in 1991.[39] However, this crisis was itself relatively short-lived and by 1994, it was over.

Obviously, the real estate and building market played a central role in Swedish economic development during the 1980s and 1990s. Together with shares, properties were the main objects of speculation and the construction industry rapidly "overheated" in the face of high land prices, a construction boom, and strong demand for labor. The housing market and housing policy were also heavily transformed during the 1980s, both as a result of the criticism directed at the Million Program and attempts to cater for demand for commercial properties and offices for the booming private service sector (itself a product of the economic policy of the time).[40] But it was not only private actors that carried out major projects during the 1980s: the municipalities were also key players. The City of Stockholm initiated a number of major housing projects during the 1980s, two of which are discussed in this book: Södra Stationsområdet (1986–91) and the Stockholm Globe City (1985–9).[41]

In most historical narratives, the transformation of the Swedish model at the end of the twentieth century is not labeled as a result of "neoliberalism." The standard accounts are, however, now being questioned on this point, with recent scholarship describing neoliberalism as a long and conflictual process that is not primarily economic but rather systemic.[42] David Harvey has described Sweden as an example of "circumscribed neoliberalization," given that it avoided the dramatic increases in inequality witnessed in the United States or the United Kingdom.[43] This may well be true, but if neoliberalization is viewed as a shift to a new rationality that is based on competition, free choice, and entrepreneurship (this would be a view which aligns with the analysis conducted by Wendy Brown),[44] then Sweden was one of the most progressive neoliberal countries, effectively paving the way in the question of how to reorganize the cornerstones of the earlier welfare state in the form of education, healthcare, and housing. The country has been described as moving from one extreme to another; from the strikes and employee funds of the 1970s to experiments in privatization of a scope unparalleled in the Western world.[45]

This book addresses the Swedish "neoliberal turn" in terms of a sequence of changes that, while they operated within and through existing policies and networks, ushered in a new political economy. The relationships between the Third Way and the knowledge economy outlined by the historian Jenny Andersson in *The Library and the Workshop* is a central theoretical reference here. Andersson argues that the Third Way "contains a distinct interventionism" that goes beyond the former social democracy in order to infiltrate the social sphere, whereby the object of regulation is not the economy but the capital that is located within the worker (and the citizen).[46] Under such a paradigm, goods that were historically considered to be non-economic, such as creativity and curiosity, were turned into new forms of capital; as she puts it: "In the Third Way, social democracy's critique of capitalism has been replaced by a theory of capital, by a theory of how to create value in the knowledge economy."[47]

Three perspectives on the neoliberal project frame the investigations outlined in this book. First, the neoliberal turn is comprehended as a systemic shift, not only in economic or political terms but also in social and even mental ones—it plays out through the introduction of a "neoliberal reason."[48] Second, I draw on scholars who prefer to use the concept of neoliberalization (over neoliberalism), which I understand as an uneven and contradictory process, the local variations of which are constructed by affirmations and resistances that occur on the ground. This position exists in opposition to the use of "neoliberalism" as an ideal and abstract concept relating to a fixed state of being. Third, in line with Michel Foucault's thinking, I relate neoliberalization to a "crisis of governmentality" and to *the biopolitical* in architecture.[49] Through the term "governmentality" (which addresses the "conduct of conduct," or the way in which individuals, groups, and institutions exercise power over one another), we can understand power as being *both* subjugating *and* emancipating, and this perspective forms a thread that runs throughout the chapters of this book: neoliberalization must be understood as *both* enabling certain freedoms *and* instilling particular limitations. Foucault's understanding of the neoliberal as "not identified with laissez-faire, but rather with permanent vigilance, activity and intervention" is furthermore essential to the argument that I will go on to make: namely, that architecture was fully involved, along with other forces, in the very process of neoliberalization.[50] The architecture assemblage has contributed to both continuation and change; it has acted as an institution supporting path-dependency and as a site for the radical transformation of thinking and acting in areas such as policy, the social field, consumerism, and housing.

I have already briefly discussed the concept of "retrenchment," but I will shortly return to it. The term came into use in comparative welfare state research in the late 1980s, and was used primarily in relation to the cutbacks proposed by the Thatcher and Reagan regimes in and around the 1980s, even if they were not fully realized to the magnitude envisaged.[51] The debates around retrenchment intensified in the 1990s with the publication of Paul Pierson's *Dismantling the Welfare State?*, which argued for welfare state "resilience" as an explanation for the lack of large retrenchments.[52] One critique of the concept of retrenchment is that it downplays the role of neoliberalization: by confining itself primarily to economic aspects, it offers a relatively limited perspective that precludes the analysis of major systemic shifts across social, cultural, and ideological registers. I wanted to provide this background, even though it is not the aim of this book

Architecture and Retrenchment

to draw on these theories. My intention here is rather to borrow the concept, with the purpose of employing it within the field of architecture, in terms of a state retrenchment but also, and mainly, as a built (and unbuilt) retrenchment. In many cases, these aspects intermingle—for example, in an urban planning discussion, I note the way in which the limited sphere of action afforded to the City of Stockholm Planning Office in an increasingly market-dominated planning system was met with the use of postmodern architecture and aesthetic regulations as a way to regain power (Site 5).

State retrenchments are in some way present in most of the sites addressed in the book (the exceptions being the first two sites, which take place around 1968), wherein they create events that contribute to the construction of both architecture and the state/society. I understand the *site* as constituting several different things at once: it is an architectural assemblage (a constellation of material and non-material agents) and a "statification" (referencing Foucault's notion of the state as a series of practices); it is also a set of transactions that modify or change "sources of finance, modes of investment, decision-making centres, forms and types of control."[53] The use of assemblage and statification supports the conceptual overlap between architecture and state formation. When looking into each site, the act of retrenchment (both as cutback and as counter-structure) is part of a given statification as much as it is part of the construction of situated, everyday life. This doubled nature reflects architecture's ability to act at a broad range of scales.

Deregulations, Reregulations

The neoliberalization of the 1980s is often described in terms of a dominant character of *deregulation*, but what were the deregulations that are actually being referred to in such accounts? For one, it is important to note that deregulations often lay the groundwork for the introduction of new regulations at a later time—for this reason, it is more reasonable to speak in terms of *reregulations*. In Jamie Peck's understanding of neoliberalization as an uneven process, the notion of initial "roll-back" phases, or deregulatory processes, are followed by constructive "roll-out" phases, which can also be called "reregulations."[54] I will confine the coming discussion of de- and reregulation in this book to four particular aspects of the process, namely: the de- and reregulation of the legal frameworks that protected the public sector (and "the public good") from the effects of market forces; economic deregulation; aesthetic reregulation; and, finally, the reregulation of the building codes.[55] All of these aspects are addressed in the material investigated in this book, and all have, as we will see, pivotal significances for architecture. In the face of the dynamic nature of neoliberalization, it is not possible to separate these processes from one another—the cases discussed here demonstrate how economics, politics, aesthetics, and building regulations are all intertwined in the architectural assemblage of practice and discourse.

While "new public management" (NPM) first made its entrance into Sweden's municipalities in the beginning of the 1980s, it wasn't until the 1990s that this new system of control broke through into mainstream usage.[56] An import from the business world, NPM was adopted in the public sector as a replacement for "progressive public administration" (PPA), with its clear opposition to the commercial interests and markets of the private sector.[57] PPA, which was meant to guarantee an effective public administration, relied on two basic conditions: first, that the public sector was radically different from the private sector and thus required different policy instruments; and second, that this form of governance should be regulated and protected in order to prevent corruption.[58] The implementation of NPM in the 1990s demanded that fundamental changes be made to the concept of "the common good," the role of the individual, and the requirements of market actors. New faith was at this time being placed in the citizen as a responsible consumer, whose power could be exerted over private and commercial markets. This reorientation affected the earlier idea, popularized under the PPA paradigm, that the role of the public sector was to facilitate, to the extent that such a move was possible, the independence of the citizen from the market. Education, health care, and housing were three of the most crucial sectors to protect—these sectors were given similar importance in the transformation toward a new public management.

The other form of deregulation to be addressed here, economic deregulation, began in Sweden in the 1980s, eventually contributing to shifts that culminated in the economic crisis of the early 1990s (Epilogue). As mentioned earlier, the property bubble which resulted from this policy led to the worst economic crisis that Sweden would face in the entire postwar period, leading to a transfer of capital from the public sector to its private counterparts. This redistribution of capital exerted a noticeable influence on urban planning, whereby public actors like the City of Stockholm's Planning Office found themselves occupying a weaker position in the planning process (Sites 4 and 5). A shift in mentality was taking place through new notions of work, leisure, and spatial organization, but also of space and organization more generally. These changes can be observed in the design and realization of a new multi-arena in Stockholm (Site 4).

The third and fourth aspects of deregulation are so deeply integrated that I will address them together: the formal and aesthetic aspects and the building code. The emergence of an aesthetic-regulatory-complex under neoliberalization was driven by a desire to emancipate architecture, and maybe foremost architects, from the alleged burdens of a normative modernism.[59] The postmodern discourse—which revolved around how to find new aesthetic and organizational frameworks—is here understood in relation to radically new economic conditions. The Swedish architectural discourse on postmodernism of the 1980s was characterized by a denial and repression of its own existence, or a "pomophobia" (postmodernism was seen as "American," commercial, and superficial) and instead ideas about returning to the roots of modernism, a search for "neo-modernism" and a "new architecture" flourished.[60] In line with Reinhold Martin's proposal that postmodernism's withdrawal from political and social engagement increased its participation in networks of power, this book shows how Swedish architects' (with few exceptions) avoidance of postmodernism paralleled an increasing engagement in new economic and political networks[61] (Sites 4 and 5). The aesthetic reformulations were thus integrated with a critique of building regulations (and of the broader welfare state bureaucracy), which were targeted by architects and planners for the limitations that they supposedly imposed upon the possibilities of experimentation and variation. Methods of designing housing became controversial. Earlier modernist prioritizations of interior functionality and organization were questioned by those who stressed the value of the exterior space as a designed "room." Socially oriented mass housing on the outskirts of town, delivered through projects that were designed from the inside out, was abandoned for the production of housing for an affluent middle class in the compact inner city, mostly through infill and renovation/rebuilding projects, which coincided with theories on "genius loci" (Norberg-Schulz), the use of historical elements, and deformations of the modernist object (often due to limited sites).[62] The Stockholm City Planning Office employed postmodernist ideas both to encourage "city-likeness" in new development and to control the private sector's increasing influence (Site 5). The Director of Swedish National Board for Urban Planning Lennart Holm accused the planning office of regulating architects against building from the inside outward, referring to the resulting "architectural drama" as a "masquerade and a panegyric over the loss of will suffered in the late 1970s."[63]

It is not, however, possible to equate postmodernism with a neoliberal turn. In the public discussion one can find very different arguments for enhancing the notion of variation and individualization, including neoliberal and anti-capitalist voices, and the arguments that converged to instigate a radical shift in architectural discourse were in themselves highly disparate. The deviation from modernism was, on one hand, seen as a subversive act directed at the capitalist consumer-oriented architecture of the suburbs, which was expendable in its repeated form, and on the other hand, the exterior and urban spaces, which were emphasized as belonging to citizens to such an extent that facades were treated as "walls" of these urban rooms. For more pragmatic economic reasons, politicians saw the diversified housing environment as a reaction to the repetitiveness of the neighborhoods that were built in the 1960s and thus as responses to the popular critique of the welfare state. In the overall call for the deregulation of the building sector, different actors (each with their own specific agenda and goals) also came together. Here, the architectural discipline and its aesthetic-spatial discourse became entangled with forces seeking profit and with conservative/(neo)liberal politicians, all of which in combination worked to fight state regulations.

The Long 1980s

This book starts in 1968 with the calls of urban activists for a new model of a "qualitative society," which would replace the allegedly "quantitative" model of social democratic regulation, bureaucracy, and expertise. The welfare model was attacked from two directions—from the left in the 1960s and from the right in the 1980s. The first critique aimed for more equality and direct democracy, while the second was founded in a vision of a new economic order characterized by a decreased public sector and increased privatization, formulated in part as a call for individual "freedom of choice." "The long

Introduction: Constructing the Supermodel

1980s" thus chart a movement from the activism of the late 1960s to the architectures of the Third Way policy of the 1980s and 1990s. The year 1994, which marks the endpoint of the book, is symbolic in relation to the breakthrough of a neoliberal rationality in Sweden. The Conservative government of Prime Minister Carl Bildt—which came to power in 1991 on the back of a neoliberal promise to bring about a "freedom-of-choice revolution in welfare politics"—had, over the course of the three-year crisis, managed to revoke the existing housing policy platform, dissolve the Ministry of Housing and reformulate the contract between the state and architecture.[64]

When the economy regained its footing in record time in order to overcome this crisis, Sweden "awoke" to a new economic, cultural, and social landscape. The state and public policy instruments that had previously existed across the social sectors, including the built environment sector, were replaced with new investment and policy strategies whereby architecture, like many other fields, was treated as a social and economic asset.[65] In this way, a shift was initiated whereby Sweden became the site of not only one of the greatest public-private debt transfers to ever occur in a Western country but also one of the most radical increases in inequality.[66] This new position, which followed broader political shifts in Western Europe, was less characterized by concrete budget cuts than by the introduction of a new mentality, described by Anthony Giddens in his 1998 *The Third Way* in the following terms: "The restructuring of government should follow from the ecological principle of 'getting more from less', understood not as downsizing but as improving delivered value."[67] This was an attitude that was also underscored at a European level by Tony Blair and Gerhard Schröder, prominent proponents of a model of government whereby "The state should not row, but steer: not so much control, as challenge."[68]

Not only is the present book framed by these two models, but importantly it also rejects the thesis that the 1968 movement paved the way for later neoliberal developments. Rather, I argue the opposite: neoliberalization was a conservative response to progressive societal critique (Site 1). The long 1980s was most often a period when a series of ideas were put in motion; movements and countermovements clashed and interacted. Concepts and ideologies floated around and were often as a result hard to pin down. And corporatist Sweden—with its politicians, business, unions, and interest organizations—rewrote the social contract in the framework of the new economy and policies of the Third Way. This contract, albeit in a more refined form, still governs the discipline of architecture to this day.

Moving through the Book

Six *sites of restructuring* are investigated in this book; these are presented in a loose chronological order—the events discussed are unfolded in time and thereby also overlapping. The first two sites demonstrate aspects of the critique that was levelled at the model, while the subsequent four sites show how neoliberalization took form through already existing institutions, materials, and actors. In each site, architecture plays the lead, although it is sometimes embedded in other disciplines and discourses. In each site, architecture is shown to have become a resource in a particular neoliberalization. I see the sites as fully interconnected in the larger nexus of societal transformation, but the book tries to unfold specific aspects in each chapter. The retrenchments (economic, social, ethical) performed by the public sector—the state and the municipality—and the concomitant responses to them construct a backbone that traverses the different narratives. Four *themes* which I see as being particularly active in the processes of transition—corporatism, human capital, code, and emancipation—punctuate this chronological narrative, vertically cutting across an otherwise horizontal reading of the sites.

Site 1, The Model, analyses urban actions in 1968 and the exhibition *Modellen* from the same year, describing these as early turning points in the discourse on the welfare state and noting the way in which these events articulated a social critique of regulations and bureaucracy. These works questioned the Swedish model, but they also provided models for the creation of a society by future generations—a promise which the 1968 generation never fulfilled. Through architectural experiences, the "system" was supposed to break and take new directions.

The second site, The Suburb, outlines the dark horizon against which the actions discussed in Site 1 played out, demonstrating how architecture and urbanism became targets in the general accusation of the social democratic welfare state government. This site highlights the importance of other actors in the corporatist Swedish system, who today are often hidden in the records. Furthermore, the role played by emancipatory forces stemming from the environmental movement and women's movement are also analyzed.

Picking up on a concept introduced in the preceding site, the first theme—Corporatism—outlines an understanding of architecture as negotiation, dissecting the role of the large-scale architectural project in a corporatist decision-making process involving public, private, and civil actors. Here, I discuss the limits and possibilities embedded in the corporatist system, including the growing emancipatory forces such as feminism and environmental movement which increasingly demanded to be heard.

Site 3, The Collective House, demonstrates how the first wave of collective housing developed in the 1930s only to collapse in the financial crises of the 1970s, and how a second wave took form in the 1980s, materializing a refigured idea of social reproduction and the distribution of labor. I outline how the feminist group Bo i Gemenskap developed a new format for living (and building) in collaboration with developers in the 1990s; the deregulation discourse here plays out in the feminist movement as an act of emancipation.

Following up on discussions in previous chapters, Human Capital elaborates on the theme's relation to architecture in the 1980s through Third Way politics. In this era, growth was understood as essentially being driven by innovation, knowledge, curiosity, and creativity and the chapter elaborates on how a "capitalization" of the social domain and the production of architectural spaces are imbricated.

Site 4 sets out a study of the multi-arena Stockholm Globe Arena in the 1980s, from its planning to its use. This site dissects the planning processes leading up to spatial re-articulations of the public good, overlapping leisure, work, and consumerism. The project saw the creation of new economic networks (public–private partnerships) wherein land became a commodity to trade for the City of Stockholm planning office, and the chapter shows how the architects, and the architecture, became the driving force in this transformation.

Starting with the building code as a practice and a project in continuous flux, the third theme, The Code, discusses how regulations interlace the micro and macro-scale in order to both control the building process and arrange everyday life. The relations between the code and the law demonstrate how two levels of decision making—the spatio-aesthetic and the economic-political—overlap. This chapter also traces the transition from prescriptive to performance-based building codes, following up on discussions raised in The Collective House and The Globe Arena.

Site 5, The Postmodern Housing Area, investigates the processes of de- and reregulation in the Södra Station neighborhood in inner-city Stockholm. Taking the formation of welfare state housing in the 1930s as a backdrop, this chapter investigates the effects of new performance-based building codes in relation to the use of postmodernism in architectural theory. It is shown that in parallel with the emerging codes, new restrictions and programs influenced by postmodernism began to regulate the public sphere and the planning process.

The last theme, Emancipation, tries to understand a series of liberatory forces that exerted crucial impacts on the very notion of architecture through their re-articulation of the relationships between civil society and the state. This chapter shows how the feminist and environmental movements in architecture were crucial, not only in the architectural discourse on postmodernism of the 1980s, but also for the development of techniques relating architecture to the forces stemming from the market. Drawing on Nancy Fraser's discussion of a "triple movement," these emancipatory forces are, I reveal, deeply related to macro-economic matters.

Site 6, The Renewal, returns to discussions from previous chapters in order to analyze the "community building" and participatory planning projects initiated by the City of Stockholm in the suburb of Tensta. It demonstrates how ideas from the civil protests of the 1970s were transferred into the sphere of new public management in the 1990s. Contrary to the intentions of these projects, the chapter shows how the discourse on participation contributed to a policy of discrimination and public retrenchment.

The Epilogue, The Elephant & Castle, elaborates on the pivotal crises of the 1990s and its effects on our contemporary situation. This chapter also gives a summary of the main topics addressed in the book.

Figure 1.1 The exhibition *Modellen* at Moderna Museet, Stockholm, 1968. Photographer: Unknown. Courtesy: Moderna Museet.

SITE 1
THE MODEL (1968)

Upon entering Moderna Museet in October 1968 one was instantly immersed in a large-scale play environment. The visit started by going through the restaurant and into a room with piles of quilted jackets and rows of shoes, where kids gathered in front of TV screens set up by researchers and educators to show a feed from the adjacent playroom. Children were pointing at one another on the screens, and took turns to run into the surveilled room while the others watched reality play out onscreen.[1] Inside the exhibition *Modellen* (The Model) it was full of playing children and a handful of adults, building, hammering, and jumping from a wooden climbing frame into a sea of foam-rubber pieces. The noise was intense; shrieks, laughter, and loud voices that drowned out most other sounds. The children of the 1960s—the generation that became adults in the 1980s and 1990s—built, with hammer and nail, a reality of their own that, simultaneously for the adults, was the promise of the future: a model for a qualitative society. Here, the children were—to use Foucault's expression—the "ability-machines," the promise for realizing what the 1968 generation never managed.[2]

Modellen, made by the urban activists Action Dialogue (Aktion Samtal) and the Danish artist Palle Nielsen, was a sharp criticism of the Swedish welfare state and its architecture for being too bureaucratic, paternalistic, and regulated.[3] Olof Palme, when minister of education and soon to be prime minister, visited *Modellen* and was pictured throwing himself headlong into the foam rubber (Figure 1.2). This was a new image for a Swedish politician, tearing himself away from rational, bureaucratic regulations to prioritize other qualities of life. In hindsight this image signifies not only a jump by an individual into the unknown, but also the "fall" of the welfare state itself, a nosedive in which the built environment played a central role. A few weeks before the photo was taken, the inauguration of the Stockholm suburb Skärholmen had prompted a storm of debate about the built environment of the welfare state, which further enforced the popular expression *betongsosse* (lit. concrete leftie) to label sluggishly old-fashioned social-democratic politicians.[4] When Olof Palme became prime minister in 1969 he had to face urgent calls to better incorporate the citizen into the creation of the built environment, and public claims for a more varied, individualized, and small-scale environment.

In this opening chapter I address how that criticism of the welfare state and its architecture, initiated by what has been called the first Swedish "environmental guerrillas" Action Dialogue, explored new formats of criticism highlighting bodily experience, media, and communication, but also how the criticism can be understood in relation to later developments.[5] The group's actions combined a critique of architecture—the

Figure 1.2 Olof Palme, minister of education, jumping into foam rubber when visiting the exhibition *Modellen*, Moderna Museet, 1968. Photographer: Olle Seijbold / DN / TT.

lack of citizen participation, the experts' dominance, the bureaucracy—with criticism of the welfare state, and garnered a great deal of media attention that popularized their views outside the profession.[6] The attack on the governance of the built environment was directed at the limitations of the social-democratic welfare state, which was constructed on the exclusion of groups such as women and non-experts and on inequalities, as revealed, for example, by Låginkomstutredningen (the official inquiry into low incomes) which was appointed in 1965.[7] There were blind spots in the criticism of the built environment, however, and a large one was the role played by private actors in a corporatist planning system.[8] In a twisted version of Manfredo Tafuri's notion of the death of modern architecture caused by the alliance between the state and capitalism, the retrenchment, if not death, of the modern welfare state was effected by the alliance between capitalism and modern architecture.[9] Thus the chapter examines several themes in Action Dialogue's practices, articulated from within a Swedish Model which was in crisis, and which reoccur in new ideological formations in relation to later neoliberalization discussed in this book. When unpacking this pre-history of neoliberalization, the tensions and interdependence of movements and countermovements are prominent, but other realities still possible to imagine are also laid bare.

In *Modellen* the children were ability-machines who could be invested in, in this case with experiences of the built environment, to generate future transformations. Much has been written about the relationship between the 1968 movement's political criticisms and the emerging neoliberal agenda in the 1990s, and a great many interpretations have been presented.[10] Some scholars stress the importance of understanding neoliberalization as a consequence of the 1968 movement, while others see it as a conservative countermovement to the emancipation and proposed new order of the late 1960s. I will take a slightly different perspective. Instead of focusing on the question of cause and effect, I return to a situation where concepts and techniques were formulated where modernist welfare society crossed with new ideological formations (and new forms of governance). In this, I follow the trajectory of struggles between ideologies as played out in architecture, to understand what different realities and proposals were put up against one another. I find it valuable today to return to moments when discourses which were diametric opposites politically and ideologically were braided together in architectural assemblages, and when the criticism of regulations, governance, and bureaucracy was bound up with notions of solidarity and equity.

The mainstream histories describe the period of the Swedish 1968 movement as confrontational, albeit less aggressively so than Paris in May 1968. In the literature the battles between the political left and right are often in focus, and 1968 has gone to history as a period of political violence, when norms, rules, and value systems were questioned and torn down. In this chapter I want to unpack another history of urban action that, instead of confrontation, used strategies based on communication, participation, and the creation of new models for a future society. The 1968 urban activists cannot unambiguously be identified with the political left, but, influenced by the "new left," they stressed the importance of redefining all criticism.[11] Aligning with what Isabelle Doucet calls "criticality-from-within," Action Dialogue deviated from a Marxist Frankfurt School tradition of critical theory based on distance. Instead, their actions expressed an "embodied criticality" that called for the subject to actively participate in the exhibition, to physically participate and become active performative subjects.[12] This was all about affirming new worlds rather than criticizing the old world, or what Jacques Ranciér would call the "demonstration of existence."[13] I will discuss how these demonstrations established new connections between formats of criticism, techniques of mediation, and forms of participation, which, besides solidarity and equality, operated in the later capitalization on the aesthetic, experiential realm.

Urban Action Takes Shape

On May 3, 1968, the same day as riots broke out in Paris, violent demonstrations took place in Båstad, a small city in the south of Sweden, against a tennis match between Sweden and Rhodesia.[14] The Båstad demonstration was soon followed by other protests, such as Kårhusockupationen (the occupation of the Student Union Building in Stockholm), demonstrations against the Swedish industrial company ASEA's involvement in constructing the hydroelectric power station at Cabora Bassa (today Cahora Bassa) in Mozambique, and a "hunger strike" in front of the Swedish Parliament protesting against low levels of Swedish foreign aid and famine in the Third World.[15] The confrontations between the demonstrators and the police led to intense discussions about the nature of societal governance, democracy, and police violence, and on to fierce criticism of the party in power, the Social Democrats.

The hunger strike was different in its political ambitions, being one of the first "category actions" to focus on a theme rather than a political standpoint. The event was described in the largest national newspaper, the liberal *Dagens Nyheter*, as "a rare fraternization that broke all traditional party boundaries."[16] The social-democratic government had to balance criticism not only from the activists, but also from the Swedish Communist Party about police violence and from the conservatives for communicating with the activists and allegedly giving into their violent methods. In a parliamentary debate in May 1968, Prime Minister Tage Erlander defended his position, which was to meet and negotiate with the protesters. He argued that there was a dividing line between peaceful demonstrators and activists, but that the Social Democrats by tradition had discussed and debated with the Swedish Communists: "Where would we have been today if we had not started a systematic struggle with them on the parapets and in basements? That's the way we beat them off and made them an insignificant sect."[17] The demonstrations and protest meetings that began that May were followed by other actions in the spring and summer, and the attacks on social-democratic governance grew more strident from both left and right, not only for the lack of ability to handle the 1968 protests, but also for their relation to power.[18]

A new type of action that was neither strike nor demonstration was introduced by Action Dialogue at the end of the summer of 1968. It was planned with the suburb of Skärholmen as a threatening backdrop and was declared the only thing to challenge "the gigantic environmental manipulation" at the time.[19] Contrary to many of the earlier confrontational demonstrations and happenings, this was about conversation, participation, and communication. Party politics was ignored, and instead the action was directed at a specific situation in an urban context. As such it had more similarities with the "hunger strike" than the Båstad demonstrations, but, however, these actions introduced a new topic by focusing on experiences and attitudes, which they saw as neglected political categories in the formation of a subjectivity to transform an "aggressive consumer" into a participating citizen.[20] And heralds of the future were children.

Children's Day

Every year since the early twentieth century, Children's Day had been organized in Stockholm to collect money for holiday camps for children and young people from poor families.[21] A few days every year, festivities were arranged for children and adults to raise money, and the event grew over the years, becoming more and more commercialized with ever-more ambitious activities and commodities to consume. The criticism of the 1967 Children's Day for being too commercialized and directed toward adults rather than children led the members of the Children's Day Committee to invite the progressive author and musician Thomas Wieslander and his collaborators to participate in the next event.[22]

The Model (1968)

Figure 1.3 A poster from Children's Day 1916. Design: Vicke Andrén.

When Children's Day got underway at the end of the summer 1968 it was in the format of a miniature reconstruction of the nostalgic environment in the middle of a Stockholm public park, Vasaparken. Sörgården was a farmhouse pictured in a famous children schoolbook from 1907 about life in the small Swedish rural village of Önnemö (Figure 1.4).[23] This idyllic place is best known to a larger international audience from Astrid Lindgren's children's books *Pippi Longstocking* and *The Children of Noisy Village*. In the center of Vasaparken a red wooden house with white windows was built, and a miniature railway, ostensibly sponsored by the fictitious Önnemo Bank, connected the farmhouse with Önnemo Station. At the farm there were craftsmen's booths with live performances by men, staged as reenactments.

Architecture and Retrenchment

Teckning av Brita Ellström.

Figure 1.4 Sörgården. Drawing by Brita Ellström 1912. Reprinted from Anna Maria Roos, *Hem och hembygd: Sörgården* (Stockholm: Albert Bonniers förlag, 1912).

Sörgården came to symbolize Sweden's position as neutral in the Second World War; an ironic picture of the country as an idyllic island in the middle of a warzone. On a much smaller scale, this was repeated on inauguration day when Sörgården saw a nearby street demonstration against the Soviet invasion of Czechoslovakia: the Swedish idyll was brutally affected by global politics. Coincidentally, Lindgren lived on the street overlooking the park and could see it all in what to her was a well-known environment. She had been invited to open the Children's Day event, and in her speech she pinpointed the complicated relationship between the rising awareness of global inequality and the downsides of the Swedish welfare state—increasing class differences, poverty, and segregation: "even though help for other children [outside Sweden] might seem more urgent, we have the right to collect money for the thousands of Stockholm children who are dependent on Children's Day to get out into the outdoors."[24] And the lines of conflicts, the expressions of conduct and counterconduct, were also drawn inside the area itself.

Thomas Wieslander and his team were very critical of this arrangement and the organizers in general. In response they set up workshops *behind* the craftsmen's booths where children could try out the crafts themselves, becoming active participants rather than observers. As Wieslander put it, "Adults wonder 'How does it look?' And kids think 'How does it feel?'" In addition to the workshops, two cottages were built to flank the main Sörgården building, one filled with hay and the other with foam rubber for the children to jump in, and a large tent was filled with "rubbish material" (tools and materials to build with) and with it a climbing frame for the kids to add to. The group had had to fight to get this space, and Wieslander expressed his disappointment, especially at the strategy of using progressive forces as front behind which to run the same conservative event as usual: "it was a smart move from the organizers to invite us, and then to limit us, as a way of silencing critical voices."[25]

By the end of the week the silhouette of Sörgården had changed. In between the red cottages a structure of wooden self-built high-rises was growing up. This was a surprise for the activists who studied the children's building processes (they continuously analyzed the kids and their behavior in a form of surveillance which I will return to). Unexpectedly, not only children but teenagers came early in the morning with packed meals and stayed the whole day. The older kids demolished the machines and "tools" provided by the adults, and the younger ones soon imitated them. In two hours, everything was smashed. The activist group analyzed the situation, concluding there was "an unsatisfied desire in this age group." They tried another strategy of bringing building timber and tools for the kids to "hit constructively."[26] Soon, the older kids together with the younger ones had built a four-level wooden city, including swings and climbing frames for the smallest kids. The activists observed that "immigrant kids ... and Swedish kids are playing together even though they do not understand each other."[27] It started with three groups building their own houses, but with some help from the adults the kids learned this strategy of building individual houses for themselves meant all newcomers were outsiders, and that it would create a "housing queue."[28] So instead they changed their methods and constructed a common *city* built together by thirty kids; "it was 'their' city." They constructed bridges, walkways, climbing frames so the city could be used by all kids. "Anyone can be satisfied in their shack, but the city is used by everyone."[29]

The Children's Day site rapidly became as a collage of different wants and environmental fantasies. The organizers' idyllic red wooden farmhouses which existed to be visited, looked at, alongside the critical response of the activists; the workshops built behind the red Sörgården booths to invite active participation; and finally the children's own high-rise area, rising up between the old-style architecture. If the adults looked to the past for small-scale communities, the romantically aesthetic qualities of Sörgården, or long-lost collaboration, anti-consumerism, and small-scale environments, the children acted out their fantasies in a contemporary city and constructed their own environment with the urban density of the high-rise format.

Despite the admiration in the daily press for the kid's self-built structures with their "unconventional architecture" and "multicolored houses," they were to be demolished at the end of the week.[30] But hundreds of adults protested and demanded that the high-rises be protected. Finally, the wooden city was saved and the City of Stockholm took over the running of it. Echoing real city life, the buildings were vandalized, alcohol and drugs became a problem, and nightly security patrols were organized—but despite this

Architecture and Retrenchment

Figure 1.5 Children building high-rises in Vasaparken, Stockholm, 1968. Photographer: André Lafolie. Courtesy: Arkiv Samtal.

it remained highly appreciated.[31] The adults who had protested against the demolition met under the name Byalagen; a group that was later involved in protests against several demolitions in the city under the umbrella of Action Dialogue.[32]

Building for Play, Building to Play

In line with *Homo Ludens* by the historian Johan Huizinga, the urban activists saw play as crucial for the formation of society in all respects—including law, war, knowledge, art. This type of playground was christened *bygglek* (building play), as in the "high-rise area" in Vasaparken, the idea being that by letting children play and build on their own it increased the chances of a playful and creative future society. The concept of building play was taken from the Danish activists in Hovedstadsaktionen, among them the artist Palle Nielsen.[33] It had a much longer history, though. The Danish landscape architect Carl Theodor Sørensen argued in the early twentieth century that children, unlike adults, appreciate messy environments. In the 1930s he developed the idea of a playground made of "rubbish," and in 1943, in the thick of the German occupation, the first *skrammellegeplads* (junk playground) was built in Copenhagen, in Emdrup. Internationally renowned, it convinced the likes of the English landscape architect Marjory Allen to construct similar playgrounds, also called "junk playgrounds" and later "adventure playgrounds."[34]

There was a wide spectrum of ideas about how, and how much, play should be framed and regulated by adults and experts such as architects and planners using playground design. As pointed out by Timothy Scott there were enclosed adventure playgrounds designed by the local authorities in mid-1960s London, for example, Parkhill in Camden and Notting Hill Adventure Park, which were controlled, secure environments. In this environment, it can be argued, the child was trained to be an entrepreneurial subject, able to handle enterprise and risk, rather than a sociable, solidary citizen.[35] At their full extent, adventure playgrounds were adventure parks—such as KidZania (started in 1999), a privately owned indoor family entertainment now in thirty locations worldwide with nine million visitors a year. In KidZania children between two and fourteen can participate in "real-life activities"—bottling Coca-Cola, working at Mac Donald's or at a Crest-sponsored dentist's surgery, and so on—and "discover all about different jobs through exciting role play, and develop decision-making, teamwork, creativity, and social skills."[36]

In Sweden, the garden designer Arvid Bengtsson introduced *bygglek* in the mid-1940s—probably the first being the one in Norrköping in 1946—and it had a great many followers in other cities.[37] When the concept *bygglek* was actualized again in the late 1960s by Action Dialogue, it was used not only as strategy to fight for better environments for children but also as ideological criticism of a society regulated by rationality and bureaucracy. The playgrounds were constructed as alternatives to individualized consumer culture; instead of conventional playgrounds with swings and slides that could only be used by one kid at a time, creating competition, *bygglek* depended on collaboration. To build a structure together the kids needed to help one another, and there were no tools or toys that encouraged individual activities. Learning was understood as embedded in the participation and collaboration, enhanced by the playgrounds. Instead of adults "teaching" and "bringing up" kids, they were supposed to set up structures, frames, for the kids to develop themselves, which would give them abilities crucial for their growth as future citizens.

Roy Kozlovsky has shown how the notion of the child, and the role of the adventure playground, were part of an anarchist project, but at same time tied into the biopolitical project of governmentality regulating the interiority of the welfare-state individual.[38] In this framework, the adventure parks were not only an experiment for an alternative social order, but simultaneously a technique producing modern liberal subjects. Action Dialogue's ambition to create active citizens able to participate in constructing society was not a break with the biopolitical project to produce liberal subjectivities— rather, it can be understood as a continuation.

Inspired by Children's Day, the professor John Lind organized a *bygglek* at the Karolinska University Hospital. Film clips from the hospital show how the playground worked in rehab situations, as visually impaired kids used tools such as hammers and saws without adult intervention.[39] In these scenes, experts express their concerns about paternalistic society not giving individuals the freedom and trust needed so children develop into responsible and experienced people, and instead play became the model for an alternative future society. The way it framed play was compared to the societal regulations, begging the question of how much freedom those societal structures allowed. However, looking at the *bygglek* in Vasaparken, play there was supervised and the adults interacted in the building process as a form of teaching.

Action Dialogue

After that first *bygglek* in Vasaparken, a week's worth of actions were organized around Stockholm in late September 1968. The same strategy was used everywhere: without warning Action Dialogue left lorryloads of scrap building materials, tools, and paint at various sites; the atmosphere was peaceful and built on dialogue, and they served coffee, buns, sausages, and so on to anyone who wanted; and they handed out flyers and organized further meetings with local actors. The message, like the format of the action, was to go against the expert knowledge prioritized over locals' experiences and know-how in the formal planning processes. The role played by the architects was ambiguous. Indeed, only few activists were architects, even though they had support from a group of them engaged in the growing environmental movement. On the other hand, the architects were self-evidently among the established experts. As it said in the flyers:

> Why are infants separated from small children, who are separated from school children, who are separated from teenagers, who are separated from young people, who are separated from the middle aged, who are separated from senior citizens ...?
> Is it easier to keep track of them this way?
> Is society built for isolation? Is society built for conversation?
> Society creates specialists. Everyone has their own specialism—1-year old child, retiree, engineer, cultural worker, politician, voter.
> Specialists know nothing about one another.
> Specialists do not have conversations.
> Through conversations we act together. Our actions build society. Through actions we change it.
> Through conversations you take responsibility for your world.[40]

The Model (1968)

When the residents of a big block of flats in Södermalm in Stockholm woke up one Saturday morning in September 1968, they looked out of their windows to see a new backyard. Instead of several small plots separated by fences, each with its own carpet-beating rack and dustbins, there was a huge yard filled with building materials, sand, paints, benches, and a large banner proclaiming "Welcome in for a coffee!" The first visitor was Bertil, aged 4, and after him came the grown-ups. The kids played and "the adults were drinking coffee and eating buns and *talking* to the activists and the others."[41] The same morning a playground in Nytorget, a Stockholm park, was refurbished and turned into a *bygglek*, and while the kids built wooden "high-rises," the parents and passers-by were served coffee and buns and discussed the city environment. It was the first event in a series of events that week.

The events were described in the daily press, presenting Action Dialogue to a larger public. Through nonviolent, non-overtly political actions based on dialogue, directed mainly at kids, they reached a broad audience with their messages, achieving something more substantial than a one-off action. The journalist Rebecka Tarschys was an important supporter of the group and her position at *Dagens Nyheter*, one of the most influential Swedish daily newspapers, helped mediate the group's messages to the public. The awareness of using the media to communicate, rather than to use violence to get heard, was significant for its "peaceful revolution."[42] Tarschys ended an article about it with a rallying cry: "Everyone who wants to talk more about a better environment for playgrounds and backyards should come to Katarina Bangata 24 on Monday at 19.00." The impact of such a message in the mainstream press cannot be overestimated at a time where there was only one Swedish TV channel and three radio channels.

On Sunday, the day after the first two actions, people who passed Slussen, a square in central Stockholm, could look down into the courtyard of the City Museum and see kids of different ages playing intently in a huge pile of rubbish—there were old stoves, vending machines, kitchen sinks, and old clothes—under a banner strung across the courtyard (figure 1.6).[43] This *bygglek*, a peaceful demonstration, went on all week and ended with a public debate on "action dialogues."[44]

The following Monday a large banner with the text "Kids under 12 are not as mature as bicycle road users. Kids under 12 must be able to bike. Where?" was put up in a suburb of Stockholm and all through traffic was stopped (Figure 1.7).[45] On a gravel space near the square there was a confrontation over the activists' methods and the pedagogy developed at the local authority's Parkleken playground, which was supervised by paid staff.[46] In one corner of the yard there was a well-organized playground with equipment such as slides and swings; in the other corner was a pile of old stuff such as boards, planks, and paint. The ordered, carefully laid out local authority Parkleken was quite a contrast to the unfinished, trashy playground part of the "environmental revolution."[47] Two different pedagogical models were literally played out, one resting on didactics, the other on anarchist ideas, resulting in a collision between two "realities." The comment from the activists, who were not especially engaged in the long-term work with children's play, was that "Over there they force a miniature image of reality onto the children with small detergent boxes and everything. One fosters them as consumers."[48] The Parkleken

Figure 1.6 The third urban action made by Action Dialogue was a *bygglek* at the court yard of the Stockholm City Museum, 1968. Photographer: Unknown. Courtesy: Stockholm City Museum.

staff, on the other hand, were "hurt" by the lack of communication about the activists' visit: "It is good to paint freely but who will collect all the paper and all plans? We will have the parents against us if it looks like this."[49]

On Tuesday the same week, Action Dialogue did a "Kids Visiting Society" workshop described in Sweden's largest newspaper, *Dagens Nyheter*, with an illustration showing kids working in an office (Figure 1.8). In the morning the kids visited different working environments. Eva and Susanne, both aged 6, worked with the typewriters; 5-year-olds Velcho and Philip used the accounting machines; and Kjell, about same age, tried using the copier. Philip "was so happy that he wanted to enrol for work on the spot," and the finance director at the office assured him he was welcome back when he was older. In the afternoon, back at the kindergarten, they simulated reality through roleplay using real materials, not models or miniatures—"a piece of reality mediated and transported."[50] "We want to have even more reality," the superintendent at the kindergarten stressed, "and we will make sure we get it!" She continued, "we would happily avoid curtains if we could get TV sets. And a tape recorder! Curtains are not necessary but TV sets, which are in every home, must also mirror the reality at a kindergarten."[51]

The last action in the urban landscape was in an inner-city schoolyard on Wednesday the same week. Once again Action Dialogue came with a lorryload of building materials

The Model (1968)

Figure 1.7 Creating banners at Valla torg, Stockholm—the fourth urban action by Action Dialogue in 1968. Photographer: André Lafolie. Courtesy: Arkiv Samtal.

to the schoolyard during morning break. The kids were immediately busy, but although the headteacher and teachers thought it was a good idea they were critical of the organizers because they had not been informed beforehand. The action led to meetings between pupils, teachers, activists, and parents for further discussions about the school environment.[52] At the meeting that ended the action week on Saturday it was clear Action Dialogue was both admired for its activities, even by the local authority, and was seen as a problem (they had been reported to the police for holding "unlawful stock").[53]

Figure 1.8 The fifth action: Eva, 6 years old, typewriting, while Philip, 5, and Susanne, 6, are watching, 1968. At Kronobergsparken's Kindergarten, Stockholm, the children were supposed to take part in the adult world. Photographer: Ragnhild Haarstad / SvD / TT.

Modellen: A Model for a Qualitative Society

The turbulent weeks of urban action and new activist groups, such as Action Dialogue and Byalagen, led to a large group of people backing an initiative taken by Palle Nielsen and the journalist and activist Gunilla Lundahl to hold a protest at Moderna Museet in Stockholm.[54] Even though the museum director Pontus Hultén showed little interest, Carlo Derkert, who was working on its educational programs, supported the idea that would result in the exhibition *Modellen*.[55] It was an ambiguous project to turn into an exhibition at an establishment art museum: it was controversial for activists to collaborate with the establishment in the shape of a major institution, but equally it was a unique possibility to communicate their message to a large audience.

"We must build our own models for a new reality, where we have taken responsibility ourselves."[56] This is in the catalogue for the exhibition *Modellen: En modell för ett kvalitativt samhälle* (The Model: A model for a qualitative society) that opened in 1968 at Moderna Museet. The format of *Modellen* was deliberately ambiguous. Its role as an exhibition depended, according to the organizers, on the visitor's ability to participate, but *Modellen* was also an experimental research project. A "model" to study, where pedagogues and psychologists filmed, tape recorded, and observed kids' playing. As the exhibition catalogue explained:

> Their play is the exhibition. The exhibition is the work of the kids. *There is no exhibition*. It is only an exhibition because the kids play at an art museum. It is only an exhibition for those who do not play. Therefore, we call it a model.[57]

Even though the exhibition was seen as a beginning of a new Swedish Model, it was also a continuation of observation research in the long tradition of *folkhemmet* (lit. the People's Home), such as the Child Psychiatric Research Institute's documentation of kids at Sven Markelius's and Alva Myrdal's famous collective house in John Ericssonsgatan in Stockholm.[58] One could either participate in the play, or watch other people participating: "people want to look at people" as its creators put it.[59] The visitor was a participant, looked at and registered, an object in an experiment—but he or she was also looking at other participants, turning the experiment into an exhibition. "It is only an exhibition for those who do not play."[60] This landscape of participation evoked private and collective experiences and created ambiguity about participation and observation, the active and the surveilled citizen, the child and the adult.

Its name, *Modellen: En modell för ett kvalitativt samhälle* (The Model: A model for a qualitative society), referred to André Gorz's *Stratégie ouvrière et néo-capitalisme*, which had been published in a Swedish translation a few years earlier: "in a developed society needs are not only quantitative (the need for goods for consumption) but also qualitative [...] the need for emancipation not only from exploitation but also from coercion and isolation at work during leisure time."[61] The exhibition layout was reminiscent of a kindergarten. In the middle of the room was a wooden structure to climb on and a large "sea" of foam rubber to play in. Around this central installation were various stations, spread out as separate activity clusters: carpentry, a scrambling net, a typing and writing studio, a wardrobe of dressing-up clothes, and a painting studio.

Installing a play structure in an art museum was a radical act, and the show was criticized (especially by the artist Öyvind Fahlström) for turning the art scene into a playground. But for Action Dialogue the show was not a playground, it was a model of a future society, and even though adults were invited to play, they could not *regulate* the play. The artist Sture Johannesson designed the poster (the only thing about the exhibition produced by the museum), which consisted of a Swedish flag overlaid by images of welfare-state housing and other fragments of the society, relating the show to the "Swedish welfare model" (Figure 1.9). Even though the criticism expressed in the exhibition and earlier actions was directed at the Swedish Model and how society was governed, the response from the authorities was generally positive. The Social Democrats were skilled politicians and had a long experience of public relations, with a deft use of rhetoric and the media. Despite their adaptability, some have argued the Social Democrats failed to notice the seriousness in the general attacks of 1968 on their governance, which also became visible in public opinion by 1970, with decreasing votes in the 1971 and 1973 elections and finally their electoral defeat in 1976.[62]

Figure 1.9 The exhibition poster for *Modellen*, 1968. Design: Sture Johannesson. Courtesy: Moderna Museet.

The picture of Olof Palme joining in was taken when the exhibition was closed for the public, just before the start of a seminar organized by *Dagens Nyheter* about children's environmental and societal conditions. Palme opened the seminar with "a scary image" borrowed from a novel by the American futurist and military strategist Herman Kahn, writing of a future based on technological and scientific developments.[63] The scene was a playground with kids playing "Capture the flag." The game was observed by the principal and an assistant, who stated there were two types of humans: the creative and the deviating. The latter was understood as a risk when they were not analyzing problems and had no overview, and might run away on his own "perhaps even out on the left-wing." As a response to this horrifying scenario Palme said:

> What does the insecure human do, closed in a misanthropic environment, manipulated by commercial interests and without a sense of influence over the problems facing them? Yes, the most important thing now is to create a community in the collective, to defend and stimulate individual particularities, to create preconditions for activities."[64]

The kindergarten could be the starting point for this practice in democracy, according to Palme, and he wanted the school to be developed not for a future workforce but for reasons of equality.

With his spirited speech, Palme anticipated the organizers of *Modellen*. But Palle Nielsen naturally disagreed, adding that it was not only a question of "environment" and being "creative"; the only way to feel part of a collective was to deviate from the norm. This was also illustrated later at the seminar by Carlo Derkert, who stood up to speak "with a car tyre around his neck" read directly from the research material, the psychologists' charts documenting the children's play every hour.[65] The most obscure incident was when the psychoanalyst Jan Bouman lost patience and rushed forward, jumping up and down in front of the group and, having kissed an unknown and surprised women, encouraging the audience to be part of a happening: "Now we're playing 'Catch-up'!"[66] The scene demonstrated the desire to break norms and "deregulate" not only the architectural environment but also the social sphere. Immediately after the seminar, however, at the end of the second week, the exhibition was closed for breaches of fire regulations.[67]

Modellen was also a research project, though.[68] An academic research group of psychologists, sociologists, and educationalists studied the children playing in the hope of finding a *qualitative* alternative to contemporary *quantitative* society and its principles of buying and selling. Instead of individualizing toys, the installation was thought of as an environment enabling collaboration and collective behavior: it was a *bygglek* in the museum.[69] The kid's activities were registered, filmed, and documented as a written report of their behavior in a logbook. The research was meant to lay the foundations for "future projects about kindergartens, playgrounds, and other child environments."[70] The psychologists were especially keen to analyze children with functional variations, noting "a group of mentally retarded boys, generally loudly happy to try out everything in *Modellen*, were especially happy with the coathangers with theatrical clothes," and that the disabled children needed less help than the researchers anticipated except for the Thalidomide children, who found it difficult to get out of the foam-rubber pool on their own and got scared. Otherwise they were "strikingly curious and eager to try out tactilely the different degrees of hardness of the foam," and the slide constructed for several kids together was popular.[71] The researchers observed that the kids who came with kindergarten groups were freer and more independent in their play than the kids who came with their parents—especially the mothers "ruled" the kids. In total forty-two kids were observed continuously from entering *Modellen* until they left one or more hours later.

Architecture and Retrenchment

Figure 1.10 Boy sawing at *Modellen*, 1968. Photographer: Unknown. Courtesy: Moderna Museet.

Gaze—to be looked at and to look at—was crucial to *Modellen*. It was gaze that created the exhibition. The research project made the site even more complex, as the techniques of observing became part of the structure. The TV screens displaying "the model" constructed an awareness of being surveilled when entering the space. The child was perceived as the potential force for future change, but at the same time the documentation objectified their play into a scientific object to be analyzed and measured. In this scientific gaze, the children were resources in a double meaning: as objects for producing new knowledge through the researcher's work and documentation; and in the ambition to use this knowledge to create future environments thought to reinforce children's abilities and skills. Yet *Modellen* was also criticized for being conservative in differentiating between children and adults, one group as active participants and the other as passive observers. The statement in the catalogue "Let the children decide, because they know what they're doing,"[72] was criticized as "bare illusionism" and created a distance to the adult world and a belief that a new generation would solve the future: "a Rousseauian wind blows across the lines of these confessions to the original and pure child-world."[73] Such an attitude saw the catalogue imbued with statements such as "adults exploit and oppress kids (emotionally, psychologically, socially) in the same way as imperialism (that is we, the Western industrial countries) exploits the so-called Third World."[74]

Modellen was a public success with 35,000 visitors in the four weeks it was open (the second Saturday there were 7,000 visitors), with a great deal of attention in the daily press, TV, and radio. The original typology that inspired the exhibition, *byggleken*, found followers in new settings after the exhibition, so that kindergartens and later shopping centers and big stores such as IKEA arranged "play spaces," and "building playgrounds." It was because of *Modellen* that a children's workshop was set up at Moderna Museet, an activity later adopted by museums around the world.[75] As the end of the exhibition approached *Modellen* was advertised for sale, and there were numerous offers, including from Vienna, London, and San Francisco. The artist Palle Nielsen was asked to set up new "models" around the world. The original, however, was ultimately sold to the Swedish city of Västerås. Here, parts of the exhibition were raised for some months as a playground in Råby, outside Västerås, as *Ballongen* (The Balloon).[76]

Experience Me: Techniques and Countertechniques

Action Dialogue formulated different techniques for engaging the public in the struggle to emancipate them from a role as passive consumers. Here, architecture was understood as an emancipatory project because of its ability to create experiences. Many of these ideas introduced in the late 1968 were coopted, responded to, mimicked, and changed by other contradictory interests in subsequent decades. Participation, like emancipation, was a concept that was vague and could shift in meaning, but on the ground often served to legitimize later neoliberalization. Here I will look into the techniques used by Action Dialogue, how they were questioned as naïve when they were introduced, but also how they can be understood as powerful counteractions.

In the journal *Zenit*, members of Archive Dialogue (the new name for Action Dialogue) reflected on the specific character of the emerging environmental movements and their own methods of practice.[77] They elaborated on the importance of experiences and attitudes, understanding the society as a feedback loop of system–experience–attitude–system: "It is a system of inequality that creates experiences of estrangement, separation, isolation. From these experiences grow attitudes of competition that later gain the system and so on."[78] A determining function of the system was the passivation of the individual that brought them up as "aggressively competing consumers" through everyday objects, such as individualized toys and the domestic environment that lacked communal spaces but had central TV antenna. To break the system, they argued, the creation of new experiences would affect, and finally break, the feedback system, and the urban actions became a way to hack the system. Inspired by new left thinkers such as R. D. Laing and Andre Gorz (extensively quoted in the exhibition catalogue), architecture and the ordinary environment—from the self-built high-rise areas in Vasaparken to *Modellen* at Moderna Museet—were seen as sites of emancipation for the urban activists. Focusing on physical participation as a way to create experiences, the urban actions introduced a new form of criticality to Swedish intellectual life beyond the left–right political scale. Full-scale installations and the built environment became key assets as media evoking emotions, affecting bodies, and transforming minds. The experiences would create new attitudes and consequently "break the system."

The strategies used by Action Dialogue were at the time thought to be easily coopted by the forces of marketization and neoliberalization. Action Dialogue was singled out as naïve in their belief in creating change through "category actions" (actions directed at a specific question or group) outside traditional left–right politics. Changing attitudes were thought insufficient, and the cultural critics Agneta Pleijel and Lars Sjögren argued there was an overconfidence in the "system's willingness to give in" and that they "underestimated the system's ability to integrate and incapacitate aberrant molecular formations," for example when a business produced "the first complete equipment for backyards with conversation-friendly objects designed in foam."[79] They compared it with how the hippie movement had been swallowed by the system "without any indigestion," and quoted US Travel Service's advertising campaign: "Oh yes. We have hippies in New York. You can see them sitting just behind Washington Square Arch. For a cent they'll happily sing and play their colourful guitars. Probably they're protesting against something."[80] Category actions obviously ran the risk that, exemplified by Leif Nylén, a progressive local authority could satisfy special interests, embrace the critics, and disarm them: "glass jars for the craftsmen, a 'drugstore' for the youths, a hotel for the retired, and rose trellis and parking garages for everyone."[81]

In the late 1990s knowledge about the built environment's ability to evoke experience and to "move" individuals was incorporated into economic and management strategies. The management consultants James Gilmore and Joseph Pine argued that companies had to go

> beyond goods and services to stage experiences and guide transformations. Experiences (memorable events that engage customers in inherently personal ways, like going to a theme park, visiting a museum, or engaging in sports activities) and transformations (experiences that change the customer in some fundamental way, like toning up at a fitness centre, resolving problems with a psychiatrist, or improving one's business through a consultant) are distinct economic offerings built on top of services, goods and commodities.[82]

Where Action Dialogue aimed at changing the world by transforming the citizen, Gilmore and Pine argued for a similar strategy to reach the opposite aim: instead of transforming the consumer into a solidary citizen, the goal was to increase profits for private corporations. The subject in focus for Action Dialogue did not desire transformation, change was instead understood as an unconscious process, but for Gilmore and Pine it was a market strategy to *fulfil* the subject's desire to be transformed. The architect Anna Klingmann elaborated on John Sherry's "brandscape" (a combination of brand and landscape) in relation to Gilmore and Pine's "experience economy" and the discipline of architecture in *Brandscape* (2007). She declared her own architectural practice as "brandism," where economic values were created by experience: "Architecture cuts through the noise, the email, the myriad of marketing messages and says: experience me."[83]

If the political perspective could be considered absent from Action Dialogue's actions, one could also, in line with Jacques Rancière's notion of the political, understand their actions as critical "interruptions" to the circulation of everyday life (which is part of the system). For Rancière "the power" (the police) keeps up circulation going so citizen and objects all have to move on, not stopping. Power says "there is nothing to see, move on." Politics, on the other hand, is to stop, to make the space of circulation "into a space of the manifestation of a subject: be it the people, workers, citizens. It consists in refiguring that space, what there is to do there, what it is to see there, or to name."[84] For the urban activists "the power" was the expert—architects, urban planners, politicians—and the methods used by Action Dialogue were a way to manifest the subject (the child, the citizen) in society. To *stop* a movement by taking action was a way to subjectivize the anonymous person (the child, the citizen) in a space of circulation where documents, plans, and decisions "moved on" from expert to expert and were never manifested for the public. The actions articulated environmental themes most often handled in spaces, without transparency, and the physical manifestations gave form to objects and actors moving on in the circulation of the authorities' processes of conduct (cleaning, throwing, limiting). For Action Dialogue, the discussion about the "citizen" was not an appraisal of the individual as solitary, as it reoccurred in the new discourses of 1980s neoliberalization; on the contrary, it was about citizens as a presence in the urban sphere, both as bodies in the city and in the direct decision-making.

The action dialogues that played out in the city and the museum not only revealed a problem, but, crucially, affirmed the possibilities of what Rancière calls a "demonstration of existence."[85] A telling example was how Alternative City, an urban activist group with connections to Action Dialogue, not only took action in the urban context, but also interacted with the decision-making process by presenting their own proposal for Karlbergsvägen, a central Stockholm street that was going to be made into a motorway. This and other direct bureaucratic actions—such as writing reports, going to policy meetings, presenting proposals to politicians, "lobbying"—meant they managed to stop the proposal, and to this day the street is a quiet dead end. The struggle to empower "the citizen" contributed to a strident criticism of experts (maintaining spaces of circulation) and undermined representation. This criticism was also directed at the heart of the Swedish corporatist model, of which more later, based on the legitimacy of representative groups, such as popular and interest movements, and political decision makers.

Emancipation Movements and Neoliberalizations

The literature offers two standard explanations for the relation between "68" and the rise of neoliberalism: it was a consequence of the 1968 movement or a response to it. Even though the relationship often resists these straightforward explanations, I will try to make my perspective in this book as clear as possible. Following scholars such as Kristin Ross, Christian Laval, and Melinda Cooper, I understand the events lined out in this first chapter as a critique that questioned established values, norms, and hierarchies in the capitalistic system with an emerging neoliberal rationality as its conservative response. Through the recuperation of radical ideas and methods, forces of neoliberalization protected the existing order under threat. Moreover, the harsh critique of the 1968 movement as a destructive force is also part of the rhetoric applied by the neo-conservative movement of today.

At the end of the 1970s, philosopher Régis Debray accused the 1968 movement of being the "midwife of capitalist revolution."[86] This was at the time a highly original statement that later, at the beginning of the twenty-first century, became an academic convention. The notion of a neoliberal May '68 made the jump from the academic world to politics, where, for example, it was used by Nicolas Sarkozy, who in the 2007 election stated, "See how the cult of money-worship, short-term profit, speculation, how the excesses of finance capitalism were carried in the values of May '68."[87] The "68" events can in this perspective either be seen as a needed modernization of society and the capitalist economy, or, as Sarkozy expressed it, as the start of a "limitless individualism that opens the way to unbridled capitalism, deregulated finance, the loss of all morality and solidarity."[88]

According to Kristine Ross this official story not only state that the radical ideas from May 1968 was recycled in the service of Capital, but rather it "asserts that today's capitalist society, far from representing the derailment or failure of the May movement's aspirations, instead represent the accomplishment of its deepest desires."[89] Further, Ross claims that this official story erases memories of alternatives, and ideas of a different future. This is also a critique put forward by the sociologist Christian Laval who describes how this story can be deconstructed through giving back authority to the actors of the 1968 movement and "refusing to see them as passive toys of history or of obscure forces acting behind their backs."[90] This does not mean that there never can be any relationships between ideas, initiatives or expressions of the "68" and neoliberalization, but it is important to state that there is no general temporal succession.

How, then, can we understand neoliberalization as a *response* to past radical movements? Following Laval, an early interpretation of neoliberal rationality as a "conservative revolution" was formulated in 1976 by Bourdieu and Boltanski. They describe, what they call a "redeployed conservatism" not about defending tradition but rather a matter of changing things and accelerating change, even though the main goal was to protect the positions and avoid elimination. This thinking was, according to Laval, rooted in the discourse of innovation and moderniszation (since the 1930s) and was structuring the notion of a "third way" between *laissez-faire* and capitalism. This new dominant ideology of neoliberalism impacted on all who were in office and had positions in power, and played out on "neutral places" beyond right and left.[91] For Michel Foucault, though, the neoliberal response produced something new, being a practical response to the generalized criticism of the modes of government in the 1960s and 1970s. The 1968 was for Foucault a crisis in governmentality and of subjectivity; a struggle for another government that was driven by new ideologies and new approaches in the shape of "counterconduct" and "counterdiscourse." Neoliberalism should therefore be understood in the framework of counterconduct as a positive and productive—not only ideological—response to the 1968 critique of government. In this sense neoliberalism was not first a response to the crises of capitalism, but a response to mass criticism of the multiple forms of governance.[92]

The Model (1968)

Also relevant to this study is the work of Luc Boltanski och Eve Chiapello who single out the "social criticism" and the "artistic criticism" of the 1968 movement.[93] The former concept focuses on "inequalities, misery, exploitation, and the selfishness of a world that stimulates individualism rather than solidarity," while the latter "criticizes oppression, the massification of society standardization and pervasive commodification."[94] Based on texts from the field of management studies, they argue that the social criticism failed during the 1980s while the artistic succeeded but had lost its edge when the artistic criticism's protagonists were satisfied with the changes that neoliberalization brought with it. Contrary to Boltanski's and Chiapello's argument, Ross stresses that when the union of intellectual contestation with workers struggle has been forgotten, the idea of an emancipatory counterculture prefiguring desire and liberation has survived.[95] In this book the notion of an artistic and social critique is not possible to separate – a role, or capacity, of architecture in these societal transformations is to intertwine the different notions of critique in the construction of a broader discourse. Another perspective on the relationship between "68" and neoliberalization is the gender critique provided by Melinda Cooper. She understands neoliberalism as a new liberalist order defined through a social and economic restructuring in direct relation to the shifted gender and race composition of labor. An alliance between neoliberalism and new conservatism grew as a response to the 1960s liberation movement that questioned sexual normativity and traditional family values.[96] I will return to this aspect in the chapter on the collective house.

When discussing the 1968 urban actions in Stockholm, it would be to neglect the importance of collective struggles and fights for equality to argue that the activists in the late 1960s embraced individual freedom and foreshadowed 1980s individualism. Instead, it is more relevant to understand how the neoliberal turn erased its own history, including its antecedents. Therefore, in this book, the activist's discourse in the late 1960s is not understood as an impulse starting a development later manifested in 1990s neoliberalism. Instead, neoliberal rationality is seen as a response to the 1968 emancipatory movements that coopted ideas, techniques, concepts, and expressions. Forces stemming from the radical rethinking of the "68" activists and from neoliberalization are not seen as part of a deterministic process of causes and effect, but rather as movements and countermovements existing in parallel. These movements created "sites of tension and restructuring," where vaguely defined concepts had varying significance. Party politics did not define the dividing lines between all the interpretations and operations, and it is impossible to describe these sites solely in terms of a political left–right dichotomy.

Sites of Tension and Restructuring

The narrative thus far has highlighted urban actions as emancipatory projects, played out in culture, architecture, and the built environment. The citizen was supposed to be liberated from the consumerist regime; the child from controlled frameworks of play; the architects and the architecture from modernist regulation. The goal was to shape an active political subject able to participate in creating the built environment. In early 1968 a state commission was appointed to revise the Swedish Building Ordinance, which was considered too bureaucratic and non-inclusive, and the importance of transforming the subject for a new future governance was explained in *Dagens Nyheter*: "We need to be trained for when the new Building law will be instigated and give space to people's opinions."[97] I will thus try to identify some topics which will later turn up in different ideological guises (often contradictory).

The first topic circles around *regulation*. To change society from the ground up, the urban activists hoped for a qualitative society not governed by the experts, bureaucracy, regulations, and norms that limited human creativity. Criticism of the built environment overlapped with that of the social-democratic welfare state, and discussions on aesthetics, building design, and building regulations were intertwined with ideas of deregulating economics and politics, even though they often were formulated separately and had very different intentions. The poster for the exhibition *Modellen* was telling: a Swedish flag with a blue background of modernist blocks of flats and a yellow cross with press cuttings such as Action Dialogue's collective swing, ironic notes on the police "leading the way in society," and critical statements about government. Together, these discussions created a discourse of deregulation and reregulation that would contribute to the transformation of the Swedish Model.

The second topic relates to *criticism* and the foregrounding of action and participation as elements in societal change. In the late 1960s the international cultural and philosophical discourse was marked by conflicts and distrust within Marxism and other left-wing movements, which resulted in new ideological constellations. Attempts to link Marx's materialism and Freud's psychoanalyses positioned the libidinal as a driving force in society, implying cultural unconscious and societal collective desires.[98] The idea of criticism and critical theory formulated by the Frankfurt School was challenged, which led to various intellectual and aesthetic experiments trying out new forms of criticality. As seen, a turn away from criticism based on distance toward experiences and physical participation was significant in the work of Action Dialogue.[99] In full-scale models, such as *Modellen*, visitors participated rather than observed, and the aim was to transform the individual's experiences and attitudes. This would break society's feedback loop of system–experience–attitude–system.

This brings us to architecture as a *medium*. The 1968 urban activists were not only alert to the importance of publicizing their actions in the popular media by collaborating with journalists or using Establishment institutions for exhibitions and discussions, but perhaps more importantly, they explored how architecture operated as a medium. Walter Benjamin had noted the role of architecture in societal transitions, or "turning points in history," where the human apparatus of perception was mastered not by optical means or contemplation but by tactile appropriation.[100] This architectural ambiguity was elaborated on in Action Dialogue's work, and common for these actions was that architecture was both the medium and the message: architectural manifestations for the individual to engage with, foreshadowing the "brandscapes," and raising issues directly critical of architecture, built society, and its environment. In this media–message complex, a reformulated notion of criticism and participation, the immediacy of sensory physical experience, and the aestheticization of the experience itself all came together to create new trajectories for the future.

The Model (1968)

The last topic is the perception of *a model,* or guidelines for future change. The child has repeatedly been a model for fantasies of possible alternative worlds. For example, in modernism the child, together with figures such as "the savage" and the "mentally ill," was a source of knowledge into the secret domain of the "other."[101] As modernism's muse, the child was an inspiring force and a role model for the free and spontaneous human, but, at the same time the child was human material who could be educated, governed, and formed into a rational citizen.[102] This duality was also present in the work by Action Dialogue. The child was not a free individual in the discourse framing urban actions; they were "regulated" to be free. The child was supposed to be a crucial transformer (of society), but in a direction already pointed out, and to reach the desirable future the child became an asset to invest in, a human resource to manage. The child was both seen as a model for the future and a human resource to invest in: a human capital.

The actions, such as *Modellen* and the Kids Visiting Society, used full-scale elements and created safe environments for children's reality-testing. Following the logic of the experience economy, this was also a technique developed in the 1990s adventure parks for children. For example, as shown by the artist Priscila Fernandes's film about KidZania, children were shown how to be employees of companies such as McDonald's, or shoppers able to handle money (paying, going to the cash machine, counting, saving, spending, etc.) in big stores and malls.[103] Both the 1968 and 1990s models for the future society were "laboratories" for creating future adults, but with contradictory goals: *Modellen* aimed at creating human value as a resource for solidarity in society, while KidZania's goal was to produce human economic capital. It was not a new phenomenon to enhance human value by upbringing and education, but with the emerging neoliberalization it becomes a resource to be conducted, not only by the state, but also by the market and the individual. In this context human investment should be understood in relation to a much broader field outside schooling or professional training.[104] Human value or capital as a theme can be traced from the discussion of the child in the late 1960s, to the interactive cities of the late 1990s where children are adapted by commercialized role play to become employees, consumers, and future actors in a world of shopping, money, and profit.

Here, I have considered culture and aesthetics as driving a rethink of architecture's role in the transformation of the Swedish model. I have unpacked a history of emancipation and participation in the 1968 urban actions, with a re-articulation of criticism as spatial, physical affirmations. This affirmative criticism, or following Foucault the productive "counterconduct," also tied into a broader criticism of architectural regulation, bureaucracy, and the welfare state that had very different ambitions. Without the struggle for solidarity and emancipation, ideas embodied in the urban actions of 1968 were later reframed by Third Way neoliberalization in the 1980s. The history of neoliberalization comprises interpretations of other realities it is still possible to imagine, and the entangled history of emancipation has informed not only contemporary architecture and planning, but also society. The twilight landscape of Swedish welfare-state neoliberalization lies before us, where, as in many other contexts, its concepts and practices shift guise and voice, and recombine in new constellations.

Figure 2.1 Ann-Marie Norman, the third person from the left, called on Olof Palme to "shoulder the mantle of responsibility" during a demonstration at Sergels torg, Stockholm, February 26, 1972. The "Housewives of Skärholmen" started a protest movement against the high food prices. In December, the government decided to introduce a price freeze on milk, cream, cheese, and some other products. Photographer: Jan E. Carlsson / DN / TT.

SITE 2
THE SUBURB (1968)*

It worried Prime Minister Olof Palme that 6,000 people were demonstrating in central Stockholm against the high price of milk. It was February 26, 1972, and the "housewives of Skärholmen" had organized a demonstration as the finale of a two-week consumer strike. The slogan rang out: "Prices rise and Palme says nothing."[1] The pressure on Prime Minister Olof Palme and the Social Democrat Party was increasing when the minister of trade, Kjell-Olof Feldt, said openly on a late-night TV show he did not care about some housewives from Skärholmen. The women, who four years earlier declared in the press, "Yes, we are the blacks of Sweden" after being stigmatized as passive victims of an inhumane housing policy in the daily papers, were triumphant and a price cap was introduced in December 1972 on milk and other dairy goods.[2] The cap was not removed until in January 1975. Instead of "becoming alcoholics" or "suffocating in their suburban kitchens" as predicted, the women formed a unique, extra-parliamentary political body that changed society.

Skärholmen, to quote Leif Nylén, was the dark horizon against which Action Dialogue's urban actions played out, and the suburb was widely thought an alienated, bleak environment typical of the contemporary welfare state. Set against all the negativity, the victory of the "wives of Skärholmen" reminds us that the suburb also was a site of transformative resistance that tied into later feminist movements in architecture. Here, I will discuss the nature of the suburb where this resistance took shape: the Skärholmen, which was part of Sweden's Million Program. The ceremony to mark its inauguration was in 1968, just a few days after Action Dialogue was formed but before any urban actions took place, the straw that broke the camel's back, for it sparked the first major public debate in which architecture was the cause of the criticism of social-democratic policy and the welfare state. "Tear down Skarholmen!" was stated in the daily newspaper the day after the inauguration, and started a critical debate on architecture, the welfare state, and government.[3]

The heated discussions painted a dark picture of the suburb as a grim slum that stifled the residents' voices. Obviously, this was also something many women from the area reacted to and even raised their voices against, but they had never been heard in the existing institutional channels for groups outside the democratic structure as part of Swedish corporatism.[4] The discourse of the dystopic suburb paralleled the colonial thinking which positioned certain housing areas as "outside"—something that still frames views of suburban areas.[5] Significant for this pessimistic attitude on suburbs as outside society was the ignorance of the criticism that came from within the areas (from Skärholmen, in other words); the criticism was often strong, but directed at other aspects of the reality framing the suburb. However, these critical suburb discussions were mainly about areas usually described as a state "program"—Miljonprogrammet or the Million Program—which portrayed the architecture as closely linked to ideals shaped by the Swedish state. This was not the whole picture of the reality of the program, as we will see. The Million Program was a decision to grant state loans to companies to build 100,000 flats every year for the decade between 1965 and 1974, and, notably, this was not only supported by the Social Democrats. Even so, the suburbs were synonymous with the social-democratic welfare state in the harsh criticism from both left and right.

Here I will look at what driving forces there were behind the final plan of Skärholmen, concentrating on the private sector rather than the state. Today fresh research has modified the picture of the suburb, but still most literature adheres to a widespread, if oversimplified, narrative of the relation between the Swedish twentieth-century welfare state and its architecture.[6] I follow the trajectory of a Swedish corporatist policy striving toward a consensus between the state, the business world, and powerful interest groups, in order to investigate the commercial influences on the planning process of a Million Program suburb that at its inauguration prompted the debate that came to symbolize all the criticism of the Swedish welfare state and its built environment. Swedish corporatism, of which more later in the book, is best described as a way of organizing public decision-making processes around the institutionalized participation of key interest groups.[7] In the corporatist system, organized interests—associations for trade and industry or agriculture, trade unions—have prioritized positions as legitimate participants in the process of public decision-making. In Sweden, these channels have typically included participation in government commissions and official inquiries, representation on ministry boards, and inclusion in political consultations.

Criticism in the debate about the Million Program focused on the lack of public transport, the explosion of consumerism and car ownership, the "dead" environment that produced alienated inhabitants, and the segregation of the poor and those without cars. The architects were attacked too. It was said that had the architects been interested in people's everyday life the architecture would have been different, and not regulated by cars and consumption.[8] I will address this criticism by discussing three important elements that shaped Skärholmen—cars, consumption, and the building industry.

The Blueprint

Skärholmen may have been officially inaugurated in 1968, but the General Plan including the suburb had been proposed as early as 1960. This was a period when the Swedish corporatist system reached its peak, and certain groups dominated the process and the outcome. In the 1960s the corporatist system would shape Swedish urban planning and large-scale architecture, not least at Skärholmen. With a privileged position in the consultation process, organizations such as the Stockholm Chamber of Commerce and the Stockholm Retailers' Association had an important impact on the democratic

The Suburb (1968)

process. Through the Civil Engineering Board (a government agency), interest groups representing the motoring and road-building industries exerted influence. The same went for the building industry, which was heavily represented in the important government commission Investigation of the Industrialization of Buildings that paved the way for standardized and centralized large-scale housing production.[9]

Many descriptions of the future Skärholmen combined an efficient rationality with rhapsodies about Nature—a technological romanticism. Planning algorithms derived from the already questioned Reilly's Law were combined with descriptions of nature (which would be destroyed by the development): "An open field and low meadowland with scattered groups of oaks surrounded by mountains in north and south" would be the place where the motorways connecting the surrounding areas intersect; the extended landscape was to be brought into the man-made structure of Skärholmen's interior.[10] This would-be shopping center would have 5,000 parking spaces and cater to the needs of 300,000 consumers, and the area itself was projected to have 26,000 residents. Reading these descriptions today calls to mind an approach where technology and efficient systems were considered second nature.

The intersection of three motorways became the backbone for the whole area and defined the basic structure. Thanks to the different level of the three roads (picking up the surrounding landscape's topography) regional traffic could access the car park from different levels at the main east entrance to the center. The car park opened into the shopping center, which in turn opened onto the main square, and so on to the

Figure 2.2 Model of Skärholmen by Boijsen & Efvergren. Courtesy: ArkDes Collection.

Architecture and Retrenchment

residential area on the northern side. It was a smooth continuation from Nature to built structures. Skärholmen Centrum was planned as one big machine made of concrete, with underground service roads providing it with all its supplies. Below the service roads, there would be district heating and a cooling plant, supplying the whole area. According to the mythology of Skärholmen, the underground area was soon inhabited by young people sniffing glue.[11]

Skärholmen was divided into five areas: the car park (on the east side); the shopping areas (in the middle); culture and social activities (on the west side); six-story blocks of flats (on the north side, on a hill); and, further west, three-story blocks of flats. Even if the area was separated into functional parts, the overall idea was to intertwine housing and other activities; the public housing company Svenska Bostäder stated "that the housing should connect and even penetrate the Centrum."[12] Skärholmen was a suburb organized through separations of functional units, but with the ambition to merge units into a more complex whole. This strategy was also used on a smaller scale in relation to individual buildings, and anticipated later planning tools used for policy colored by neoliberalization. A community center was proposed but this was canceled, and instead the local schools were to be opened at night to serve the community.[13] The library was also seen as providing the functions of a community center. This strategy of multiprogramming was cheaper and saved space, and was later in 1980 called *radikal samordning* (radical coordination) by the City of Stockholm.[14] A "hotel" for elderly people incorporated into the main structure, with use of both the school and the library, shows the ambition to overcome functional separation.

Consumer Organizations

In the corporatist consultation process, which started as early as 1960, the proposed General Plan for the Sätra area (where Skärholmen would be located) was sent by the City Planning Office to various bodies for comment.[15] The Stockholm Retailers' Association noted in its response that the association had been an important actor in the planning of Vällingby, with a "proposal that led to the construction of Vällingby Centrum and consequently to the breakthrough of the large commercial centres in the planning of the Stockholm region."[16] The association criticized the plan as it preferred "old principles," and warned new solutions should be found otherwise small independent shops would soon disappear. Rather than as proposed splitting shopping between two centers, there should be a single large-scale commercial center next to the motorway. Although the downside of this development was pointed out—for example customers' walking distances and inconvenience would increase—this "future was inevitable." In the association's view, it was "no use in the long run to neglect adapting urban planning to the changed habits and reactions of consumers." Another issue on which the association had strong views was the proposal for areas of mixed housing, where garden city typologies were combined with a more dense urbanity. In their view the explosion of motoring had created the preconditions for a more "homogenous urbanism," as in the United

The Suburb (1968)

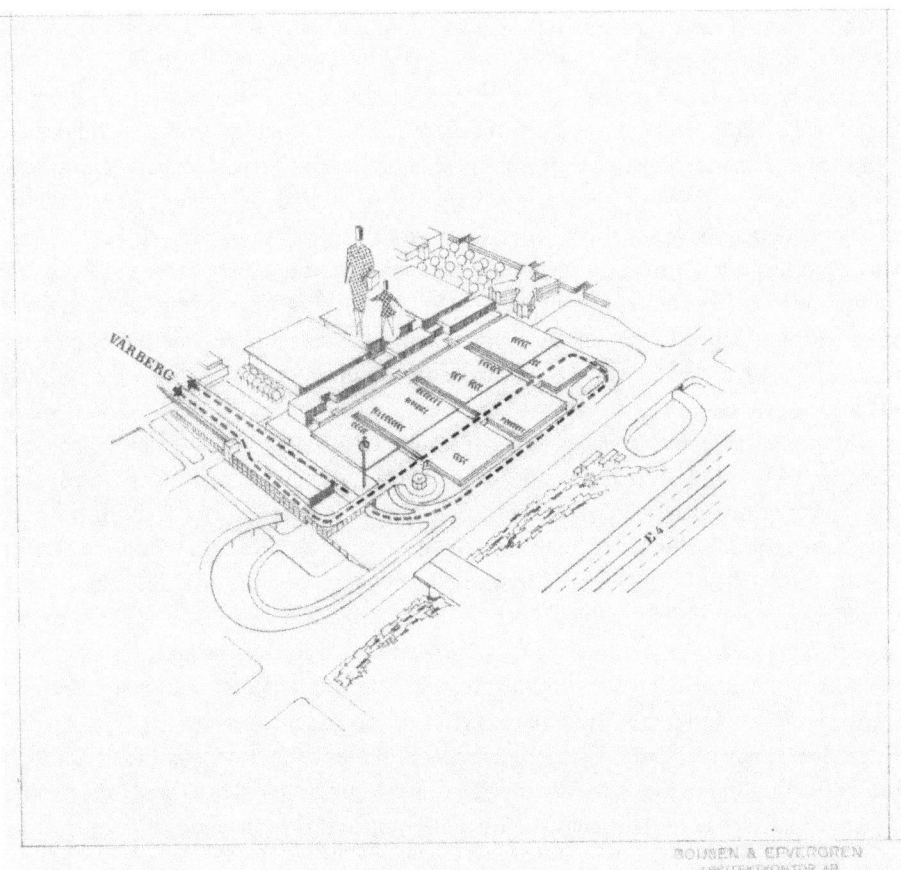

Figure 2.3 Skärholmen Centrum. Drawing by Boijsen & Efvergren. Courtesy: ArkDes Collection.

States: "If the different housing types—single-family houses and blocks of flats—were separated into different neighbourhoods a more adequate environment would likely result."[17]

The response from the Stockholm Chamber of Commerce was similar to the Stockholm Retailers' Association's. But in addition they stressed that the change in modes of travel—from public to private—would give more freedom to planners, since the walking distance between areas of housing and the public transportation network would no longer be a major issue.[18] Not everyone agreed, but the only complaint (backed up with a list of signatures) found in the files came from property owners in the area who believed the planning of public transport to be poor: "Generally, a distance of 1,500 metres between the stations is too long and will lead to an increasing use of private transportation. In keeping with the City's traffic policy the distance between the stations should be less than that."[19]

Architecture and Retrenchment

The General Plan underwent repeated revisions until the final version was produced in 1963. Toward the end of the process a report into consumer factors, ordered by the Stockholm Chamber of Commerce and produced by the Stockholm School of Economics, had a major impact on the final result. A combination of Reilly's Law and their own statement that everyone should be expected to own a car—a dramatic increase—meant providing 5,000 parking spaces instead of 3,000.[20] Put together, the main demands from the business and retail organizations sent to Stockholm's City Planning Office were to have one large commercial center placed next to the motorway instead of one center in each of the two housing areas; to cut the number of small, local, independent shops; to a put distance between houses and blocks of flats; to have greater distances between stations; and to dramatically increase the number of parking spaces.

The organized interest groups were institutional experts and their opinions were objective facts based on science and mathematical formulae, and so most claims from the consumer organizations were incorporated into the final General Plan. In this way the planning process, and eventually the built environment, became a fulfilment of their visions, rather than of the ideas of architects, planners, or politicians. Even though the planning process of Skärholmen was run by the City, and was understood in media as a "public project," one can argue that the built environment was more connected to the flow of private capital than to ideas about society. It was not mainly architectural ideologies that shaped the new suburb: rather, it was the interests given power via the corporatist model. Nonetheless, architecture still served as an important tool. Through the materialization of ideas into architectural forms, differing interests could merge into concrete plans for a future society. Architecture was in this sense a precondition for the corporatist regime to operate the planning process.

The Swedish Roads Association

In the mid-1950s, Sweden was the European country with most cars per capita, and its ascendant car industry argued that society simply had to mobilize for the inevitable further increase in car ownership. By the end of the 1960s, motoring was at the top of the political and public agenda. Measured by value of output, the car manufacturer Volvo in 1970 was the largest company in Sweden.[21] The privileging of motoring in the late 1960s was visible in several official documents that regulated construction.[22] The ruling principle was that norms for how to build and plan cities became looser, while traffic planning was regulated by more precise norms, and city planning had to adapt to roads and infrastructure rather than the other way round.[23] The building layout therefore had to be elastic and adapted to the road system. But how were the roads planned? Beyond the traffic engineers working with the plans, again, organized interests had an important role. The Swedish Roads Association, which led the car lobby, was a central actor in corporatist policy. It is telling that one of the most influential lobby groups in Europe—

The Suburb (1968)

European Roundtable of Industrialists—was initiated in 1983 by the former CEO of Volvo, Pehr G. Gyllenhammar.[24]

An alliance was established in the 1950s between the Swedish Roads Association and the main state agency, the Civil Engineering Board, and together they worked for a "Taylorization" of the roads. In this way, the potentially controversial policy area of traffic became a scientific and objective field for the experts. The new subject of "traffic engineering" was introduced, and engineers were sent to the United States to study at source. In the *Vägplan för Sverige* ("Road Plan for Sweden") of 1959, this scientific and depoliticized approach provided the rules to regulate not only the roads but also city planning and housing.[25]

What about the architects? What kind of architectural response did the car create? The answer was if traffic was turned into a scientific subject for engineers, then it became an aesthetic category for architects.[26] Transport systems were investigated and treated not only as technical problems but also as architectural issues.[27] It is as if in the 1960s, architecture and planning were stigmatized and infrastructure made up a new creative field of freedom. Despite the discourse based on numbers, rationality and expertise,

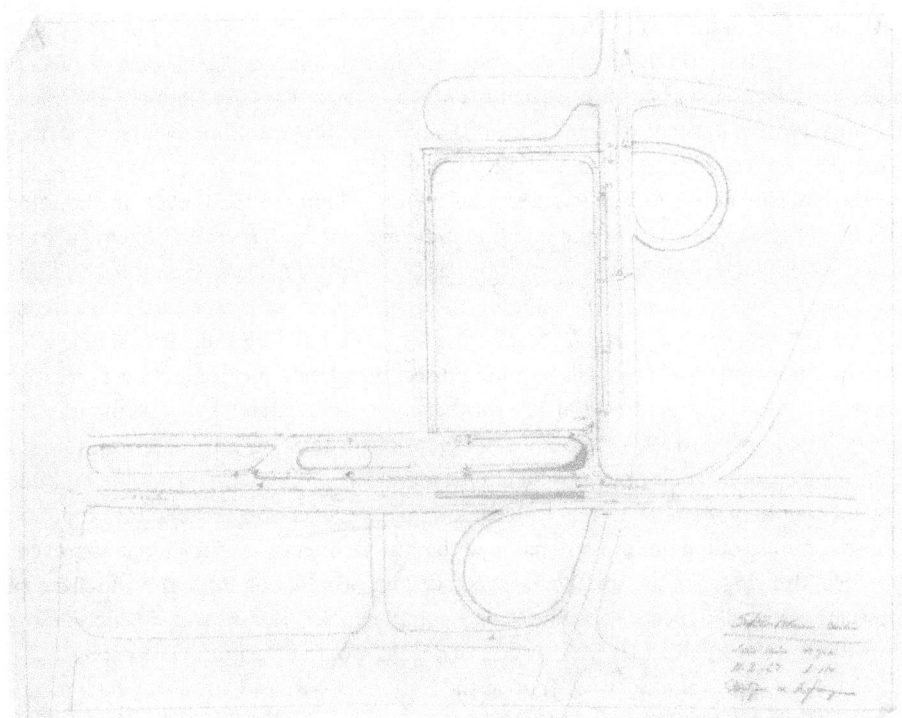

Figure 2.4 Skärholmen Centrum, sketch over traffic circulation. Drawing by Boijsen & Efvergren. Courtesy: ArkDes Collection.

Architecture and Retrenchment

at Skärholmen infrastructural elements such as motorways, communication systems, streets, arterial roads, underground culverts, street decks, and terraces were all treated with high architectural ambition. Skärholmen as a structure could be read as a gigantic machine made up of infrastructure and transport flows. The levels taken from the dramatic topography of the natural landscape were intertwined into a complex network that formed the backbone of the area.

The Building Industry

Skärholmen Centrum was constructed of 25,000 prefabricated building elements, while 50 kilometers of piles reinforced the muddy soil below. A single company, Byggproduktion AB, partly owned by Landsorganisationen (LO, the Swedish Trade Union Confederation), undertook the construction. If motoring and consumer lobby groups were two strong forces in the formation of the architecture of the suburbs, the building industry was another. There have been no state-owned Swedish construction firms, and, contrary to what is often believed, Sweden has had fewer state-owned companies than most other European countries.[28]

In the mid-1960s, there was still a shortage of housing, even though the standard and the supply had dramatically increased in the previous fifteen years, and housing policy was an urgent topic on the political agenda. The idea of building 1,000,000 dwellings in a decade was discussed both in Parliament and by Stockholm City Council. The Social Democrats were hesitant to commit to this very large program, but eventually started what later was called the Million Program.[29]

As shown by Kristina Grange, a fierce debate erupted in the 1950s over "the building troubles."[30] It was initiated by the building industry, which argued that state regulation made building too complicated. The result was that some of the largest national building companies pushed through a simplification, ensuring that technical evaluations should be similar in all Swedish local authorities. The building industry's struggle for simplification and type-approvals became a direct threat, not only for architect's creative ability and social engagement, but also for the wages, as illustrated by a statement in the Swedish Parliament in 1964: "It cannot be defensible to allow an expensive workforce to continually produce new drawings for almost identical buildings."[31] A report on building costs a couple of years later was to have a damaging effect on architectural practice. Those commissioning buildings demanded that the architects add "or similar approved" on their drawings so the architect's specifications would not limit the purchase of alternative (usually cheaper) products and components.[32] This was to downgrade the drawing and the architect's work—price, not design, would determine the final result. In 1967 a "type-approval unit" was set up at the National Board of Planning, which meant that a building detail, or a whole building type, could be approved nationally, and the possibility for local variations ended. This paved the way for the massive, centralized housing production that characterized the Million Program.[33]

The Suburb (1968)

The building industry also put pressure on the official Investigation of the Industrialization of Buildings (1965–71). As a result of the investigation, to maintain continued building production and employment, the government adopted a policy of signing five-year contracts with construction companies. New factories for prefabricated concrete elements were set up by the industry to fulfil these contracts and to meet the demand created by the Million Program. But before the end of the 1960s the Million Program was already running into problems, with flats standing empty; yet because the contracts could not be broken, large-scale housebuilding operations continued into the 1970s.[34]

The Public Debate and the Decision-makers

The critical narrative of the suburbs, as the new locus for the welfare state, told the story of residents caught in a misanthropic architecture that destroyed human individuality. The debate that followed the inauguration of Skärholmen came at a crossroads, just before major changes took shape, and constituted the horizon against which a countermovement was formulated, including the urban guerrilla group Action Dialogue. The role of the architects in this period was ambiguous, as it was a profession covering the whole spectra of experts, civil servants, craftsmen, and activists. In the design of Skärholmen, the project architects were brought on board late in the process and they were given the job of elaborating on a plan that had already been settled, materializing what already had been planned, but they were not to engage in the political and societal questions which to a large extent determined what was being designed. As a group the architects had no institutional channel in the corporatist decision-making process for Skärholmen, and seem to have acted more as craftsmen simply doing a job of work.

Later criticism was directed at explosion in consumerism and motoring; it was a "dead" environment beset by alienation, segregation, and transport poverty. If architects were interested in people's everyday lives, it would all have been different, with no priority given to cars and consumption.[35] Here too, of course—as in the planning process—the architects' voices were absent. In most of the press coverage the planning and decision-making processes were not apparent, so they seem to have been attacks that missed the real targets. The author Lars Gyllensten, however, did not subscribe to the dystopic cliché of the suburb. He instead argued that democracy was being sidestepped in the urban planning and architectural processes.[36] He saw Skärholmen as a symptom of larger problems of democracy and argued that questions relating to the living environment—architecture, urbanism, housing—must be taken back into the political sphere where they belonged. The environmental movement, of which Gyllensten was part, was a new voice in the discussion of urban planning and architecture, and, like the urban activists, transcended the ordinary positions on the left or the right. So, to

Architecture and Retrenchment

Figure 2.5 Skärholmen Centrum, contact sheet. Photo: Sune Sundahl. Courtesy: ArkDes Collection.

follow Gyllensten, the problem was not, as the popularized narrative trumpeted, politicized social-democratic welfare-state building, but rather that architecture and planning were located *outside* politics.

The Suburb (1968)

Figure 2.6 Skärholmen Centrum. Photo: Sune Sundahl. Courtesy: ArkDes Collection.

The Price of Milk

There is an oft-repeated notion that in postwar welfare-state social democracy the government worked through architects to design the everyday life of its citizens. This gives too much credit to the assumption that Swedish functionalism and, later, large-scale building structures were formed mainly by the social-democratic state. When highlighting other actors in the construction of Skärholmen, which became a symbol of a dystopic future in the criticism of the welfare state, I would instead point to the influences of the market and business as being the main forces behind the most criticized aspects of the suburb. The strong market forces operating in the Swedish Million Program strengthened the criticism of the welfare state. The corporatist character of the Swedish system meant that organized interests played a crucial role in the policy process, but as this chapter shows it became a question of whose interests were represented. The corporate system enabled organized interest groups from civil society and business to influence the political decisions. But how and why was a group recruited to the process?

It also raises general questions about the role played by the corporatist system for the realization of larger architectural projects, and the other way around, the role architecture played in the corporatist system. In Skärholmen, consumer and motoring organizations and the building industry were essential to the planning process while the architects were notable by their absence from the decision-making. However, architecture—its

Architecture and Retrenchment

Figure 2.7 Prime Minister Olof Palme (left) and Minister of Agriculture Ingemund Bengtsson meet the "Housewives of Skärholmen." Photographer: Olle Wester / EXP / TT.

drawings, models, and plans—was an important tool in arriving at a consensus between the various interests and pressure groups. The corporate system influenced the design of the architecture, from housing to larger infrastructure, but architecture as a discipline played a crucial role in the consensus-making of the corporatist system.

When the "wives of Skärholmen" demonstrated in central Stockholm to make their voices heard, they created their own channels to the power, such as direct actions and using media to raise public opinion. They used similar techniques as Action Dialogue in their struggle to change existing living conditions by successfully manipulating the system. Such extra-parliamentary actions demonstrated the shortcomings of the corporatist decision-making system. The protests were not only to demonstrate for lower milk prices, they also made "citizens" visible, framed as victims of architecture and planning. The women took direct action that exposed the limitations of the corporatist democracy, which had not only hiked milk prices but also lay behind Skärholmen's urban plan and architecture.

CORPORATISM

In the 1974 article "Still the Century of Corporatism?" Philippe Schmitter brought life to the concept of corporatism connected to the fascist regimes of the 1930s.[1] Reflecting on the verdict passed forty years earlier by the economist Mihaïl Manoïlescu, a Romanian politician and fascist, Schmitter argued for the renewed relevance of the statement "the nineteenth century was the century of corporatism."[2] No longer solely connected to fascism or dictatorship, corporatism could signify practices which democracies promoted under labels such as "participation," "collaborative planning," and "mixed representation."[3] By labeling postwar corporatism as neocorporatism, Schmitter wanted to give the concept a new significance. Today, almost fifty years on from Schmitter's article and with neoliberalization in the rear-view mirror, the corporatist system has transformed from within, and perhaps even contributed to neoliberal transformations.

Architecture and planning have both been affected by these changes, but also been the sites where these shifts have taken place. When corporatism reached its zenith in the Swedish Model, the business and commercial sphere exerted a great influence on postwar architecture, and when the shift to lobbyism came in the 1980s it too had repercussions on architecture. There has been little examination of the relationship between architecture and corporatism, and more studies are needed in order to theorize it successfully. Instead, I will outline a possible starting point for further research. Drawing on analyses of the Million Program area Skärholmen, collective houses, and Stockholm Globe City, I will consider architectural projects as sites of societal transformation in the corporatist decision-making process, involving public, commercial, and private interests. This chapter elaborates on the limits and possibilities inherent in the corporatist system for giving a voice to those often excluded from the built environment's decision-making processes.

Sweden, a Corporatist Democracy

The societal changes of the 1980s were characterized by issues of participation and emancipation, with those forces directed at the state or the public sector, stemming both from civil society and from business. The recalibrations of the corporatist system not only reflected these changes but also contributed to them. In welfare studies and political science, the Swedish Model is famous for being a corporatist democracy characterized by economic prosperity and political stability with no, or very few, strikes or mass protests. However, the 1990 report *Demokrati och makt i Sverige* (itself an example of corporatism) by Maktutredningen (the Power and Democracy Commission) established that Swedish corporatism had died with the Swedish Model in the 1980s.[4] This was in line with the remarks by the early international advocates for postwar corporatism such as Philippe Schmitter and Wolfgang Streeck, who saw corporatism as bound to disappear in a neoliberal world of free markets and welfare-state retrenchment. They were certain that when the basis on which corporatism operated was eroded, corporatist behavior and patterns of governance would disappear.[5] Yet this was not the case in Sweden or internationally, and instead there was a continuation to other forms of bargaining framed in a new economic and political context.[6] Most scholars agree there has been a significant shift in Swedish corporatist democracy from an institutional participation to more informal channels, making democracy more reliant on lobbyism. The mechanisms and effects of the transformations on the corporatist system are not at all obvious, but there can be no doubt the changing conditions have affected architecture, and the sites discussed in this book are examples of this.

What, then, is characteristic of corporatism? With origins in the Latin *corporare* (to make into a body), the concept of corporatism describes society as an organic body striving toward social integration and minimized conflict in order to hold the body, the corpus, together. This view, with a long tradition dating to the medieval guild system, stresses the individual's participation in social groups (corporations), whatever they are centered on—family, profession, politics, ecology, finances, and so on.[7] The French Revolution swept away the tradition of corporatism, and held there should be only two extremities to a society: the state and the citizen. To attain equality, the only channel to the Parliament was the citizen. This revolutionary structure directed the citizens' will and desire with no intermediary levels to the Parliament, which resulted in violent confrontations.

Throughout the nineteenth century, the ideology of corporatism became a way to create political stability and avoid unrest among the workers.[8] Corporatism is often associated with the Italian Fascist Party. Benito Mussolini introduced the ideology in the mid-1920s, and it was implemented in 1939 when the lower house was replaced by the Camera dei Fasci e delle Corporazioni (Chamber of Fasces and Corporations) with representatives appointed by the corporations (the unions and the employers' associations) and the Fascist Party. As an alternative to this and to Lenin's confrontational politics, reformist social-democratic policies had built on negotiation and the legitimization and organization of class compromise by the state. In Sweden this came after violent strikes led to the famous Saltsjöbaden Agreement of 1938, where the Trade Union Confederation (LO) and the Swedish Employers' Association signed an agreement which was the model for future wage negotiations.

In the 1970s the concept was reframed and new research traced the rise of neocorporatism after the Second World War. Following Schmitter and others, corporatism may be described as a way of organizing the public decision-making process based on the institutional participation of key interest groups.[9] Scandinavia and Austria were often singled out as typical cases of corporatist democracies. When civic associations and organized interests—such as associations for trade and industry, trade unions, or the agricultural sector—are given a direct opportunity to participate in the formulation of public policy it is usually called corporatism. Some organized interests are given special status by the state, institutionalizing its contact with them and elevating them to legitimate participants in the public decision-making process.[10] The question is whose voices are institutionalized. In Sweden, these channels have typically included participation in government commissions, representation civil service boards, and inclusion in political consultations. If this participation dominated the decision-making process, the system could hardly be termed democratic, but as one practice in a functioning parliamentary democracy it can be considered a "democratic system with some unclean elements."[11]

Architecture and Postwar Neocorporatism

How to understand the relationship between architecture and corporatism? The four pillars in the universal system of welfare were education, health care, social safety, and housing—and all these sectors, not only housing, were intertwined with architecture and planning of the public institutions connected to these sectors. When studying architecture's relation to state projects, both it and planning were pivotal for the construction of the egalitarian welfare state, in both theory and practice, but it is also clear that architects have less influence than might be expected of their roles as experts in a technocracy. I would suggest one reason for this is that architects as an interest group have not been especially assertive in the corporatist system, and that architectural expertise has been downplayed by the groups which *are* included. As a result, architects and planners (and the built environment as a field) too often became a tool for other groups' interests.[12]

To prepare for political reform such as the Million Program, or new legislation such as the Planning and Building Ordinance, the government appointed official commissions of inquiry consisting of representatives from various sectors: politicians, experts, representatives from interest groups for business, or civil society. The inquiries' findings were published as Statens offentliga utredningar (SOU, Swedish Government Official Reports), which many of the studies in this book are based on, among them the reports by the Collective Housing Committee. Another form of participation was submitting a formal response to the reports: SOU reports are always circulated to democratically elected representatives and nonelected organizations, such as relevant professional associations or other experts or groups. Public architecture and planning projects are always referred to representatives of pre-agreed groups. The submitted responses demonstrate how corporatism allowed for special interest groups to dominate certain aspects of government, and demands from powerful actors intent on protecting business interests rather than the public good hide in the records. The harsh criticism of the state often had its origins in demands made by business, often contrary to advice of planners, architects, and sociologists in the state planning agency.

Architecture and Retrenchment

Corporatism, however, also makes it possible for voices to be heard. One example was the 1948 Collective Housing Committee, which included several women even though they had difficulties making themselves heard.[13] To be included in the corporatist system demanded a certain level of organization. For example, when women working in architecture and the built environment came together in 1980 to found the Kvinnors Byggforum (Women's Building Forum or KBF), they soon became a referral body, and thus submitted formal responses on a proposal to revise the Building Code and Building Ordinance. They were also a referral body and part of the expert group for a new suburb of Stockholm—Hansta—in the early 1980s. The KBF's contribution to the process was the manifesto "It is about our lives" taken from a 1976 exhibition about Alva Myrdal and her work for an equal society.[14] Obviously, it was crucial whose representatives had access to the institutional channels.

Scholars of democracy theory talk about the "intensity problem" when explaining the benefits of corporatism for political stability.[15] In a "clean" democracy all voices are counted, and not given extra weight for being strident, which can lead to a situation where a group that cares a great deal about an issue has to stand back for a majority that cares little. This can result in conflicts, demonstrations, and violence, and corporatism is a way of mediating between groups of wildly differing sizes or intensities. When following the discussion in relation to architecture and planning from 1968 to 1994, it seems clear the corporatist system did not work as well as it could have. Not including the new urban movements of 1968 was a missed opportunity, leaving them to act outside the system by taking direct action and shaping opinion. The same could be said about the women's movement in relation to housing. If their voices had been integrated—heard better in institutional channels—the welfare-state housing sector would have been open to experiments in collective living, developing alternative models to large-scale service solutions and mass-produced housing developments. The institutional channels to the decision-making were used by groups geared by strong desires, but the "intensity problem" in too many instances was driven by profits rather than solidarity and equality. The housewives of Skärholmen had to demonstrate in Humlegården and be humiliated in the press, while the representatives of the Swedish Roads Association sat at the negotiating table.

Pluralism, Lobbying, and Neoliberalization

If corporatism was not dead in the 1980s, it was certainly altered. In the official report *Avkorporatisering* ("Decorporatization") the old system was described as "hollowed out from within," and some argued that Swedish society became even less democratic in the late 1990s.[16] In their view, corporatism was still alive, but eroded on the inside: the government commissions became smaller and political reforms were no longer drawn up as an official report, written by a committee with representatives from different sectors. Instead, the trend was toward the new format, one-person inquiries written in a much shorter time. Paradoxically, however, the more groups which were involved in a decision-making process, the less power they had. The alternative way to exert pressure on politicians, far more common now than in the 1980s, is to attempt it from outside the system, through lobbying and direct action. When it came to architecture and planning, the 1980s was the period when new networks in economics and politics were created, resulting in areas of negotiation that were not transparent for the public, although, interestingly, architects could obtain a new, more important role in the decisions.[17] The history of Stockholm Globe City shows the key role of architecture as a communication medium in negotiations, with aesthetics a powerful tool evoking the actor's personal vision of the future.

Corporatism and lobbyism differ, but there are also similarities, and the institutional participation of interest groups representing traffic, roads, and transport shows strong continuity from corporatism to lobbyism.[18] In the Swedish post-corporatist system, the favored mode for political pressure is still direct contact with politicians and the media. This smooth transformation was not a force threatening corporatism from the outside; it was something that happened from within. As the historian Maiju Wuokko has demonstrated in the Finnish context, it was not a question of whether business supported corporatist institutions, or whether they came together in a neoliberal assault on these institutions; instead, it was through these different approaches that business advocated and realized neoliberalization.[19] In the Swedish context, one can find parallels. Dissecting Stockholm Globe City as one of the large architectural projects in the 1980s in the Stockholm region, demonstrates how the old institutional channels were used in new ways as platforms for lobbying, closed negotiations, and new forms of bargaining. The coming neoliberal planning policies such as planning by negotiation and public–private partnership advanced by using the welfare state and its consensual, corporatist policy-making traditions to the full.

Figure 3.1 Doll's house made by Bo i Gemenskap (Living Together) at the exhibition *Boplats 80*, 1980. Scale 1:12. Photo: Kerstin Kärnekull.

SITE 3
THE COLLECTIVE HOUSE (1935-94)

In 1980, the same year Dolores Hayden asked for "a new paradigm of the home" in her article "What would a non-sexist city be like," a group of Swedish women proposed a reorganized version of the traditional collective house to fit the society of the 1980s.[1] Like a playful nod to what Hayden stated was the most critical (and often implicit) principle of architectural design and urban planning in the last century, "A woman's place is in the home," they stayed at home and made it a room of their own. Domestic work was revalued; from seen as a burden that women should be liberated from, to a resource of human and social capital including men and women on equal terms. At the 1980 exhibition *Boplats 80* (Habitat 80), the fiftieth anniversary of the Stockholm exhibition which had introduced functionalism, the women's group Bo i gemenskap (Live in Community or BiG) presented a furnished doll's house on a scale of 1:12, complete with children, adults, teenagers, and cats and dogs.[2] The interiors were carefully designed with woven carpets, wooden tables, hand-made lamps, and patterned wallpaper.

The doll's house model was an iteration of the modernistic *smalhus* (narrow block) from the 1930s—a *barnrikehus* (large-family homes) for families with many children first built in the Stockholm suburb of Traneberg.[3] This housing typology resulted from Bostadssociala utredningen (the Social Housing Commission), which laid the ground for Swedish housing policy in the postwar period. The model demonstrated the interior of a living-community where the residents activated spaces—there were sewing machines, workshops, bedrooms, large kitchens, and so forth. Being part of the playful postmodern discourse, the doll's house was not only a reaction to modernist large-scale planning, but also a provocation to the professional culture of architecture and urban planning with its strict limitations of norms, taste, and quality. But more important here, BiG stressed the need to rethink social reproduction in such areas as care and housework, and its position in society, which resonated with contemporary Marxist–feminist theories. The position taken by BiG, however, differed from the struggles for "wages for housewives."[4] With among the largest number of women in paid work in the world and the first non-gender-specific parental leave in 1974, the harsh criticism was primarily reserved for large-scale social services commodifying social reproduction and care.

In the Swedish modernist manifesto *acceptera* (1931, "Accept") it was predicted that in the future one of three important forms of housing would be "family hotels" with collective functions.[5] However, despite the influential architects' and politicians' positive words, the collective house as a program and a building typology was never incorporated into the welfare-state system of subsidies and housing norms.[6] The result was that very few were realized, and here I argue that the collective house became more important as a discursive object (in debates, investigations, and reports) from the 1930s to the 1980s in discussions about how to organize housing services and social reproduction. This site brings the *service question* to the fore, elaborating on distributing social reproduction and care in relation to housing, and it shows how housing services have been at the center for strident conflicts between the public, private, and civil sectors since the formation of the welfare state in the 1930s to its decline in the 1980s and 1990s.[7] In the extensive discourse on housing services in the daily press and among politicians, architects, sociologists, and other professionals in this period, the collective house was a concrete example of how to materialize and spatially distribute the often-abstract notion of services. With this focus, the chapter highlights the home not as a private entity with strict borders, but as a fluctuating territory—a space of conflict—whose borders are constantly negotiated.

My inquiry into the collective house builds on scholars such as Dick Urban Vestbro, who have significantly contributed to the knowledge on the field. Further, the readings of this site draw on Nancy Fraser's discussion of capitalism's foreground–background relations: how social reproduction, ecology, and political power are necessary background conditions for capitalism's economic front story. She argues that the "hidden abode" (the background conditions) has political potentialities and "harbours distinctive ontologies of social practice and normative ideals."[8] In the past, and especially in periods of crisis, these institutional divisions of capitalism have often been a focus, with boundaries challenged and changed, such as between social reproduction and production, paid labor and nonpaid labor. Here, I will investigate forms of collective living and large-scale services as two poles in these "boundary struggles," and how social reproduction worked as "new ontologies of social practice," intertwining histories of emancipation, participation, and neoliberalization. When Fraser maps the boundary struggles historically she outlines three regimes: the nineteenth-century regime of liberal competitive capitalism that created a new bourgeois imaginary of domesticity stressing production and reproduction as separate spheres; the state-managed capitalism of the twentieth century that internalized social reproduction through state and corporate provision of social welfare; and finally the globalizing financialized capitalism of the present that has promoted state and corporate disinvestment from social welfare.

Here, I will focus on the passage between the second and the third regimes, and trace three waves of the "collective house." Each wave articulates a specific boundary struggle, negotiating the organization of social reproduction and collective services in relation to the architecture of the domestic. The first takes its starting point in the formations of the welfare state and covers small-scale collective houses with paid staff. The second wave is defined by institutional large-scale services (combining public and private actors) and the compartmentalizing of social reproduction in the 1960s and 1970s. Finally, the third wave is framed by rethinking social reproduction as a resource in the 1980s co-housing movement.

It was not until new forms of governance emerged that the collective house was supported in policy decisions and in public debates, and this site investigates how notions of self-regulation were implemented in "local" co-housing. The chapter shows how the new model of collective houses formulated a radical imaginary to marketization and privatization, but also how the discourse of deregulation was played out in the feminist movement as an act of emancipation. It is demonstrated how the shortcomings of the patriarchal welfare state, perceiving the collective house as a threat toward family values and the universal notion of welfare, never opened for emancipatory alternatives of housing inside the public welfare system, and so contributed to the decline of the same system.

But first some terminology. In Sweden the same term, *kollektivhus* (collective house), is used for both the early projects in the 1930s and the projects with a new organization from the late 1970s. Internationally, however, the terminology often distinguishes between two types of organization. In collective houses, employed staff provide the services, whereas houses where the residents share services and household work between them are instead called collaborative housing or co-housing. One can be even more specific and use collaborative housing when referring to collaborations among residents, and co-housing when referring to housing with communal spaces and shared facilities. Sometimes the word "co-house" is used when focusing on the physical building and organization.[9] I will use the term "co-housing" to denote this second wave of collective houses, except where collective house was specifically indicated. "Intentional communities" is a label for many of the collective ways of living based on residents' intentions.

The Collective House Writ Large

It is not far-fetched to look back on the twentieth-century discourse of the collective house as a mirror of wider society, showing the contested politics of social reproduction and care work. The collective house became a device for transforming abstract discussions about "social services," "communal spaces," and "care" into material spatial organizations. It also mirrored the conflictual site where multiple projections, often in opposition, were overlaid. Notions of the family, gender relations, housework, regulations, and the role of the state were just a few of the pressing issues that came together in an architectural assemblage of politics, regulations, spatial organization, and design. This chapter unpicks some of the strands in this intertwined history, beginning with a brief introduction to the role played by the collective house on the level of the population, in this case the national welfare state, *folkhemmet*, or the People's Home.[10]

Since the Industrial Revolution, the trajectory of experimentation with collective housing has tracked the radical impact capitalism had on social life, gender relations, labor division, and family structures.[11] "Intentional communities" have been test beds for organizing welfare and reproductive services, and they worked as litmus tests for how social and economic life was played out (enhanced, directed, limited) in society, often revealing the shortcomings of the organization. Early examples important in developing welfare services were the nineteenth-century utopian socialist communities such as Robert Owen's textile mill town New Lanark and Charles Fourier's kibbutz-like *phalanstères*, whose legacy was resuscitated by Swedish social democracy.[12] The role played by social reproduction in production and economic growth was consciously explored through architecture and spatial layout in these "living-machines" with educational systems, domestic areas with common activities providing social services.[13] New Lanark and the *phalanstères* were autonomous communities, little related to the surrounding world (in New Lanark the interface to the outside was addressed through "visitors").[14] These communities created their own utopian worlds closed off from society, and provided welfare for all residents or workers. In a smaller scale, they foreboded the national welfare states, which combined in a system of social security, biopolitical upbringing, economic thinking, and growth.

If the collective house is a mirror of the society, the Swedish People's Home can be interpreted as a collective house on the level of the population. When the social-democratic leader Per Albin Hansson used the concept in a famous speech in 1928, the People's Home had already existed since 1898 as a collective urban space for all citizens, independent of political or religious affiliation, class, and gender.[15] Around 1900 an infrastructure of urban commons emerged all over Sweden, from People's Homes, to People's Kitchens, People's Houses, and People's Parks.[16] These collective spaces, along with the Swedish popular movements (e.g. the temperance movement, the labor movement, the women's movement), created channels of distribution and communication the welfare state could build on, but they were gradually transformed and increasingly regulated by the state from the 1930s to the 1970s.[17] The domestic sphere tied into this network of commons and became part of the political scheme to liberate, foster, and govern citizens. The cooperative housing movement paved the way for several welfare-state functions in relation to housing, such as kindergartens, communal laundries, rubbish chutes, and individual bathrooms.

The slowing of Sweden's population growth was an urgent political issue that the social democrats Alva and Gunnar Myrdal addressed in *Kris i befolkningsfrågan* (*Crisis in the Population Question*) in 1934.[18] By connecting social policy to economic policy, the Myrdals laid out a new direction in Swedish politics, using housing norms and reform as the seminal tools for regulating the social domain and producing a healthy population and a growing economy. For young people to find childbearing and childrearing attractive, they argued, the family must be "broken up" for the working day and gather again in the evening. The family should not be dissolved, but reorganized in a more open form, connecting the individual to the societal order. As pointed out by Sven-Olov Wallenstein, the housing model introduced in *acceptera* and by Alva and Gunnar Myrdal can be read as a form of biopolitical power not based on prohibition or discipline, but on "a vital force that traverses the body politic, running from the individual through the family up to the level of the population."[19] In the Myrdals', and especially Alva Myrdal's, vision of the housing of the future, with architects such as Sven Markelius, the collective house was a typology frequently used. If the crisis in the population issue was one urgent problem, another was the shortage of labor,

The Collective House (1935–94)

one solution for which was for women to take paid work—and the collective house providing services could respond to both these quests. Though most often rejected, the collective house featured repeatedly in discussions about the welfare state. Like an itchy scab, it and its contested themes—threats, promises, control techniques, radical fantasies—were always there. In constructing a welfare society, how was one to organize family life? What was the responsibility of the state versus the individual or family? How to provide "universal welfare"?

One cornerstone of the Swedish welfare-state housing policy as it was first formulated in the 1930s was a generally oriented policy without individual assessments, dominated by public housing companies, *allmännyttan*.[20] This was part of the "universalism" significant for the welfare-state policies including the whole population and not just targeted groups, with the ambition of "a higher level of social equity than selective or stratifying policies."[21] The first wave of early collective houses serving a small community was understood as inimical to universal welfare goals, which hindered the authorities from subsidizing services in collective houses. This resulted in large-scale service houses (I do not consider them collective houses) in the 1960s with changed relations between resident communities and the surrounding communities. These houses were not only supposed to provide resources for the residents, but the services provided were instead assets for the larger community, or as urban commons for a larger community.[22] The relation between the interior of the collective house and the exterior society has been analyzed in terms of "inward-oriented community" and "society-related detachment," and this relationship had an important impact not only on the collective house, but also on the city at large.[23]

Small Collective Houses with Paid Staff

Before the first collective house became a reality in Sweden in the early 1930s, there had been earlier experiments with forms of collectivity. In 1892, the teacher and philanthropist Agnes Lagerstedt organized cheaper housing with collective functions for the working class, and the 1906 Hemgården *Centralkök* (communal kitchen), managed by a private company, provided services to the emerging middle class.[24] In these initiatives, the main focus was to increase the living standard and liberate (often privileged) women by providing services, such as a cooperative shop, a restaurant, and a laundry.[25] In the early 1920s a strong housing cooperative movement took form, introducing collective functions associated with housing, such as kindergartens, laundries, and rubbish chutes.[26] The first collective houses were true to type and had paid staff to serve residents, inspired by Russian blocks of flats, such as the Narkomfin Building.[27] The collective house described here was a response to the insufficiency of the separation of the two spheres—production and social reproduction—with the effect that it consolidated class differences. This organization stood in stark contrast to the collectives in old Moscow proposed by the Soviet ambassador in Stockholm Alexandra Kollontay, where household work was shared between the residents and the focus lay on community life and the reorganization of the family.[28] Yet it was the organization with paid staff which was further developed as the first Swedish collective houses to be realized.

The architect Sven Markelius, in close collaboration with Alva Myrdal (then president of the Professional Women's Club), designed a large-scale project in the Stockholm suburb of Alvik. The project consisted of three modernist 12-story blocks of flats, each containing 200 flats with collective services provided by hired staff, such as a dining room with a collective kitchen, dumb waiters, laundry, and cleaning. There was also place for gymnastics, sun bathing, and a large nursery in an annex connected to the flats where children could stay overnight. Sven Markelius described how the building provided a life-pattern that imitated the upper classes and protected social class hierarchies, and he wanted to spare working mothers the difficulties a family without a maid had to live with; a system that repeated the favored methods of rich people all over the globe.[29] On the one hand, the early collective houses were often more expensive to live in than other rented accommodation, but it had the potential to be state-financed and run by the local authority housing companies or the housing cooperatives.[30]

The Alvik project was never built; instead, a smaller modified version was realized in John Ericssonsgatan in Stockholm in 1935 (Figure 3.2).[31] It was difficult to find a construction company to build the house, but armed with a list of future residents, many famous and influential, and organized as a tenant–owner association, they did find the builders Gumpel & Bengtsson. A kindergarten, a laundry, a restaurant with dumb waiters up to the flats, and shops were among the collective activities in the house (Figure 3.3). The interest which Alva and Gunnar Myrdal shared with many others in designing a modern social and family policy demanded knowledge about how the lives of communities, families, and children unfolded, and the child became a device or model for a new social order. This was (as showed in Site 1) later repeated in the 1968 struggles to change the system, but that time it was the child who possessed the primitive natural forces that went *against* the order and bureaucracy of the welfare state.

As argued by Jacques Donzelot, the family is a privileged space for modulating individuals' most private behavior and for controlling the forms of the family within a societal transformation, and in this sense the family is a basic element in political issues. Furthermore, Donzelot argued that the "social worker" was a crucial profession in the process of "normalization," because they identified families at risk using interrogations and questionnaires—and the technique of intervention was not prohibitions but corrections.[32] At John Ericssonsgatan it was not the social worker but "the educator" who mapped behaviors that could be compared and understood in relation to normalizing interventions. In 1958 Barnpsykologiska forskningslaboratoriet (the research laboratory for child psychiatry) was inaugurated on the first floor, and with the maternity nurse Gunhild Frendelius they ran the "Frendelius" kindergarten (Figure 3.4). Using one-way mirrors and sound recordings, the children's behavior was observed (similar to the observations in conjunction with Moderna Museet's exhibition *Modellen* ten years later).

The Collective House (1935–94)

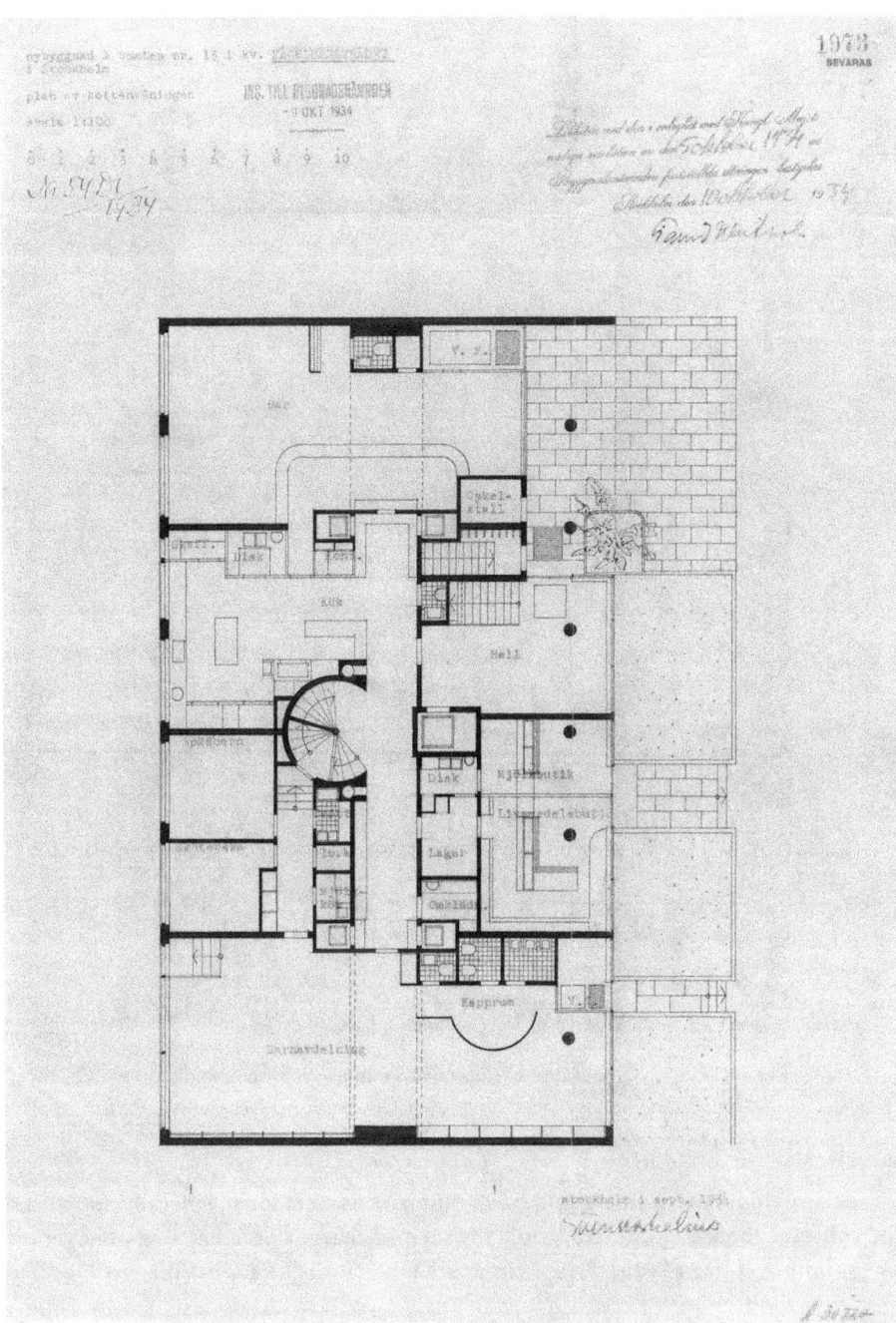

Figure 3.2 Sven Markelius' drawing of the collective house at John Ericssonsgatan in Stockholm, 1934. Stockholm City Archive. Courtesy: Stefan Markelius.

Figure 3.3 A dumb waiter in the collective house at John Ericssonsgatan. Photographer: Unknown. Courtesy: ArkDes Collection.

Social-democratic women, and other women's associations, generally supported the collective house movement, while the men in charge of the housing policy most often did not.[33] In 1939 the Yrkeskvinnors Klubb (Professional Women's Club) had erected a modernist collective house of their own, YK-huset, designed by Hillevi Svedberg and Albin Stark, with a restaurant, gymnastics, and a nursery. Despite that, politicians, public housing companies, and cooperatives hesitated to back up the realization of collective houses; the private developer Olle Engqvist developed the typology and built seven collective houses between 1938 and 1955, designed by well-known architects in a Swedish postwar style known as "new empiricism"

The Collective House (1935–94)

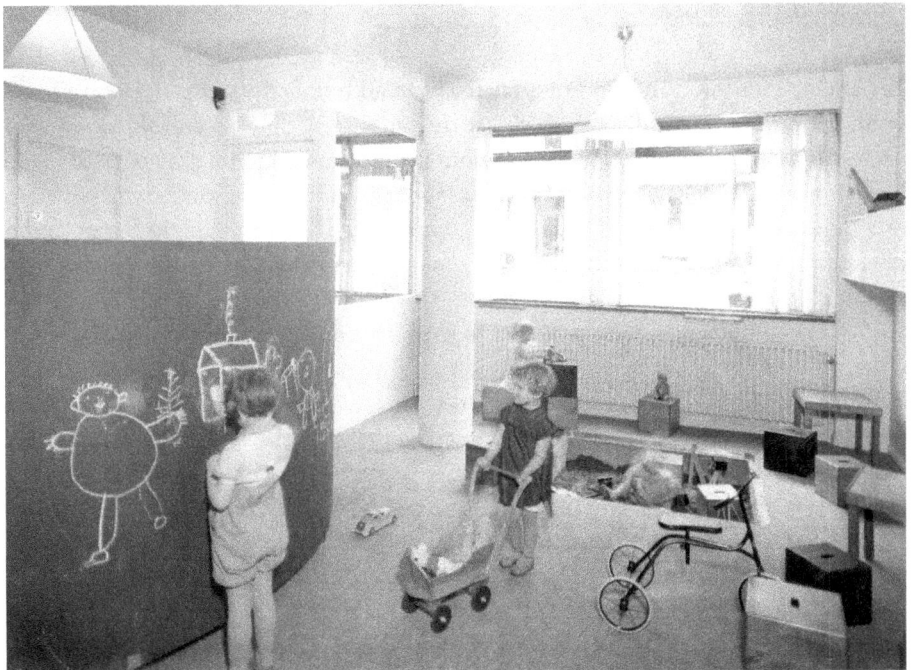

Figure 3.4 The kindergarten at the collective house at John Ericssonsgatan. Photographer: Unknown. Courtesy: ArkDes Collection.

Figure 3.5 Dining room at the Marieberg Collective House by Sven Ivar Lind (left), and the exterior of the collective house Elfvinggården by Backström & Reinius (right). Photographers: Unknown (left), G. E. Kidder Smith (right). Courtesy: ArkDes Collection.

(saddle roofs, bricks, and other elements with a more vernacular style).[34] All of the postwar collective houses before 1980 were based on a labor division with employed staff and mandatory purchase of meal tickets, and even though some women were liberated from housework, the structure protected a class- and gender-unequal system (Figure 3.5).[35]

Architecture and Retrenchment

Compartmentalizing Social Reproduction

In parallel with the realization of a relatively small number of collective houses, the typology turned into a discursive object in state investigations, policymaking, and professional and public debate. This discourse highlighted the relationships between "housing" and "services," such as domestic labor and care. How should domestic work and care be organized? Privatized or/and commodified? How should the organization operate in reality as architecture? Who should be responsible for the provision of services—the state, the private sector, or the civil society? Instead of focusing on the well-explored housing question, I want to shed light on the adjacent *service question*, closely connected with the collective house and impossible to separate from housing, but have not received the same attention in architectural histories. In the postwar years until the 1980s several committees, investigations, reports, and publications were instigated and produced by many actors. Comparing the early reports with the later ones indicates several shifts. First, there was a shift in the level of decision-making, from the state as the sole actor to the local authorities; second, the reports reveal two perspectives on collectivity from service to collaboration; third, the increasing number of women authoring the reports. This implicates that the phenomenon of the collective house, around which hovering the larger question of social services, has a much greater importance than the small number of completed projects would suggest, and I would suggest the collective house had even greater importance as a symbolic object.

In the reports and discussions following the publications, the collective house was an example of how to spatially articulate the often-abstract term "service," and it demanded precision (spatially, socially, economically) in how to define the boundaries between social reproduction and production. A pivotal circumstance for the service question were universalism in welfare-state policy that pushed the format of the small collective house providing services for the inhabitants of the house, toward large-scale service centers offering services to a larger community. Several proposals were presented for how to organize a service market providing care and domestic work, compartmentalized into bits and pieces which required a certain price.

In Sweden, the housing service question came to the fore in 1948, at the instigation of the Collective Housing Committee.[36] It had been tasked with investigating a "community facility that directly complements the homes and facilitates families' daily lives, and provides better conditions for association life (föreningsliv) and social gatherings, leisure activities for different age groups, etc."[37] As the quote shows, the organization of services had an important role to play not only for communities but also on the level of the population—how to foster a healthy, sound and responsible citizen. The committee was in operation for eight years and published four interim reports on home care, on collective houses, on laundries, and on communal spaces and the final report in 1956, *Hemmen och samhällsplaneringen* ("Homes and urban planning").[38] The Collective Housing Committee was followed by a great many

Figure 3.6 Some of the reports that were published on services, collective functions, and collective houses. From top left: *Kollektivhus. Bostadskollektiva kommitténs betänkande II*, Government Official Report SOU 1955:8; *Servicekommitténs utlåtande* by Konsum, Stockholm, 1968; *Boendeservice 1*, Government Official Report SOU 1968:38; *Serviceverksamheter i Stockholms innerstad*, Stockholm stads fastighetskontor/City of Stockholm, 1970; *Boendeservice 4*, Government Official Report SOU 1971:26; *Kollektivhus*, SABO (Swedish Public Housing Association), 1984.

reports on services, collective functions, and collective houses in the 1960s and 1970s, not only by the state, but also by local authorities, public housing companies, and corporations.

The Collective Housing Committee reveals a shift in how to solve the service question, from a focus on the realized small-scale collective houses to notions of a more general large-scale service provision. The committee advocated more state-funded experiments with collective houses to provide them for a broader population, but they also stressed the importance of the collective house to serving the larger community, not only the residents of the building.[39] Collective functions in the building were to be shared and combined with activities in the area, although it remained unclear how that should be organized. In the final report (1956), the collective house was described as a *service center* with employed hostesses who could give advice and mediate services from the surrounding neighborhood. In line with the arguments that social services should be available for everyone, the new category, *familjeservice* (family service), was invented that provided all households with paid domestic work, such as delivery services, cleaning, shopping, housework, and laundry. The existing regulations sent conflicting messages. On the one hand, state loans were given to public or cooperative housing companies, including collective houses;[40] on the other, they did not cover the common premises, so the possibilities for developing the benefits of living together by reducing flat sizes (and the individual cost) and having more communal spaces were anything but enhanced.[41] What we can see taking shape in the committee's proposal was a new market for social services related to housing.

The market for services was quickly established and expanded, as several investigations show, for example, the 1965 state report *Höjd bostadsstandard* ("Improved housing standards") that laid the groundwork for the Swedish Million Program. The report recommended *not* developing collective houses, but instead providing area services not limited to certain buildings.[42] The government reports tell us something about a new understanding of the concept. From being inscribed in a physical and social context in the form of architecture (the collective house was physically articulated in space and related to a social group), services had lost their physicality and specificity (no defined function and no site) and existed more as a commodity in the market, in the *service sector*. Following the pattern of organizing and running industrial companies, commercial, social, and cultural services were planned in the centers of suburbs and urban districts, intended to be available for everyone.[43] In the late 1960s and early 1970s, several reports on services were published, and a new official committee on the service question in housing was appointed in 1967, and in 1968 the *Boendeservice* report (housing services) was published to spread "information and raise awareness about service questions."[44]

Similarly, the Swedish Cooperative Union initiated a committee on services in 1969 and advertised their own large-scale solutions: *serviceknutar* (service points) and *servicecentraler* (service centers) combining goods and social services.[45] In an article in the daily press, the Swedish American architect Judith Turner referred to Bertrand Goldberg's mixed-use building in Marina City, Chicago, as a model for organizing services in a Swedish context, namely, rendering services as a commodity on the free market.[46] Turner pointed out the crucial question of who took responsibility for the services: Who was paying and who was providing? The nongovernment Swedish Cooperative Union Committee proposed that the service should be publicly funded through large-scale *serviceinstitutioner* (service departments, see Figure 3.8). However, no one took responsibility for the financing, and the governmental report *Boendeservice* stated that public financing was nothing to take for granted: Was it

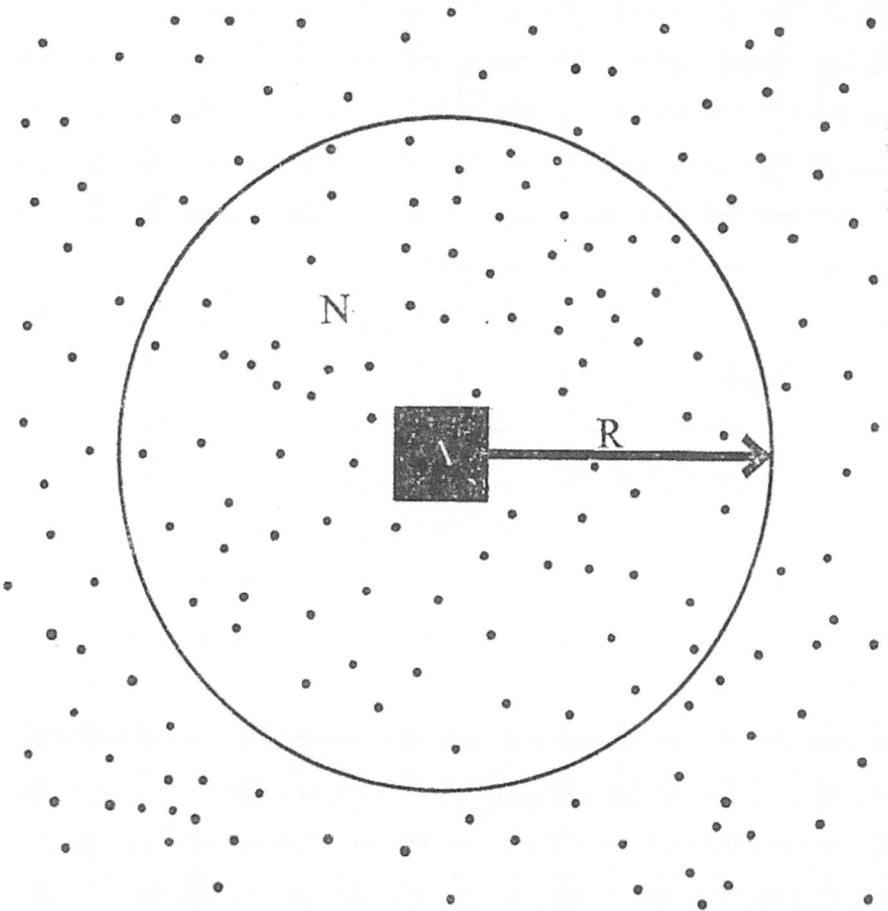

Figure 3.7 "For all service functions, which require buildings or facilities, you can make this principal figure. The service facility A must be 'sufficiently large' to be able to function efficiently and the distance R to the furthest resident user must be acceptable. The circle must then be home to the number of users N that corresponds to the facility's desired base. If you cannot achieve this ideal condition, you must either reduce the facility, stretch the distance R or find another form of service offer." Citation and diagram from *Boendeservice 1*, Government Official Report SOU 1968:38, p. 15.

the public or private sectors or civil society which would take responsibility for these services?[47]

The discourse on services in government reports was characterized by two overlapping organizations of collective functions: first, *the collective house*, incorporating services for a smaller group (dining halls, childcare, etc.) as an "inward-oriented" community; and second, *large-scale social services* (service centers, service points, etc.) available to the community. The first was criticized for being self-sufficient and closed off from

Architecture and Retrenchment

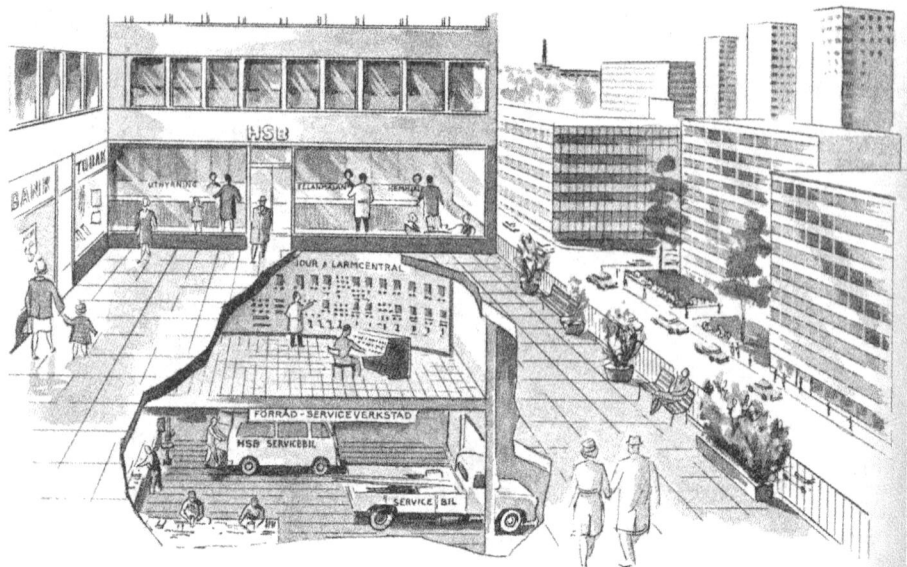

Figure 3.8 HSB Service Center—a sketch from 1965. Reprinted from Dick Urban Vestbro, *Kollektivhus från enkökshus till bogemenskap* (Stockholm: Statens råd för byggnadsforskning, 1982).

the surrounding community, while the second was accused for being too large-scale and impersonal, thus missing the ability to build a sense of sociability and community. The large-scale solution was partly a result of universal welfare thinking, but also a way to rationalize the service question. Seen as two extremes, these figures were also combined into forms of service house. One was Sollentuna service house (1972, see Figure 3.10), in a Stockholm suburb, followed by Fältöversten (1973, see Figure 3.9) in the city center, both of which combined large-scale complete service solutions spread out in a housing area with a single collective house.[48] Sollentuna service house was a megastructure: it combined ten nine-story blocks of flats and some lower buildings, amounting to 1,250 households, and serviced by a network of restaurants, shops, and household services (Figure 3.10). It was criticized for not differing greatly from living in a suburban center with ordinary facilities nearby, however.[49]

Services as a Resource, a Countermovement

In response to the large-scale service solutions, there were countermovements. For example, in the late 1960s the author and journalist Ingrid Sjöstrand had already proposed an alternative model to large-scale service centres, *samhem* (co-home).[50] She argued for communal spaces in all housing areas with 75–100 people. Co-homes should be open

The Collective House (1935–94)

Figure 3.9 Fältöversten—an inner-city Service House in Stockholm. Photographer: Unknown. Courtesy: ArkDes Collection.

Figure 3.10 Sollentuna Service House. Photographer: Per Adolphson.

Figure 3.11 Sollentuna Service House. Women queuing for the collective laundry (left). The signs in the hallway (right) show the directions to the collective functions: "Kindergarten," "Health Care," "House Hold Appliances," "Men's Fashion," "Mother- and Childcare," "Radio and TV," "Physiotherapy," "Hobby Workshop," "Tobacco and Toys," "Exhibition," "Womens Clothes," and "Medical Station." Photographer: Bengt af Geijerstam (left and right).

to multiple functions such as spaces for gymnastics, dances and parties, and films; a large kitchen for 15–20 people; workshops; a sauna; and rooms where one could stay overnight. Counteracting social separation, co-homes mixed generations, ethnicities, and functional variations.[51] Byalagen and other groups from the 1968 movement had been fighting for communal spaces in housing areas for many years, raising the subject with the housing-sector authorities and politicians. Byalagen's and Sjöstrand's proposal finally gave a result, and in 1970 it was decided that to get state loans to finance new buildings a 100-square-meter "warm and sound-proof" communal space with cooking facilities *must* be erected for every 40–50 households.[52]

A similar rethinking of collectivity, services, and affinity was formulated in the 1975 publication *Service och gemenskap där vi bor i Stockholm* (Services and community where we live in Stockholm) by the local authority board's committee for women's issues, and in the exhibition *Det gäller vårt liv* (It is about our lives) and a debate at Kulturhuset in Stockholm.[53] In May 1976, *Svenska Dagbladet* stated that "more and more people want to live in collective houses."[54] The same message was to be read in the feminist Fredrika Bremer-Förbundets magazine *Hertha* and the Social Democrat Women's Union's *Morgonbris* that month. Here, service and collective functions were not seen as produced by one part and consumed by another, but as activities that strengthened the social network of services. From being a burden converted to a commodity in the market (for public and private consumption), "services" were framed as a resource and human capital that must be managed in the best way. In 1977, the authorities even showed a new interest in collective houses, and *God Bostad 5*, the volume on collective houses, set out guidelines for how to realize a collective house with 250 flats.[55]

The first example of a local authority collective house influenced by ideas of small-scale services and shared labor was Stolplyckan in Linköping in 1982, which comprised 180 households (Figure 3.12). Stolplyckan was a mix of the two ways of organizing services and collective functions. Kindergarten and service flats for the elderly were integrated in the housing block with staff available for all residents; a restaurant served food during the day and at night the residents organized dinners, and the premises assigned to children or the elderly could be co-used by everyone living in the house. However, the developer and Linköping local authority were breaking new ground by incorporating small-scale services managed by residents into the building structure and the relatively small community. According to the architects Höjer-Ljungqvist, the project had been made possible by the special conditions afforded by the ongoing work of *socialförvaltningen* (the local authority social services) to integrate small-scale care leisure activities into the housing areas as part of the revaluation of large-scale schemes together with the new guidelines for collective houses in *God Bostad 5*.

In the 1970s, the qualitative aspects of housing were seen in a new light. It was not the lack of housing but the lack of community, the growing alienation, and the cultural superficiality which were criticized, and different variations of collective housing as services emerged as possible solutions.[56] In the 1980s, housing became "a social project" rather than a technical one, focusing increasingly on the "realization of qualities of life."[57] The architectural competition *80-talets boendeformer* (The 1980s Forms of Housing) showed the move from form and aesthetics to social aspects: for example, it was not elaborated on how to build *for* a community but, rather, on how to *build* a community; on how to create a production of housing that enabled citizens and experts to collaborate in the planning process.[58] This focus on creating strategies for building communities spread like wildfire in the 1980s, affecting not only housing companies but also authorities. Socialtjänstlagen (the Social Services Act) from 1982 introduced the idea that social services should primarily strengthen community and solidarity, and the local environment was said to be as crucial for developing individuals' and groups' own resources.[59]

This rethinking of services in relation to the built environment coincided with a larger societal transformation related to the service sector. Around 1970, the service sector (not including unpaid housework) for the first time employed more people than the industrial and construction sectors, at the end of the 1970s, more women were working in the public sector than with unpaid housework. However, in parallel with the many women moving from unpaid domestic work to paid work in the public service sector, the rate of public investment halved from 1970 to 1980. A new labor market with public services, such as childcare and eldercare, enabled women's emancipation, yet the decline in investment in the public sector called for new ways to think about services and public governance. As the literature points out, remarkably, the structural transformations hit the sector producing human capital that became increasingly important for growth, such as education and care. Instead of creating an innovative expansion in a sector through investments, these savings resulted in a lack of initiative and creative space.[60]

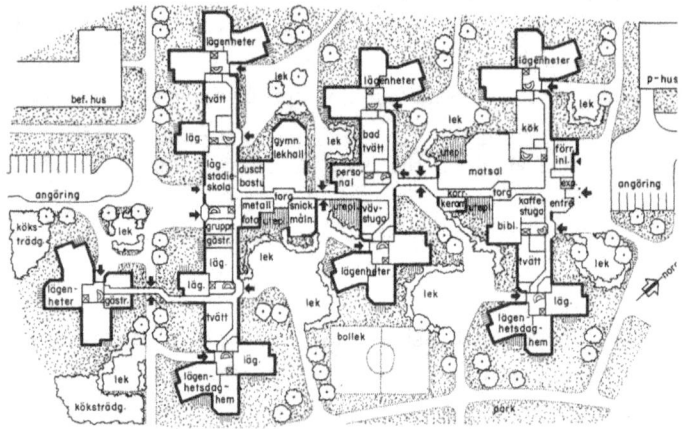

Figure 3.12 The Collective House Stolplyckan, Linköping. Photographer: Sune Sundahl. Courtesy: ArkDes Collection (top). Site Plan reprinted from Dick Urban Vestbro, *Kollektivhus från enkökshus till bogemenskap* (Stockholm: Statens råd för byggnadsforskning, 1982).

Melinda Cooper shows how the critique and dismantling of the public sector in an American context was a backlash for women's emancipation—why pay for something (through taxes) that was for free?[61] Also in a Swedish setting the austerity in public care and education (mainly governed by male-dominated politics) resulted in limited resources for the service sector (and the collective house movement), which hindered

The Collective House (1935–94)

innovative thinking in relation to services and new small-scale formats, and instead left it to women and the market to remedy the problem. Consequently, the turbulent shifts taking place in domestic work and services with the emerging economic crises in the public sector left "services" in urgent need of inventions, new investors, and a general rethink. In the mid-1970s, for the first time, the percentage of women with paid work in the public sector was higher, and still increasing, than the percentage of women doing unpaid domestic work. At this precise moment, the feminist criticism of large-scale services was being articulated in parallel with the collective house managers cutting housing services for financial reasons.

The Italian philosopher and one of the founders of the operaismo movement, Mario Tronti, described in the beginning of the 1960s a situation in which all social relations were subsumed under capital and the traditional distinction between society and factory was collapsing: "the whole society lives as a function of the factory and the factory extends its exclusive domination to the whole of society."[62] For Tronti, this shift emerged with the construction of the welfare state and when state regulations pursued a singular rational plan in the service of capitalist reproduction, a well-known position also taken by Manfredo Tafuri.[63] In line with both Tafuri and Tronti, the large-scale domestic service sector in the 1960s and 1970s was a way of capitalizing on social reproduction and simultaneously turning it into a field that lost its progressive force.

Feminists such as Mararosa Dalla Costa, Selma Jones, and Silvia Federici were strongly influenced by Tronti and the operaismo movement to build a new type of political subjectivity where the spatial and functional organization of social reproduction was in focus.[64] However, starting with Tronti's notion of the collapse of the barriers between factory and society, the feminist notion of a "social factory" gave agency to architecture and social reproduction. The circuit of capitalist production and the production of the social factory was understood as "centred above all in the kitchen, the bedroom, the home … and from there it moved on to the factory, passing through the school, the office, the lab."[65] Mariarosa Dalla Costa (and Selma Jones) labeled it the "woman question," referring to the role of women as it had been produced by the capitalist division of labour.[66]

Before moving on to the Swedish feminist response to the women question around the 1980s, we will look more closely into the events at Hässelby Familjehotell that mirrored, but also contributed to, this rethinking, paving the way for politicians to initiate a second wave of collective houses—co-housing—organized on a collaborative basis.

The Battle for Hässelby Familjehotell

Hässelby Familjehotell (Hässelby Family Hotel), built by the private firm of Olle Engkvist and designed by the architect Carl-Axel Acking, was at the time the largest collective house in Sweden. Four high-rises connected with lower buildings (and a 750-meter-long corridor system) contained 340 flats, four inner courtyards, one restaurant with two

Figure 3.13 Hässelby Familjehotell (architect Carl-Axel Acking) inaugurated 1955. Photographer: Studio Gullers. Courtesy: Nordiska Museet.

dining rooms, a large space for gymnastics, a youth club, supermarket, kindergarten, a garage for eighty cars, and a chapel. In 1976 Hässelby Familjehotell thus became a battleground for intertwining public, commercial, and private interests. It generated public debates and articles, and was part of the larger criticism of postwar housing policy.

When collective houses were part of the general waiting lists for public housing, individuals who had no intention of living collectively were assigned flats in collective houses.[67] In the example of Hässelby Familjehotell, this created conflicts and revealed class differences. When newly built, the company Olle Engqvist provided empty premises to the residents in Hässelby Familjehotell—three spaces in the basement and one canteen—to use as they wanted as a step toward the tenant's participation.[68] After a short, but intense, collaboration between tenants, the individual financial preconditions created a deep divide within the group. Two factions emerged: the largest fought to lower rents, which were higher in Hässelby Familjehotell than in many other buildings (many in this group had not lived collectively before); while the other group focused on developing communal activities. The latter group gave themselves the middle-class-sounding name Nytta och Nöje (Benefit and Pleasure), collaborated with the owner on questions regarding the house, and decided the rules for social interaction in the house for the first years. For example, everyone was to change for dinner, had their own tables, and helped encourage the more active kids to behave during meals. Benefit and Pleasure organized activities in communal spaces and laid the ground for future collaborations among tenants, but soon new conflicts emerged. Finally, at the end of the 1950s, all cooperation between the residents and the housing company was shut down, and the company took back its premises.

In the late 1960s, the development diversified in two directions as a new generation moved into Hässelby Familjehotell who were more used to working collectively, but after the death of Olle Engqvist in 1969, capital interests came to steer the decisions to a larger extent. The new management of the housing company included the lawyer Claes Sandels from the largest Swedish bank (Skandinaviska Enskilda Banken, or SEB).[69] In the early 1970s, the housing company started the process to close the restaurant and all associated services, which was achieved, after lengthy legal proceedings, in 1976.[70] The story did not end there though. Services were reorganized by the residents to allow household tasks performed by hired staff to be shared. To their surprise, the residents found this work attractive and a long-term management model took shape.[71] In 1979, three years after they started to collectively run the food service, the residents were reported to the authorities by the owners for using the dining hall (Figure 3.15).

Figure 3.14 Hässelby Familjehotell when the restaurant was still in service. The residents' personal napkins were placed in a wallboard. Photographer: Unknown. Courtesy: ArkDes Collection.

Architecture and Retrenchment

Figure 3.15 Hässelby Familjehotell. Cooking together in the kitchen (left) and the dining room with the banner "Build more collective houses. Save Hässelby Familjehotell" (right). Photographers: Unknown / Pressens Bild / TT (left), Gudmund Mårtensson / TT (right).

At 16.00 on Friday, July 20, 1979, there was what the press called a "police raid" on Hässelby Familjehotell: the dining hall was stormed, the press were thrown out, and eleven people were taken to the police station.[72] The police were unexpectedly violent and handled the press with a degree of aggression which led to speculation about a new strategy to prevent the media from documenting the police. It should also be understood in relation to the two, similarly violent, police actions the year before against squatters at Mullvaden and Järnet in Stockholm.[73] Police behavior caused a stir in the daily press, and photos from the police raid were published and elicited a strong reaction from the public.

These turbulent events meant politicians became involved in Hässelby Familjehotell, leading later to negotiations between residents and the politicians in City Hall over buying the property, which the owner rejected, but after further legal proceedings the residents were able to open the collective dining hall in new premises. Following a private bill, presented by a member of the liberal Centre Party, the City Council in 1980 formed the Stockholm Committee on Collective Housing to "prepare ideas and proposals for collective forms of housing."[74] In a comment on the bill, three Social Democrats on Stockholm's *fastighetsnämnd* (property board) declared: "The history written thus far of Hässelby Familjehotell has meant a major defeat for private property ownership. We note that the objectives of private property owners are not in line with a socially oriented housing policy."[75]

Social Reproduction as a Resource

The Swedish feminist movement in architecture which emerged in the late 1970s with groups such as BiG (Live in Community) and Women's Building Forum (Kvinnors byggforum or KBF) responded to the "women question" (Dalla Costa) and positioned

The Collective House (1935–94)

Figure 3.16 "The police strike – against the family hotell. They are thrown out of their dining hall." Facsimile from *Aftonbladet* July 21, 1979, 3.

itself as a countermovement, struggling against services framed as large-scale, rationalized assets.[76] They stressed the domestic sphere as central to the circuit of production and capital flow, and contradictory to feminist voices such as the Wages for Housework Campaign, when advocating *collaborative* nonpaid domestic work.[77] The Swedish feminists were mainly struggling against domestic labor and care being an asset on the market and aiming at inventing structures that did not compartmentalize and commodify social reproduction. One of the largest events to mark this turn was the exhibition was the exhibition *Boplats 80* (Habitat 80), where women groups stressed the value of sharing domestic labor and care instead of dividing the work

85

and "outsourcing" it to paid staff.[78] BiG presented the doll's house to show a collective lifestyle to counter large-scale service, and KBF exhibited a full-scale environment for the visitors to move through, to counteract the abstraction of the text-and-image exhibits hanging flat on the wall. They built an entrance and a hallway: collective in-between spaces they claimed were often neglected or treated routinely. The KBF also suggested rough areas where one could paint, do crafts, and fix things in contemporary flats. Like BiG, the KBF invented new collective spaces and new uses in the living spaces of 1980s flats, and both groups encouraged individuals to decide on the organization of their own space.

At a witness seminar in 2019, BiG members revisited 1970s feminism to discuss their reasons for engaging in questions of collective living, housework, and care work.[79] As already noted, Sweden had internationally speaking a large proportion of women in waged work.[80] Lifestyle and gender roles changed, but according to BiG's members, the organization of everyday life and built space did not. Looking back, most are struck by their life situations, with children, absent men, intense work, and dwellings not supporting their way of living. Similar to how the 1968 urban activists criticized the welfare state for generational segregation separating young and old, BiG reacted against the suburban planning which enforced similar segregation. One member remembered:

> It was not planned for children and adults to socialize. Mothers were supposed to sit on the bench and the children should be in the sandpit, and the swing sets were not made for adults ... It was astonishing, so I longed for another way of living with kids.[81]

Starting from their private situations and an *intermediary level* between family and society supporting the infrastructure of everyday life, BiG elaborated on the spatial conditions of everyday life in their search for new models.[82] BiG identified three crucial shifts where

Figure 3.17 Bo i Gemenskap at a witness seminar arranged by Action Archive in 2019. Photographer: Mariette Parling. Courtesy: Action Archive.

The Collective House (1935–94)

social reproduction and domestic space and their organization were key for initiating change: first, changing the gender division between paid and unpaid work; second, reducing social segregation; and third, switching to sustainable energy consumption and an environmentally friendly living environment.[83] They searched for alternatives to the two dominant ways to manage the conflict between paid and unpaid work in welfare-state policy—either to turn domestic work into waged labor "bought and sold as time units on the market," or to procure technological devices.[84] Instead, collaborative care and housework was a *creative* realm where a supportive physical infrastructure could be constructed through shared work; it was not only a site where certain domestic functions (cleaning, cooking, caring) were performed, but perhaps more importantly a site for producing and maintaining feelings.[85]

> [to] break with the traditional way of focusing all planning and all housing policy measures on the household. Today, the household is not only the smallest planning unit, but the only one. The block, the neighbourhood, the residential area remains at most fictions in the planners' imaginary world, as long as they lack content.[86]

Conceived in response to this lack of content, an intermediary level developed into a *bogemenskap* (living-community) that resonated with Ingrid Sjöstrand's *samhem* and the regulation issued in 1970 to provide communal spaces. The size of a *bogemenskap* was somewhere between the traditional collective house and the "large-family" block of approximately 20–50 households. A number of care and household functions were supposed to move from the little household of the family to the intermediary level of the *bogemenskap* with the possibility for the community to take over specific functions, such as eldercare, but it was not primarily thought of as a building: "bogemenskapen is an idea, not a house."[87] In 1982 BiG articulated this idea as a model in the handbook *Det lilla kollektivhuset: En modell för praktisk tillämpning* (The small collective house: A model for practical implementation). The handbook was influential for the realization of the new collective house with shared housework and care in Sweden. The first co-housing example of the new generation was a refurbished high-rise from the 1960s, Stacken, realized by a group from Chalmers School of Architecture led by Lars Ågren.[88] The BiG manual was used, not only by action groups and housing companies, but also by politicians such as the Stockholm Vice-Mayor and City Commissioner of Social Services Mats Hulth, who worked in the late 1970s on various models of collective housing.[89]

A decisive aspect of the model was the management of the building: What kind of lease was appropriate? In international discussions in the period the importance of "self-made processes" was often stressed, but BiG advocated a mix of self-organization and public support, with the experience from Hässelby Familjehotell (and other collective houses) where profit-making had destroyed the collaboration, they highlighted models where in first hand public or cooperative housing companies took initial responsibility.[90] The rental flats, managed by local authority housing companies, were not a saleable asset (unlike the owner flats), which guaranteed the collective house's flats would not end

Architecture and Retrenchment

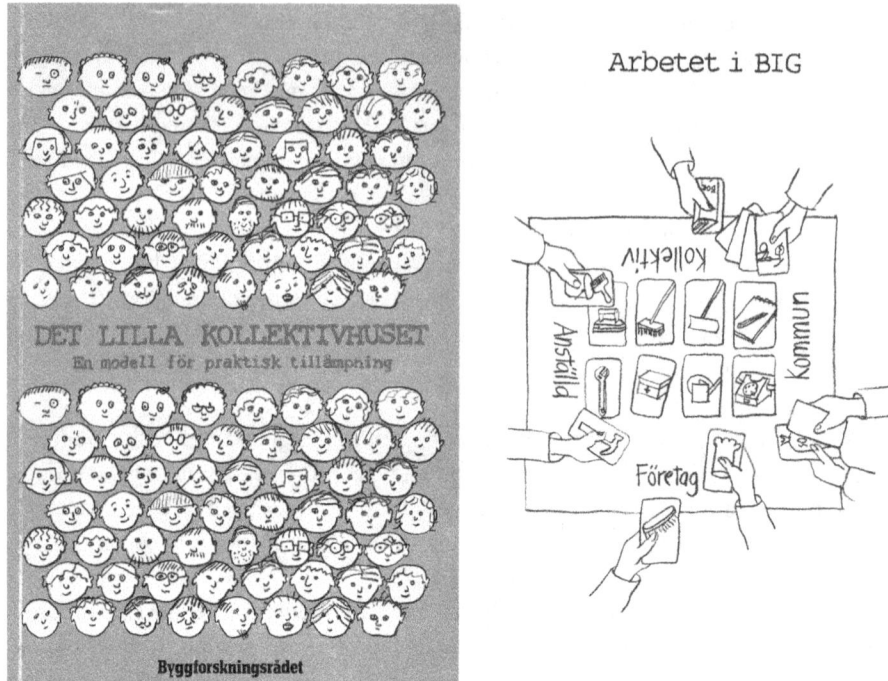

Figure 3.18 Publication on co-housing Bo i Gemenskap 1982. The drawing to the right illustrates the "play" between different actors: The Collective, The Municipality, The Private Sector, The Employee. Reprinted from BiG, *Det lilla kollektivhuset* (Stockholm: Statens råd för byggnadsforskning, 1982).

up on the open market. The 1980s collective house movement put great store by the experiments in new forms of tenure between the rentals and those owned.[91] These efforts ceased abruptly when the conservative majority in Parliament got a new law passed 1982 by one vote, which prohibited all effective measures to regulate rampant housing prices.[92] The local authorities in Stockholm supported the development of new tenures that made "cooperative living" possible, but they had to reject the application under the 1982 law.[93]

A New Everyday Life

The feminist movement not only highlighted architecture as a designed lived environment but also brought new discussions to the table about power structures and discrimination. Bureaucracy, regulations, and management (as with new forms of tenures) therefore became important sites for progressive architectural practices, and they continued a longer tradition of instigating norms and regulations as the social contract of architecture. This was highlighted in the Nordic research project New Everyday Life, which started in the early 1980s. Its aim was to address how discrimination of women was built into architecture and urban planning, and the neglect of developing reproductive functions in the built environment. With the participation of Birgit Krantz, a professor of building function theory, the project was grounded in the Swedish research environment, and its two BiG members, Kerstin Kärnekull and Inga-Liisa Sangregorio, secured the links to the collective house movement.[94] Following the strategy to be productive rather than critical, and to work for direct change in the face of existing conditions which were significant for the postmodern feminists, the New Everyday Life was "future studies" research, in line with biologist Rachel Carson's "handbook" for the future of life, *Silent Spring*.[95] The research project pointed to the experiential aspects of the built environment and social reproduction, and how emotional relations were played out in the intersubjective field.[96]

In an article on women's visions of their new everyday lives, Birgit Krantz articulated the complexity of, and difficulties with, the new landscape of small-scale services. She stressed what she labeled *local housework* and *local care* organized collectively by a group of households in collaboration with the public sector providing services not only for the collaborating households but also for a larger public. According to Krantz, the service house Stolplyckan, discussed earlier, was a materialization of local care at a level in between the individual and the society, such as the parent's organization of childcare as a cooperative endeavor. She pointed to the ongoing dismantling of the public sector and parents' wishes to engage more with their kids everyday life.[97] The parent's kindergarten cooperative was a collaborative example, into which civil society put its time and the local authority its money. This was at the time a new model where the public sector financed civil society to organize social care, and the research group saw even further possibilities of transferring functions to the local situation. In 1983, the creation of the first private kindergarten in Sweden, Pysslingen Förskolor, sparked a political row about the private provision of education. In 1984, the Lex Pysslingen law was brought in to prohibit the government from financing childcare managed by a private, for-profit company, but this law was abolished in 1992. The ambiguity about the new social field of *local* care and housework that attracted new actors, including the "market-oriented sector," had already been articulated by Krantz in the early 1980s:

> We are now experiencing how the public sector in all Western industrialized countries is cut, and how care and the local environment, traditionally women's areas, are affected. We must ask ourselves what role the state should have and in what way we should request public services from the state. Are there reproductive areas which, without entailing disarmament and without us losing land, can exist independently of the state, the public sector?[98]

The sociologist Birte Bech-Jørgensen understood the fresh interest in the concept that gave its name to the research project, "everyday life," as a reaction to the somewhat hackneyed notions of "community" and "local environment." And, importantly, she pointed out that it was not in conflict with "the direct and open self-centredness characterizing the lifestyles and thinking of the 1980s." "Everyday life" became a concept that bridged large-scale societal structures and private life, creating a zone where people had to deal with, live with, and change these structures.[99] The new rhetorical figures contributed to emancipation in a new "self-centered" world without questioning the societal transformations of the time. This was the thin line which the 1980s feminists trod between direct action and criticality.

The ideas presented in the New Everyday Life research project were disseminated in a broader European context by the EuroFem Gender and Human Settlements Network (1994–2000).[100] In EuroFem's research, there was a similar ambivalence about self-governance as in the earlier Nordic work. Their arguments tied into a neoliberal discourse of the importance of transferring functions from the public to the civic, or private, sector. In line with the economic discourse of the 1990s, EuroFem stressed how the infrastructure of everyday life, picking up on Hazel Henderson's "economy of love," could contribute to economic life (collective organizations, recycling, goods, and services) and they accentuated the positive effects of fragmentation in postmodern society that helped redefine the plural nature of communities.[101] In their efforts to move away from the functionalist view of spatially separating people and functions, EuroFem took Tronti's "social factory" one step further when arguing, in a typical postmodern manner, that "as individuals we have to fuse in ourselves our work and leisure, working life and family life, the public and the private as one life totality."[102] Not only were the boundaries between the factory and society erased, but also the boundaries between the outside living environment and the inner space of subjectivity.

The 1980 Collective Housing Committee

The women's movements in architecture were never highlighted in the dominant professional discourse (and most often excluded from architectural postmodernism), but interestingly, they influenced politics all the more. BiG's handbook and the conflict at Hässelby Familjehotell resulted in the appointment in 1980 of Kollektivhuskommittén (Collective Housing Committee) by Stockholm's local authority to come up with proposals for collective houses that could quickly be realized. The Committee found that in recent decades the common social functions had been transferred either "into the private home" or "out to society at large," and following Rita Liljeström and BiG, among others, they stressed the importance of developing the intermediary level in peoples' everyday lives. To reach this goal they organized a competition, open to all, to "increase interaction between people and stimulate affinity" and debate.[103] Interest in the competition was considerable and 132 proposals were submitted, and were taken as a starting point for the "new development of individual buildings as well as entire residential areas."[104] The wind had turned for collective houses, at least when it came to the attention in the press and other media.

The Collective House (1935–94)

The renewed interest in collective houses with new organizations—co-housing—came at much the same time as neoliberalization and was a double-edged response from politicians to the co-housing movement, but also to the societal formations initiated by cuts in the public sector. It chimed in with the opposition to social privatization, yet it came with government retrenchment and a wave of economic privatizations. In the Committee's final report, the centralization and specialization of care and nursing were questioned from a humanitarian perspective, but also in terms of finances, and more demands were made for greater participation and dissolution of the boundaries between home and institution. The collective house was seen as a response to several demands through "decentralized administrative responsibility and an increasing personal responsibility for the residents."[105] The pilot projects presented by the committee were valued as "*knowledge for collective elements in housing in general.*" In this way the collective house, once again, became a model for society—this time, how to decentralize and increase self-organized services and moving responsibility from the local authority to the civil society. In this way, the radical potential of rethinking the ontologies of social practice to be found in the hidden abodes of social reproduction, to quote Fraser, was limited.

As shown, after many years of resistance toward collective housing, the authorities, including the public housing companies, changed their minds, and in 1981 the first queue system for collective houses was established by Stockholm's Bostadsförmedlingen (Public Housing Agency). The local authority housing companies also invested in collective housing: six "collective villas" in Upplands Väsby, each containing five flats with kitchenettes and a communal kitchen, dining area and an inner yard, were ready for occupancy in 1983, and two years later in 1985 the first tenancy of Prästgårdsåkern in Älvsjö was built by the local authority housing company Familjebostäder. Over a period of ten years, 24 co-houses were built in Stockholm, and totally in Sweden, 64 houses more or less following the BiG model (37 of them built by public housing companies).[106] After a period of stagnation there was a third wave in the 1990s, when the majority of houses accommodated those in the "second half of life" (for people over 50 and without children), with Färdknäppen in Stockholm as one of the better-known projects (Figure 3.19).[107]

After the collapse of the government's housing policy and the financial crisis in the beginning of the 1990s, BiG published *Femton kollektivhus* in 1992 about fifteen collective houses built according to BiG's manual in the preceding decade.[108] The model for the little collective house had arrived in a political new landscape. In reviews of the book, the collective house was described as a possible solution to declining public services, such as child and eldercare, as citizens had to be prepared to pay more and contribute in a more hands-on fashion.[109] New loan rules and reduced subsidies were predicted to result in speculative housing projects driven by developers, and the collective houses were of a type that would do well in such a competition. However, what was not taken into consideration was that houses built as rental flats were later sold off and became part of the commercial market. This marketization made it difficult to keep the collective community intact, and many collectives had been shut by 2000.

Architecture and Retrenchment

Figure 3.19 The collective house Färdknäppen, Stockholm. Photographer: Mattias Tydén.

Threatening the Order of the Welfare State

The Swedish welfare state had never been opened to experimenting with collective living forms as part of the state housing policy. This was a decisive direction to take, and missed out on the chance to invent a new spatial and functional organization of the home beyond the core family, and indeed new forms of financing and ownership. There were several reasons the collective house was not included in the housing policy and never received the subsidies that allowed it to be explored and developed. A general issue was that housing was one of the most important biopolitical tools to use in the process of normalization, and that collective housing forms often threatened this. The built environment, and especially homes, had an important function in the formation of families from the early welfare state in the 1930s to the end of the twentieth century. As shown by scholars such as Michel Foucault and Jacques Donzelot, housing regulations, norms, and codes (some written in to the law and others related to financial support) were techniques used by the state to foster and govern family life.[110] Donzelot demonstrates how "policing the family" (in a French context) suppressed the working class, and describes a situation true even in the Swedish context. The role of sociologists, conducting the research and analyses, became crucial to the processes of normalization and the architects' work forming domestic spaces.

One argument for not supporting collective houses was that the typology was understood as supporting a middle-class minority, rather than workers. As architect and researcher Dick Urban Vestbro has argued, this idea was initially based on media images, and became a reality precisely because collective living was excluded from systems of subsidies, turning it into housing for more privileged groups. One characteristic of the collective house has been its separation from the surrounding city, in both an architectural and a functional sense, with spatial interiors and services only for the residents.[111] This separation was palpable from the nineteenth-century utopian communities to the small-scale collective houses of the 1930s, and the larger arrangements from the 1950s. The support of collective functions for a small community (often accused of being bourgeois) went against universal welfare provided to all citizen, and was therefore condemned in state reports as an act of inequality. This resulted in the 1960s in spatial hybrids and the concomitant commodification of (outsourced) services. The direction chosen—large-scale housing services, compartmentalized and moved from the house or home or the smaller communities to service points, service centers, and service houses serving a larger area—contributed to the criticism of the postwar welfare state as marked by social privatization.

While the universal model of welfare was one reason the collective house movement was never integrated into the official welfare-state housing policy, there were other causes. Although the collective house aimed at increasing welfare, the typology simultaneously constituted a threat to society. For example, the military psychologist Jan Agrell argued that the future in Sweden looked bad when large families and collective ownership destroyed their willingness to bear arms.[112] Core family values also guided how to organize a home in large and influential political associations, such as housing cooperatives and labor unions.[113] The reorganization of the core family values did not fit into the patriarchal policy structure; rather, it was seen as a potential risk to that power structure. Although the state report *Kollektivhus* (1954) pointed out that it was unreasonable for women to be forced to give up their careers and move to domestic work on marriage, one can read in the preparatory documents this statement was not self-evident. The Stockholm City planning director Göran Sidenbladh had proposed to cut the high cost for paid housework in the collective house by engaging "the housewives without recompense to serve in the house with for example domestic help, food walking, washing dishes."[114]

Another threat was the working-class home. Even though one criticism was that the collective house was primary not for the working classes, it was exactly the goal to erase the working-class habits that lay the ground for rejecting collective living. Policing the family, to use Donzelot's expression, using housing regulations and housing services suppressed working-class living habits. Overcrowding in the domestic sphere and floating borders between housing functions, especially within the working-class family, led to unsound, unhygienic living conditions. Housing inspections meant living standards, overcrowding, and the spatial organization of the domestic sphere were mapped out nationally as the groundwork for housing regulations and building codes. The norms were still visible in *God Bostad 5*, which set out how to realize collective living forms. It was impossible to reduce the size of private housing areas, such as the kitchen, hygiene areas, or storage, yet increase the size of the communal areas. Instead, the National Board of Housing, which was behind both the norms and the publication of *God Bostad*, itself had to by-pass it by proposing the use of retractable walls to extend the number of rooms at the expense of the kitchen and living room.[115]

The sociologist Helena Ekstam shows how codes regulating overcrowding changed from expressing the paternalistic and prescriptive politics of the 1930s to a consumer-driven norm in 1960s, and the norm system defined by rights (and segregation) in the 1980s.[116] From defining the home's physical design (size and space) as a *bostadsbehov* (housing need), understood as objectively and biologically determined in the 1930s, crucial health arguments were exchanged for socioeconomic welfare arguments of individual rights (the right to choose) in the 1980s.[117] These periods more or less coincided with the different organizations of social reproduction, here outlined as three regimes of boundary struggles over how to organize social reproduction.

The role of sociologists in conducting the research and analyses was central to the processes of normalization, as was the architects' work translating it into domestic spaces. Both the architect and the sociologist were decisive for interpreting official housing surveys and evaluating what was important or not—for example accommodating the wish for larger flats but rejecting the call for more storage space (it was unnecessary to collect things that served no useful purpose).[118]

The notion of educating citizens in housing "morals" still ruled decisions in the 1960s and 1970s, and it was only with the 1980s norms of the individual's right to choose that a new era in co-housing began. The collective house was a prism of family policy from the 1930s to the 1980s, and went from being a threat to the nuclear family to being the solution for emancipatory movements working against the nuclear family as the only norm. But co-housing also offered solutions for those who advocated a neoliberal, conservative policy under which the state's responsibilities were to be transferred to private individuals, to families, and to the community.[119]

The Restructuring of Social Reproduction

Here, I have tried to unpick the entangled history of emancipation and neoliberalization by using the collective house as a site of political and spatial restructuring.[120] The collective house was denied subsidies such as state loans and positioned outside mainstream housing policies, but became important as a discursive object. In a contradictory way, by excluding new forms of living, the Swedish Model of universal welfare contributed to the marketization, and later outsourcing, of social reproduction and care work. This marks a shift toward a situation, described by the historian Premilla Nadasen, where the crisis of social reproduction we are still living through becomes "a source of profit-making for the private sector, government agencies, non-profits and individuals, in contrast to Marxist–feminist analyses that see social reproduction as a precondition for capitalist profit."[121] It is a development which contributes to new class divisions and inequalities, where social reproduction is commodified for those who could pay and was privatized for those who could not.

The Collective House (1935–94)

By mapping the intricacies of the postwar discussions about collective function and societal service, from the collective house to the service center, I have circled the "social" field between the individual and the collective, and demonstrated how it was compartmentalized and separated from everyday domestic life. The small collective house, or co-housing, represented a countermovement, because it stressed social reproduction as an infrastructure of care that cannot be separated from the close community, whether spatially or socially; it was also both criticism and immediate response—a "utopia in reality"—to what they called social privatization (social isolation) in housing in the 1970s. But at a point when neoliberalization aligned with new public management, these countermovement, in a contradictory way, contributed to government retrenchment and ushered in the first wave of economic privatization.

The *intermediary level* was a basic prerequisite for re-establishing a lost community and a way to enhance the inner resources in each citizen. The Swedish Social Democrats' turn to the Third Way in the 1980s introduced new relations to capital, focusing on the accumulation of human and social capital.[122] Here we see it playing out in the domestic sphere and the rethinking of social reproduction. For the politicians of the 1980s, co-housing was a means to economic rationality and an enrichment of the social sphere. Co-housing was an emancipatory project for women; for politicians (and the private sector) it was an argument for a decentralized administration to hand responsibility to residents—a strategy that goes under the umbrella of responsibilization or devolution.[123]

When women worked in the public sector, mainly with tasks relating to social reproduction, investment was cut, and around 1980 the crisis in the public sector was underway. The need for pressured politicians to find techniques to enhance the social sphere by their policymaking in a period of less and less investment in public services seems obvious. The responsibilization and disinvestment in domestic work and care can be compared to the renewal projects and citizen participation in the suburbs of the 1980s and 1990s. As the Collective Housing Committee noted, the centralization and specialization of care and nursing had been questioned for both humanitarian and economic reasons, and higher demands were placed on increasing participation and the removal of boundaries between home and public institutional work. The moral imperative of the housing policy of the early 1930s and the consumer-driven policy of the 1960s and 1970s was rearticulated as neoliberal housing imperative in the 1980s, urging private engagement in the name of solidarity. Yet the rethinking of social reproduction by the feminist movement in the 1970s still has much to teach us, and should be remembered as a response to approaching privatization and individualization; a "pragmatic utopia."

The deregulations of the 1980s opened for spatial experimentation in domestic spaces that affected not only the solitary building block and its interiors but also the housing areas' arrangement. The "home larger than the house" presented by BiG and other feminist groups at Boplats 80, with new housing regulations, allowed for greater fluidity between domestic functions (cf, Site 5: The Postmodern Housing Area), compensating for smaller flats with communal spaces in the blocks of flats. Ideas once only associated with the collective house were picked up by politicians, developers, and planners and implemented on a greater scale of the housing block or the housing area. This generated

Architecture and Retrenchment

a new housing typology with large, covered, interior gardens and communications systems. Spatial sequences connecting the private dwelling with collective spaces, semi-public gardens, and the public streetscape created a "city in the city," for example at Södra Station (Site 5). Such transformations of the relationship between the exterior and interior, between the most private and public, between the dwelling and the city, were bound up with the history of the collective house—as a built reality and as a discursive object.

HUMAN CAPITAL

When the Chicago School economist Gary Becker was awarded the Nobel Prize in 1992 for having extended the domain of economics to a "wide range of human behaviour," that thinking was included in Third Way architectural policies since the early 1980s.[1] Human capital, the concept Becker was most famous for, had been introduced to a broader Swedish audience by Theodore Schultz, the Nobel laureate in 1979 for his "particular consideration of the problems of the developing countries."[2] Becker had visited Sweden before at the invitation of the Royal Swedish Academy of Sciences and the Centre for Business and Policy Studies, giving advice how to govern the country: in 1984, a year before the deregulation of the Swedish credit market, Becker noted his concern at the "irrational" growth of the public sector and advised the adoption of "public choice," shifting the role of political science and political economy from correcting the problems caused by the market to identifying problems in the public sector. It was no surprise that he was a harsh critic of the Swedish Model; he had said as much to *BusinessWeek* magazine, in speeches to the Mont Pelerin Society, and in reports for Eastern bloc countries.[3]

The dystopic images of life in the modernist suburbs were at the forefront of the criticism of Swedish Model in the 1970s, and the search for a new architecture was also a search for other living environments to partake in the formation of subjectivity. It was a new focus on enhancing the individual capacities of each person, on other human aspects than before. Now primacy was given to creativity, knowledge, initiative, and social networking. The question is how this new attitude resonated with the concept of human capital in the societal transformations of the 1980s. Although "human capital" was already part of the idiom of the earlier-twentieth-century welfare state, it took on new meaning with the introduction a Swedish Third Way in the 1980s. This policy included politico-economic and cultural modes of government, which, instead of controlling the economy, attempted to control the human capital in each individual. Here, I will outline a theoretical framework for a theme introduced in the first site The Model and discussed in several of the following sites, such as the social organization of the masses in the Stockholm Globe Arena, and the notion of the "individualization" in the planning of the postmodern housing Södra Station.

Framing the Concept

The concept of human capital has been controversial because of its association with nonhuman values. Adam Smith, in his *Wealth of Nations* (1776), included under "fixed capital," besides equipment, buildings, and land, "the acquired and useful abilities of all the inhabitants or members of the society," and he compared an educated man to "an expensive machine."[4] When Becker published his *Human Capital* in 1964 he hesitated to use the concept of human capital in the title, because of the strong antipathy to talking about people as capital, and equating humans with machines, with its associations with slavery. But by the time Becker reached the third edition in 1993 things were different: "My, how the world has changed! The name and analysis are now readily accepted by most people not only in all the social sciences, but even in the media."[5] Even in the formation of the welfare state, certain institutions had invested in enhancing human capacities, such as education and health, but, as Foucault demonstrated, it was only when the American neoliberals weighed in that human capital became a field of economic analysis, rendering a strictly economic interpretation of a whole domain long thought to be noneconomic.[6] One can distinguish between it in its more idealistic form, human worth, and human capital as an economic resource.[7]

The human capital theory was presented by the Chicago economists Theodore Schultz, Jacob Mincer, and others in the 1950s, but was popularized by Becker, who was Milton Friedman's student.[8] Foucault describes his "homo economicus" in the context of human capital theory, not as a partner to an exchange (as in classical economics), but as an "entrepreneur of himself": "being for himself his own capital, being for himself his own producer, being for himself his own source of earnings."[9] In the framework of human capital theory, investments go beyond education to include such things as social stimulation, interaction, play, and cultural stimuli.

Sweden's Third Way policies in the 1980s introduced the theory of human capital combined with a policy orientation toward a knowledge economy. Traditional material investments in buildings and equipment decreased, and instead investments in research and development started the decade at 15 percent, the same level as in the 1960s, and soared to 35 percent by the mid-1980s.[10] However, in line with the Schumpeterian idea of clusters of innovation, new resources and design efforts were put into architectural environments such as Stockholm Globe City, but also areas near communication hubs, such as Arlanda City.[11] The transformation from an industrial economy to a knowledge economy was quick, and Sweden was soon a European center for information technology—and marketed itself as such.[12]

As demonstrated by Jenny Andersson, Keynesian-era social democracy was concerned with the workforce, and in the 1980s the Third Way knowledge economy's focus was the rationalization of human capital.[13] Unlike earlier national capital resources such as steel and coal, knowledge as the new national resource is embedded in each individual. New methods were invented, so instead of extracting capital from nature, capital was extracted from within people. Human capital theory was introduced as markets became more globalized, and the government had to provide frameworks (regulations, taxes, social security) and physical infrastructure (architecture such as offices, living environments, housing areas) to attract capital. Andersson argues that "new cultural governance aims at creating this capital" which was embedded in labor, "changing the values and dispositions within the knowledge workers—in other words, 'build human capital.'"[14] The macro strategy is to attract financial capital; the micro strategy is to create "brainpower." In this new complex of creating capital on different levels, architecture can be added as an aspect of cultural governance, supporting this growth. It is telling that the Swedish wage-earner funds, conceived in the 1970s to increase wage-earner influence over business profits, came to an abrupt end in 1991.[15] In line with the new ideas of human capital, money was invested in research and innovation funds, with KK-stiftelsen (the Knowledge Foundation), which was founded to boost Sweden's competitiveness, including architecture and built environment in its remit.[16]

Human Capital Theory and Architecture

A new narrative of modernization gained ground in the 1980s. Instead of stressing rational, industrial production methods (including housing, hospitals, and schools), knowledge, whether lifelong learning, innovation, or entrepreneurship, came to characterize the process of progress. This turn had effects on the relation between the state and architecture. First, building had shifted from a public investment—the Keynesian belief in building as a resource in periods of economic stagnation by creating work opportunities and national capital—to a tool for the state (and the municipalities) to create efficient frameworks for the private sector to meet society's needs in times of crisis or economic boom. Through architectural projects new forms of collaborations between the public and private sector took form, while the state retrenched from design and organization of the built environment. Second, architecture found a new role in biopolitics. Where once it was a means to create the modern citizen (and reasonable consumer) with its functionalist ideals implemented through state regulation (hence *God Bostad*), architecture no longer existed to foster citizens, but rather to *enhance* every individual's human abilities.[17] Learning, creativity, social interaction, and innovation were mutually supportive factors that could drive economic growth. In this economic project, 1980s architecture and the built environment found a new role, providing the setting where such human qualities could only improve. Architecture's altered role went hand in hand with rethinking the modernist project in Swedish architecture, which had been criticized by professionals and the popular media for creating dysfunctional citizens, often with the Million Program as the warning example. An important task of the "postmodern" aesthetic in all its variety was to enhance those aspects of the human character that could generate creativity and innovation as assets for the future society. The new discourse of architecture was to create value and boost the market for architecture with a capital A as lending increased.

The rethinking of social reproduction, domestic space, and collective living in the 1980s did also resonated with human capital, and was a possible in building it up. When the sociologist James Coleman elaborated on what he saw as the most important developments in economics since the 1950s, among his answers was human capital, adding "social capital."[18] Where human capital "is created by changes in persons that bring about skills and capabilities that make them able to act in new ways," social capital is created "through changes in the relations among persons that facilitate action."[19] Social capital exists in human relations, and, in the same way as physical and human capital, it facilitates productive activity. The models formulated by BiG and the New Everyday Life research group for how to materialize the intermediary level of care in co-housing echoed Coleman's ideas that enhancing social relations would strengthen human values. The politicians could see the potential of human capital as an economic resource in the co-housing model, aiding state retrenchment and public savings. Like Coleman, Third Way growth theories leant toward a logic of "capitalizing the social"—a policy that capitalized on social structures and processes as a source for growth.[20] This policy had repercussions for how architecture was interpreted as an asset, a new thinking that understood the social domain, constructed in spatial organization, as an economic resource. This was demonstrated by co-housing, but the same strategy was evident at Stockholm Globe City, where the arena amounted to a machine for a new logic of consumption. The ability to produce living environments on different scales—home, community, city—became part of a new interventionist policy designed so the individual could operate in a manner that was creative and innovative (human capital), but also at the level of the group to construe a community (social capital).

The aims to construct, and capitalize on, these new social infrastructures were present in descriptions of architects, planners, and politicians—and the city became the umbrella for these innovations. It was, using the historian Håkan Forsell's word, with a "dazed ascertainment" that the Swedish political debate in the late 1980s found that the urban environment shaped people's circumstances and contributed to societal development.[21] As Storstadsutredningen (the Commission on Metropolitan Problems) stated in 1988, "The metropolitan environment, by dint of its intense contact with the outside world, carries the seeds of changing social and political barriers—new political dividing lines, new values and lifestyles, and new patterns of participation throughout the country."[22] When planning the Stockholm housing area Södra Station, the ambition of most involved—politicians, architects, bureaucrats, and planners—was to turn its "spatial Keynesianism" around.[23] The use of postmodern aesthetics and a new spatial organization (spatial sequencing), new regulations, ideas of an "intermediary" level (taken from the collective house movement), and rearticulations of private and public responsibilities (care, health, education) were all techniques related to architecture, and all found physical expression in living environments supposed to enhance forms of human capital.

For Welfare or for Economic Capital?

For the 1968 urban activists, it was a creative strategy to invest in the next generation. Their architectural actions were "models" for change, and children were the hope for the future, who should be invested in to create a qualitative society. The exhibition *Modellen* was the test bed where adults protected the children's qualities (from consumer culture and individualism) and worked to enhance their solidarity and creativity. Architecture was a resource in this, because it created experiences that would foster future adults (and break "the system") as "free" individuals, and it was not a question of creating human capital to economic growth and prosperity (on the level of the individual or the population), but rather about a more idealistic notion of "human worth." The urban activists understood architecture to be an emancipatory project with the ability to create experiences and enhance human abilities; later, as shown in relation to the coming sites, architecture was used to create economic human capital.

Architecture, by creating spaces, saw activities such as sports, leisure, work, and shopping interwoven to create "city-likeness" or Schumpeterian "clusters" (Södra Station and Stockholm Globe City), and was equally a means of constructing human capital. All spaces that enhanced human creativity and innovative thinking supposedly generated economic capital, personal prosperity, and national growth.[24] Another example, as already mentioned, of how human capital or social capital played out in architecture (and domesticity) was in the field of social reproduction and care. In the case of co-housing, the social domain, in terms of building social infrastructure, was capitalized on in the state's strategies of retrenchment. The Tensta renewal project pointed to another aspect of human capital, combining public retrenchment with "the neoliberal moral" by leaving responsibility to the individual citizen, family, or community.[25] This was a new form of governance in the 1980s, sometimes called "responsibilization," that expected citizens to develop (or invest in) their ability to take responsibility—to take the initiative—to the point where it was a moral duty.[26] Architecture became a project by which human abilities such as morality, knowledge, and care were supposedly refined and increased. This process of enhancing human capital was intended to increase public economic capital by passing responsibility (and work) to residents in the name of participation.

The project to increase human capital according to the Third Way knowledge policy obviously had its downsides. Human capital, after all, can be a "potential waste," or it can be an argument for "putting people to use, tapping the potential of us."[27] It was certainly a process where architecture and the built environment could operate to "build human capital." The meaning of human resources had gradually shed its idealism, leaving only the economic, and putting architecture in a vulnerable position. From having served the common good, architecture now had to serve public retrenchment and financial savings too. From being a resource when building human worth that centered on solidarity, architecture now neatly tied in with neoliberal human capital theories and processes of responsibilization.

Figure 4.1 From "James Hund och den djävulska stadsplanen" (James the Dog and the City Plan from Hell). Cartoon series by Jonas Darnell and Patrik Norrman, *Dagens Nyheter*, August 18, 1991. Courtesy: Jonas Darnell and Patrik Norrman.

SITE 4
THE GLOBE (1982-9)*

"Too late. The Globe's come free. Wait! It's going to flatten the tax office!" This, screamed from a helicopter hovering over the newly built Stockholm Globe Arena as it rolls off down one of Stockholm's main roads in a comic strip from 1991.[1] In the first frame, the Globe Arena—or the Ball, the Bump, the Bruise, the Baldie, the Speech Bubble, the Bowling Ball (just some of the nicknames for this controversial project)—has just started its journey through Stockholm. As it rumbles along, it squashes government buildings, obliterating the government agencies that run the country. The Globe Arena leaves society in ruins. Like a rubber ball, the Globe rolls unscathed through the very structure of society, while the old, obsolete, vertical, and oh-so static institutions are flattened. No war, no conflict is necessary—the inexorable progress of the new (societal) body creates its own world. Once set in motion nothing can stop it, and in the end it demolishes the democratic heart of society: Parliament.

This was just one of many myths that made up the daily rhetoric of the Stockholm Globe Arena in the 1990s. The simple and banal shape made it a gift for storytellers, a source of endless metaphors, and shortly after its opening the building became a symbol for the societal changes in Sweden in the 1980s and 1990s. Its form, the abstract sphere of a globe, was free of fixed connotations and symbols, and allowed contemporary fantasies, perceptions, and critical readings to be projected onto its shiny surface. But there was more to it than merely its simple shape. A long process of political negotiations and aesthetic decisions from 1982 to its inauguration in 1989 involved a broad range of actors and changed the conditions for planning, articulated a new era in the logic of consumerism, and remodeled the common good. This chapter will demonstrate how new financial networks and planning techniques were created in the planning process, and how, once it was a realized cultural object, it resonated with both the global cultural industry and the experience economy. The Globe Arena was not a solitary building, though; it was part of a larger complex of shops and offices, which at a time that saw something of an urban renaissance was named Stockholm Globe City.

The area, which combined a sports arena with offices, shops, a hotel, public spaces, and culture, was built on two axes: north–south and east–west. The entrance was marked by two "portico buildings" that were part of the office blocks alongside the arena and created an exterior public space in between the sport facilities and the shops. The arena was connected to two slabs with related activities, such as VIP areas, a hotel, and a restaurant, which formed the north and south façades and entrances. Its strict formal expression of simple geometric bodies and detailing in bright colors

Architecture and Retrenchment

Figure 4.2 Globen and The Globe City. Photographer: Bengt Ohlsson. Courtesy: Berg Arkitektkontor.

made historical references to early-twentieth-century Russian constructivism and 1930s Italian rationalism. The sphere was an iconic architectural form, and the arena building explicitly refers to many of the examples of Claude-Nicolas Ledoux's and Étienne-Louis Boullée's utopian architecture from the eighteenth century to Richard Buckminster Fuller's early-twentieth-century geodesic domes. There were also references closer to home, such as Peter Celsing's 1969 proposal Guldkulan (The Golden Ball).[2]

Even though Globe City marked a clear break with modern architecture and planning, and thus could be taken as an example of a postmodern building, the architects were careful to point out that it deviated from international postmodernism.[3] One of the architects, Svante Berg, said the project was modernist, and had nothing to do with

The Globe (1982–9)

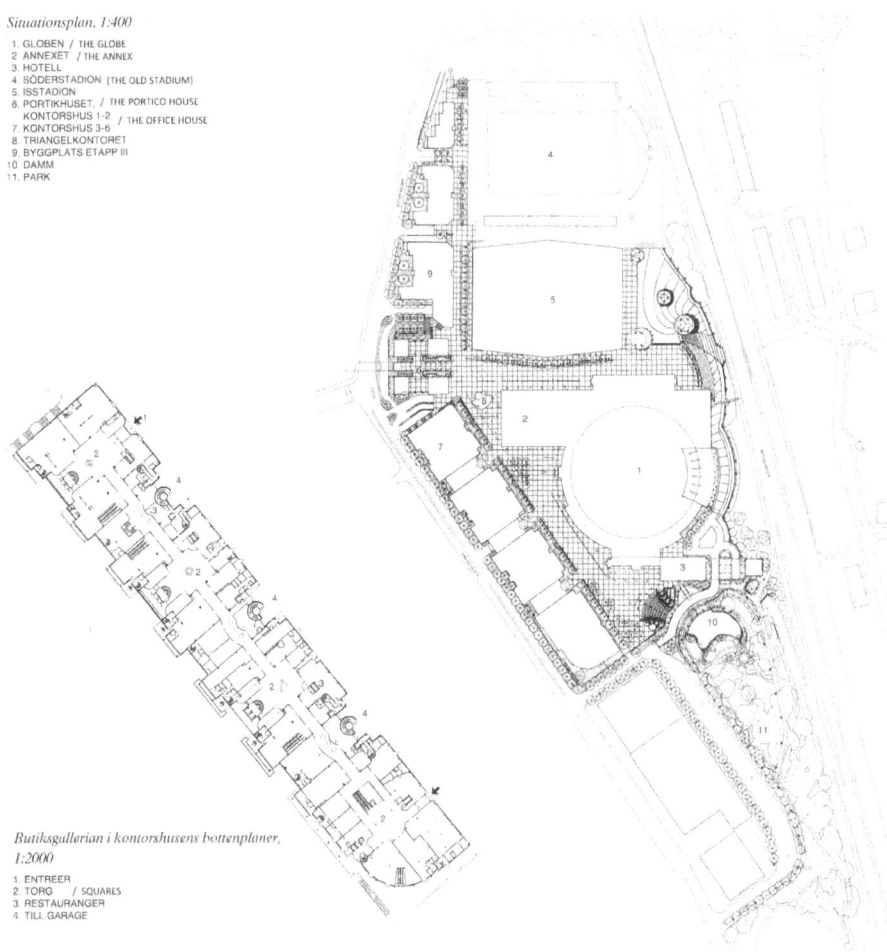

Figure 4.3 Site plan, The Globe City. Drawing by Berg Arkitektkontor. Courtesy: Berg Arkitektkontor.

postmodernism. The cultural journalist Leif Nylén, on the other hand, described Globe City as "neomodernism," adding that "the modernist styles are reduced to one style—something you borrow and drape yourself in without taking the theoretical claims seriously," which meant he was not far from the American cultural geographer Allan Pred, who broke the tacit agreement that postmodernism was "non-Swedish" when he argued that the project solved the commission "by falling back on the full register of postmodern devices—pastiche, irony, eclecticism, the appropriation of 'local history', citing of historical forms."[4] As pointed out by Catharina Gabrielsson, the rejection of postmodernism as style can be understood as a denial of "conflicts and trauma linked to architecture's loss of familiar ground."[5]

The globe as a shape had a symbolic, iconic significance for the project, but the spatial organization played an at least as important role in shaping its imagined future. Contrary to its exterior expression as a single space, the interior of the Globe Arena had spatial divisions that individualized the mass audience into social strata. Overall, it was a site where leisure would mix with work, and sport with culture, to create what the City Planning Office called *cityfilialer* (lit. branch cities). The rise of the service sector and the growing property business had increased the demand for office spaces, which could be combined with already existing housing areas to create the 1980s *ABC-stad* (lit. ABC city), the acronym of *arbete* (work), *bostad* (housing), and *centrum* (centre).[6]

The Globe project was part of the worldwide return of architecture in the 1980s, though, and the functionalist language of efficiency and rationality was replaced by architectural form, color, and aesthetic. However, the new aesthetic of postmodernism was, as argued in the book, soon set in play by the city in larger networks of power. This site shows how the architecture with an A was used by the municipality to create new financial networks and private–public collaborations, but also to put Stockholm on the map, as the Stockholm City Commissioner put it: "it's about much more than just getting another arena."[7]

The West's economic revival in the 1980s under Ronald Reagan in the United States and Margaret Thatcher in the UK was the starting point for an extensive political and economic transformation, and Sweden was one of the earliest social-democratic governments to take on the new political direction, the Third Way.[8] Reduced state ownership and state control and the emerging new high-growth sectors, such as digital technology and biotech, transformed the relationships between the nation state and the private sector. The innovations in the media, information, transport, and technology nexus fueled the internationalization of corporate business, and marked a turn toward a globalized market and a "global cultural industry" described as permeating everything, from production to consumption and beyond.[9] The importance of enhancing experiences neatly tied into a new cultural mode of governance that, instead of controlling the economy, attempted to produce "human capital" that resided *within* individuals.[10] The Stockholm Globe City, I argue, was a part of neoliberalization on different levels: through its "Architecture," through negotiations within the corporatist model, and through spatial compartmentalization and capitalizations on the social domain.

The 1980s was the era of the grand architectural vanity project—think Euro-Lille, Docklands, and Mitterrand's "Grands Projets" in Paris—which, being large, complex, and often chaotic, had a transformative impact on economic and political habits, structures, and rules, because of the number of actors and the sheer money involved in setting up the new collaborations and routines.[11] In Stockholm there were several large projects underway in addition to Globe City, all known for their dynamic, complex planning processes and mix of public and private funding: World Trade Centre, Överkikaren, the Södra Station area (see Site 5). In fact, these three projects were literally connected to Globe City by Söderleden, an infrastructural tunnel project cutting through the city centre.[12]

The Globe (1982–9)

Production and Transformation

The result of the vote was 34–26, and it ended Sweden's hopes of hosting the 1987 Ice Hockey World Championships. Among the delegates at the International Hockey Federation's 1984 congress in Austrian Pörtschach am Wörthersee there had been uncertainty whether the planned facilities in Johanneshov in the south of Stockholm would be ready in time. Stockholm's politicians were blamed for the embarrassing failure of Sweden's bid, and hopes was now pinned on the 1989 World Championships.[13] A few months later, the social-democratic City Commissioner Ingemar Josefsson and the conservative Barbro Ekdahl led a Stockholm delegation to Vancouver, where they were photographed outside the Pacific Coliseum: "We want an arena like this."[14] Except for the far left there was political agreement at City Hall, and later that autumn the final decision to build a new arena was taken. Another eight months on, in the spring of 1985, Josefsson produced the architectural competition brief, complete with drawings, to show Günther Zabetski, the Chair of the International Hockey Federation—a meeting described in the press as "Stockholm is now fiddling around in the corridors of the elegant Intercontinental Hotel in the heart of Prague."[15] Josefsson got what he wanted: an informal promise that the other main candidate, Paris, was out of the running and the 1989 World Championships would take place in Stockholm.

It was back in 1982 that Josefsson had first hit upon the idea of developing the area around the existing sports arenas in Johanneshov, hoping to attract the championships.[16] There were other good reasons, though: to regenerate the south of the capital with a combination of multiplex sports arena and business complex; to attract tourists and money; and to market Stockholm with a spectacular new building that would enliven the city's silhouette. All these agendas counted on it being part of a larger mission to create a new type public space with a mix of functions. Even if differently phrased, the expectations of the actors involved—sports associations, the City of Stockholm, the building industry—followed the recent trope of human capital plus creative spaces equals new urban discourse.

The location in the south of Stockholm was part of a larger decentralization program of *cityfilialer* (lit. city branches), which were densely built office blocks outside the city center where communications were good.[17] In 1982 the City commissioned two authorities—one responsible for the planning of commercial premises and the other for recreation—to investigate how *cityfilialer* could be developed, with two goals in mind: build office space for the new service sector; and "promote the development of the region as a tourist attraction."[18] By overlapping work, leisure, and culture, the plan would deliver attractive, creative public spaces to the capital's periphery. The spatial ideology framing the project echoed the ideological rhetoric of the new social-democratic policy. In the party manifesto of 1984, much was made of the "free individual" and "free choice" as a new civic right.[19] *Cityfilialer* and the proposed arena's flexibility should be viewed in the light of this turnaround; here, the individual would be offered greater freedom to choose between types of entertainment, and the City of Stockholm would have the long-awaited monument that would reflect the new Sweden. Aesthetics, architecture, economics, and marketing coincided there, so it characterized the consumer logic of the 1980s, which tracked an internationalized and extremely competitive market in goods—including cities and regions.

"Creative financing—A must for the Globe project": that was a 1988 advert where the state bank Stadshypoteket promoted itself as a creative, flexible, and market-oriented credit institute.[20] The difference in rhetoric from the 1970s with its largely state-regulated economy was striking. It was true that creative financing was a precondition for the Globe City project in the sense that financing from private investors was combined with the City's financing in a more integrated collaboration than before, but the project itself—and its architecture—was as much a precondition for the creative financing, where the city used land as its key financial asset in negotiations. Significantly, the finances saw innovations both by the City of Stockholm early in the planning phase and later by financiers in the implementation phase. The Stockholm politicians had proposed that an architectural competition be held which would involve designing the finance as well as the architecture.[21] When the open competition was announced in April 1985, the program contained three parts. In addition to the design of the arena and the entire area, a third part requested a proposal for the management and financial conditions for the commercial buildings and a financing offer for the city of Stockholm. Money thus played a major role at the competition stage and, like the architecture, had to be sourced and organized; architecture and finance were two fields to be "designed," and that required a creative effort from the bidders.

The Swedish economist Jesper Blomberg and other scholars of large-scale building projects like Globe City have established how important the creation of new collaborations and networks can be when reorganizing society.[22] The role of architectural representations in these transformative processes has not yet been studied in any real detail, but the Globe City project demonstrates the importance of materialized visions in weaving the private and public actors together. From the start, Scandiaconsult AB, among four other companies, had been asked by the City to organize a bid. Greger Ahlberg, an architect at Scandiaconsult AB, put a group together with former fellow students at Berg Arkitektkontor.[23] The financing of the project was uncertain, both the competition entry itself and realizing their bid if they were to win. Scandiaconsult AB ultimately lost faith in the project, and, having decided to pursue other work, withdrew, dissolving the competition group. Berg Arkitektkontor still believed in the project, however, so Scandiaconsult AB passed everything to them through Svante Berg and left them as the project lead.[24] The result of the turbulence was that the architects were left in the unusual position of being responsible not only for designing the competition entry but also for raising the funds needed for the entry and its realization.

The architects, left without backers, had to come up with an idea to bring in the financiers and construction companies they needed to compete. Their design was, as we know, a huge globe, which they promoted with the arguments that it would give the arena a theatrical ambiance, and it would give the city a distinctive logo.[25] As Svante Berg said, they based their design on several of the original requirements, which together gave them the final cohesive globe: the desire to concentrate the space to give it a sense of atmosphere; the plans for indoor projections (to create a starry sky) and daylight (originally the upper part of the globe was to be light-transmitting); controlled smoke movement in the event of fire; and ease of evacuation. The simplicity of the resultant abstract form created a powerful image that was easy to remember, manifested in an "imaginary object" that was smoothly internalized and supported (Figure 4.4).[26] Armed with their architectural proposal and a rough costing, they contacted 150 possible partners and competition sponsors, and within two months had agreed terms with the competing construction company SIAB, which reduced the numbers of bidders.[27] They joined forces with a number of construction firms, insurance companies, and other financial institutions in a consortium they christened Hovet (lit. the royal court), in a play on Johanneshov's nickname. They duly called their competition entry Prins Bertils Arena (Prince Bertil's Arena) after the king's uncle.[28]

In October 1985, the bids were submitted and four were put on show a few days later: the spectacular Prins Bertil Arena (Hovet); Skanshov (Skanska and VBB), which followed the local authority's brief most closely and was easiest to implement; Kronan (Diös and Fabege), which was influenced by the Colosseum in Rome; and the Cathedral (Skandia and FFNS), which was a high-risk project financially. Despite the technical and financial uncertainties, Hovet was rumored to have won the first round, partly down to its aesthetic and architectural qualities, but also because it was presented unusually, with a popular version exhibited that included slide shows, brochures, and other carefully chosen displays.[29] As for the oral presentation, Gunnar Jonsson from the Recreational Activities Administration (later Stockholm Globe Arena) said that "Svante [Berg] went above and beyond with the enthusiasm," while the others sent "finance directors and such boring people" who did not have the same "fire" about them.[30] The architects, together with the entire Hovet consortium, gave their project the edge by pitching it with a distinct sense for the market. It also signaled the advent of a new type of glamorous starchitect, with promises of what the development would bring to the area.

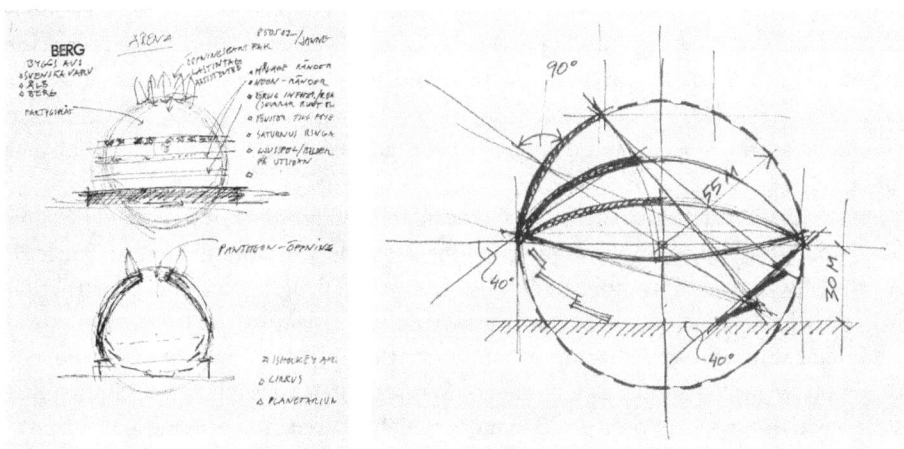

Figure 4.4 The Globe – a first sketch. Courtesy: Berg Arkitektkontor.

Architecture and Retrenchment

After two months of consortium negotiations about the financial format, the jury appointed Hovet's Prins Bertils Arena the winner. Hovet's financial proposal had clinched it because it was more profitable for the City, but also because the proposal had extended the level of exploitation far further than the others.[31] According to the competition brief there was to be 75,000 square meters of offices and shops, which would finance the whole development.[32] Although there were complaints from some political parties—not the Conservatives and Social Democrats—145,000 square meters were ultimately included in the final contract.[33] The conditions of landownership were also changed. At the start of the project it was decided that the private companies would have site leasehold rights from the City to build commercial buildings such as offices and shops, in exchange for covering the construction costs of the arena.[34] This was where the most striking effect of the project can be seen, for instead of leasehold rights the participating companies were given ownership of the land, and in return the city was freed from all construction costs.[35] The City of Stockholm provided the consortium with a large loan to cover costs, which would be paid back when the office space was leased out.[36] The Globe project pioneered "planning by negotiation," where for the first time land was up for negotiation.

Factors for the success of the Globe City project were the limited time frame, which made it possible to push through decisions, and a site which had clear physical and legal boundaries. According to Jean-Paul Baietto, the director of the research company Euralille-Métropole, the result of these temporal and spatial limits created the processes of large architectural projects, what he called the *dynamique d'enfer*, "the process from hell," playing with *dynamique de paix* (peace process). The limitations created sites where "the interconnections, the mutual dependencies, the proliferation of interfaces, the superimpositions of users and owners" were so complex they "form a group of prisoners, shackled together by mutual obligation."[37] Without a shared ambition it is too complicated to realize a large-scale project, given the financial realities—and in this particular process, the common vision was Globe City. According to Berg, the project would never have come about had Scandiaconsult AB not pulled out.[38] The conditions changed radically for the winning architects when they became project leaders. The architectural proposal came first, and was used to attract investors to join the new consortium. Besides the architecture, the architects' personal networks, their ability to communicate their vision, and their skills in design were crucial for setting up the new group.

In the jury evaluation of the Globe City competition proposal, it was asked whether Stockholm was "capable of building the largest spherical building in the world."[39] Admittedly, it was a complicated project, and challenging for the construction workers who had to finish the arena in short time to be ready for the Ice Hockey World Championships in 1989. It is important to note the enormous interest at the time for this sport, regarded almost as a symbol of Sweden and the social-democratic welfare state—which made the project a far more widely shared concern and helped push it to completion. The construction process became a public event, an urban theatre in the media and visible all over the city. Globe City was theatrical even before it

The Globe (1982–9)

Figure 4.5 A section of The Globe (left), Lasse Wretblad and Esbjörn Adamson, Berg Arkitektkontor (middle), Ingemar Josefsson, the social-democratic City Commissioner and Svante Berg, Berg Arkitektkontor (right). Courtesy: Berg Arkitektkontor (left), Photographer: Tommy Pedersen / EXP / TT (middle), Photographer: Tomas Oneborg / TT (right).

was inaugurated, in a phase when the central players on stage were the construction workers, a group of almost 700 people. The workers were visible in adverts, in the press, and later in books about the Globe City project.[40] The workers' media presence was crucial for positive publicity, but also for the public good. Criticism of the City of Stockholm (for spending too much money, for taking decisions behind closed doors, for selling off tax-payers' land) was neutralized by people's sympathy for the workers.[41] The project became an important investment that Stockholmers paid for together and built together. It is telling that the press conference for Globe City's topping off ceremony, marking its very obvious completion visible across the city, was set for January 4, 1988, but the builders on duty in late December finished before New Year's Eve. The final shift they worked through the night and called the evening paper *Expressen* to say the last panels were about to be mounted (Figure 4.6). This was described as their New Year present for the project management and for all of Stockholm.

The political processes behind Globe City show how architectural proposals, being chains of decisions, can finally result in built architecture, changed ideas, values and preconceptions, and new collaborations.[42] The site plan, other drawings, and models materialized ideas in an architectural form, shaping the actors' wishes and desires, while different interests could merge with concrete plans for a future society. In this way the architectural tools became subject to negotiation. The site plan set out territories, ownership, and levels of exploitation, and the models and drawings represented ideas, dreams, and desires for a future that materialized a common goal—but the representations not only mirrored the future as rational material for decision-making, but also as material to conjure up collective fantasies and images for the future. In the

Architecture and Retrenchment

Figure 4.6 In the final days of December 1987, the last plate was put in place at the Globe's top, 85 meters into the air. The construction was to be ready for the Ice Hockey World Cup 1989. Photographer: Jacob Forsell / EXP / TT.

1980s the flow of new investment with the public sector slowed and the local authority planning apparatus weakened, which increased the role of architectural representations in negotiations to find collaborators and financiers.

Shifting the Corporatist Model

The Swedish Model has been characterized as being a corporatist democracy.[43] If the influence of interest groups over the decision-making process becomes too great, it cannot be a democratic system, but if used in a well-functioning parliamentary democracy, it can rather be "a democratic system with certain impure elements," to refer to the official inquiry into the decline of the corporatist system in 1999.[44] The Swedish corporatist system reached its peak in the 1970s, and in 1980s gave way to a system more dominated by non-institutional participation of interest groups, like lobbyism.[45] This change in the decision-making process had consequences for democracy and the influence of the public sector, and should be viewed against the Swedish principle of openness, which "means that the public and the mass media have the right to transparency in state, local authority, and county council activities."[46]

The Globe project both mirrored and contributed to this transformation of the institutional channels for decision-making in the corporatist system. The process leading to Globe City was colored by discussions and negotiations behind locked doors without public documentation, something that also was criticized in the press.[47] Before the competition there had been open discussions between the City and thirty of the most important construction firms, which were narrowed down to the five companies invited to bid: Skandia, Scandiaconsult AB, Diös, SIAB, and Skanska.[48] The jury was appointed by the City Council and consisted only of representatives from the City, so an internally recruited "expert group," more knowledgeable about technical questions, was also established. The Swedish Association of Architects (SAR) proposed that they should have two representatives in the expert group, but the city declared "it would not be appropriate."[49] Instead, the two named architects were offered payment to formulate their evaluations.[50] Through closing the institutional channels the City transformed the role of the architects into paid consultants, which meant that they could be much more easily overlooked in the democratic process.

The decision to make the SAR representative a consult might be explained through the tight schedule—all possible obstacles had to be removed.[51] Right from the start, time was short. In the minutes of the City board meeting months before the competition was announced, some stated that a "precondition for this tight schedule is that all decisions are taken with no delay."[52] Even when the final decision to build Stockholm Globe City was taken, it was rushed through because of the time schedule. It was with a new political rhetoric of Third Way policy, drawing on finance, innovation, and international fame, that Ingemar Josefsson made it possible for Globe City to be built.[53] Comparing site plans from different dates shows how public land was sold off to finance the new area as an innovative "meeting place" and boost for economy. The land was considered by the City Planning Office as a valuable natural environment designated *protected* in the competition brief.[54] In the final plan, after the negotiations with the Hovet consortium and the architects the protected green space with a pond was replaced by offices, with no further discussion documented (Figure 4.7). The bulldozing of the site and marketing of the arena had begun before the final plan acquired legal force.[55]

Another effect of the transformation in the corporatist system and its institutional channels for decision-making processes was illustrated by the dual role of one of the main players in the project. Hans Liljeroth, the manager of SIABS's Stockholm division and the deputy director of the Hovet consortium, was also a member of the City Council. He was initially involved in setting up the conditions for the project, then participated in the competition, and ultimately was among the winners. As he said himself after the Globe City was built, "I was involved before almost anyone else, because I am on the City Council."[56] In the second part of the competition, Hans Liljeroth and C.-G. Pettersson, from the property developer Nisses, were negotiators for the Hovet consortium, making all the deals with the City.

In their first meetings with the City, the Hovet consortium had to specify their proposed design and clarify their deviations from the competition brief, but these discussions soon turned into tough negotiations. The City's representatives were impressed by the architecture, but they wanted the consortium to put price tags on different parts

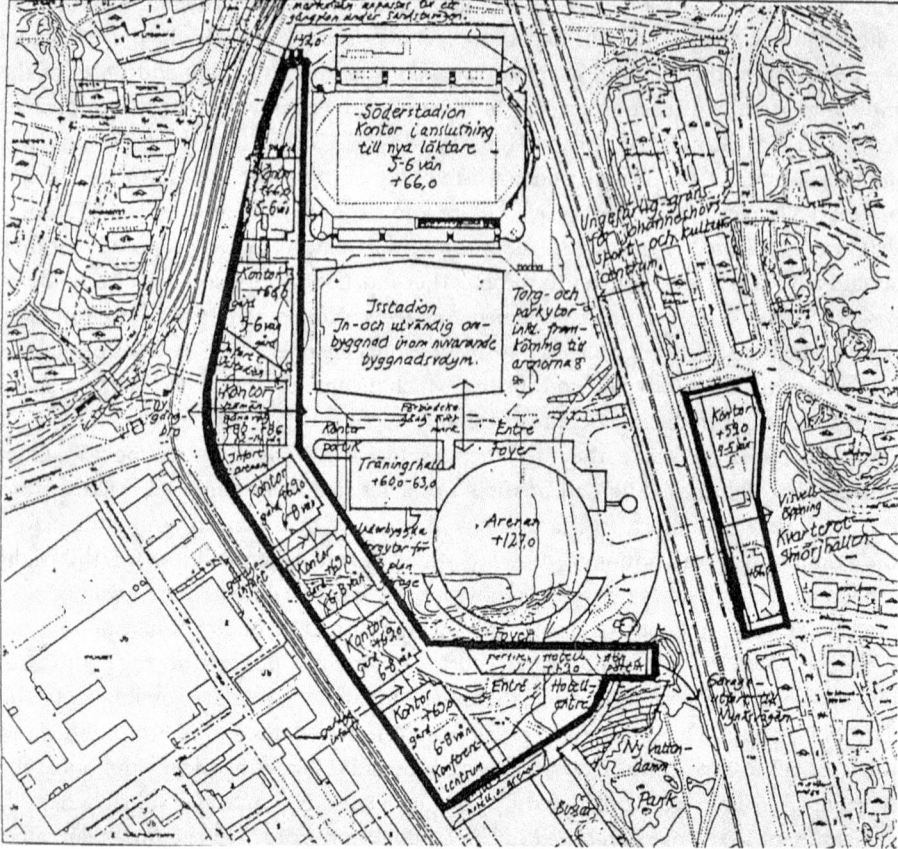

Figure 4.7 Site Plan showing the proposal that was eventually decided. The marked area shows the land which the consortium Hovet would get ownership of. Courtesy: Stockholm City Planning Office.

of the proposal.[57] This was a new strategy where planning proposals were presented in "packages" that each had to be financially self-sufficient through a collaboration between the public and private sectors. The City had to recoup on the deal even if it meant selling their property. However, the consortium never actually met the City's demands to create packages, as they first wanted to agree on a common business plan and then solve the details. At the end of the process, the City ended the collaboration with Hovet and instead started negotiations with Skanska. But Hovet turned the situation around, and after one night of unminuted discussions with the two City representatives they worked out a "letter of intent." All parties signed it the following week, even though the drawings and details were reduced to vague statements such as "they were going to build a world-class arena."[58] Discussions behind locked doors and off the record gave way to new forms of negotiation in Swedish planning, and the City Globe project was the beginning of an era of "planning by negotiation".[59]

Capitalizing the Social

When the Globe Arena was inaugurated in 1989 it was known to the Swedish public as the world's largest spherical building. On a rainy evening in February the public was invited to an outdoor performance. "Colourful strangeness," as the press put it, fluttered across the white sphere, which measures 85 meters high and 110 meters in diameter, and a psychedelic light spectacle filled the dark Stockholm sky. The façade of the globe was transformed into a giant screen, and the show was compared to a cinema performance with the entire city's inhabitants as audience, but with the difference that the commercials were shown last, not first. Of course, advertising was included in this public performance, which introduced a new space not only for sports and culture but also for mass consumption in Stockholm. The Globe was the new cathedral that all Stockholmers paid for, and it was important for the social-democratic politicians' marketing that the building gave something back to the public on its inauguration.

Interest and emotion, conjured up with form and aesthetics, were used in adverts and design, and even, as shown here, in the new field of city branding. The architectural object, the globe, did work as a logo used for marketing Stockholm on the international scene and was a main argument when deciding on the project, as Ingemar Johansson said:

> Stockholm with its functions as a capital and its role as a meeting place and engine for growth is primarily competing with other foreign metropolitan areas. Because of that it is an advantage for the whole of Sweden if Stockholm asserts itself internationally. … It's about much more than just getting another arena.[60]

Designed as an entity, a recognizable thing, the curve of the arena was visible from most of the major sites in Stockholm. Its height distinguished the Hovet bid; while the other proposals used flags or high-rises to advertise the site, it was the arena itself that became the selling symbol in this proposal.

The 1980s were marked by a turn toward a knowledge society, enhancing "human capital" as a driving force in the economy.[61] Culture, creativity, and social networking became the prime tools in the production of human capital, and architecture materialized places and environments to enable these themes. Stockholm Globe City was built as a new entertainment center combined with offices, which was a way of intertwining the quickest growing sector in society, the service sector, with culture, sports, and events. Through the spatial techniques of dividing and connecting functions in the arena and in the area, architecture could regulate social behavior and capitalize on personal wants.

One spatial strategy used in the project was to merge work (knowledge) with events and consumerism in the buildings separate from the arena, in the arena, and in the public space between the buildings. The office block with an interior commercial street intertwines offices and entertainment together in a city-like environment. The notion of the city as a creative space is often theatrically expressed in arranged situations and compositions. Inside Globe City the foyer was like an open field where different

Figure 4.8 The Globe. Photo from inner city street Götgatan. Photographer: Jan Jordan. Courtesy: Berg Arkitektkontor.

episodes—shopping, selling food, selling event merchandise, adverts, information—floated into one another and created what I elsewhere call an "event zone."[62] This way of merging different functions and imbuing them with consumerism was a new way of organizing public spaces in a sports facility: experiences and desires were turned into financial entities.

The spaces in between the arena and the surrounding facilities, like the hotel and the conference space, were also places for merging functions, specifically sport with food and VIP privacy. For example, the restaurant was hooked into the arena like a tentacle, only possible to reach from the independent hotel building not connected to Globe City, so the restaurant was physically separate from the arena. There was a visual connection through big glass walls with curtains that made it easy to close off events. The restaurant was a functional mix of eating and entertainment, a multi-experience built into the

The Globe (1982–9)

structure and visible in the format of the ticket and its price. The spatial differentiation easy to play with—either separate the rooms (pull the curtains), or interlink the restaurant and the arena (draw the curtains) for its economic equivalent in the ticket. One could buy multi-tickets including both food and sport, or only food or sport, and in this way the space enabled a differentiation of both food and price. By perforating the boundary to the sports arena from other interior spaces, which earlier had been absolute (you were either inside or outside), there was the possibility to capitalize on attendance inside the arena too.

The spatial composition of the arena also articulated the relationship between public and private in new ways compared to earlier sport facilities. Traditionally, the public terraces were a communal space, and the individual, regardless of personal wishes, became part of a common sociality—as an audience, everyone was part of a collective. In the Globe Arena it was possible to have your own space and still participate in the event. One could even have a private TV feed to follow the event more closely. There were also luxurious private boxes, much like opera boxes, on the top floor up under the roof where private parties could be held while still participating in a match, out of sight of the rest

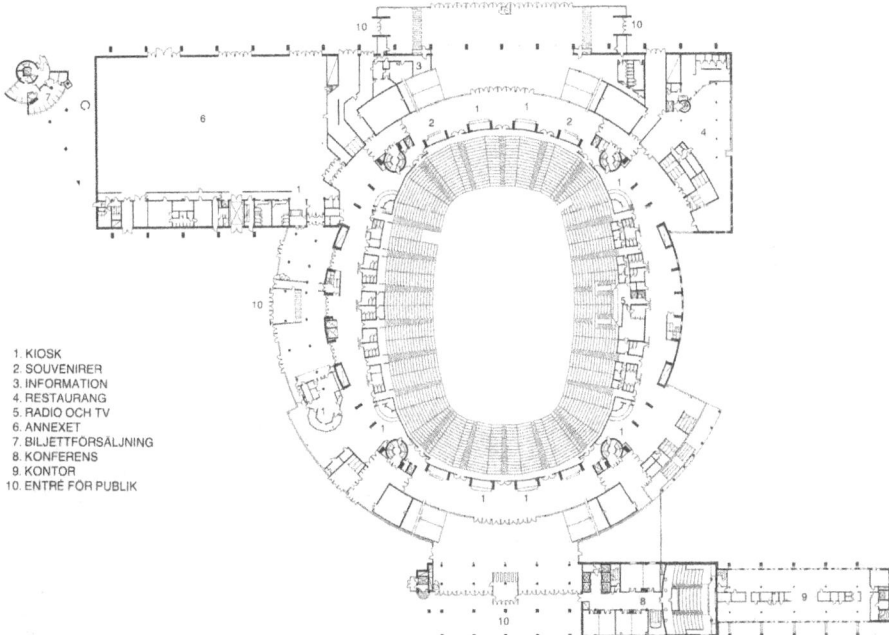

Plan 4, entréplan, 1:1600 (+49.20)

Figure 4.9 The Globe City. Plan of level four (entrance) by Berg Arkitektkontor. The image shows how the interior and exterior of the globe are connected through the perforated boundaries which were made into a flexible space possible to differentiate. The transformative space did also support the differentiation of the audience. Courtesy: Berg Arkitektkontor.

of the audience. This meant that the space of the new arena itself offered a variety of experiences, in contrast to the socially cohesive communal space which contributed to strong collective feelings and experiences. This departure from the usual democratic organization of Swedish sport facilities, which was a core component in the former popular orientation of the welfare state, was a subject of public discussion.[63] Symbolically, collective sports event had been important by creating a communal space where everyone, regardless of class, was equally valued and united in the strength of emotion. This was changed in the Globe Arena, which asked questions about individuality and freedom contra equality and collectiveness.

Like the restaurant's spatial organization, the design of the arena corresponded to the variations in ticket price that were a way of individualizing a mass public and dividing citizens into categories and groups. The differentiated space and the range of tickets were a spatial expression of aspirations for a society based on "freedom of choice," which could

Figure 4.10 The Globe Arena. A glazed private box at the top floor. Photographer: Jan Olsson. Courtesy: ArkDes Collection.

be capitalized on to generate more profit. There was also a social side to the differentiation of the space and the tickets where "besuited businessmen become a counterweight to the more noisy audience"—a kind of individualization of the audience where the crowd is divided into categories and groupings. Semi-public spaces had a different permeability in relation to the social domain, and you were allowed into certain spaces because of your employment, your sponsorship, your status, or your interest—if you had paid enough for a certain experience. In the Globe Arena there were three different luxury boxes, some glazed (a way of getting round the prohibition on drinking alcohol in a public space), some smaller boxes, and boxes connected to the restaurant where you could have dinner in private (Figure 4.10). The VIP box was the most exclusive and was intended for the royal family and other VIP guests and sponsors. All the boxes shared a "package logic": it was the differentiation between ticket packages, with combinations of food, drinks, add-ons, access to private or semi-private rooms, certain lobbies, restaurants, and entrances.[64] Strategies for increasing profits by creating packages with added experiences were developed through the project, but also by commercial messages immersed into the architectural environment, adverts on tickets, on the front of shops and foods, on pillars, walls, and leftover spaces. Each event in the Globe Arena produced additional things—gadgets, food, and the like—which also could be combined into packages. The tendency to "thingify," to produce things out of culture, has been described as typical of the global culture industry.[65]

That the Globe Arena offered each visitor a variety of choices before each visit and the opportunity to position themselves in relation to other visitors was a departure from how earlier arenas and sports halls gathered spectators in a shared space with a symbolic cohesive function, and where all visitors met on the same level regardless of class and wealth. It may seem ironic that the Globe Arena advertised itself as a unitary symbol—an entire sphere—while the exact opposite is introduced; the divided room. But that may be part of it—a shift from a modernist ideal (where the outside reflects the inside functions) toward the "schizophrenic" postmodern expression (where surface and content are separated).

Stockholm Globe Arena "capitalized on the social domain" through its architectural organization, but also through the arena as a medium. The surface arena was a communication board to transmit messages to a mass audience. Culture got thingified, but everything got mediatized in the era of global culture. The Globe Arena was an abstract form designed to project messages on, and described by the architects as one gigantic TV studio where new worlds could be created through events, and mesmerizing atmospheres made by projecting onto the smooth surface of the dome.[66] The inside surface of the dome had no beams or traces of building material: it was designed as an immaterial media interface.[67] The Globe was at once an empty sign ready to be filled, but also a characteristic landmark. "A ball is only a ball, it is how you play with it that counts," as one reviewer put it.[68] In the same review the Globe Arena was seen as part of the invisible media construction of the city and its interior spaces, and has more the character of a background than of its own identity. It is primarily an apparatus for a multiplicity of events and the white interior and exterior surfaces are only for projections.

Figure 4.11 The Globe Arena. Photographer: Jan Collsiöö / TT.

The building could even communicate what was going on inside on the outside. More than being a sign, the building was an interface with the global network because of its function as a space for broadcasting, and the personal experiences could be delivered as images. "Authenticity, belonging, and honesty are lost in these performances" but, instead, experiences not yet even thought of could be created.[69] And as a prolongation of the TV studio, the architects wanted to develop the whole area into a media center for telecommunications, computer hardware, and software production and distribution, which had strengthened the network character of the surrounding buildings.

Architecture as Service

Innovation, personal relations, and creativity were all supposed to support the knowledge society and architecture was part of building a new landscape enabling this future. Instead of being subsidized and regulated by the state, and seen as a cornerstone of the nation's economy, architecture was rather considered a service to buy in order to conjure this anticipated future. In the Stockholm Globe City architecture contributed to this shift in two ways: through the production processes and through the spatial organization as a cultural object.

First, through the architectural production process new economical collaborations and negotiations between the public and private realm were set in place. In the processes leading up to the realized architecture, involving all decisions from the competition brief to the built structures, ideas of the common good were rethought. To create meeting places, to put Stockholm on the global map, and to mix culture, sport, and shopping with offices were all seen as promising strategies to create the new knowledge society. In this striving toward a new political economy architecture became a significant tool to conjure desire and engage all parties involved in the process that also opened for what is often referred to as planning by negotiation. Aesthetic sensibilities had a major role in the creation of a public radical imaginary contributing to a common goal intertwining public and private desires and wishes.

Second, the Globe City contributed to new ideas of a common good, new habits and values through its presence as a cultural object, and as a biopolitical tool; that is, through the multidimensionality of architecture the Globe City contributed to the "new spirit of capitalism."[70] The way space was materialized in the Globe City, combining the service sector (offices) with culture, sports, and consumption, constructed a concrete vision of the creative life as well as of societal growth. Innovativeness, entrepreneurialism, and freedom of choice were all values created consciously or unconsciously through this environment, foreboding the coming event economy turning experiences into commodities. Through material articulations, as spatial compartmentalization, integration, and overlaps, different forms of environments created new possibilities of uses, as well as of aesthetic sensibilities. The arena's interiority was divided differently than in earlier sport facilities. Through a spatial differentiation—open terraces, different forms of luxury boxes including a diversity of facilities—the citizens were divided into categories and groups. This was on the one hand a "freedom of choice," but on the other hand it was an individualization of the collective, dividing the public in relation to economy and status. The exterior of the blank abstract unified symbol branding Stockholm enclosed a compartmentalized interior. This inner space, governed by the consumerist "package-logic," was turned into commodities through ticket prices.

In 1992, two years after the inauguration, the Globe City consortium went bankrupt and suspended payments. All partners withdrew. This is significant for the deep economic crisis in Sweden in the beginning of the 1990s. It was a crisis deeper than in most other European countries, and it had major impact on future development. New forms of collaborations, and networks, between the public and private realm, often seemed to be the only solution during the recession. When the economy was once again turning up at the end of the century society was reorganized in profound ways. More than only being a brand for the City of Stockholm the Globe City project reveals how architecture has the capacity to enable profound transformations through its alliance with economics and politics in the production process as well as through its engagement with personal desires and behaviors as cultural objects.

THE CODE

When discussing "actually existing neoliberalism," Jamie Peck, Neil Brenner, and Nik Theodore argue that neoliberal restructuring strategies interact with preexisting and coexisting institutions.[1] Building codes were one such institution, where new forms of governance co-acted with existing frameworks and created a slow change, in Sweden's case over the course of thirty years. The first comprehensive, legally binding regulation in architecture, *Svensk byggnorm* (SBN, the Swedish Building Code), was in force between 1967 and 1989. The radical deregulation introduced by Boverkets byggregler (BBR, Boverket's Building Regulations) in 1994 was the result of a long transition that involved a wide range of actors.[2] The new code was not a surprise, hitting the ground hard; it had a smooth landing in what was a soft field of regulations.

In this chapter, I want to highlight the role played by the building code in the transformation of the welfare state and its architecture. It is not only the changes of the code itself, from prescriptive to performance-based, that is in focus, but also the building code as a field of practice, part of the Swedish corporatist system. The building code, I argue, is a practice and a project in continual flux; what I call a *soft field*, which enabled neoliberalization from within. The law and the instructions, standards, recommendations, manuals, investigations, committees, and so on relating to the legal system created a field of intense negotiation.[3] Despite regulation in architecture being under-researched, there are several recent important studies on which to draw.[4]

Since the Second World War there has been a critique of building regulations for impeding growth and innovation, a discourse that grew strong with what Foucault calls a "state phobia" emerging in the late 1970s. As demonstrated by Rob Imrie and Emma Street, this criticism was largely based on "anecdotal or incomplete evidence" that served to "caricature the interrelationships between regulation and the design and development process."[5] The pressure to delimit regulations with an often romantic desire for spatial and aesthetic freedom laid the ground for the emerging discourse of deregulation that affected not only the field of architecture but also the notion of the welfare state. Importantly, deregulation resulted in reregulations that shaped new regulatory apparatuses. Government was still present, but acted at one remove. For the Swedish welfare state, scholars have described how new regulations made deregulation legitimate, and how the transformation to an "advanced liberalism" contained a mix of neoliberalism and conservatism.[6] Instead of withdrawing, the state actively introduced governance that followed the logic of the market. Almost immediately after the deregulatory rollback, a rollout phase[7] followed, with performance-based regulation and the expansion of the code into new areas of life, regulating a larger territory, such as public space (parks, traffic infrastructure, neighborhood areas), and cultural heritage.

Architecture and Retrenchment

The regulations now applied to new areas of life, but on the other hand the government pushed responsibility down the hierarchical channels of power, handing power over to other actors and instead acting remotely, as in "regulated self-regulation."[8]

The discourse on building codes was part of an emancipatory movement in architecture. In the formation of the welfare state, the codes were supposed to create individual freedom by providing social protection. Later, though, they were understood as a threat to liberty: from being a provider of freedoms, the state became a hindrance, and instead the individual would find free choice in the market.[9] However, regulations that abolished freedoms were the work not only of the forces of neoliberalization, but also of actors who welfare-state thinking had excluded, such as women. Nancy Fraser's theory of a triple movement (largely concerned with feminism), coined when discussing how emancipatory forces can align with the forces of either marketization or social protection, is helpful in relation to the complex of building codes.[10] Despite not being excluded in the welfare state, and in a parallel to Fraser's feminists, a large group of architects "liberated" themselves aesthetically from what they found to be the limitations of modernist welfare-state regulation.

The Swedish Building Code, 1967–89

In Sweden, as in most other European countries, there is a long tradition of regulating building. In Sweden's case it began in the seventeenth century, but it was first in 1874 that a national law, the Building Charter, was instituted. This law was general and intended to safeguard "safety, health and welfare." In 1947, parallel with the implementation of a postwar welfare-state housing policy, the Building Charter was complemented with specifications that regulated housing.[11] Designed to promote universal welfare and with housing policy as one of its cornerstones, the creation of a national building code was an essential tool for the country's politicians. The period when regulation went hand in hand with state housing policy, securing a high living standard for all citizens through subsidies, was surprisingly short, however. It spanned the recommendations *God Bostad* (Good Housing) after the Second World War, and the legally binding *Svensk byggnorm* (SBN, Swedish Building Code) of 1967–89. These forty years were the crucial precursor to the radical changes to housing policy and the new relationships forming between the state and the discipline of architecture in the 1990s.[12]

God Bostad and SBN, as all other regulations, were part of a network of entities governing building, such as the informal community norms, the market, and the infrastructure that organized the world. The regulations were closely tied to standards and norms, enforced in contracts and budgeting by the National Board of Public Building (1918–93), advisory documents, or commercial actors such as IKEA.[13] The legal scholar Lawrence Lessig demonstrates the extraordinary role of the law (such as the building code) in this complex, and how it affects the other modalities regulating an object or behavior.[14] Obviously, changing the building code affected many areas and actors outside the specific field of architecture, as is revealed by the official opinions submitted as part of Sweden's corporatist decision-making processes. The building code therefore became a topic of interest for many actors.

God Bostad, as the recommended housing norms, predated SBN, and illustrates how the state norms were intertwined with the market. If nothing else, to receive state loans, builders and developers had to meet the recommendations.[15] The norms in *God Bostad* were not legally binding, but a collection of instructions for how to obtain financial support. By regulating measurements and spatial relations through these norms, the state operated as the market, operating through prices, contracts, and offers rather than imposing prohibitions. *God Bostad* not only governed the biopolitical domain by means of the spatial organization of domestic life, but it also implemented governance through the power of free choice. The "de-commodification" of housing was achieved with a typical market method—competition with the best offer in a free market.

When SBN replaced *God Bostad* in 1967, it introduced regulations that were more prohibitory. Parliament delegated the detail of the general law to Statens Planverk (the Swedish National Board of Urban Planning), a state authority with architectural professional expertise.[16] SBN was published as a volume of instructions, some legally binding, others only recommendations. The many revisions of the building code were instigated by Parliament, but it was the National Board of Urban Planning that brought in architectural offices and individual architects, who did the architectural examinations and investigations of the existing code using drawings, models, and full-scale experiments.[17] Their work resulted in proposals for revised codes that, as part of the standard corporatist process, were sent out for consultation to representatives of several special interest groups. The consultation process created a zone where an architectural discourse marked by spatial–aesthetic topics overlapped with political–economic issues. In the early 1980s, for example, politicians considered the deregulation of the building code, claiming it would save money and reduce complications, while the profession's arguments had aesthetic preferences and were based on housing's functional and spatial disposition. I would argue that the interaction of these two instances of decision-making—the political and the architectural, or Parliament and the National Board of Urban Planning—contributed to a broader discourse about deregulation and neoliberalization.

Considering the multilayered functions and levels of decision-making, the consultation process for building codes became a site where resistance and affirmation co-mingled through negotiation and deliberation, creating a politics of consensus that prepared for coming changes in the law. The interaction between the two levels of decision-making—Parliament and the National Board of Urban Planning—was often conflictual due to the different cultures and the language used, for example, between the building industry and the architects, or planners and politicians. Interest groups in the building and construction industry were skeptical of the strong influence of the architectural profession, claiming that it created bureaucratic challenges and blocked development.[18]

According to Gösta Blücher, the first general director of Boverket, the calls for a deregulated economy and politics did not extend to the deregulation of the SBN.[19] In the field of architecture, the wish to deregulate was instead driven by the intention to privilege knowledge over building codes, in the certainty that the codes contributed to reducing knowledge that then fell into oblivion.[20] That the calls to deregulate the building code had different aims than to promote Third Way neoliberalization is also confirmed by articles in the professional press.[21] As demonstrated in the discussion of the postmodern housing area Södra Station (Site 5), the discourse of deregulation was closely connected to the reaction against modernism that had a strong impact on the Building Charter.[22] The architectural profession took on the emancipatory role in Fraser's "triple movement," with its ambivalent relationship to neoliberalization.

Toward Performance-based Codes

The history of the SBN, from 1967 to 1989, was one of transformation from prescriptive codes towards the performance-based codes, BBR, in 1994. If a prescriptive code regulated a solution, a performance-based code outlined "general requirements of quality and performance." It was thus a shift from means to ends, or from what a building is to what it does.[23] The engineer Greg Foliente exemplifies this with how to manage fire safety: the prescriptive code regulates both material and spatial qualities, while the performance-based code states that the building should be able to withstand fire. Foliente presents typical arguments for introducing the new regulatory framework when he describes how prescriptive approaches "serve as a barrier to innovation."[24] That may be true, but the shift to performance-based codes removed the innovative space from the architect and gave it to the developer or builder. This had consequences for building construction and processes, and for spatial organization especially in relation to the domestic sphere.[25] The first Swedish Building Code, SBN 67, integrated two earlier regulations—*BABS* and *God Bostad*, the first regulating building construction and material and the latter spatial organization of housing—which in SBN 67 were supposed to be merged into "functional requirements," to simplify and "coordinate all rules in building design and construction."[26]

The introduction of the new performance-based codes affected both the construction and building processes and the architectural space. In relation to architectural objects, Erik Sigge has demonstrated how function was not perceived as a stable quality of the object, but supported a structuralist thinking of function as a performative flexibility of the object's ability to support functions.[27] Performance-based thinking disrupted the aesthetic object, comprehended as a unit, in favor of a formless performative structure, with the object as a material modulation of a structure in time and space. This marked a turn away from the modernist paradigm in both architecture and economics, and, as Sigge shows, a new supply-sided economy enforcing deregulation, tax-reduction, and neoliberalization was introduced to the building industry by performance-based thinking.[28]

Performance-based codes influenced the spatial regulation of the domestic sphere slightly differently, as they resulted in a deviation from the modernist way of separating functional units, in contrast to the premodern working-class home. In the welfare-state housing policy, the lack of boundaries between functions, such as eating and sleeping, had been unhealthy for hygienic and sexual reasons (primarily incest), but, as argued by Lennart Holm in the 1980s, this separation was no longer needed when housing standards had dramatically improved.[29] Instead of stating measures and spatial relations, the codes, by dint of revisions and investigations, such as in the realization of Södra Station, increasingly came to specify requirements for performativity. For example, the spatial notion of a "kitchen" represented in drawings was exchanged for a text-based code that stated the space must enable "kitchen fittings" to perform. That is, prescriptions of defined spaces gave way to requirements for functions to perform, such as eating, sleeping, or socializing. This shift opened for almost existential questions left to the assessors. What was required for socializing or eating? What spaces did life require? Performance-based codes also affected the size and organization of space. In general, the size of blocks increased but flat sizes decreased, which had knock-on effects on the organization of the city and the relationships between public and private spaces.[30]

With the introduction of performance-based thinking, the SBN moved away from the language of representation linked to architecture, such as drawings, defined measures, and spatial relations, toward simplified, scientific, text-based communication. The form of representation used to mediate codes is reproductive and has repercussions for thinking about codes and architecture: the architect Marja Lundgren understands representations "as generative in acts of intellectualization," and argues that performance-based codes have contributed to a shift to scientific questions in relation to the built environment, at the expense of architectural issues.[31] In a study of the UK's first national codes, Katie Lloyd Thomas finds a similar development, arguing that the NBS 73 dropped descriptions of the building process, including specifications of materials in a "prose-like language," for a more open form of specification that left the selection of solutions to the contractor.[32]

In a Swedish context, "functional requirements" enforced efficiency, leaving specifications open and flexible for the producers in the building industry, and manufacturers were given greater responsibility for finding solutions. The creative process fell to the producers of the building more than to its architects.[33] Consequently, the divide between architects and other actors in the building sector increased with the introduction of performance-based codes. The committee that drafted a new Building Ordinance stated in 1974 that "qualities not corresponding to the requirements in an assignment should be accepted if the functional requirements in the regulations are fulfilled."[34] This attitude meant producers and constructors could often decide to invent their own, often cost-cutting, solutions, which was pointed out by a researcher at the time: "the producer's maximal freedom to use cost-cutting rationalization and to use production methods, materials and designs that for him give the lowest cost. … The society was putting the responsibility of products developments and design, the 'creative process', on the producers."[35] Another effect of the performance-based codes was that they resulted in new forms of assessment. Town planning committees needed

Architecture and Retrenchment

expertise for the complex task of evaluating the objects' ability to perform, and another consequence was the internalization of government regulations by developing systems of self-regulation.[36]

Existing Institutions of Restructuring

The SBN and other regulations, specifications, and instructions constructed a field of practice where resistances and affirmations co-existed; a field transformed from within, which demonstrated neoliberalization as embedded in the existing institution of the SBN. In this transition between forms of governance, a rational idea of efficiency as characterizing the modernist welfare state was mixed with, and contributed to, neoliberalization.[37] When rational structuralist thinking in architecture (and the building sector) set aside the aesthetic object to prioritize cost efficiency and budget calculations in the regulatory infrastructure, a shift in power followed, leaving the architects to lag behind in an emerging supply-side economy, where the creative part increasingly fell to producers and manufacturers.

Understanding building codes as a soft field that enabled restructuring also reveals them to be a creative field where it is possible to act. As shown by Liam Ross, their history has several telling examples, for example, Ove Arup's participation in the fire codes.[38] Another example is the Swedish Women's Building Forum's engagement in developing the domestic building code. One interpretation of building codes and regulations, not primarily as limitations or tools for a negative, repressive biopolitics rationalizing everyday life, is offered by Peg Rawes, drawing on Félix Guatttari and Rosi Braidotti.[39] As shown in this chapter, the shift toward performance-based codes has left architects weaker, while enhanced efficiency and cost-cutting has handed more of the innovative space to builders. But could we think about the code in another way, more like Rawes's description of a space for maneuver for groups that fought for emancipation, but also for alternatives? Instead of focusing on the dichotomy between resistance and protection, does it have the potential to be a field of creative practices?

The calls by urban activists to rethink Sweden's Building Ordinance and the SBN were not a campaign to throw out the codes altogether, but to remodel them. That had begun as early as 1968 with a parliamentary commission of inquiry, Bygglagutredning (BLU), which had raised the key question of the day: citizen democracy. In the late 1960s, thanks to the campaigns to give the individual the chance to influence the formulation of architecture and planning, the field of rules and regulations was framed as a future hope in the public debate. As *Dagens Nyheter* put it, "We need to be trained for when the new building law is instituted and will give space for people's opinions."[40] The determination to strengthen the role of the individual citizen can be traced both to the 1968 discourse, marked by activism and resistance to authority, and to the discourse of the new politics of marketization in the 1990s. From the first parliamentary commission of inquiry, it took almost twenty years for the new law, PBL, to be passed—a law that stressed the individual's rights and importance of local authority self-governance, and embodied the complex interplay of emancipatory forces, business, and neoliberalization. Somewhere along the way, the possibility of framing the code in another, more flexible, way was lost.

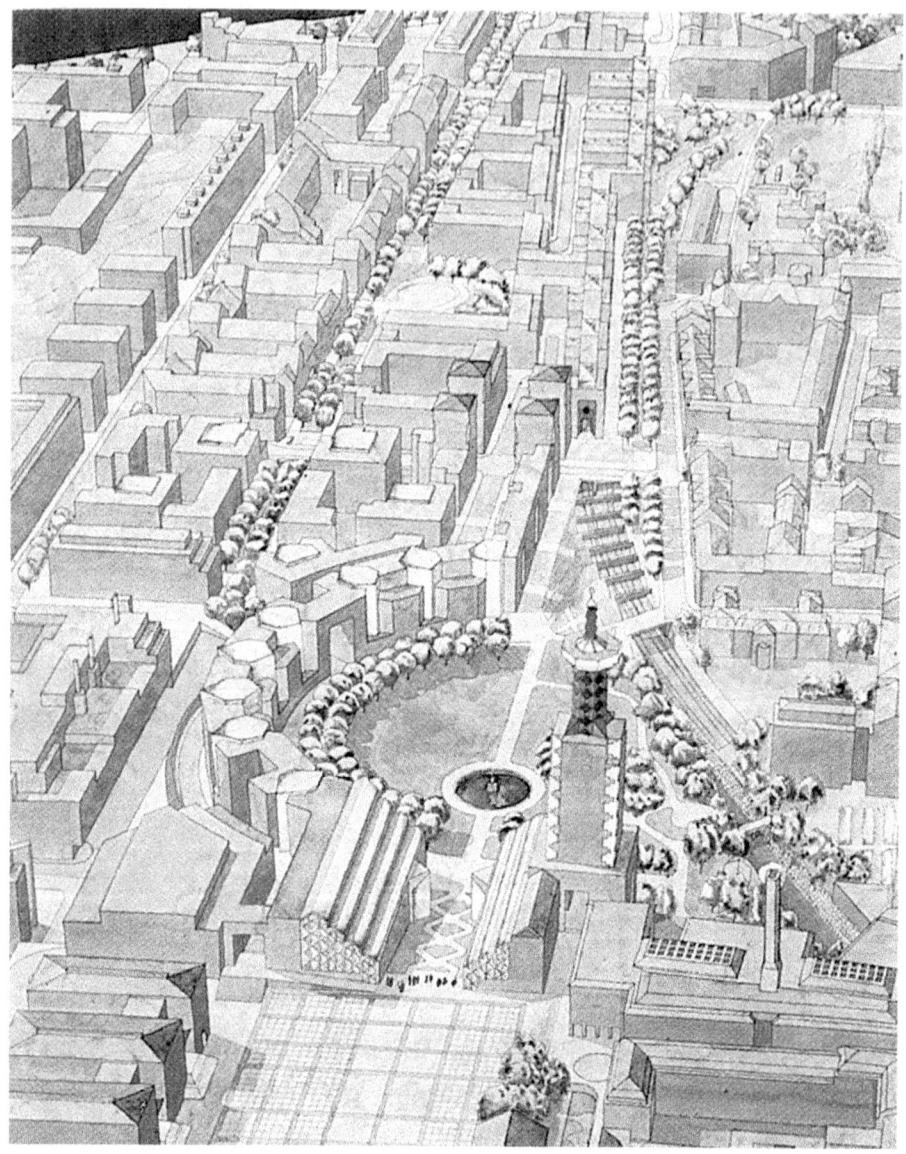

Figure 5.1 Axonometry showing the area of Södra Station (Södra stationsområdet) as published in the program for Södra Station (1984). Reprinted from "Södra stationsområdet. Program," June 1984, Stockholm City Planning Office.

SITE 5
THE POSTMODERN HOUSING AREA (1981-7)*

When Léon Krier visited Stockholm in 1980 to prepare for an architectural competition, he was welcomed by the influential Swedish architect and planner Jan Inghe-Hagström, from the City Planning Office, with the words, "Dear Mr Krier, I will now entertain you for about 20 minutes by reviewing on screen the greatest imbecilities we have been committing in Stockholm over the last thirty years."[1] Krier recalled this in his article about designing the new inner-city housing area in question, Södra Station (South Station), published in *Architectural Design* in 1984.[2] Against the background of his competition proposal, Krier launched a determined attack on building regulations: "We refuse to occupy ourselves with ideal and abstract measurements. Such preoccupations are characteristic of merchants and policemen; they always confuse type and standard, of normality and norm."[3] Krier's attacks on architectural norms and regulations were echoing the heated discussions in Sweden around 1980, and they framed the abandonment of the functionalist paradigm for new economies and new aesthetic styles. The criticism of regulations and rules in the early 1980s dominated not only contemporary architectural debate, especially about functionalism, but also the criticism of the social-democratic welfare state.

The discourse on regulations, norms, and the welfare state was captured by Michel Foucault in his 1979 lectures at the Collège de France, where he identified the excessive attacks on the state as a "laxness" that framed contemporary debate, and he argued that "state phobia" was a symptom of a "crisis of governing" and not of the state itself.[4] In the context of Södra Station, the criticism was primarily framed in terms of aesthetics and architecture, and the aim was not to condemn the state per se; it was rather the starting point for an investigation of new living forms and new social and spatial organizations. Compared to contemporary criticism of the Million Program, which was much closer to criticism of the state, the discussions in the 1980s were more directed toward new aesthetic expressions and constructive proposals. In that sense the architectural discourse paralleled the emerging political discourse on new forms of governance initially of the 1980s. The call for change came from a variety of groups—such as feminist architects, environmentalists, and neoliberal marketeers—and could not be understood or explained from a single perspective. In 1980 it was the anniversary of the 1930 Stockholm Exhibition, which was marked by exhibitions, articles, and public debates on how best to reinvent modernist housing to suit contemporary life.[5] What made the architectural criticism of regulations and building codes in the early 1980s an explosive societal force was that it fed into the restructuring of the Swedish welfare state, fueling the political discussion of "freedom of choice," individuality, and variations.

Architecture and Retrenchment

Figure 5.2 Jan Inghe-Hagström and Leon Krier. Collection of Jan Inghe-Hagström, Stockholm City Archive. Courtesy: Maud Livén.

In this way, the discourse on aesthetics and architecture overlapped with the broader political discourse of "state phobia," as Foucault put it, even though this was not always the intention. The Södra Station housing project was planned and built at the crossroads of different forms of governance—Keynesian policy versus the Third Way policy—and reveals how crises of governance played out on different levels: in government policy, in local authority policy in Stockholm, and in the planning system.[6]

The competition entries for Södra Station presented by Krier and many others in 1981 charted the full range of options that offered an alternative to functionalist planning. Yet only architects did not consider the site a blank page on which to sketch the outlines of the 1980s "brave new world"; politicians, bureaucrats, and legal experts all came to revise their frameworks for arranging life, and they tested them on the site. Parallel to the aesthetic turn toward postmodernism, another less remarked regulatory turn took place in most sectors. The Swedish Building Code (SBN) was under review in the early 1980s, not only from an architectural standpoint but also for economic and political reasons, and a proposal for a new deregulated performance-based code for housing (interior spaces) was tested with a new regulation of form and spatial design of the exterior urban space at Södra Station.

The history of the restructuring of the Södra Station area in the 1980s should be understood in terms of the rise of the welfare state in the early twentieth century. Housing was an economic and political cornerstone of the welfare state. Sweden's housing policy did not revolve around social categories, with cheaper housing for the less well off; it was part of a biopolitical scheme to create a uniform housing norm for

The Postmodern Housing Area (1981–7)

the entire population. Central to the move toward an equal society, besides changing the country's economic circumstances, was the redirecting of the individual's wants and need. The proletariat's subjectivity would thus be reshaped, and the attributes which were the result of a long history of oppression would melt away, leaving the workers to adopt a combination of wants and needs that coincided with those of modern, middle-class citizens.

To effect a radical change in the housing stock without having to nationalize construction, a state loan system was introduced where the borrower (the developers) had to meet the agreed housing rules and norms (the norms were nonbinding at first, although that changed). The requirements—set out in *God Bostad* (Good housing), between 1954 and 1964—marked the same process of "de-commodification" that characterized the welfare state and was designed to separate living standards from pure market forces.[7] Using *God Bostad*, the authorities could steer future housing stock to a high standard of living and a high commercial value, and the needs and values of the resident (consumer) would not only be reflected in the regulations on dimensions, quantities, and ratios but also be shaped by them. The welfare state's housing policy was realized in under fifty years, running from the 1930s to its dismantling in the 1980s and complete restructuring in the 1990s. The early 1990s brought a complete about-face: a system change as radical as the one in the 1930s. The Ministry of Housing was abolished and its remit divided between seven ministries.

The planning and construction of the Södra Station area came just before this total reversal of housing policy, and heralded several of the changes to the regulations. The political upheaval of the 1980s left its mark on housing construction and views on housing, but it is less evident how the relation between those political realities and the design of housing and local surroundings found expression. Where previously it was the proletariat's subjectivity which was to be refashioned, adopting the new structures of wants and needs of a modern middle class, from then on there was a new "postmodern" individual, whose inner qualities and impulses were rather assets in the new economy then taking shape. How to understand the new aesthetic sensibility and design experiments of the 1980s, there to be seen in the Södra Station area, in terms of neoliberalization and deregulation? How did the deregulation of housing standards relate to other types of deregulation at the same time, whether in economic policy or the public sector with its new public management (NPM)? Unlike political and economic deregulation, in architecture it had other purposes—as two processes, one based on economic–political arguments, the other on aesthetic–architectural grounds, which went on to coincide in a major societal transformation.

Laws, norms, and standards, just like lived space, the everyday environment, and the home, are all sites for organizing life, and all express the shifts in how life and society ought to be governed and experienced. Here, I therefore not only discuss the spatial and architectural aspects of Södra Station but also look at the legal framework governing design in the shift from prescriptive codes to performance-based codes. Even though Södra Station marked a shift away from the housing structures of the late 1960s and 1970s, the old functionalist typologies still determined its form, resulting

Architecture and Retrenchment

Figure 5.3 View over Södra Station in 1982 before the development, showing housing areas from the 1960s in the background. Photographer: Erik Zetterström. Courtesy: Stockholm City Museum.

in what might best be called a hybrid of planning ideologies. Bridging the various aesthetic preferences, political ideas, and planning systems, Södra Station showcases how architecture as a discipline not only mirrors such shifts and contributes to them but also resists them.

Postmodernism and the Crisis of Planning

Södra Station was designed as "a city within the city," and it remains so to this day. However, the final result was very different to the "city of communities" that was Krier's ideal.[8] The area is developed as an enclave, with a formal inner organizational logic that differs radically from its surroundings.[9] Although the intention was the opposite, the housing area was cut off from the old city pattern by the traffic separation typical of functionalist planning—lowered streets or streets closed to vehicular traffic—which shows the ambiguous planning ideals. The architectural language is coherent in its diversity and has a spatial precision with elaborated corners, pillars marking lines of sight, paths and roads creating a geometry with long lines of sight, diagonals cutting through the structuring grid, intimate plazas, and large public squares.

The Södra Station project was preceded by long, difficult negotiations between the City of Stockholm and Swedish Railways (SJ), which had started as far back as the 1950s.

The Postmodern Housing Area (1981–7)

Figure 5.4 Aerial view over Södra Station. Photographer: Martin Naucler.

It was only in 1979 that the city bought the land from SJ, after the decision was made to turn the site into a housing area that would consist of 2,650 flats, for 7,500 residents, and 70,000 square meters of commercial space. Unsurprisingly, the planning process for the area was hotly contested: a large area of housing in the inner city was certain to be controversial, and public interest was intense. To meet public pressure while still achieving its stated political goals, the city adopted a wide range of strategies for citizen participation, including setting up an information and consultation office and arranging seminars, debates, and exhibitions. Proposals for the area by leading local architects were first at the Boplats 80 exhibition in downtown Stockholm in the summer of 1980 and later that year at the consultation office. The exhibition was also important for helping prepare the brief for the international ideas competition in the spring of 1981.[10] The competition expressed the emerging interest from the authorities to engage the public, and it was criticized for not taking professionals seriously because it was

135

open to everyone resulting in many proposals by non-professionals that did not include drawings, only written ideas.

Out of 124 submissions, however, 25 were chosen by the city as inspiration for the final plan presented and approved in June 1984, the same year construction started. The first residents moved in a mere three years later. By then the economic and social situation had changed radically since 1979, when the land was bought, and implementing the plans and ideas framing the process both mirrored and contributed to this shift. The program for Södra Station proposed by the City Planning Office was made under financial pressure. The chosen development plan for the area was described as "an *opportunity* for realization" when the "difficult economic situation dictates greater land use in the physical planning, which also applies to other elements which may be decided later in the process."[11] Consequently, the plan, though approved after a period of public consultation, remained unclear, and some recognized that standards for the flats could be lowered, as could the "housing supplements and services." The senior architect at the City Planning Office, Lars Brattberg, was frustrated. He reiterated that the lack of resources made it impossible to draw up visionary plans (nor could they be designed and then put on hold for better times) and that the focus should instead be on *how* to achieve the project. Instead, he and others favored a more flexible process of negotiation: "We have to be able to act now, we must be able to change and develop the city even if money is lacking."[12]

That there was general turbulence in the field of urban planning is also evident from the public debate after the proposal by the City Planning Office for the Södra Station area was sent out for comment (in the summer and autumn of 1983). The proposal, which attracted much criticism, was defended by Brattberg, who talked of "annual model planning," led by investors and builders, which would be "driven by economics-related norms and rules" and which would raise their profiles in the market.[13] He argued that Stockholm's finances, with a resurgent construction industry, would increasingly influence planning in the 1980s, with the consequence that instead of focusing on visions and goals, the emphasis would be on planning. Brattberg expressed his confusion about the role of the private market and the effect of regulation, both criticizing the market's irresponsible attitude to planning and claiming that city planning was "paralysed by excellent control mechanisms."[14]

The City Planning Office organized study circles and lectures between 1979 and 1981 to discuss the international architectural debates because, as they put it, "something was happening." These events had a special focus on postmodernism, urban space, the renaissance of the city, and the concept of "city-likeness," and they had a significant impact on the planning of Södra Station.[15] The importance of postmodernism for the planning of Södra Station was also obvious through Krier's work, whose proposal was one of the strong references in the chosen city plan but also through Norberg-Schulz, whose theories of form and place were crucial for the City Planning Office; and Ricardo Bofill, who designed one of the most significant parts of the area. The local discourse of postmodernism, or the "new architecture," in the early 1980s was equally important.[16] In the public debate, one can see very different arguments in favor of pursuing variation

The Postmodern Housing Area (1981–7)

and individualization, which shows how disparate the arguments were that converged on a radical shift in the architectural discourse. It was, on one hand, seen as a subversive act toward the capitalist, consumer-oriented architecture of the suburbs, expendable in its repeated form; on the other hand, the new urban space, with all its variety, was said to enhance the liberation of the individual in the emerging Third Way Sweden.[17] And for the Stockholm politicians, the diversified housing environment was a welcome response to the popular criticism of the welfare state.[18]

Södra Station was one of the last housing large areas to be developed before the radical reorganization and deregulation in 1991, when housing and the planning process became openly part of the commercial market. Lars Brattberg and Jan Inghe-Hagström at the City Planning Office spoke up strongly against this emerging new ethos of public management during the planning of Södra Station, although Inghe-Hagström at the same time argued for "deregulating" the functionalist norms.[19] When the discourse of aesthetic deregulations was tied into the processes of economic and political deregulations the architects often ended up in situations marked by contradictions and frustrations. However, Brattberg's and Inghe-Hagström's response to the "threats" to the planning system was to use aesthetic deregulations, postmodernism, as a weapon against the effects of economic and political deregulations, and they invented new aesthetic regulations to adapt the system to prevailing conditions in the early 1980s. These "postmodern regulations" were formulated as "quality programs" that controlled the formal spatial aspects of Södra Station.

The role played by aesthetics in planning was reliant on the legacy of functionalism stressed by the architect Torsten Westman, director of the City Planning Office, who was behind one of the most comprehensive functionalist projects in postwar Europe, the Stockholm city renewal in the 1960s. He argued that only through form could the high plot ratio be controlled, and indicated that elimination of functional boundaries must be superseded by strong design (*gestaltningskonst*).[20] Here postmodernism played a multifaceted role, enhancing deregulatory societal forces, but also "protected" the architectural order from the forces that menaced traditional architectural values.[21] There seems to have been considerable confusion about the planning system's transformation: norms and controls could be thought positive (for example, housing standards as a guarantee of quality) but also limiting and paralyzing.

The long-term state housing policy began to be dismantled in the 1980s, and it was reorganized in 1991. As part of this comprehensive reorganization of the housing sector and state housing policy in the early 1990s, a new set of regulations replaced the Swedish Building Code SBN 80. A study of the changes to the codes over time reveals three evolving themes: a shift toward a focus on the individual user and citizen participation; a shift toward performance-based regulation; and a regulatory shift away from interiors to exteriors such as streets and public spaces. Citizen participation and performance-based regulations were centered on user experience and the determination to strengthen the role of the individual citizen and can be traced to the 1968 activism and criticism of authorities, and to the 1990s discourse of the new politics of marketization.[22] The realization of Södra Station came halfway between the 1960s and 1990s, and the discourse

Performance-based Building Codes

Just before the Social Democrats came to power in 1982, Minister of Housing Birgit Friggebo, of the Liberal Party, stressed in the government's budget the correlation between regulation and high building costs, and she instructed the Board of Urban Planning to investigate the Swedish Building Codes for housing.[23] That same year the board presented a final proposal, which two architectural offices—FFNS and White— were commissioned to test.[24] In the end the proposal never gained legal force since it had no determinable impact on building costs, but it would prove important for introducing open-plan flats and the overall organization of the Södra Station development. The area became in effect a full-scale laboratory for many proposals on how to re-regulate housing—proposals that only later came into force in the new regulations, Boverkets byggregler (BBR, Boverket's Building Regulations) in 1994. In this way the architecture of Södra Station anticipated the legal shifts that would marketize Swedish housing policy and pave the way for the radical neoliberalization to come.

Lennart Holm at the Board of Urban Planning argued that the existing norms' strict requirements for differentiation in the dwellings' inner spaces (i.e., for separating out the domestic functions) had been formulated to counteract a lack of suitable personal living space. Thanks to much higher living standards and larger flats, these regulations were no longer considered necessary. In historical terms, this meant a step away from the modernist ideal of separating the functional units of the premodern working-class home. The lack of boundaries between sleeping and eating, for example, was perceived to be unhealthy, both mentally and physically. For hygienic and sexual reasons (the incest taboo), the space was differentiated. In the new proposal, spatial differentiation and specific measurements were replaced by requirements for performativity.[25] For example, the concept of a *vardagsrum* (living room) was replaced by the performative reality of *sittgrupp* (seating area). Under SBN 80, the living room, bedroom, and kitchen had been defined as separate units, but under the new disposition they were integrated into the concept of one continuous *bostadsrum* (lit. dwelling space). Instead of "kitchen," the term "kitchen fittings" was used to signify products (furniture) rather than spatial relations.

Through this regulatory shift, the clear prescriptions that had defined spaces and measurements (often visually demonstrated in drawings) were replaced by spatial requirements for functions such as eating, sleeping, or socializing. Although this change might have left the design more open to alternatives, it nevertheless also created more intrusive assessment tools and put them in the hands of the city planning committees, who had to evaluate design proposals in relation to the norms.[26] It is also questionable whether the proposal presented by the Board of Planning did reduce regulation. One

The Postmodern Housing Area (1981–7)

new regulation stipulated that both the dining space and living room had to have natural light and a view. This affected the plans for Södra Station: for Bofill's housing, for example, it caused a conflict between the City Planning Office and the architect when the composition of the façade was distorted.[27] Taken together, the inquiries into the codes and all the proposals formed a field of negotiation, deliberation, and constructive resistance.

The proposal's reregulation of the flats also affected the reorganization of spatial relations on a larger urban scale. The City Planning Office announced that the new codes would result in smaller flats with a new open social area with a mix of functions, which would affect both privacy and people's ability to furnish the space. The result of cutting both the flats' size and the building costs was that each staircase had to serve many of the flats (up to thirteen), which implied large building volumes and many "one-sided" flats. In order to organize Södra Station without abandoning what the City Planning Office called a good living environment, "more spatial typologies such as streets, entrance squares, and parks would bring variety to the environment" in combination with strict limits on traffic.[28] The expectation was then that an emphasis on exterior qualities would compensate for the lack of interior qualities, meaning that the proposed new codes had implications for the relationship between individual homes and urban spaces, for the organization of the communal space within each block, and for the courtyards and public urban space.[29]

To extend the homes to encompass the exterior areas had already been attempted in the exhibition Boplats 80, for example, by feminist architects who stressed in their call for new forms of collective housing that the home was larger than the individual flat and not limited by its walls.[30] A related tendency was also evident in the Södra Station competition entries years before the proposed new codes were published, as they showed different versions of how to move activities out of the inner space of the blocks of flats and into the public spaces of the blocks—to integrate public and private spaces, or to blur the boundaries between public and private. This transgression of spatial borders was accompanied with a transition of responsibility, with the City Planning Office noting that the competition entries showed how the "boundaries for the dwelling are extended to incorporate common functions of the housing block, and are institutional activities modified to let activities and premises be run by the residents."[31] And in the preliminary plan for the Södra Station housing, the City Planning Office stressed that "sharp boundaries must be erased between the private home and the public environment, between activities in the home and in public institutions such as preschool and school, and that the individual should be responsible for activities that the public sector took care of before."[32] These claims by the politicians during the planning process required the architects to spatially articulate a new social situation, one in which the residents were meant to take over the responsibility for social-care services until then run by the public authorities. This was a step toward the reorganization of public and private services, characteristic of the NPM turn, by which citizens were to become active consumers or producers in the market. The idea was to combine different functions such as schools and smaller workplaces to create new social networks that spanned generations and

Architecture and Retrenchment

social groups, while the shared premises designed for most of the blocks of flats were thought crucial to the new social organization.

Five housing companies were invited to develop their competition entries regarding aspects of the "extended dwelling," such as the possibility to create social groups and develop collectivity on different levels in the housing area, and strengthening the relationship between the interior and exterior environments.[33] This found its most radical expression in BGB's proposal (never realized), in which "school" as a building of its own was deconstructed into individual rooms that were departmentalized, scattered, and integrated with housing functions (Figure 5.5). These spaces were supposed to have multiple uses. The rooms assigned for schooling could also serve as communal spaces for residents and care centers for the elderly.[34]

Another example was Röda Söder (Red South) by HSB, a nod to the early-twentieth-century social-democratic Red Vienna. The Röda Söder housing was to be a combination of high-rises and slabs, integrating larger units of communal spaces such as laundries, workshops, sports facilities, and *festvåningar* (party rooms).[35] This proposal was a revised version of the provocatively rhetorical proposal Söders Manhattan (Södermalm

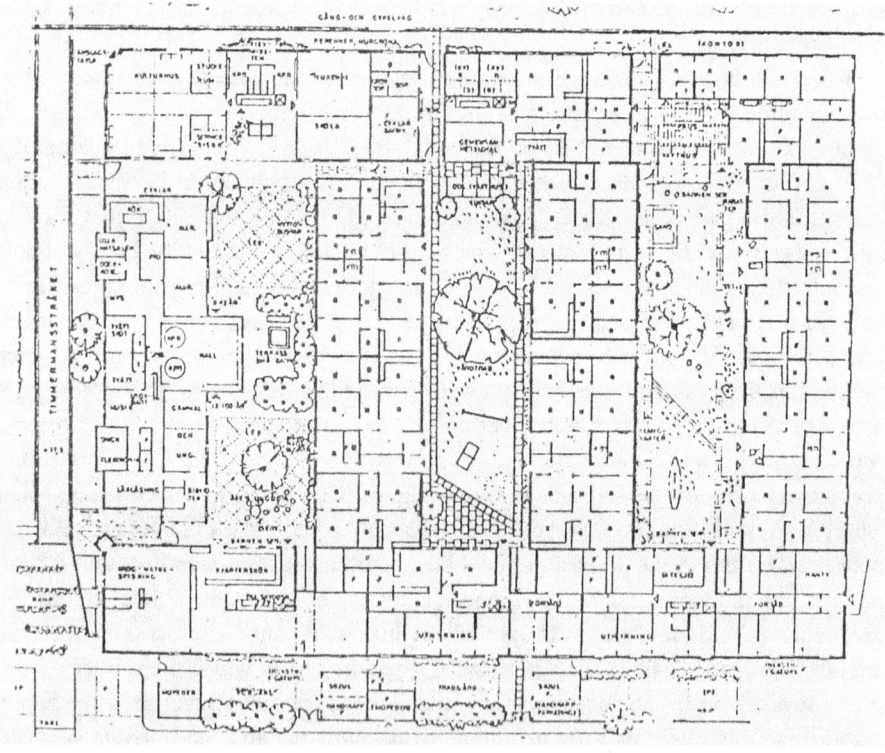

Figure 5.5 BGB:S proposal for an "extended dwelling," 1983. A school was deconstructed and integrated with housing functions. Reprinted from "Boendeprogram 5," February 1983, Stockholms fastighetskontor. Stockholm City Archive.

140

Manhattan), put together with the journalist Björn Rosengren, which had presented the communal spaces as larger units mostly intended for recreation, leaving the flat sizes unchanged. This resulted in more expensive flats and was judged unrealistic by the City Planning Office.

Stockholmshem's proposal, by the architect Bengt Lindroos, had the interior and exterior spaces of the blocks of flats as one continuous floating space—a spatial articulation also found Lindroos's proposal for the flats built under the new codes. Stockholmshem and Lindroos demonstrated the different ways to arrange communal spaces inside the blocks of flats or outside in the courtyards, which also had semiprivate spaces labelled "house gardens."[36] There was a noticeable shift in the 1980s in the graphics and visual representations in the plans discussed here compared to the functionalist drawings of the 1960s and 1970s, confirming how the sensibilities and imaginaries of "sequences of spaces" were expressed in aesthetic drawing techniques—the insides and outsides of the blocks of flats were articulated as one expanded field, with dynamic spatial differentiations floating into one another.

The proposals by BGB, HSB, and Stockholmshem show how the demands formulated by the City Planning Office came together in a new architectural language and a new organizational order. The Södra Station development was a hybrid of various planning ideologies and political paradigms, and the collective spaces integrated into its blocks of flats, with their collective multifamily homes, had one foot in the older paradigm of the 1968 movement (and further back to the 1930s) and the other in a world where social services were privatized and managed by the residents themselves.

If the interior organization of the flats following the introduction of the new building codes had a close relationship to a new organization of the exterior collective spaces and social services, it also tied into the city itself. In the program for the area some stated that the previous decade had been marked by a concern for the existing environment in the city center, "but lately the debate has new elements, and wants something new and different." Therefore, "the nickname Södermalm Manhattan became synonymous with an expectation for an inner-city environment that never has been experienced before."[37] The City Planning Office indicated that the existing streets and public spaces were currently just the "backsides of the built structures" because of the heavy traffic and the spatial arrangement of courtyards, and therefore they stated a new spatial layout was needed.[38] Brattberg, as the head architect at the City Planning Office, stressed it was not enough to increase the exploitation of the land or to design flats of the "new low standard" and force people out on the streets, in the best case into some collective urban arrangement.[39] Instead, semi-public spaces would connect the streets with the inner courtyards, and dynamic differentiated spatial sequences—urban rooms leading into one another—would create what according to Norberg-Schulz is a precondition for urbanism in the Nordic countries: the "romantic Nordic landscape."[40]

This romantic space, described by the planning office as having "spots of light and shadow instead of sharp contrasts," was supposed to mirror the local situation much better than classical designs. "Haze, dusk, the low light are elements that should form the urban space" that was supposed to evoke the "Nordic human being's closeness to

Architecture and Retrenchment

Figure 5.6 Atrium in a residential building, Södra Station. Photographer: Mattias Tydén.

Figure 5.7 Exterior semi-public spatial sequences connecting the street-scape with courtyards, Södra Station. Photographer: Mattias Tydén.

The Postmodern Housing Area (1981–7)

nature" through trees and vegetation as symbols and experiences in the city.[41] In this way a peculiar image of a postmodern city appeared: urban nature governed by NPM, with the homes, courtyards, and urban spaces the segments in a spatial sequence. The spatial reorganization of social services, in transition from the public sector to the private, took the form of a "romantic Nordic landscape," naturalizing what was a radical transformation of modern Swedish society.

In the discourse of Södra Station, the urban space signified both a material and a conceptual space, an "interiorized" (internalized) space open to projections, images, and fantasies.[42] This duality was evident in a contemporary review, which singled out the urban space as the "property" of all citizens and the façades as the "walls of the urban room."[43] The exterior space took on a new significance by expressing aesthetic variation, and the citizen's right to choose and the exterior walls were often prioritized in the design process. The exterior acquired a symbolic value that earlier was primarily assigned to the interior. This attitude came under heavy attack from the functionalist old guard, an example being Lennart Holm in his article on Skarpnäcksfältet, another housing project planned in the early 1980s outside the city: he accused the City Planning Office of forcing architects to plan from the outside in, "ignoring knowledge, habits, and values."[44]

In its aesthetics, historical references, use of symbolic forms, and new expression of monumentalism, Södra Station runs the style gamut of the postmodern urban renaissance. It was planned in the early days of welfare-state retrenchment and the transition to greater individual responsibility (especially regarding social services). A new political economy was taking shape, along with a new knowledge society and a focus on "human capital" such as sociability, creativity, and knowledge—societal resources that citizens had to regulate by themselves, with support from society.[45] The new human capital that resided *inside* the individual and depended on social capital (created in social interactions such as norms, values, and trust) had to be supported and *built* by new cultural modes of governance.[46] In the 1980s it was the citizen, the individual, who held the symbolic power in the architectural and political discourse, which created the ideological framework for a new social-democratic policy. Metaphorically speaking, the human and architectural body was turned inside out; the new focus on human capital meant that the citizen's internal capacities were now the measure of growth rates and economic welfare, and the qualities of the architectural interior, whether the conceptual space of imaginaries and projections or the material space, now turned outward to the outside urban space, creating an urban living room with inner walls that expressed the "image of the city."

Quality Programs, Regulating the City of Performance

Inghe-Hagström may have dismissed the earlier functionalist planning in his conversation with Krier in 1980, but, as we have seen, that did not stop him as an architect at the City Planning Office from being sternly critical of the planning system taking shape in the mid-1980s. When the program for the Södra Station was approved in 1984 and the more detailed phase began, the architectural challenge was, he said, to create a coherent environment rather than to create variation—"the risk of chaos is greater than the risk of monotony."[47] In order to control the design, and thus the private contractor, five "quality programs" (later renamed environmental programs) were put in place for Södra Station, each regulating one part of the area.[48] The planning office negotiated the programs with the developers, formulating them as a way for all parties to collaborate and act in unison throughout the process—which also meant controlling all the individual actors. The aesthetic preferences expressed in the programs came from Inghe-Hagström, and in his private collection one can closely follow his readings of Norberg-Schulz's *Genius Loci*, and his notes and comments reveal ideas that appear later in programs and documents for the area (Figure 5.8).[49] The postmodern framework expressed in the quality program, securing not only *genius loci* but also *stability loci*, controlled the private builders and architects concerned.[50]

The five quality programs treated the individual housing areas as objects, with their own internal geometries and relations, so that each building was regulated in form, size, color, and proportion, as were the relations between buildings, extending to the streets, yards, parks, and other urban spaces. As a governance strategy, the quality programs can be compared to building codes, and although the interior space of the flats was "deregulated," new regulations were imposed on the exterior sphere. In times of deregulation and private capital, these programs were an attempt to regulate the city through forms rather than norms.

One of the five areas with its own quality program was designed by Ricardo Bofill (Figure 5.9). His project, nicknamed Bofill's Arc, was a toned-down version of the dramatic Espaces d'Abraxas in Seine-Saint-Denis on the outskirts of Paris.[51] His design, adapted to Swedish regulations and the Nordic light conditions, was a locally situated version of postmodernism: an arc transferred from the southern classical plaza to the "Nordic romantic" urban landscape. This meant, for example, revising the profiling of the façades—instead of a surface articulated in three dimensions, the façade is "flat," to avoid obstructing light from entering the flats—and, as mentioned earlier, after a long struggle between the architect and the Swedish authorities, the dining areas were given windows (Figure 5.10).

"City-likeness" has been a topic of intense discussion among professionals and the public, and that heated debate marked the vivid search for a new urban sensibility. The goal to be city-like, articulating the ideal of a city, was also continually repeated in the quality programs.[52] Expressions such as "design motifs" and "backdrop motifs," when applied to urban space, indicated an elaborate new theatricality, sharply focusing on the semiotics of architecture. The fact that the set designer Sören Brunes' competition entry for Södra Station was titled *Staden som teaterscen* (The city as a stage) is a telling example of this relation to urbanity. The idea that Södra Station should be city-like, with its connotations of image, fantasy, parody, and unreality, was often brought up in public criticism of the area but was rarely framed as something postmodern.[53] It was claimed that the new period of "associativeness" in architecture followed on the heels of

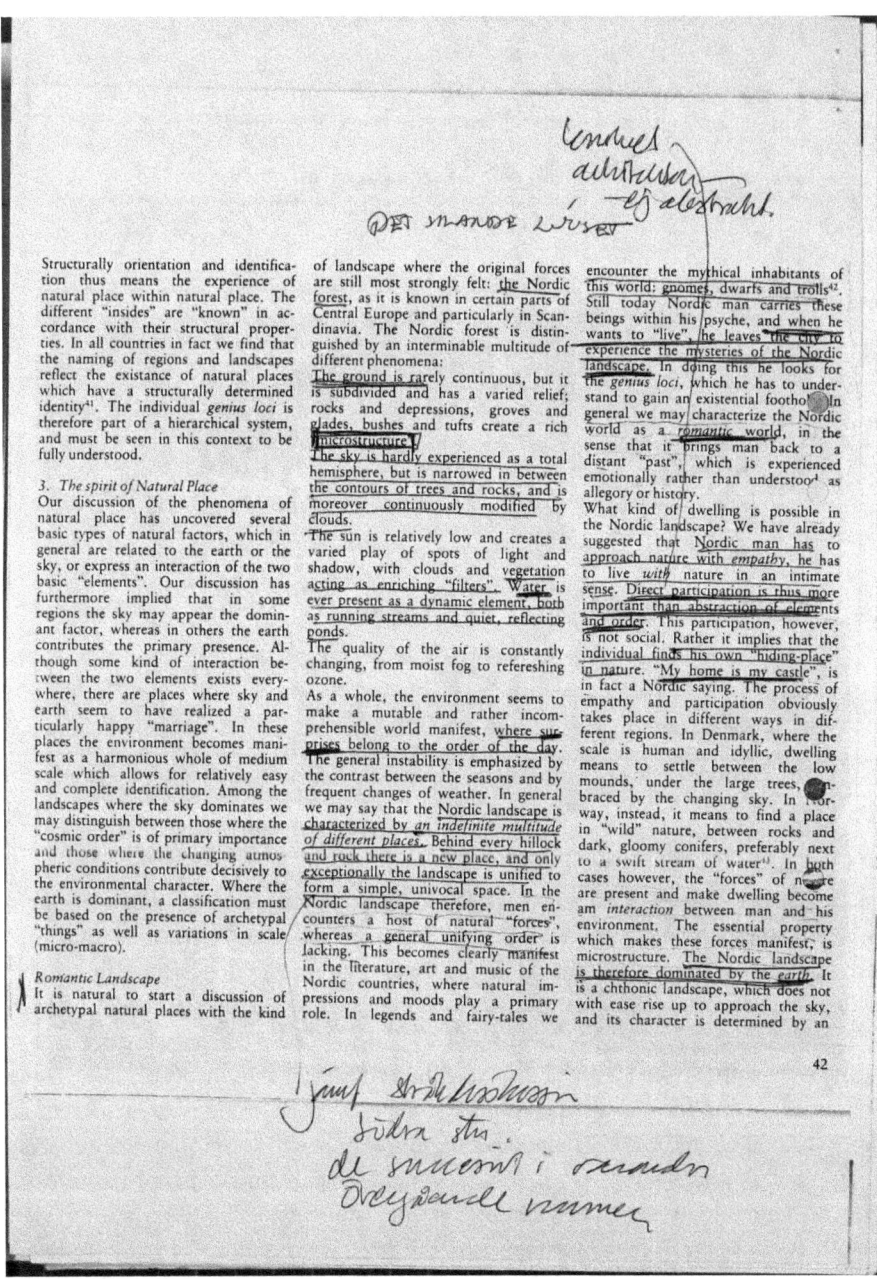

Figure 5.8 Jan Inghe-Hagström's private notes in Norberg-Schulz's *Genius Loci*. Inghe-Hagström compares the pathways at Södra Station with Norberg-Schulz's "Nordic landscape" where the "Nordic man has to approach nature with *empathy*, he has to live *with* nature in an intimate sense." Collection of Jan Inghe-Hagström, Stockholm City Archive. Courtesy: Maud Livén.

Figure 5.9 Ricardo Bofill showing his winning proposal for Södra Station in 1984. The project was later named "Bofill's Arc." Photographer: Lasse Olsson / DN / TT.

functionalism.[54] This was mentioned in relation to specific buildings or other elements at Södra Station, such as the fake creek or buildings that "pretended" to be something they were not (the covered market that looks like "two houses in a public square, but is one house over a motorway"), as well as to the activities, such as the sausage vendor wearing a butcher's apron.[55]

The new aesthetic sensibility of the urban had an impact on how people understood the area as a whole: it was a staged object in the city, "performing" city life. Reinhold Martin talks about the urban as a mode of cognition, and with Södra Station the concept of "city-like" becomes a framework for "speaking a certain kind of performative truth about how humans live together such that certain historical possibilities come into view and others disappear."[56] The discourse of how the city was to become a lively environment (a social meeting place, and a creative milieu) made the radical societal shift, and the concomitant rearticulations of the relationships between the private and public realm, into an issue of secondary interest.

In line with Norberg-Schulz's theories inspired by Gestalt psychology, the quality programs contributed to a concentrated image supposed to make the environment "meaningful" for the user.[57] As already noted, performance-based thinking was the framework for re-regulating the housing building codes, and "functionality" was

The Postmodern Housing Area (1981-7)

Figure 5.10 "Bofill's Arc," Södra Station. Photographer: Mattias Tydén.

extended from being decided in terms of measures to including potential performances. And just like the regulations, the city was turned into a performance-based system, with more than a nod to Kevin Lynch's "performance dimensions" set out in *Good City Form* (1981).[58] The quality program made most objects perform, and form communicated and "move" the individual subject. A 7-meter-tall ventilation station, for instance, was thus a "powerful backdrop motif," intended to create the effect of a sculptural staircase, camouflaging its service function.[59] Similarly, the ordinances for Södra Station regulated the street furniture to be used in the urban space, including benches, lamps, and fencing—what Bofill himself calls *meubles urbaines*—as well as the lighting.

Södra Station's urban space was articulated in such a way as to offer different scales of intimacy, carefully elaborated and often very detailed, as befitted the new planning ideology. This made the area a self-contained unit, repeating the language of the private space—the home—with its exterior walls toward the surrounding city and interior spaces decorated and interiorized. The importance of the concept "dwelling" for architecture and planning, pointed out by Norberg-Schulz, was thought dependent on both orientation and identification (Lynch's "environmental image"), which implied that the environment was experienced as meaningful.[60] For Inghe-Hagström, it seems the challenge primarily was *identification*, not orientation, and in the quality programs much effort was put into how "to feel at home," how to "become friends with a particular environment."[61] For Norberg-Schulz, "true freedom" presupposes belonging and identification, and making public space "a property of the citizens" is also a way of creating true individual freedom. The postmodern aesthetic in the quality programs was not only the new way to regulate the city space through decoration, sculpture, color, and street furniture; it was also a way to enable the citizen to self-orient and identify; the tool with which to activate the urban space and perform new scenarios of individual freedom and creativity.

In a Swedish context, Södra Station came to represent the new notion of the city as furnished and personalized, where urban space had become the "property of the citizen," not yet in economic terms (although that was to come), but through architectural materiality; it was an interiorized space, a space in which to feel at home.[62] This image of the city was also bound up with a new notion of a public good, where private initiatives and interests were to take greater responsibility for public obligations, while the state withdrew from the scene (but was still governing), and all came together in the new life of the Swedish Third Way.

Deregulation and Postmodernism in a Landscape of Surprise

The City Planning Office imagined the new housing area at Södra Station as a specifically Nordic residential landscape, where urban spaces would float into one another—spaces merging streets with courtyards, and courtyards with dwellings—creating spatial sequences with exciting surprises around the corners. The urban experience was compared with walking in Nordic nature at dawn, with diffuse low light, haze, and long grey shadows, but instead of finding stones and glades the 1980s citizen discovered societal elements organized in new ways, such as social services in new places, schools scattered out and mixed with eldercare in the blocks of flats, and responsibilities moved from the public sector to the private.

Here, I consider this obscure landscape in the light of the debate about architectural regulations, norms, and aesthetics that coincided with criticism of the welfare state. I try to understand how postmodernism was translated to a local context and was

The Postmodern Housing Area (1981–7)

Figure 5.11 Söder Torn, Södra Station, by Henning Larsen who left the project in the middle of the process because of too many compromises. Photographer: Mattias Tydén.

operationalized politically and economically, by investigating the complex discourse of "deregulations"—a constellation of material and nonmaterial agents such as built objects, decision-making processes, drawings, programs, guidelines, models, and financial transactions—an assemblage that fueled the notion that the state was in crisis.

Architecture and Retrenchment

The demand in the 1980s for new regulatory strategies can also be understood in relation to a knowledge society and a new political economy predicated on "human capital"—knowledge, creativity, social competence—and governed by new techniques.[63] The 1980s city, a site for these techniques, reorganized the relationship between the public and private spheres, between home and urban space; it was a place for arranging life and for governing habits and everyday existence.

The architecture and planning of Södra Station was both a response and a contribution to Foucault's crisis of governance. The redistribution of capital from the public to the private sector—driven by the 1982 social-democratic "politics of crisis"—weakened the role of the City Planning Office, which had to invent new forms of regulation and techniques of governance. This coincided with changes to the housing regulations under strong pressure from industry and the political right and center, and together these developments changed the basis for architecture and planning, and the way life was arranged in spatial and social terms. The planning and building of Södra Station demonstrated how architecture and the built environment were part of what Foucault calls "statification," or state formation, in the way they retargeted sources of finance, modes of investment, and decision-making, and ultimately invented new forms of control.

The building code has always existed in a state of flux, and it is used to test new formats of practices and regulations, thus anticipating the far larger changes legislated into existence to impact economic policy. I have singled out three stages in the evolution of the building code since the late 1960s, and how each stage was intertwined with aesthetic shifts and with architecture as a cultural signifier: the move toward performance-based systems; a turn toward the individual actor; and a shift in focus from the interior to the exterior urban space. These shifts, because they had both spatial and social effects, directly affected the planning and building of Södra Station. This performative turn can be traced in the organization not only of the flats but of the city itself and the creation of a landscape built up by spatial sequences where the dwelling and "the urban" constituted segments in the sequence, a sort of postmodern organization echoing a Fordist organization in the manner of Ludwig Hilberseimer. It was the new "postmodern citizen" (replacing the "modern subject of functionalism") who had the knowledge and creativity to perform city life in the 1980s.

EMANCIPATION

In *Fortunes of Feminism*, Nancy Fraser suggests that emancipatory struggles in the postwar welfare state "challenged oppressive forms of social protection" and aligned with neoliberal strategies of marketization.[1] More specifically she is talking about the women's movement and how the dreams of women were harnessed "to the engine of capital accumulation." Fraser calls for a new alliance between social protection and emancipation, a position that has been criticized for leaving emancipatory struggles "in a conservative position where resistance takes on a restoring role."[2] Without doubt, the projects discussed in this book can be related to Fraser's theoretical framework. I will, however, avoid the dichotomy between marketization and social protection, and instead pick up on the notion of ambivalence. The sites discussed here show how emancipatory practices operated in a contested field of restructuring forces, and how the proposals presented opened for possible worlds not yet included in the welfare state. Rather than understanding these practices as paving the way to neoliberal marketization, I see them as part of the architectural assemblage constituted of entangled forces of social protection *and* marketization in the midst of a process of societal transformations.

The concept of emancipation is elusive and broad, which risks emptying it of meaning—and it is so often framed as an abstraction, further diluting the concept. Yet it is a concept that evokes a strong response, frequently used in emotional political situations in times of radical change. With its shifting significations, Janus-like, it has a powerful agency in different ideological contexts. It is a concept with a long history in political theory that has taken on many meanings; a keyword in the 1968 movement and again in recent theories of neoliberalization, and neoconservative, racist, and gender discourses.

Emancipation was one of the most contested concepts in the changes to architecture and the built environment in the 1980s, and central not only to women's lib and the environmental movement but also to Third Way neoliberalization, at a time when the key issues centered on *who* should be liberated, from *what*, and *how*. Whose emancipatory projects would have the deciding say? The point here is not to discuss architecture's emancipatory power, but rather to consider how architecture was perceived and the effect it had as an emancipatory project, and how that tallied with the restructuring of the welfare state's policies.[3] How could architecture be a means to an end for emancipatory projects in a welfare state? The idea of liberation from a controlling, restrictive state was a constant, but the voices and arguments instrumental to the project were different, whether they were environmentalists, urban activists, or liberal planning officers, women's libbers, reformist social democrats, or business people.

Architecture and Retrenchment

Normative, Evolutionary, Self-reflexive

The reforms of the 1960s—a historic class compromise—were based on the incorporation of the initially recalcitrant labor movement, reinforced by certain gender and ethnic or racial exclusions, which were the basis of the postwar emancipatory movements.[4] As indicated in the discussion of Skärholmen, collective houses, and Stockholm Globe City, this duality of inclusion and exclusion was formally institutionalized in Swedish corporatism, where trade unions and the larger special interest groups were included while others were excluded. Of course the women's liberation movement was not absent, for example, but they did not enjoy the same access to formal channels of influence, and had to operate in other arenas. We can view developments from the perspective of movements and countermovements, on the inside or the outside of institutional decision-making. Looked at as institutional channels for a street-based study, the housewives in Skärholmen do not feature at all and the motoring organizations' activism is background noise. Although the Swedish Roads Association was not an obviously emancipatory movement, its advocacy was still the result of a discussion about release from restrictions and individual freedom of choice. Thus both groupings pursued their policies in an emancipatory project framework, even though they had widely differing intentions and channels. Before turning to the women's movement, a key emancipatory movement in Swedish architecture in the long 1980s, I will run through the history of the concept, concentrating on three aspects: normative, evolutionary, and self-reflexive.

Historically speaking, emancipation has gone from legal act to political concept. In Roman law, emancipation meant a father declaring his son to be of age; in thirteenth- and fourteenth-century France and Italy it took on fresh meaning in the sense of "to emancipate oneself." As the historian Reinhart Koselleck has demonstrated, this denoted a decisive change in mentality that gave the individual a new active role, because of the concept's overtones of self-liberation: the passive declaration "to be free" was replaced by "self-authorization." It could be a person or a group who was emancipated, but it could also be future governments freeing themselves from their predecessors.[5] Emancipation was later used in the sense of both self-liberation (entailing a normative requirement to be legalized by the state) and natural maturity (which generations went through as they grew up). Koselleck demonstrates how emancipation acquired its contemporary significance in the French Revolution, with a normative aspect (emancipation entails new legal rules or rights), an evolutionary aspect (the natural process of growing up), and a self-reflexive aspect (individual or collective self-authorization).

The threefold meaning of emancipation highlights those aspects of liberation where architecture has been involved. Emancipation reveals the connection between the micro and the macro, both self-reflexively and normatively; the self-reflexive principle, grounded in the individual, entwined with the socio-regulatory framework of the law.[6] The connection between the self-reflexive and normative poles was clear in events in the 1960s. Architecture was tool of emancipation because of its ability to create emotional landscapes, which it was thought would alter the individual's experience of reality (and of self) and be significant in the self-reproducing loop of life. It was all about changing "the system" by changing the individual. There was an idea about maturity, not only for the individual, but for entire generations. The child to whom it was addressed was the future generation who would carry the experience with them in the next phase of humanity's advance to maturity. Emancipation's normative side was also prominent in the 1968 movement's demands for better living standards: the investigations by the official inquiry into the Building Act that began in 1968 were closely monitored, and there was continual pressure throughout its lengthy proceedings until the 1980s. The opportunity to exert civic influence and the determination to give the individual a greater say in decision-making meant there were high hopes they would legally secure this emancipatory project.

Their actions were designed to "wake" citizens from the passivity instilled in them by the welfare state, with its overly bureaucratic regulations. As in most projects where architecture was used as a tool of emancipation, it was not the authors of the campaign who were to be emancipated but other people, often the welfare state's beneficiaries. In this was a crucial paradox for architecture if it were to emancipate anyone—a paradox that was even plainer in the Million Program, which was run as a top-down emancipatory project that was anything but "self-reflexive." A regeneration program which relied on introducing *boinflytande* (resident involvement), it was pushed through by politicians, housing associations, and architects. It had a normative aspect, but rather than create new laws to secure newly won rights, it was about setting a moral framework. The temporal aspect was very much present: the process by which generations of new arrivals would grow into integrated citizens was there in the project from the start.

Feminist Emancipation through Architecture?

The feminist movement in Sweden coincided with the introduction of the Third Way in politics and postmodernism in architecture. Texts such as Mary McLeod's "Architecture and Politics in the Reagan Era" lay the ground for understanding postmodernism (deconstructivism, poststructuralism, formalism) in relation to the political and economic transformations at the same time.[7] Yet the role played by women's lib (and other emancipatory movements) was not elaborated on, even though McLeod points to the fact that "women, blacks and other minorities have been notably silent voices" in the theoretical discussions.[8] Despite the major impact of feminism on postmodernism, feminist emancipation's position in neoliberalization is still poorly formulated in architectural history. Here, Nancy Fraser's contribution to the field can help us work through this problem area.

The Swedish feminist movement's involvement in architecture began in around 1980 with the groups such as BiG and the KBF.[9] Through their membership there was continuity with the 1968 movement, but now the rethinking of criticism was taken further and developed into strategies for constructions, models, and handbooks.[10] BiG saw the extended home or habitat as an emancipatory space while the KBF located the emancipatory project in larger societal structures and decisions. Both campaigned for gender equality in decision-making and in the building sector as project managers, builders, and developers, and both demanded that women's studies in architecture should be included in the country's curricula. Swedish feminist history resonates with Fraser's demonstration of how feminism's stance on forms of subjection rooted in welfare-state policy overlapped with other initiatives, but formulated from other ideological standpoints.

Fraser's "triple movement" draws om Karl Polanyi's seminal work of 1944, *The Great Transformation*, in which he described a double movement of marketization and social protection, and "disembedded" versus "embedded" markets. He argued that until the nineteenth century economy was understood as embedded in society (subordinated to politics, religion, and social relations), but with the classical economists' introduction of self-regulated markets, or disembedded markets, social relations were instead seen as "embedded in the economic system".[11] For Polanyi, the disembedded market was a utopia which could never be realized, and if left to themselves the self-regulating markets would destroy society. The answer was political regulation. Contrary to marketization, forms of "social protection" were duly created, and together these antithetical forces created a double movement, which impelled societal transformation. Fraser formulates a feminist response of "a triple movement" to Polanyi's theory, adding emancipation as the third pole, in order to analyze the "second great transformation" of our times: neoliberal capitalism.[12] She argues that Polanyi has a blind spot about social protection, as he ignores it is often the same as social dominance. Fraser's scheme thus differs from Polanyi's by being more dynamic and transformative in its ambitious attempt to chart the shifting relations between these three political forces, whose projects frequently stumble or collide.

In Fraser's hands, emancipation is above all *ambivalent*, able to side with the forces of social protection or of marketization, though she argues for the need to find new alliances between emancipation and social protection. That is where we part company, for where she finds distinct assemblages of social forces and (feminist) emancipation aligning *either* with marketization *or* with social protection, I find it resists such tidy definitions, let alone schematics with three poles. When applied to architecture, Fraser's theory, which outlines a theoretical framework relevant for *all* emancipatory movements, is too general an abstraction to serve our purposes of understanding the specific cases discussed here.[13]

Fraser's argument that the criticism of the American family wage has resulted in the two-earner family aligning with marketization rather than social protection is relevant to the co-housing projects discussed in this book. She demonstrates the ambiguities of criticizing the family wage using two strategies: one is the feminist campaign for women's full access to employment—universal breadwinners—and the other is to reenvision social arrangements to enable everyone—men or women—to perform both sets of activities as universal caregivers. The first is the more common, and keeping pace with marketization has already resulted in the exploitation of women in the workforce, according to Fraser, while the second aligns with social protection.[14] The emancipatory notion of co-housing operated in multiple ways in Third Way neoliberalization, employed differently by different actors.[15] Co-housing was an example of Fraser's universal caregivers aligning with social protection, but it was also used as a strategy on the political macro level and thus speaks to state retrenchment and the rearticulation of the relationship between civil society and the state (Site 3).

A situated reading of feminist co-housing in the 1980s shows the difficulties of distinguishing between alignment with either the market or social protection, and ultimately the risks of reducing the emancipatory project to good or bad, according to one's definitions of promoting neoliberalization or protecting the welfare state. The cases in this book demonstrate that emancipatory projects in architecture were part of a multiplicity of discourses on as many different levels. It could be a specific proposal for how to organize the domestic sphere on a local level for a group of individuals; it could be the decentralization of social care, retrenchment, and public savings. Faced with the realities of architecture, Fraser's generalized abstractions meet equally complex specificity, engaging all three poles simultaneously.

From Emancipation to Responsibilization

Increasingly, scholars are identifying the links between neoliberalization and emancipation. Erik Swyngedouw has pinpointed how a redefinition of emancipation has undermined democracy by being part of a neoliberal ideology. By understanding emancipation as the wish to be free in the sense of autonomous, democracy is threatened from within: "unhinged from the rights and obligations of life in common, free of oppression and able to choose one's identity."[16] However, there is another side to it, where self-reflexivity is reduced to the moral call to "Liberate yourself!" This was a strategy used by politicians, housing associations, and public utilities in running the resident involvement projects of the 1980s. Joan Scott raises another question in "The Vexed Relationship of Emancipation and Equality," showing that "emancipation" is a characteristic of groups rather than of political struggle: it has become part of a policy of discrimination, above all against Muslim women who have not aligned themselves with Western notions of emancipation.[17] Emancipation is a requirement for obtaining one's rights, replacing "We want" with "We demand that you want." This is emancipation as a categorizing, differentiating tool; a (moral) call to action.

As will be shown in the next chapter, Tensta's participatory planning project was part of a larger urban renewal scheme project, the Million Program, where participation initiated from the public sector was required in order to give residents more power—to emancipate them. Behind it all was responsibilization, a determination to transfer responsibility that was (and is) part and parcel of NPM and the Third Way's eager reorganizations. Architecture was ideally suited because it was both the site and the means for an imposed emancipation project. Janus-faced emancipation—on the one hand elusive and broad in its significations, on the other a forceful abstraction operating on an emotional level—allows it to work in a variety of ideological contexts. Architecture reveals emancipation's trickle-down, following the lines of decision, passing through actors, and finally materializing on the ground.

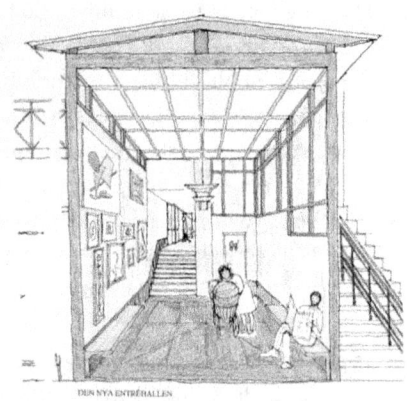

Figure 6.1 Proposal for renewal of Glömminge gränd, Tensta, 1991. LOGGIA arkitekter ab. Courtesy: LOGGIA arkitekter ab.

SITE 6
THE RENEWAL (1985–94)

The last weekend of April 1991, an urban renewal proposal went on show that Loggia Arkitekter had designed with the residents of the suburb of Tensta outside Stockholm. Kvarteret Glömmingegränd was a Million Program housing estate with seven-story blocks of flats built in 1969. The owners, the public housing company Familjebostäder (Family Housing), had received a great many complaints from residents over its twenty-year existence, and these days it was generally thought run-down. But now at last the tenants could see what the three long years of meetings and discussions had resulted in, and whether their ideas recorded in numerous "contribution books" had been acted on. "I am their pencil and interpreter," explained the architect Ylva Larsson, adding that she did not sketch at first, in order not to take the initiative from the residents.[1] Familjebostäder's housing estate manager said something similar about keeping a low profile so tenants would feel it was their proposal. The project had two cornerstones: "the residents" know-how and participation combined with delegated management.[2] It was a large commission for the architects, as it involved the complete renovation of 930 flats at the behest of Tensta's politicians and the estates owners. It had not been easy, and as one of those involved said, "Things can get pretty bumpy when you can finally put a face to a name."

In 1988, two years before Loggia had started work on the renovations, one Tensta resident had reported the suburb to the director of the Stockholm Traffic Department:

> The centre has litter everywhere with so much rubbish up against the houses and blowing around the alleys. The square by the loading dock on the lower level is basically a tip, with piles of black bin bags full of rubbish and litter all over the square. What kind of street cleaning schedule does the Traffic Department have these days? Do something about it, now![3]

The answer shows that there was neither the money nor the interest to do things differently: "Improvements in street cleaning in central locations by introducing a weekend schedule is not possible, primarily for reasons of finance, but also because under the Working Hours Act the use of existing staff at weekends would mean a corresponding loss of hours in the working week."[4] Some of Stockholm's suburbs had got a bad name for rubbish and littering, and the Traffic Department was quick to point out things were worse in Tensta/Rinkeby than elsewhere. They had tried "improvement initiatives," which meant giving residents more responsibility, and in the spring of 1986, 20 school classes and 200 associations had joined in, litter picking for the local authority.

Regarding street cleaning, the Traffic Department claimed that the high proportion of residents with foreign background might be one reason the anti-littering message had not got through, and wrote that it was important to "encourage residents in these districts to litter less."[5] According to The City it was "almost more important to try to encourage residents in these districts to litter less" than it was for it to improve its street cleaning in the suburbs.[6] Both examples—the housing renewal project and the littering campaign—were signs of the new form of governance introduced in the 1980s, which assumed active civic participation, and had been strengthened by the new Planning and Building Act 1987 (PBL 1987). There were a great many projects, which, predicated on resident participation or civic participation, reformulated the relationship between the individual and society, and raised questions about responsibilities and obligations. How much responsibility could be shifted onto individuals and groups? Which obligations and responsibilities remained with the authorities?

This book opened with urban activism in 1968, which in Sweden was a response to the criticism of the Million Program suburb Skärholmen, south of Stockholm. We have come full circle, arriving at another Million Program suburb, Tensta, but now twenty years on. In the mid-1980s, a decade after the Million Program ended, Stockholm launched a new initiative, of which the work in Tensta was part: an urban renewal program it dubbed Miljonprogram för miljonprogrammet, or Millions for the Million Program. The "first" Million Program (1965–75) marked the end of the Keynesian era; the "second" Million Program (1985–92) marked the beginning of the Third Wave's new Swedish Model. The period of change which is the theme of this book is thus perfectly bookended by the two housing programs. Thus far I have considered a range of sites that have something to tell us about the processes of change in architecture and the built environment. The long 1980s also stood out for its demographic changes, which will be examined here, with a significant shift from labor migration to refugee reception that saw Sweden increasingly open up to the outside world.[7] In the mid-1970s there had been a debate about "multiculturalism," which had picked up on the idea of a "mixed city" and made it into a political policy at the national level.[8] Ultimately the trend is perhaps best described as a racialization of the discourse about the city, construction, and housing.[9]

The authority in this new Swedish Model, like the participation, ideally came from below, and its welfare strategies were supposed to be combined with a dramatic decentralization in politics and in the built environment.[10] The sweep of its political ambitions, however, saw a broad range of results. Jennifer Mack's study of Södertälje shows how a more flexible planning apparatus made possible new professional planning practices, with "urban design from below" run by Syrian immigrants.[11] Here, I will address a different top-down development, in which the 1968 movement's emancipation projects were increasingly appropriated into the public apparatus. This could have positive effects, such as when individual citizens gained in influence, but the fact remained that often "resistances" were becoming part of a public machinery that was designed to create consensus and perhaps even "compliant citizens."[12] In shifting responsibility to civil society organizations, the public authorities pushed through a policy of "activation," as Magnus Dahlstedt would have it, while any dissatisfaction was channeled into well-controlled, institutionalized forms of communication.[13] A variety of techniques and concepts were developed when dealing with architecture, planning, and the built environment, ranging from advocacy planning, equity planning, and participatory planning to community design and, a priority here, resident participation.[14]

By returning to a specific renewal project where residents were involved in the planning and design, the chapter addresses the consequences of a new form of governance on a local community, and how the project could operate on several levels by riding on the coattails of a major political enterprise that spanned retrenchment and neoliberalization. The Millions for Million Program brought together architects, planners, residents, and politicians, whose societal ambitions for the project were curbed from the very start by local government cuts. The government's interest in handing off responsibility to civil society organizations and private individuals was seen in many other places in Europe and elsewhere in the 1980s and 1990s, but in Sweden's case it was against the background of a distinctive welfare model. True to type it had top-down central planning, which made the change of direction even more extreme.

The historical perspective is central to the argument here, highlighting the importance of historiography in the construction of people's—and places'—identities. Ever since the Million Program, a variety of time-limited projects have experimented with new methods and ideas, the majority on the authorities' initiative, in the hope of "changing" or "renewing" rather than getting to the bottom of it. This "projectification" has meant reorganizations, staff reshuffles, and changes of strategies, to the detriment of the documentation and archiving of key documents, and, eventually, to a loss of local history.[15] The Millions for the Million Program shows the historic results when market-based governance sets new agendas for the suburbs, and architecture played a crucial role in the changes.[16]

Tensta, a Million Program Suburb

The City of Stockholm bought the open fields of Järvafältet to the northwest of the city in the early 1900s, but it was left undeveloped until 1962 when the City declared that it was going to build housing for 160,000 people there. Several competition briefs were assembled into a master plan for the area, and Tensta was built between 1966 and 1972 as part of the Million Program. However, it was not long before the country quiet was shattered by a motorway, rolled out between the fields and the new residential area. Tensta was designed to be a traffic-segregated linear town with comparatively few green spaces between the low blocks of flats. There were three parallel bands of buildings: higher-rise blocks of flats in the north facing the motorway; communal facilities in a middle zone and low-rise residential buildings in a band toward a valley in the south (see Figure 6.8). It was a "city-like" development with dense residential areas and a grid street plan, and a wide variety of building types betraying the number of architects and builders involved in its design.

Architecture and Retrenchment

Figure 6.2 Children playing in Tensta, 1971. Photo: Lennart af Petersens. Courtesy: Stockholm City Museum.

Figure 6.3 Tensta, 1971. Photo: Lennart af Petersens. Courtesy: Stockholm City Museum.

The Renewal (1985–94)

Like in many other suburbs built in the 1960s and 1970s people moved into Tensta before it was finished, and newspaper reports from the time described the failures of a social-democratic policy. The alleged problems with the suburbs were frequently blamed on politicians while the residents were usually portrayed as victims. This was reinforced by *Rapport Tensta* from 1970, a special report written by three reporters at Sweden's largest evening newspaper, the center-right *Expressen*. The authors described the area as turning from being a building site to being a permanently unfinished, run-down, litter-strewn housing estate. The report had photos of children playing on building sites and finished by saying Tensta was "a byword for the failing community-building of today."[17]

The late 1970s saw an emerging narrative of residents' antisocial behavior, with photos to back up news of crime and alcoholism, but it was not until the 1980s that residents, often referred to as "immigrants," were described causing their own problems, as in the example of the littering. This changing media image has been described by researchers such as Irene Molina as one of the steps in the stigmatization of suburb; first, permanently unfinished; then, dirty with rubbish littering the place; next, ridden with crime and alcoholism; and finally, immigration and immigrants are to blame.[18] This process, too, has contributed to the passing of responsibility from the authorities to individual residents, which has further increased segregation and driven the neoliberalization process.

From the start there has been a sense that the Million Program estates are enclaves in society, both socially and building-wise, but the descriptions have changed. When people discussed the suburbs in the late 1960s they talked about domestic migration, but twenty years on it would have been global migration and refugees.[19] Today the term used is *utsatta områden* (vulnerable areas), which frames the suburban discourse in terms similar to the Danish *ghettoer*, drawing a causal link to the number of immigrants and foreign-born residents, and with relocation as the solution of choice.[20] As Jennifer Mack has shown, the Million Program's positives have been called into question since the very start, and many suburbs had a long history of short-lived urban renewal projects and improvements. From 1975 there were government improvement grants available [miljöförbättringsbidrag] for the housing estates' public places, so coinciding with their completion.[21]

Resident Participation, New for the 1980s

In the early 1980s, the Swedish public housing companies faced a complete reorganization, and thus a fundamental change in view on residents' roles and theirs. The decisive step was the change in the law in 1982, permitting the sale of a proportion of council housing stock. Tenant-owner's flats could already be sold on the open market and mortgaged in the same way as other private property, but tenants in public housing had no corresponding financial benefits. This difference in housing tenures was thought to fuel segregation. Thus, the new paradigm, selling out public renting apartments, was done in the name of tackling growing regional inequalities, rather than for the sake of privatization. The law was changed in the early 1980s, but few flats were sold until the 1990s and the first major wave of privatizations; however, the 1980s saw a view on society which held the solution to the challenges of community-building, such as segregation, was financial.

At the time when the sale of public housing was legalized, the interest organization for public housing companies Sveriges Allmännyttiga Bostadsföretag (SABO, Public Housing Sweden) launched its new management philosophy, which was predicated on resident participation, decentralization, and upskilling. Today, SABO says the idea of resident participation had already altered from the collective influence of the 1970s to the "individualization" of the 1980s, the focus moving "from buildings to people and from tenants as a collective to tenants as individual customer," though "not all tenants had the financial means to act as customers."[22]

Familjebostäder, part of SABO, had begun to work on its resident participation in Tensta in 1984. It organized workshops about resident participation, conferences, and courses for residents to practice running advisory groups.[23] In one of its housing estates, Glömmingegränd, residents had started an advisory group, and as a result they took over one of the communal rooms and decorated it with the young people who were "causing a nuisance" in the stairwells, or as Familjebostäder put it: "The premises will now be used by both young people and adults from the estate to everyone's benefit." Much of what was said to residents was utopian in its idea that their problems would be solved if only they joined in, while often the opposite was true, as one resident said: "We felt we'd been steamrollered. We sat in meetings and planned. We knew exactly what we wanted, but that's not how it worked out." They had tried to arrange a barbecue area but failed, because Familjebostäder thought it would attract litter: "It was like they declared us incompetent."[24]

Millions for the Million Program

In the mid-1980s, the City of Stockholm was not satisfied with how Familjebostäder and the Park Service were running some of the Million Program estates.[25] Many of them were thought to be doing well, but in Södra Järva, which includes Tensta, radical change was needed. When the social-democratic Stockholm Vice-Mayor and City Commissioner of Finance, Mats Hulth, responded by drawing up the Millions for the Million Program in the autumn of 1985, only a decade had passed since the original Million Program ended. In the intervening years there had been urban renewal projects which focused on the structural engineering, design, and appearance, but Millions for the Million Program would combine social, cultural, physical, and administrative improvements in everything from the quality of the buildings (rot, damp, wear) and design (large scale) to social segregation and lack of community spirit.

Decentralized decision-making would encourage district loyalty, and the local authority social services paid for two coordinators to secure the social factors were not missed out from the renewal project. The ambition was to mobilize Tensta's residents. It was assumed the "radical change" in mind would only be possible by marshalling the residents' own resources and initiatives. The City saw possible synergies in the decentralization of architecture, community planning, and social work, carried over from the resident participation set up by Familjebostäder in its transition from manager to administrator.[26]

When the decision was taken to launch the Millions for the Million Program, a local reference group was appointed with representatives from many of the City's departments.[27] In a sitrep a year after the project started, the management team said significant improvements to the shared and public spaces would be needed, especially in the center of Tensta, and noted the buildings' construction failings were a reason for excessive wear and tear. Despite the scale of the problems and the lack of money, the sitrep concluded it was still possible to implement all the measures provided the residents were prepared to contribute: "The high costs make it particularly important to involve the residents. They ought to be able to take responsibility for the management of the housing estate." The management team added that resident participation should be extended to "give residents their own responsibility," especially in places with "social difficulties and vandalism."[28] The wording said everything, for instead of residents taking responsibility they were to be *given* it by the City. A new vocabulary was evolving for resident participation projects, and I will return to the way language created the rules for participation and helped to shift responsibility to the residents.

Recent coinages which set the tone for the new era were also evident in the local authority's new strategies, which largely came down to financial austerity, although described in language that said something else. Coinciding with this major urban renewal project, further cuts were imposed on all of Stockholm's local authorities. The management team's response was to introduce what they called *radikal samordning* or "radical coordination" of services and premises (in schools, social services, and leisure) to streamline existing community services.[29] Another new concept was *frikommuntänkandet* (the autonomous approach), which saw financial decisions delegated to the city districts. Another solution was also to pass responsibility from local government to civil society organizations (and residents). The renewal project's finances were increasingly strained, to the point where the question of citizen and resident participation went beyond democratic influence to some sort of financial factor. The shifts in terminology fueled a utopian discourse about local democracy, decentralization, and resident participation, which, rather than changing reality, was used to justify the authorities' lack of responsibility and ultimately their increasingly neoliberal political thinking. Responsibility was passed from decision-makers and management teams to professionally and personally committed "renewal workers" (e.g., citizens, local authority staff, architects). It is often said that nothing advances capitalism like a crisis, which seems borne out in this case.[30] Once the urban renewal project was underway, there were strong incentives for those running it to see it finished come what may, which forced them to adopt "innovative solutions."

It is evident looking back that government aid policies could at times be counterproductive when it came to Tensta's rejuvenation. Between 1986 and 1992, a government renewal grant was available for flats and public spaces in areas with major societal problems. To qualify, at least 10 percent of flats had to be empty or the annual tenant turnover rate had to be at least 30 percent. In Tensta, there were not "enough" empty

Architecture and Retrenchment

flats, nor was the tenant turnover large enough for the government grant. Paradoxically, it was doing too well, with most of its flats occupied and a low turnover. Without the government grant the renewal project continued to be a drain on local resources, and the neglect that was the original cause of the problem simply deepened. There was palpable frustration among local Social Democrat politicians who had approved the scheme, and they raised the question of funding at the national level. The renewal funding was also briefly extended to *all* Million Program housing estates.[31]

The government subsidy was phased out in the spring of 1989, and at the local authority level the grant the Social Democrats proposed for "active renewal" projects in estates such as Tensta was cut by the center-right majority in the autumn of 1990.[32] Urban renewal projects in a time of change were instead used to argue for neoliberal forms of governance, and the public housing companies were forced to sell flats to raise money to pay for the renovations that had already begun.[33] Other arguments were used, taken from the 1968 movement's campaign for political influence; by passing on all responsibilities, it could finally realize its ambitions. The dominant discourse of the local authorities' withdrawal was thus based on the notion that only by handing public responsibility to civil society organizations could *true* local democracy exist, bringing together local communities, city subcommittees, and the local authorities. Then in the discourse of the 1990s, terms such as "resident participation," "local democracy," and "community spirit" acquired conflicting meanings among the actors involved. Such shifts in terminology gave citizens a new place in the machinery of local government, where influence and participation became synonymous with the moving of responsibility—and workloads—onto residents.

The Swedish Model Seen from Outside

As part of the urban renewal project, the City of Stockholm decided to gauge Tensta's situation in an international perspective, and so in 1989 an international housing seminar was held there with experts from the United Kingdom, France, Turkey, Finland, the United States, Denmark, and the Netherlands.[34] The guests studied Tensta for a week solid and went on to present several targeted suggestions for improvements. At first, to their surprise, they found functioning housing estates, but eventually they got to "the bottom" of the problem: there was "no soul." "Why are there so few people out during the day? [...] Where are all the kids who live here? The public system is rigid."[35] What they found was a kind of "stewardship" that stifled the residents' own initiatives, and they noted that the Swedish welfare system's public sector was ill-adapted to a multicultural society. The French housing expert and consultant in social work, Florence Ostier, cited Freud in order to compare participatory housing projects with psychoanalysis: just as patients paid for analysis, so citizens would pay for urban renewal. Ostier believed individual commitment and unpaid work were crucial to how individuals were engaged in the renewal work, which in turn would guarantee continuity. And perhaps even more importantly, the project would help foster self-sufficient individuals who had no need of financial support.[36]

The Renewal (1985–94)

Figure 6.4 Participants from The Housing conference in Tensta, 1989. Photo: Anna Hesser. Courtesy: City of Stockholm.

Figure 6.5 A walk in the area. The Housing conference in Tensta, 1989. Photo: Anna Hesser. Courtesy: City of Stockholm.

Architecture and Retrenchment

As a solution for the supposedly "rigid organization" that obstructed dynamic development, the guests proposed making Tensta an "autonomous district" analogous to the "autonomous approach" of the Millions for the Million Program. A kind of economic free zone to promote trade and entrepreneurship could be set up where a diversity range of industries and private initiatives could take root. The experts recommended instituting local self-government under an apolitical district council with a range of subcommittees, right down to each block of flats, so that residents took over both local government and the management of their public housing. They argued that residents should begin by being "self-reliant" as they would not have access to public funds because of the looming cuts. They pinned their financial hopes on transforming Tensta into Sweden's very own Hong Kong—a free trade zone where companies could be treated with a light hand, which, it was thought, would stimulate the emergence of "craft enterprises" and in turn finance urban renewal. Careful management and commerce would be combined in a neoliberal utopia and save Tensta's tottering local economy. The physical environment, the architecture, was also to be "liberated." Tensta should become an architectural free zone. Pitched roofs, external stairways (to replace the outdoor corridors), penthouse flats, roof terraces: it would make the estate more vibrant and the residents more creative. Physical changes to the architecture could remedy the lack of individuality that bedeviled Tensta, because even though "time is short," as Florence Ostier and Rod Hackney put it, "there is still a chance to catch the train" (Figure 6.6).[37]

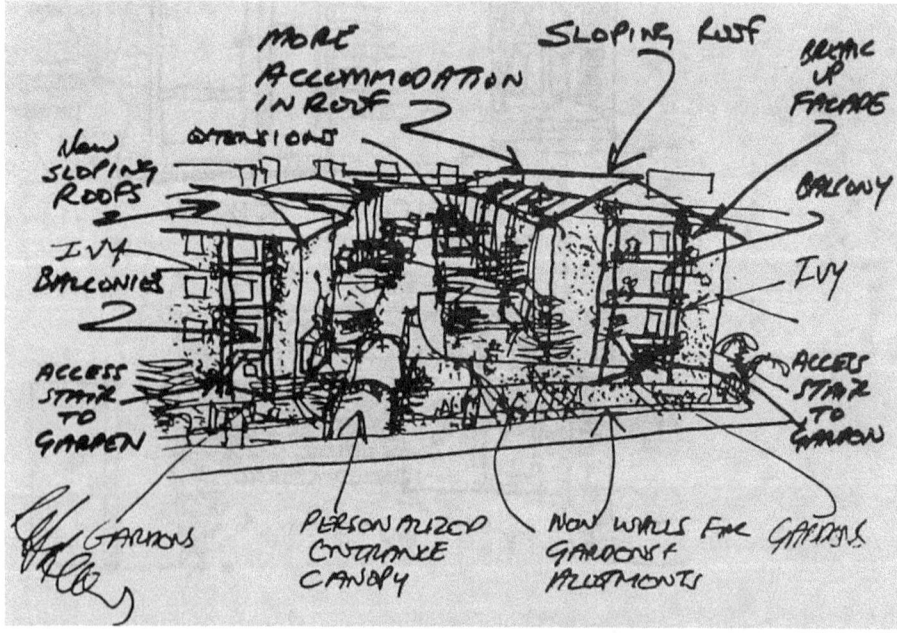

Figure 6.6 Proposal for a renewal of a three-level building and a courtyard at Husingeplan, Tensta, by Rod Hackney, 1989. Reprinted from "Seminarium om förnyelse av bostadsområden, Tensta," 1989, Stockholms fastighetsnämnd. Stockholm City Archive.

The Renewal (1985–94)

The way the international experts envisaged the Swedish Model, its architecture, aesthetics, and political governance were part of the same (modernist) edifice: rigid, rational, inflexible. They saw standardized, conformist aesthetic, and "soulless" architectural designs in an uneasy combination with criticism of the mode of governance. The effect was a discourse of "emancipation" that could be applied in a great many contexts—architecture, economics, and politics. That despite ambitions to the contrary (formulated by architects, politicians, tenants, and so on) the result of this emancipation was ultimately to "liberate" the public authorities from their (financial) responsibilities does not seem to have struck the visitors. It is unclear if the conference findings satisfied the organizers or helped them draw up new guidelines that might reverse Tensta's downward spiral and all the other late modern Stockholm suburbs.[38] Perhaps the most important outcome of the housing conference was the initiation of a urban renewal project that Familjebostäder and Loggia Arkitekter would work on for three years.

Resident Participation at the Planning Phase

Kvarteret Glömmingegränd in Tensta was one of the first housing estates to have a resident participation project. It stood out from the surrounding estates for the residents' strength of feeling about their shared and public spaces such as stairwells, entrances, courtyards, and laundry rooms.[39] In 1987, Familjebostäder trialed *arbetsboksmodellen* (the logbook model) of property management, and a preliminary study of the residents' experiences of their local environment was carried out by a sociologist and an architecture student.[40] All residents received a "logbook" in their native language with open questions about their flats and the estate which they could answer as they wished (Figures 6.7 and 6.9). Their interaction with Familjebostäder was colored by their previous experiences, with a feeling of disappointment and disempowerment well to the fore. Despite this there was a considerable response from the tenants, even if "men and immigrants" were noticeable by their absence.

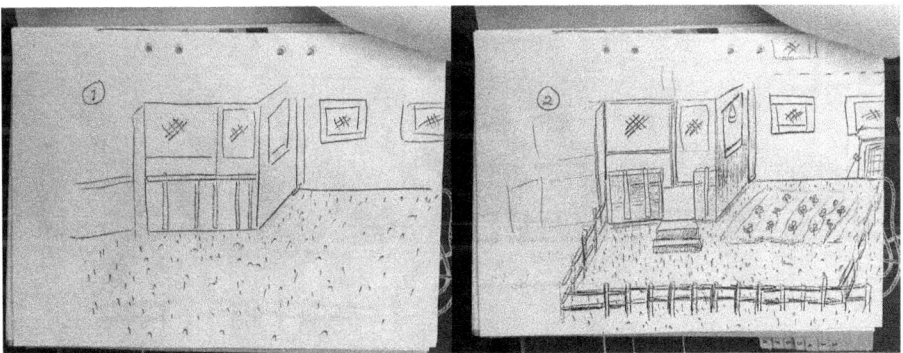

Figure 6.7 Sketches from Familjebostäders *arbetsbok* (logbook) showing residents proposal for renewal of gardens. Collection of Familjebostäder, Stockholm City Archive.

Architecture and Retrenchment

Loggia Arkitekter—Ylva Larsson and Johanna Wiklander—were brought in in 1990 by Familjebostäder to work with residents to design the ideas documented in the logbooks. The project covered seven clusters and 930 households.[41] Using the 60 percent of logbooks which were returned with comments, the architects worked with residents to draw up discussion papers (what they called "collaboration books") with sketches and plans ready for the next phase. The architects then distributed a set of proposed building alterations to all residents. The societal issues were addressed in a separate set of documents, the "result books." As may be imagined, this was not without its complexities—Larsson has described the hours pouring over the details of the project and the meetings with residents in the evenings. Although it was difficult to reach all the residents, there was a very active group who put in at least as much time as the architects.

Kvarteret Glömmingegränd, which is bordered on one side by a motorway, consists of three 7-story high-rise blocks of flats, placed in a row on a single-story foundation containing a car park that connects the buildings.[42] The whole housing estate with its three blocks had 152 flats before the renovations, 4 commercial premises, and a car park with 64 parking spaces. Between the buildings, on top of the parking garage one floor up from street level, were two courtyards. The housing slabs, perpendicular to the suldu-sac that ran next to the block, turned their entrances to the pavement. The entrances

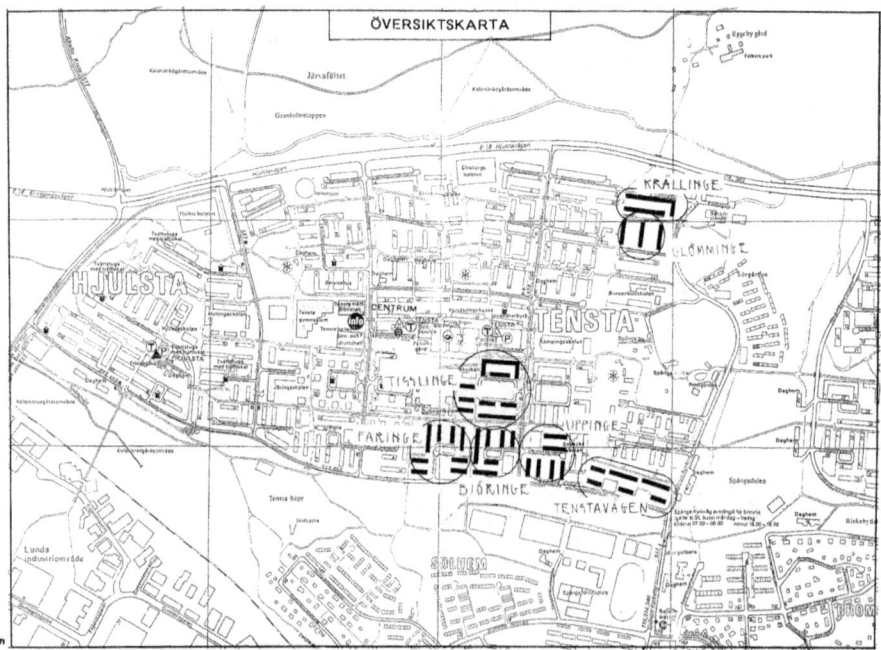

Figure 6.8 Tensta. Plan by LOGGIA arkitekter ab. Courtesy: LOGGIA arkitekter ab.

The Renewal (1985–94)

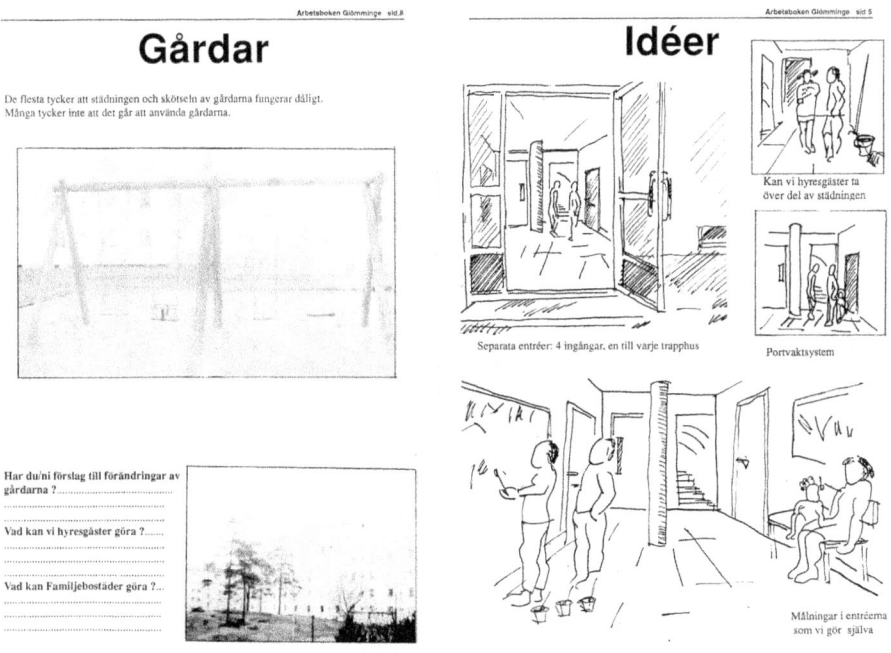

Figure 6.9 "Arbetsboken: Glömminge, no. 1, January, 1990," Familjebostäder in collaboration with Hyresgästföreningen Södra Järva.

originally were simple entryways between the garage doors that led into culvert-like corridors from which one reached the building's four stairwells, laundry rooms, and storage spaces. Many residents said they avoided the dark corridors, basements, and laundry rooms where youth gangs liked to hang out. They thought the buildings and local environment looked shabby, the ways in resembled delivery entrances, and the main doors were difficult to find.[43]

The redevelopment plans comprised five separate elements: the addition of smaller buildings between the main blocks; new entrance buildings facing the street; the refurbishment of the basement corridors and laundry rooms; larger kitchens; new balconies and, on the ground floor, terraces; and new penthouses on the roofs (an idea that was later abandoned). The resulting idea after the collaboration between architects, inhabitants, and the housing company, was to open up the buildings to bring daylight down into the corridors and other dark shared spaces. Finally, three new entrance halls extended out from the existing entrances toward the small cul-de-sac of Glömmingegränd, breaking the earlier murky monotony with bright, generously dimensioned entrances. A new space was added that served as a well-lit porch to the entrance corridors, with benches and public art. The corridors themselves now opened inward onto the stairwells with glass dividers to maintain the flow of light.

Architecture and Retrenchment

Figure 6.10 Glömmingegränd, before and after renewal. Photo: Ylva Larsson / LOGGIA arkitekter ab.

The Renewal (1985–94)

Figure 6.11 Glömmingegränd, before and after renewal. Collaboration meeting with residents (top right) Photo: Ylva Larsson / LOGGIA arkitekter ab.

Implementation

When in 1992 Familjebostäder approved the proposal Loggia Arkitekter had drawn up with the residents, the local council had changed hands and Sweden's new Conservative government had got off to a flying start by changing, or rather shutting down, the country's national housing policy and the few remaining grants and programs.[44] These new circumstances meant the various collaborations struck up between residents, architects, the public sector, and other actors had even fewer resources to call on, and so they could not continue as planned.

The main blocks were refurbished in 1993 and the project entered its management phase. The architects' work was done, and the main responsibility had been passed to a "residents service manager" from Familjebostäder and a tenants' ombudsman. A housing estate in deep crisis had resolved its finances and cumbersome bureaucracy to make way for a new administrative and bureaucratic structure. Under the new mechanisms for resident participation, residents received far more information and could be appointed to several positions, including member of the local housing board, where residents and the residents' service manager set budgets and oversaw the estate's finances. There were clusters of communal spaces or "family nests" planned for one of the new detached buildings on the street side of the estate, to contain laundry rooms, a large laundry room, guest accommodation, and retail space on the bottom floor. In the other detached house, the plan was for a kindergarten, but for financial and local government reasons this was changed to a health center that also never was realized when the County Council withdrew. A key part of the work was to recruit *kvartersvärdar* (building wardens) from among the residents, to take the lead on the maintenance of the shared and public spaces—something which did not always appeal, it seems. It was one of the clearest examples of the paradoxical situation likely to arise after a refurbishment in a period of rampant neoliberalization: few were much interested in looking after garden furniture, sweeping stairwells, or managing bookings for the guestroom and laundry.[45] When Loggia Arkitekter left Tensta in the early 1990s, Larsson underscored the importance of learning from previous experience, but a lack of documentation following a series of reorganizations has proved inimical to a successful knowledge transfer from the early resident participation projects.[46]

In late 1993, errors during the implementation phase of the project were listed in memory notes from a meeting between the architects, the tenants, and the housing company. There were reports of deterioriation of some flats: "When you look out of our living room window all you see is a black roof."[47] Other flats now had stairs outside their bedroom windows, and Larsson, on inspection, suspected they might have used the same balcony brackets as in Flemingsberg, where the balconies fell down. There were rumors the stairwells and lift lobbies would be left undecorated because the money had run out, whereupon Familjebostäder said it would "provide the paint and brushes if the residents themselves could do the painting." The language is carefully chosen to frame what in reality was the shifting of responsibility as an invitation to wield influence. The residents were also dissatisfied with refurbishment itself, with the basement storage sloppily built and none of the building waste cleared away. Even Annika Johansson of Familjebostäder seemed concerned when she asked whether "there really isn't any money for cockroach elimination in one of the flats, because renovations have had to stop completely because of it."[48] In a letter to Familjebostäder in 1994, one of the residents wrote that the whole housing estate was a "building yard and machine park," and when he had visitors he said that it "felt bloody awful for his guests to see his home like that" so he tidied up himself as best he could. He added that he saw no possible way the tenants and their backgrounds could be used as an excuse for the mess, and that the blame fell squarely on Familjebostäder, the site manager, and the contractors for shoddy work: "It's not just *svartskallar* [literally 'black heads', a Swedish pejorative epithet for immigrants] and people on welfare who live here, who you don't have to show any consideration to."[49] We cannot be certain what the letter writer meant by that— and heavy irony does seem possible—but it is still a clear example of how environment and discrimination can feed off each other.

Discrimination by Stealth

The juxtaposition of ethnicity, race, and the built environment cannot be denied in Tensta, or in any similar Million Program estate, as the casual racism of the remarks about origin and littering showed. What is less clear, though, is *how* the built environment contributed to the construction of a racist discourse that grew ever-stronger as the nature of immigration altered. Molina, as we have seen, has demonstrated how the media have contributed to the stigmatization of the suburbs, which having been on the margins of welfare-state Sweden in the 1970s are now relegated to a place outside the national—and nationalist—tropes of Swedish community.[50] Representations of the built environment have fueled the construction of social exclusion, for example with images of litter-strewn, run-down, and dysfunctional suburban environments. Though not a truthful impression, it nevertheless helped cast the suburbs' inhabitants as "permanent nomads" who were left excluded from the rest of society.[51]

It was not only the representations of the suburb which were stigmatizing; as this chapter has shown, the very built environment itself in its realization had the same effect. When the Million Program was launched in the mid-1960s, it was in response to deficiencies in the housing market, in terms of both supply and standard. By the time of the second Million Program, however, there was, if anything, a surplus of flats, and instead it was the deficiencies in the built and societal environments which were to be remedied.[52] An awareness of these shortcomings and the hopes for suburban renewal were intertwined with the realities of immigration in the 1980s. The special conference in Tensta in 1989, too, demonstrated the confusion about how the "shortcomings" might be managed. Was multicultural suburbia a positive? Or was it a segregation issue which should be addressed? The politicians rejected all rules that distinguished between ethnicities, and yet there was still an interest in demographics and how best government propaganda should be communicated to different groups.

The social-democratic politicians and officials responsible for the second Million Program underlined that the problems were nothing to do with who was living in Tensta; the program existed to improve residents' homes and lives. There was to be no special treatment; no instructions that only applied to immigrants, for example. Yet even so, there was an interest in redistributing the population. Rather than issue political regulations, it was left to marketing to persuade more Swedish-speaking families with children to move to Tensta and "to encourage immigrants to choose other places to live."[53] New marketing techniques would see residents internalize the political messages as never before. The official line was to improve living conditions, but the actual measures focused on bringing more Swedish-speaking people into the area and fewer migrants. Notions such as the "autonomous districts," promoting trade, entrepreneurship, and "craft enterprises," also convey discrimination of a kind, based on preconceived notions of groups and their skills and interests.

Ambivalence about group affiliations and the right to a home was very much part of the urban renewal projects, adding to the complexities of what was meant by a "good social living standards" and what the desired outcomes might be. Tensta, of course, was not given any of the renewal grants in the mid-1980s because it did not meet the criteria, with too low a turnover and not enough empty flats. The architect Ylva Larsson, who designed much of the refurbishment, had the impression the authorities saw Tensta as a "transit area," where new arrivals would not put down roots—a significant problem for the second Million Program: "they were not supposed to live here [in Tensta] for a longer

Architecture and Retrenchment

time, they were supposed to be integrated. They should go somewhere else in Sweden to be Swedish."[54] This was confirmed by a resident in the mid-1980s, who said most immigrants were worried and thought they would be thrown out of Tensta, which was going to become somewhere for engineers and "better people."[55] Although the premise of urban renewal was specifically to make life better for the people already living there, many residents' concerns about having to move were confirmed by Familjebostäder's regional manager: "Of course, it's the residents who will be paying for all this through their rents."[56]

In the 1980s, in other words, things had moved on from the protests against relocating northern populations from Norrland to the big cities, summed up in the Norrland Association's 1960s slogan "We ain't moving!" to the newly arrived immigrants' "We don't want to move!" The protest against moving to the suburbs of the Million Program had thus been replaced by the protest against moving from there. From being the place without history in the 1960s, the suburb was established for many people as the 1980s new homeland, which perhaps even then meant an "impossible nostalgia."[57]

Twenty-five Years Later

In 2014, five of the international community planning experts who participated in the 1989 housing conference came together at a public seminar in Tensta.[58] Beforehand they revisited the housing estates. The event brought back memories of the recent past's neoliberalization, with its dramatic economic downturns and new forms of citizen governance. The conflicts of 1989 stalked the seminar, exposing the hurt done by mismanaged resident participation in a suburban renewal projects.[59] The seminar was tense, emotional, and even confrontational at times—a sign of the deep divides between different interests and perspectives. The frustration, disappointment, and anger were not limited to the speakers and the audience, but extended to the international experts, local architects and planners, local politicians, citizens, and administrators:

> Local politician: "All the ambitions were shut down. It was a massive problem. We could not handle it the way we should have because of shifting political majorities."

> An international expert: "Today I saw no happiness. All the faces were gloomy, the facial expressions, they were deep in thought, perhaps for financial reasons."

> A citizen: "How are we meant to know, like you said, what we should do or not do in Tensta, or if the power really should be given to the people? Is that just another expert statement, or what?"

> A citizen: "It was decided twenty years ago [to build a road link to neighbouring suburbs] and now it's been taken away. It happens all the time. And the people

of Tensta, many don't even know about it, but perhaps they sense how things are decided here; they are depressed."

The seminar revealed a metanarrative of feelings that still frame its long history of renewal projects, and heard not only from individuals but also from collective memory. Projects started in the mid-1980s and formally ended in the 1990s lived on in the collective consciousness as a *trauma of neoliberalization*. When the subsidies and state-financed projects abruptly ended, the community was left hanging in what Meike Schalk has conceptualized as "an unfinished situation," picking up on Paul Goodman's term.[60] Even if the renewal projects were terminated on paper, they were never properly complete in reality. Poor project record-keeping and archives have always discouraged a historical understanding of the effects of neoliberalization on the suburbs. Instead, the lack of evidence has left us with a suburb without a history.[61]

Cleaning Up the Dirt

The government and local authority urban renewal projects discussed in this chapter started in 1985, the same year as Sweden's financial markets were deregulated, and ended with Social Democrats leaving government and the Conservatives coming to

Figure 6.12 Twenty-five years after the renewal project. Witness conference at Tensta Konstall, 2014. Photo: Axel Lieber.

power in 1991. It was a period when the guidelines for the "new welfare state" were drawn up, heavily influenced by notions of civic empowerment and bottom-up rather than top-down authority. Changes were characterized by shifts of responsibility (at the national and the local levels) and shifts in terminology, where the meaning of, say, emancipation, local democracy, or individual freedom could be interpreted in new ways. The introduction of the new mode of governance depended on arguments and a new vocabulary of participation, and, as events in Tensta around 1990 show, on how architecture and ideology were interwoven in the discourse of resident participation. The urban renewal projects took shape where the civil society organizations' demands for influence (inspired by the 1968 civil rights movement and urban protest groups) intersected the new Third Way's control techniques, incorporated the emancipatory movements, and redirected them from resistance to consensus. This site shows how the discourse and practice of architecture are not only embedded in discriminatory policies, they are active participants.

Events in Tensta around 1990 can, of course, be understood in broader terms about the effects of neoliberalization. As Wendy Brown has argued, the devolution of decision-making and authority is a hallmark of neoliberal governance and criticism of central government. What follows is not solely local self-government: there are serious problems in the shape of financial crises, unemployment, and environmental problems in the pipeline, on their way from central government to the local authorities, communities, and individuals, and finally to "small and weak units unable to cope with them technically, politically, or financially."[62] Instead of labeling the subject (or institution, or authority) as responsible, the linguistic term *responsibilization* better exemplifies the process, shifting it from an individual capacity to a governance project expecting "the reflexive moral capacities of various social actors."[63] Responsibilization is the missing link from the abstraction of governance to the real practice on the ground.[64]

The lawyer Sara Schindler writes of architecture and the built environment as a form of regulation that the judiciary often overlooks. The built environment is usually seen as "functional, innocuous, and prepolitical," which means that any segregating and discriminatory "architectural exclusion" often eludes the legal system. It is also a form of regulation that lends itself to the workings of neoliberalization, often in silence as a stealth revolution. Schindler examines at several such categories in the built environment— physical barriers, transit stops, highways, one-way streets, parking permits—but in this chapter I have addressed another type of architectural exclusion, which is more about the processes of realizing architecture, and the effects of that, both of which are perhaps even easier to ignore.[65]

By withholding financial resources, formulating high social ambitions, and passing the responsibility to residents, the public authorities in Tensta created an impossible task, far beyond the residents' abilities to solve, and instead strengthened the idea there was a causal link between race, ethnicity, and poor housing. To pursue a program of urban renewal based on resident participation while denying them the necessary resources is a discriminatory and even racist policy, even if it was unintentional. From being victims, the residents were made responsible for their situation through the techniques of responsibilization—a shift closely bound up with changing demographics.⁶⁶ However, that is not to say there was a direct causal relationship between migration and changing control techniques, but the combination of these two factors was in itself discriminatory.

The urban renewal project not only shifted responsibility from the public sector to the residents, it also gave the architects greater responsibility. In this case, Loggia Arkitekter was given new professional powers and responsibilities to mediate between the residents and the public sector, but equally between ethnic and cultural groups and their wishes.⁶⁷ The upshot was a paradoxical situation in which committed individuals of high ideals—architects, planners, administrators, residents, politicians—all participated in a development that contributed to an exclusionary and discriminatory discourse. Architecture was central to this discursive turn, and the lived, built environment had a contradictory role. From a micro-political perspective, the lived environment improved in many respects, while the urban renewal project pursued new counterproductive solutions at the macro-political level, such as rent rises and the sale of public housing. There is another story to tell, too, and an important one, about Loggia Arkitekter's work and positive, strengthening effects of their long collaboration with the residents, but my aim here has been to identify how this suburban renewal project was embedded in neoliberalization.

Magnus Dahlström has written of "the politics of activation" and how it contributed to a macro-political shift in Sweden from a state-centered to an individual-centered regime; a shift that is also reflected in changed views on democracy in, for example, the new Planning and Building Act, the official Commission on Democracy, and also the "multi-ethnic suburb."⁶⁸ Decentralization, participation, and responsibility: three concepts central to the policy of empowerment, whose meaning altered over the course of the Tensta refurbishment.⁶⁹ The determination to empower residents created a "truth regime" where the local authority's role was to step aside, making way for voluntary, independent actors. The ambition was to "mobilize" Tensta's residents and create social capital—a sense of district loyalty, complete with social cohesion.⁷⁰ In the 1980s, housing was a social project intended to improve quality of life (rather than quality of housing), focusing on how to build a community rather than how to build *for* a community.⁷¹

As we have seen, it was typical of neoliberalization to shift responsibility to the residents just as resources were cut. In Tensta, the result was that socially and economically vulnerable groups were left exposed. There is a tendency to talk about places being vulnerable rather than people, which has been used to justify urban renewal projects such as in Tensta. We should ask ourselves what exactly these places are vulnerable to. All too often the impression is given that the threat comes from the residents, when the reverse is true; there is a long history of exposing residents to diverse sociopolitical projects which in the long run not seems to have raised the quality of life. In conjunction with the urban renewal project discussed here, a moral vocabulary was drawn up: what was good and what was bad; who was responsible and/or guilty—two concepts that often overlapped.

We will end where we began, in a litter-strewn public square in Tensta in the late 1980s. The Traffic Department is out cleaning Stockholm's city center every day, but only on weekdays in the suburbs, and the solution to the residents' complaints was that they should do it themselves. According to the local authority, it was more important to change attitudes than to improve the service they provided. In Tensta, as in so many other suburbs, a discourse of dirt and litter was created which asserted that the residents and their immoral, careless behavior were the problem, whether because of ethnicity, culture or lack of language skills. Litter was not the only thing residents were "offered," nay "encouraged," to take personal responsibility for. Housing, management, architecture: it was all there, the duties and concepts, trickling down through the bureaucratic machinery to the residents who were expected to sit on councils and attend meetings, whose voluntary work replaced paid labor as building wardens. Unpaid work and dumped responsibilities were framed as expressions of solidarity, morality, and guilt—a moral debt that in many places would soon be compounded by a financial one when the residents were left with all the responsibility of becoming tenant-owners. In the market's backyard, in neighborhoods such as in Tensta, most residents could not, however, afford to buy their flats; rather than symbols of home ownership these flats would become assets that instead circulated on the global financial market.

*

This chapter is not only a historical narrative. It is as much a comment on Sweden's suburbs today as it is on their pasts. The same can be said of the book as a whole, which has been written from a contemporary perspective looking back over an extended past to understand the myriad workings of architecture.

EPILOGUE: ELEPHANT & CASTLE

In June 1990, the Swedish real estate investor Leif Nordqvist canceled payments on a loan that his company had obtained for the purpose of investing in a new office building at Elephant & Castle in the south of London. The deepest recession to have hit the Swedish economy since the interwar years had just begun; 1992 witnessed a 500 percent rise in Sweden's marginal rate of interest, a hike that affected millions of Swedes; the country's overheated property market imploded, resulting in a series of bankruptcies and shutdowns. The realpolitik of the architecture field and the construction, real estate, and finance sectors had started to threaten the stability of the entire Swedish banking system.[1] Whilst many of the cornerstones of the Swedish Model caved in, behind its crackling surface a new armature was already more or less in place. So, after an unexpectedly short period of "market injections," a new and remodeled welfare state—the supermodel—took to its feet, its spirit one of neoliberalism.

As this book demonstrates, the crisis of the 1990s has an important pre-history. Architecture and real estate played a central role both in the bank crisis and in the longer-term societal changes that swept Sweden during the decade spanning from the mid-1980s through to the mid-1990s. Architectural deregulations—involving aesthetics, spatial organization, building materials, measures—aligned with a series of other deregulatory initiatives which reached their peak in the mid-1980s. Several months after the opening of the "norm-breaking" Bo 85, a housing expo located on Stockholm's periphery that for the first time engaged in large-scale experiments in designing "beyond the code," the Riksbank (Sweden's central bank) proposed that all remaining regulation of the Swedish credit market be removed. When Finance Minister Kjell-Olof Feldt presented this measure for Prime Minister Olof Palme, explaining that what he was suggesting might be interpreted as "the final stage in an ideological retreat," he was met with the response "Do what you want, I don't understand any of this anyway." And with that, on the 21st of November 1985, the country's finance market was deregulated, in a moment that came to be known as the "November Revolution."[2] In the two-hour period between his discovery of Feldt's decision and its formal announcement at a press conference, Lars Wohlin, a former director of the Riksbank who was at the time director of Stadshypotek, an institute that financed residential development, took out loans to a total value of 300 million crowns.[3] A speculative borrowing hysteria set in immediately. The Riksbank, which had long opposed such deregulation, had given in to the deregulatory impulses of the Thatcher and Reagan governments. Through this shift, and further deregulations that occurred in the closing years of the 1980s, capital began to flow more freely over national borders—the "globalization" of economy and business had begun.

Architecture and Retrenchment

In Feldt's view, the transfer of power from the nation state to the financial market, like the shift from state-led regulation to private initiatives, could not only be attributed to the deregulation of financial markets. Beyond the capacity of banks to grant loans, these changes required that borrowers really believed in the projects that their loans were to fund,[4] and this is where architects entered the picture. Architecture's ability to materialize ideas, futures, and imaginary realities, in tandem with the aesthetic boom that had accompanied architecture's "emancipation" through the desire-inducing visual languages and experience economies of postmodernism, meant that in these newly deregulated financial conditions, projects that had previously been confined to the drawing board could now suddenly be realized. While the changes sweeping Sweden echoed those seen internationally, the unfolding crisis was rapidly escalating. It is telling that one of the pioneering figures in property speculation in the 1970s was anchored in architecture: Adam Backström, who was not only educated as an architect but was son of one the most well-known "welfare state architects," Sven Backström (one half of Backström & Reinius Architects). The younger Backström's successful maneuvering on the housing market, which was in part predicated on reducing or even withdrawing maintenance in relation to the buildings he owned, led to the "lex Backström" law, which introduced new powers for municipalities to steer the allocation of rental housing and thus reduce speculation on the rental market.[5]

In this way, the international market opened up to Swedish architects at the end of the 1980s: suddenly, it was possible to finance building projects on the basis of loans that radically exceeded the value of the initial investment. The drawing board negotiations of the 1960s and 1970s became a thing of the past, and business meetings instead took place on aeroplanes or over a glass of champagne in an airport lounge. Architects were given prominent roles in project teams and traveled the world in search of inspiration for the environments they were tasked with designing. The construction of Stockholm's first World Trade Center (Vasaterminalen) reflected this ethos of internationalization. When the property world exploded in the 1980s, the (partially imaginary) budgets upon which the design phase rested skyrocketed, and the architecture discipline was able to expand in ways that were previously unimaginable. This increased capital brought with it opportunities to raise the standards of architectural projects, meaning that many projects were in fact still being designed when construction started. Arne Hilton, a consultant with Electro Engineering (previously FJ Injenjörsbyrå), remembers the hasty nature of the decisions that were taken by the leadership of the Stockholm World Trade Center, who—when arriving back from one their many international study tours—were given to making announcements like, "From now on, we're going to do it like *this*."[6] The impetus for these changes, according to Hilton, seemed to be a desire to raise the level of architectural ambition, by, for instance, replacing brick with polished granite, or upgrading other materials, or the specification of more exclusive finishes in lobbies and entrances.

In the midst of this moment of euphoria within Swedish architecture, which liberated architects not only from aesthetic regulations like SBN80 but also from the confines of their offices, Leif Nordqvist's thirst for new investments momentarily intersected with Margaret Thatcher's penchant for deregulation. The amalgamation of the London Council in 1986 and the subsequent introduction of the "Regeneration Area," a policy instrument which aligned with sympathetic taxation conditions for private investors, had led to a building boom around the tube station Elephant & Castle in South London. As a result, a number of large plots in the vicinity of the station were put on the market without any planning guidance regarding their redevelopment. In the spirit of the times—and backed by loans that were secured by the property portfolio of his company, Allhus AB—Leif Nordqvist decided to purchase one of the plots. The office building that Nordqvist had commissioned from British architect Paul Clayford was clad in fashionable pink marble and polished granite, and when it stood completed on site in 1992, it had already become a significant building for Sweden, albeit as a harbinger of crisis rather than success.[7] When in 1990 Nordqvist suspended payments to Nyckeln, the property and financial services company financing the project, Nyckeln deferred on payments to their bank, which led to an avalanche of other deferrals: within two years, a thousand Swedish companies had been declared bankrupt.[8] Leif Nordqvist later commented to the newspaper *Dagens Industri*, "We should have given overseas a wide berth. But at that moment, Swedes were behaving liked wild animals when it came to foreign investment. You just had to pick up the phone and you had a loan."

*

Finally, we might ask whether it is in fact possible to succinctly summarize the role that architecture played in the enormous societal changes addressed here. On one hand, architecture clearly played a central role in relation to these transformations. The years between 1968 and 1994 witnessed the birth of countless movements and countermovements alike within architecture—and in society at large. This was, however, also a period in which corporatist Sweden, with its politicians, businesses, unions, interest organizations, and other actors, rewrote architecture's social contract, shifting the terms of the fine print and revising its overarching aim from being *to serve the common good* to rather *acting in service of the asset economy* (understood as comprising both tangible and non-tangible assets). It is precisely this revised contract, albeit in an even more refined version, that holds at present, dictating the terms of a "derivative trade" whereby architecture's form is primarily decided on the basis of its future economic value as property. The idea that the value of a currency decays over time implies that to offset these losses, property must increase in value; this is to be achieved with the help of architects, either through the construction of new buildings or through the renovation, restauration, or transformation of old buildings. Mathematical equations secure a good rate of return in these games: their calculations reward low investments that give high returns, and as a result architectural "burdens" such as the Million Program housing areas are re-evaluated as "assets."[9]

Is it then possible to fully describe the role that architecture has played in these changes? The answer is, upon reflection, perhaps "no." Nevertheless, I would like to highlight a number of apparent tendencies that cut across the specific examples discussed previously. The first concerns *architecture's complicity*, which takes us back to two ideas that I introduce at the start of this book: assemblage and statification. These terms, according to their respective creators, describe *compositions* that are made up of both tangible and intangible things. When considered in and through the field of architecture, these concepts help the reader to gain an appreciation of the scope of the discipline. Assemblages constantly participate in statifications and vice versa; when building regulations suddenly become "negotiable" or the "design guidelines" of postmodernism appear in the void left by an absent planning apparatus, architecture is revealed as being both a practice and a politics, which operates at scales that span from the microscopic to the planetary.

When it comes to neoliberalization, which forms the book's primary object of inquiry, *Architecture and Retrenchment* has emphasized architecture's role in contributing to the removal of institutions and regulatory frameworks, and in materializing a range of seemingly abstract political and ideological operations within the most banal of local environments or everyday situations. The transformations of the 1980s and the crisis of the 1990s undisputedly contributed to the marketization and financialization of sectors that were previously "protected" from market logics; upon close scrutiny, architecture, with its close links to real estate speculation and debt, can be seen to have acted as a field through which these transformations passed. By the time that the construction boom had begun to gain momentum in the private sphere, the effects of the public-sector cuts of the 1980s were becoming visible: these were particularly apparent in architecture's changing relation to the state and municipalities. What remains underacknowledged, however, is the architecture field's active participation in the implementation of austerity and the introduction of new forms of governance. Beyond their economic consequences, these changes also reformatted subjectivities, remodeling ways of thinking and, at their outermost limit, ways of being human.

Architecture has an ability to operate on a number of levels simultaneously; this characteristic makes it difficult to determine in advance how the discipline might act or what it might end up contributing to a given situation. To return to Fraser's three—the market, social protection, and emancipation—it can be noted that architectural projects often engage all three poles simultaneously. Two concrete examples that show this can be found in the collective house and in the participatory renewal of Tensta. In the case of the former, ideas about collective living were formulated in line with progressive ideas about how a society can be organized in order to support household types other than the nuclear family—although it had been advanced by the women's liberation movement for decades, this was an issue that had not been given much thought within the structures of the welfare state. The innovative and revolutionary thinking around social reproduction that occurred in the 1980s was soon recognized by politicians, though, as providing a way to solve the political and economic crisis of the present. *Kollektivhuset* became a large-scale model for the new forms of governance that were being put forward by politicians and bureaucrats at the time. Similarly, the renewal of Tensta witnesses a similar strategy: here, ambitious and experimental architecture was also enrolled in the task of producing new social forms, the significance of which lay well outside of the local situation and its buildings. The user influence that many actors had demanded throughout the 1960s and 1970s, which eventually entered legislation through revisions to the Planning and Building Act, was transformed in Tensta into a requirement accompanied by strong moral overtones. In both cases, architecture was a means to implement radical social changes, which in turn ultimately transferred responsibilities onto either the individual or groups of individuals.

Architecture as resource is another theme that cuts through many of the discussions that are staged in this book. During the long 1980s, architecture was increasingly viewed as a resource—not just economically but also in terms of its "human" values (creativity, innovation, and entrepreneurship), in this way it was seen as embodying Anthony Giddens's dictum of "getting more from less."[10] Architecture was thus not only financialized and marketized during this period, but also acculturated. Culture under neoliberalism ceased to be something to be observed and became rather more like a laboratory wherein "social products" (material or social) could be developed, or particular qualities of individuals could be strengthened, without state intervention. This newfound interest in creativity and innovation cannot, however, only be understood in terms of the operations performed by individuals in order to make themselves more employable or to create their own employment opportunities.[11] Architecture's increased relevance as a producer of human and social capital was at this time tested in a number of sectors within society, from health to sport and recreation. These tests were nothing new in themselves—in the heyday of the welfare state, culture had played a crucial role in disciplining and emancipating citizens. What was new was the fact that architecture was being deployed as an economic and political resource: something that could be delivered through and support market mechanisms. Architecture was suddenly expected to be able to prevent or ameliorate economic crises, aid in making funding cuts, dilute social tensions, improve health and knowledge, and function as an incentive for economic growth.[12]

But these shifts in architecture's role also took on another expression; from being a figure integrated in the economics and politics of the public sector, the architect became ever more entwined in matters of "aesthetics" and the task of raising "value" (which could denote anything from worth, understood in economic terms, to human, aesthetic, or social values). Architecture, it was proposed, created added value. In 1987, Sweden launched its first architecture policy, *Framtidsformer*, the greatest contribution of which perhaps lay in the emphasis that it placed on the "aesthetically pleasing" aspects of architecture. Once detached from social planning (including the design of schools, kindergartens, and healthcare facilities), the architectural apparatus was redirected toward the production of aesthetic values, a development which is echoed in the "design guidelines" that were developed for the Södra station neighborhood (Site 5).

The final theme foregrounded in this book is that of architecture's *historiography*— understood not only in terms of the methods required to explore events within the architectural field at large, but more specifically those needed to trace the maneuvers that architecture made (and continues to make) in the almost-present-day landscape of neoliberalization. A wide range of sources must generally be consulted when writing architectural history—these include archival materials from state institutions and boards, protocols and minutes from committees that address architectural matters, and the personal archives of private actors, particularly those involved in voluntary work or activism. The archive of the 1980s is, as I comment previously, oftentimes simply missing in action, and for this reason the study of this period demanded that new methods be developed to reconstruct archives, collect material, and engage existing narratives. Participatory historical methods were in this sense particularly pertinent. I would argue that the most central of the methodological orientations to emerge in the writing of this book was a commitment to searching for openings within the tangled terrain of contemporary history. Within such openings lie, I discovered, a range of possible techniques, elements, and operations that might again be deployed in the service of initiating societal change through and with architecture.

NOTES

Introduction

1   "The Next Supermodel," *The Economist* 406, no. 8821 (2013): 9.
2   "The New Model: A Bit More Unequal, A Lot More Efficient," *The Economist* 405, no. 8806 (2012): SS20–SS21.
3   "The Next Supermodel," 9.
4   The bank crisis that took place between 1992 and 1994 and had its origin in the first rise and fall of the asset economy resulted in a systemic shift, making a fortune for some and plunging others into lifelong debt. See the Epilogue.
5   This is a perspective taken by many scholars, including: Luc Boltanski and Ève Chiapello, *The New Spirit of Capitalism* (London: Verso, 2005); Wendy Brown, *Undoing the Demos: Neoliberalism's Stealth Revolution* (New York: Zone Books, 2015); and Jamie Peck, *Constructions of Neoliberal Reason* (Oxford: Oxford University Press, 2010).
6   Thomas Piketty, *Capital in the Twenty-First Century* (Cambridge, Mass.: Harvard University Press, 2014).
7   Lisa Adkins, Melinda Cooper, and Martijn Konings, *The Asset Economy: Property Ownership and the New Logic of Inequality* (Cambridge: Polity Press, 2020).
8   Adkins et al., *The Asset Economy*, 34, 144.
9   I will come back to my use of the term "neoliberalization," but for discussions of the concept, see, for example: Neil Brenner, Jamie Peck, and Nik Theodore, "Variegated Neoliberalization: Geographies, Modalities Pathways," *Global Networks* 10, no. 2 (2010): 1–4; Peck, *Constructions of Neoliberal Reason*.
10 Nicholas Gane, "The Governmentalities of Neoliberalism: Panopticism, Post-Panopticism and Beyond," *The Sociological Review* 60 (2012): 613.
11 See, for example: Esra Akcan, *Open Architecture: Migration, Citizenship, and the Urban Renewal of Berlin-Kreuzberg by IBA—1984/87* (Basel: Birkhauser Verlag GmbH, 2018); Kenny Cupers, *The Social Project: Housing Postwar France* (Minneapolis: University of Minnesota Press, 2014); Catharina Gabrielsson and Helena Mattsson, guest, eds., Special Issue: "Solids and Flows—Architecture and Capitalism," *Architecture and Culture* 5, no. 2 (2017): 157–341; Miles Glendinning, *Mass Housing: Modern Architecture and State Power* (London: Bloomsbury Academic, 2021); Tahl Kaminer, *The Efficacy of Architecture: Political Contestation and Agency* (London: Routledge, 2017); Anne Kockelkorn and Reinhold Martin, *Housing After the Neoliberal Turn: A Sample Atlas* (Berlin: HKW, 2015); Sandra Karina Löschke, ed., *Non-Standard Architectural Production: Between Aesthetic Experience and Social Action* (London: Routledge, 2019); Jennifer Mack, *The Construction of Equality: Syriac Immigration and the Swedish City* (Minneapolis: University of Minnesota Press, 2017); Kim Moody, *From Welfare State to Real State: Regime Change in New York City, 1974 to the Present* (New York & London: The New Press, 2007); and Florian Urban, *Neo-Historical East Berlin: Architecture and Urban Design in the German Democratic Republic 1970–1990* (Farnham: Ashgate, 2009).

Notes

12 For example, see: Frida Rosenberg, *The Construction of Construction: The Wenner-Gren Center and the Possibility of Steel Building in Postwar Sweden* (diss. Kungliga tekniska högskolan, Stockholm: KTH, 2018); Helen Runting *Architectures of the Unbuilt Environment* (diss. Kungliga tekniska högskolan, Stockholm: KTH, 2018); Guttorm Ruud, *Sites of Crises: Histories of Satellite Town* (diss. The Oslo School of Architecture and Design, Oslo, 2021); and Erik Sigge, *Architecture's Red Tape: Government Building Construction in Sweden, 1963-1973* (diss. Kungliga tekniska högskolan, Stockholm: KTH, 2017).

13 See, for example: Kenny Cupers, Catharina Gabrielsson, and Helena Mattsson, eds., *Neoliberalism on the Ground: Architecture and Transformations from the 1960s to the Present* (Pittsburgh: University of Pittsburgh Press, 2020); Christian Hiller et al., eds., *Housing After the Neoliberal Turn: International Case Studies* (Leipzig: Spector Books, 2016); Tahl Kaminer, Miguel Robles-Dúran, and Heidi Sohn, eds., *Urban Assymetries: Studies and Projects on Neoliberal Urbanization* (Rotterdam: nai 010 publishers, 2011); Johan Pries, *Social Neoliberalism through Urban Planning: Bureaucratic Formations and Contradictions in Malmö since 1986* (diss. Lund University, Lund: Lund University, 2017); Hossein Sadri, ed., *Neo-Liberalism and the Architecture of the Post-Professional Era* (Cham: Springer, 2018); and Douglas Spencer, *The Architecture of Neoliberalism: How Contemporary Architecture became an Instrument of Control and Compliance* (New York: Bloomsbury Academic, 2016); *Critique of Architecture: Essays on Theory, Autonomy, and Political Economy* (Basel: Birkhäuser, 2021).

14 Cf. Peggy Deamer, ed., *Architecture and Capitalism: 1845 to the Present* (London: Routledge, 2013), 1.

15 Mark Swenarton, Tom Avermaete, and Dirk van den Heuvel, *Architecture and the Welfare State* (London & New York: Routledge, 2015).

16 Mary McLeod, "Architecture and Politics in the Reagan Era: From Postmodernism to Deconstructivism," *Assemblage*, 8, no. 8 (1989): 22–59.

17 Peck, *Constructions of Neoliberal Reason*; Jamie Peck, Neil Brenner, and Nik Theodore, "Actually Existing Neoliberalism," in *The Sage Handbook of Neoliberalism*, eds. Damien Cahill et al. (New York: Oxford University Press, 2010). Peck compares the "long transitions" of Sweden, Singapore, and China with the crises-driven shift in Britain, 21.

18 "Minnesanteckningar förda vid ett möte mellan Glömmingegränds lokala hyresgästförening, Familjebostäders distrikt och NCC samt Loggia arkitekter" (memory notes from a meeting with Glömmingegränd's local tenant association, the public housing company Familjebostäder, the construction company NCC and the architects Loggia), October 11, 1993, AB Familjebostäders arkiv, box E2b:3, Stockholms stadsarkiv (Stockholm City Archive).

19 Recently calls for a history of the welfare state from the perspective of groups not included in the mainstream narratives have been raised by scholars such as for example Stephen Pimpare, "Toward a new Welfare History," *Journal of Policy History* 19, no. 2 (2007): 234–52.

20 My use of the term "assemblage" draws on Gilles Deleuze and Felix Guattari's descriptions of constellations of material and non-material agents, exemplified for instance in "the knight-machine": man, lance, horse, and stirrups all together forming an assemblage, distributing new possibilities of movements and affects, and creating a whole new geography of war. Gilles Deleuze and Felix Guattari, *A Thousand Plateaus: Capitalism and Schizophrenia* (Minneapolis: University of Minnesota Press, 1987), 351–423.

21 I have been inspired by methods in contemporary history, for example the format of the witness seminar. Two chapters—"The Collective House" and "The Renewal"—use material from witness seminars organized by Action Archive (Sara Brolund de Carvalho, Helena

Mattsson, and Meike Schalk). For more on witness seminars in architecture and other "participatory history writing" methods, see Helena Mattsson and Meike Schalk, "Action Archive: Oral History as Performance," in *Speaking of Buildings: Oral history in Architectural Research*, eds. Janina Gosseye, Naomi Stead, and Deborah van der Plaat (New York: Princeton Architectural Press, 2019), 94–113.

22 See Reinhold Martin, "Epilogue: Neoliberalism and Architecture, Backward" in *Neoliberalism on The Ground*, 415.

23 See, for instance: Niels Finn Christiansen et al., eds., *The Nordic Model of Welfare: A Historical Reappraisal* (Copenhagen: University of Copenhagen & Museum Tusculanum Press, 2006); Urban Lundberg and Mattias Tydén, "In Search of the Swedish Model: Contested Historiography," in *Swedish Modernism: Architecture, Consumption, and the Welfare State*, eds. Helena Mattsson and Sven-Olov Wallenstein (London: Black Dog, 2010); and Bengt Larsson, Martin Letell, and Håkan Thörn, eds., *Transformations of the Swedish Welfare State: From Social Engineering to Governance?* (New York: Palgrave Macmillan, 2012); Nils Edling (ed.), *The Changing Meanings of the Welfare State: Histories of a Key Concept in the Nordic Countries* (New York: Berghan, 2019).

24 While the concept of *Folkhemmet* was popularized by the Swedish prime minister Per Albin Hansson in the famous speech of January 18, 1928, where he argued that the class society should be replaced by the "People's Home," the idea has a longer history, for example appearing in the conservative Rudolf Kjellen's vision of a corporatist-styled society. It has been argued, however, that *Folkhemmet* actually was not used as a key political concept by the Social Democrats until the 1980s when it was resurrected as defense for the "good society" against the attacks by the 1980s neoliberals. See: Nils Edling, "The Primacy of Welfare Politics: Note on the Language of the Swedish Social Democrats and Their Adversaries in the 1930s," in *Multi-layered Historicity of the Present: Approaches to Social Science History*, eds. Heidi Haggren, Johanna Rainio-Niemi, and Jussi Vauhkonen (Helsinki: University of Helsinki, 2013), 125–50.

25 Marquis W. Childs, *Sweden: The Middle Way* (New Haven: Yale University, 1936).

26 Bostadssociala utredningen, *Slutbetänkande* (Stockholm: LiberFörlag/Allmänna förl., 1945).

27 Thomas Piketty, *Capital and Ideology* (Cambridge, Mass.: Harvard University Press, 2020), 162 (ebook). Piketty opposes the notion of Sweden (and other countries) as having always been *inherently* egalitarian. Instead, he argues that Sweden was more sophisticated than most countries in organizing its inequality and more systematic in expressing its proprietarian ideology (see: 186). See also: Erik Bengtsson, "The Swedish *Sonderweg* in Question: Democratization and Inequality in Comparative Perspective, c. 1750–1920," *Past and Present*, 244, no. 1 (2019): 123–61.

28 At the end of the 1980s and beginning of the 1990s, all these institutions closed down; they were either melted together or spun off as state-owned pseudo enterprises or simply ceased. The periods that the institutions existed were: Bostadsstyrelsen 1948–88, Svensk Byggnorm 1967–89, Byggnadsstyrelsen 1918/67–93 (in 1967 the name changed from Kungliga Byggnadsstyrelsen to Byggnadsstyrelsen), Statens Planverk 1967–88, and Bostadsdepartementet 1974–91.

29 Jenny Andersson and Kjell Östberg, *Sveriges Historia 1965—2012* (Stockholm: Norstedts, 2013), 29.

Notes

30 Saltsjöbaden was a fashionable suburb of Stockholm where the Trade Union Confederation and the Swedish Employers' Association met for negotiations in 1938. The implications of "the Spirit of Saltsjöbaden" can, of course, be discussed. The negotiations were definitely a way to avoid strikes and at the same time secure wages through institutionalized negotiations; however, at the same time, these were top-down agreements that were handled by a few men, which became binding for most Swedish wage earners.

31 Gøsta Esping-Andersen, *The Three Worlds of Welfare Capitalism* (Cambridge: Polity Press), 3; Swanerton et al., *Architecture and the Welfare State*.

32 Wigforss, not himself a trained economist but having a PhD in Nordic language, was close to the economists of the Stockholm School, a group which included figures such as Gunnar Myrdal and Bertil Ohlin. The latter argued that the Stockholm School did not only anticipate Keynes General Theory (GT), but was also superior to it. See, Bengt Ohlin, "Some Notes on the Stockholm Theory of savings and Investment I," *Economic Journal* 47 (1937): 221–40. This has been criticized by many scholars, who argue that the complete edifice of GT was beyond the Stockholm School. See for example D. Patinkin, "On the Relation between Keynesian Economics and the 'Stockholm School'," *Scandinavian Journal of Economics* 80 (1978): 135–43. It has recently been argued that Wigforss was more important than the Stockholm School for the development of the Swedish economic policy through his connections with British liberals and Keynes in the 1920s. Martin Kragh, "'The Wigforss Connection': The Stockholm School vs. Keynes Debate Revisited," *The European Journal of the History of Economic Thought* 21, no. 4 (2014): 635–63.

33 Cf. Helena Mattsson, "Designing the Reasonable Consumer: Standardisation and Personalisation in Swedish Functionalism," in *Swedish Modernism: Architecture, Consumption, and the Welfare State*, eds. Helena Mattsson and Sven-Olov Wallenstein (London: Black Dog, 2010).

34 The historian Klas Åmark has argued that social democracy aimed at strengthening the role of the workers in the market, rather than making them independent of it. Klas Åmark, *Hundra år av välfärdspolitik: Välfärdsstatens framväxt i Norge och Sverige* (Umeå: Boréa, 2005), 67.

35 This process of exclusion is not specific to Sweden, but applies to most Western welfare states. Cf. Nancy Fraser, *Fortunes of Feminism: From State-Managed Capitalism to Neoliberal Crises* (London/New York: Verso, 2013), 8.

36 Yvonne Hirdman investigates what she calls *genuskonflikten* (gender-conflict) in the Swedish postwar context; see for example Gertrud Åström and Yvonne Hirdman, eds., *Kontrakt i kris* (Helsingborg: Carlssons, 1992), 9.

37 See for example Mack, *The Construction of Equality*; Irene Molina, *Stadens rasifiering: Etnisk boendesegregering I folkhemmet* (diss., Uppsala university, Uppsala: Uppsala University, 1997); and Magnus Dahlstedt, "The Politics of Activation: Technologies of Mobilizing 'Multiethnic Suburbs' in Sweden," *Alternatives: Global, Local, Political* 33, no. 4 (2008): 481–504.

38 Ingvar Carlsson, *Så tänkte jag: Politik & dramatik* (Stockholm: Hjalmarson & Högberg, 2003).

39 Bengt Dennis, *500%* (Stockholm: DN, 1998).

40 A parliamentary decision to build one million apartments in Sweden in ten years, 1965–74.

41 Dalen (1979–82), Skarpnäcksfältet (1981–), and Södra Stationsområdet (1986–91), but also major commercial projects such as Globen City (1985–9) and Cityterminalen (1985–9).

42 See, for example: Bengt Larsson, et al., eds., *Transformations of the Swedish Welfare State*; Pries, *Social Neoliberalism Through Urban Planning*; and the research project run by

Jenny Andersson, "Neoliberalism in the Nordics: developing an absent theme," financed by Riksbankens Jubileumsfond (https://nyliberalisminorden.se); Jenny Andersson, "Drivkrafterna bakom nyliberaliseringen kom från många olika håll," *Tidskriften Respons*, no. 1 (2020), accessed May 8, 2022, http://tidskriftenrespons.se/artikel/drivkrafterna-bakom-nyliberaliseringen-kom-fran-manga-olika-hall/.

43   David Harvey, *A Brief History of Neoliberalism* (Oxford: Oxford University Press, 2005), 115.
44   Brown, *Undoing the Demos*.
45   Andersson, "Drivkrafterna bakom nyliberaliseringen kom från många håll."
46   Jenny Andersson, *The Library and the Workshop: Social Democracy and Capitalism in the Knowledge Age* (Stanford: Stanford University Press, 2010), 42.
47   Andersson, *The Library and the Workshop*, 157.
48   Cf. Peck, *Construction of Neoliberal Reason*.
49   In six lectures between January 31 and March 21, 1979, Foucault discussed the emerging neoliberal state; see Foucault, *The Birth of Biopolitics*. For a discussion of the state phobia and crisis of governmentality, see, for example, 76–7. On biopolitics and architecture, see Sven-Olov Wallenstein, *Biopolitics and the Emergence of Modern Architecture* (New York: Princeton Architectural, 2009).
50   Foucault, *The Birth of Biopolitics*, 68.
51   See Peter Starke, "The Politics of Welfare State Retrenchment: A Literature Review," *Social Policy & Administration* 40, no. 1 (2006): 104–20. For early scholarship on retrenchment, see for example Michael K. Brown, ed., *Remaking the Welfare State: Retrenchment and Social Policy in America and Europe* (Philadelphia: Temple University Press, 1988).
52   Paul Pierson, *Dismantling the Welfare State? Reagan, Thatcher and the Politics of Retrenchment* (Cambridge: Cambridge University Press, 1994).
53   Foucault declares that the state is "nothing else but the effect, the profile, the mobile shape of a perpetual statification (*étatisation*) or statifications, in the sense of incessant transactions which modify, or move, or drastically change, or insidiously shift sources of finance, modes of investment, decision-making centers, forms and types of control, relationships between local powers, the central authority, and so on." Foucault, *The Birth of Biopolitics*, 77 (87).
54   Peck, *Constructions of Neoliberal Reason*. See, for example, the diagram "Relational Spaces of Neoliberalism," 26.
55   On these matters, I especially want to thank Catharina Gabrielsson for stimulating discussions and collaborations within the research project "The Architecture of Deregulation," KTH School of Architecture, and all participants in the conference "Architecture and Deregulations: Postmodernism, Politics and the Built Environment, 1975–1995," held at KTH in 2016.
56   On the introduction of New Public Management in Sweden, see Roland Almqvist, *New Public Management: NPM om konkurrensutsättning, kontrakt och kontroll* (Malmö: Liber, 2006); and Stig Montin, *Moderna kommuner*, 3rd ed. (Malmö: Liber, 2007). According to Montin, the marketization of the public sector was carried out faster in Sweden than in neighboring Nordic countries, but not as forcefully as in Britain.
57   Christopher Hood, "A Public Management for all Seasons?," *Public Administration* 69, no. 1 (1991): 3–19; and Christopher Hood, "The 'New Public Management' in the 1980s: Variation on a Theme," *Accounting Organizations & Society* 20, no. 2/3 (1995): 93–109.
58   Hood, "The 'New Public Management' in the 1980s," 94.

Notes

59 Significant for understanding this complex is that modernist ideas were written into the Swedish building code already in the 1930s (and stayed there until the 1980s) and came to dominate the built environment through legislations. Monica Andersson, *Politik och stadsbyggande: Modernismen och bygglagstiftningen* (diss., Stockholm: Statsvetenskapliga institutionen, Stockholm University, 2009).

60 Cf. Helena Mattsson, "Revisiting Swedish Postmodernism: Gendered Architecture and Other Stories," *Journal of Art History* 85, no. 1 (2016): 109–25; Catharina Gabrielsson, "Through the Anxieties of Style: The Triggering of Neoliberalism and the New Vasa Museum in Stockholm,", in Cupers et al., (eds.), *Neoliberalism on the Ground*.

61 Reinhold Martin, *Utopia's Ghost: Architecture and Postmodernism, Again* (Minneapolis: University of Minnesota press, 2010), xiv.

62 Mattsson, "Revisiting Swedish Postmodernism," 116.

63 Mattsson, "Revisiting Swedish Postmodernism," 118.

64 Prime Minister Bildt ended his first Government Declaration in 1991 with the following statement: "Too often, the state and the public powers have been perceived as the same thing as the society. But now the time of collectivism is over. In our Sweden, the society will always be greater than the state. We strive to make the 1990s a decade of change and renewal for Sweden." Swedish Parliamentary Papers, Chamber Protocols, 1991/92, no. 6 (October 4, 1991), accessed February 28, 2022, https://www.riksdagen.se/sv/dokument-lagar/dokument/protokoll/riksdagens-snabbprotokoll-1991926-fredagen-den_GF096.

65 The dismantled housing policy, and associated government economic instruments (such as subsidy and loan rules), and a number of government agencies that were previously linked to the development of the built environment were replaced by new strategies formulated by the state. Policy documents were, for example, introduced that highlighted aesthetic values, such as "Framtidsformer" (Future forms) in 1998. Moreover, the planning of public spaces and housing was transformed, to the extent that "planning" more or less was replaced by "investment" in the private sector (in the form of consultants).

66 See, for example: Thomas Piketty, *Capital and Ideology*, trans. Arthur Goldhammer (Cambridge, Mass.: Belknap Press, 2020); Erik Bengtsson, *Världens jämlikaste land?* (Lund: Arkiv förlag, 2020).

67 Anthony Giddens, *The Third Way: The Renewal of Social Democracy* (Oxford: Polity Press, 1998), 74–5.

68 Tony Blair and Gerhard Schröder, "Europe: The Third Way/Die Neue Mitte," 1999, quoted in Philip Arestis and Malcolm Sawyer, "Economics of the 'Third Way': Introduction," in *The Economics of the Third Way*, eds. Philip Arestis and Malcolm Sawyer (Cheltenham: Edward Elgar Publishing), 6–7.

Site 1

1 Lily, "Moderna muséet: Lek i plast död i sammet," *Hudiksvallstidningen*, October 21 1968, 5.

2 Michel Foucault, *The Birth of Biopolitics: Lectures at the Collège de France, 1978–1979*, ed. Michel Senellart, trans. Graham Burchell (Basingstoke: Palgrave Macmillan, 2008), 226.

3 On the exhibition Modellen, see Lars Bang Larsen, *The Model: A Model for a Qualitative Society* (Barcelona: Museu d'Art Contemporani Barcelona, 2010); Helena Mattsson, "Demonstrations as a Curatorial Practice: The Swedish Exhibition Scene from She to ARARAT, 1966–1977," in *Exhibiting Architecture: A Paradox?*, eds. Eeva-Liisa Pelkonen,

Carson Chan, and David Andrew Tasman (New Haven: Yale School of Architecture, 2015); Helena Mattsson, "1968 Modellen: En modell för ett kvalitativt samhälle" and "1976 ARARAT," in *Exhibit A. Exhibitions That Transformed Architecture 1948–2000*, ed. Eeva-Liisa Pelkonen (New York: Phaidon Press Ltd, 2018); Maria Lind and Lars Bang Larsen, eds., *The New Model: An Inquiry* (Berlin: Sternberg press, 2020).

4   See for example Jennifer Mack, "Hello Consumer! Skärholmen centre from the Million Program to the mall," in *Shopping Towns Europe: Commercial Collectivity and the Architecture of the Shopping Centre, 1945–1975*, eds. Janina Gosseye and Tom Avermaete (London: Bloomsbury Academic, 2017).

5   Leif Nylén, "Aktioner, alternativ," *Paletten* 29, no. 4 (1968): 12.

6   Bjereld and Demker show how urban criticism was intertwined already with the *Provierörelsen* (related to the Dutch Provo-movement) in 1966, but they did not focus on the urban and environmental like later groups did, such as Action Dialogue. Ulf Bjereld and Marie Demker, *1968: När allt började*, paperback ed. (Stockholm: Hjalmarson & Högberg, 2018), 192. There had been earlier substantial architectural postwar criticism, for example, in relation to the housing situation in the 1950s.

7   The "historical class compromise" was based on inclusion of groups such as radical labor movements but also on gender and racial-ethnic exclusions. See for example Nancy Fraser, *Fortunes of Feminism: From state Managed Capitalism to Neoliberal Crisis* (London: Verso, 2013), 8.

8   See Site 2: The Suburb and Corporatism in this book.

9   The private actors influenced on the heavily criticized modernist housing areas fueled the critique of the welfare state, and the links between architecture and capitalism will be elaborated on in Site 2: The Suburb, cf. Lucy Creagh, "From *acceptera* to Vällingby: The Discourse of Individuality and Community in Sweden (1931–54)," *Footprint* 5, no. 2 (2011): 5–24.

10 See for example Luc Botanski and Eve Chiapello, *The New Spirit of Capitalism* (London/New York: Verso, 2015); Kristin Ross, May '68, and it Afterlives (Chicago: The University of Chicago, 2002). In relation to architecture see for example Tahl Kaminer, *The Efficacy of Architecture: Political Contestation and Agency* (London: Routledge, 2017) and *Architecture, Crisis and Resuscitation, The Reproduction of Post-Fordism in Late-Twentieth-Century Architecture* (London: Routledge, 2011); Douglas Spencer, *The Architecture of Neoliberalism: How Contemporary Architecture Became an Instrument of Control and Compliance* (London: Bloomsbury Academic, 2016). On the Swedish context see for example: Kim Salomon, *Rebeller i takt med tiden: FNL-rörelsen och 60-talets politiska ritualer* (Stockholm: Rabén Prisma, 1996); Kjell Östberg, *När allt var i rörelse: Sextiotalsradikaliseringen och de sociala rörelserna* (Stockholm, Prisma/Södertörns högskola, 2002); Bjereld and Demker, *1968*.

11 Conflicts and distrust in Marxism and other left-wing movements resulted in new ideological formations. Rethinking Marxian materialism in relation to Freud and the role of subjectivity positioned the libidinal as a driving force in society, see for example Herbert Marcuse, *Eros and Civilization: A Philosophical Inquiry into Freud* (New York: Vintage, 1955); Wilhelm Reich, *The Mass Psychology of Fascism* (New York: Orgone Institute Press, 1946); and Erich Fromm, *Marx's Concept of Man* (New York: F. Ungar Pub. Co., 1961); Gilles Deleuze and Félix Guattari, *Anti-Oedipus: Capitalism and Schizophrenia*, trans. Robert Hurley et al. (Minneapolis: University of Minnesota Press, 1996 [1972]) and Jean-François Lyotard, *Libidinal Economy*, trans. Ian Hamilton Grant (Bloomington: Indiana University Press, 1993 [1974]).

Notes

12. Isabelle Doucet, *The Practice Turn in Architecture: Brussels after 1968* (Farnham: Ashgate, 2015), 22–3.

13. Jacques Rancièr and Mark Foster Gage, "Politics Equals Aesthetics: A Conversation Between Jacques Rancièr and Mark Foster Gage," in *Aesthetics Equals Politics: New Discourses Across Art, Architecture, and Philosophy*, ed. Mark Foster Gage (Cambridge, Mass.: The MIT Press, 2019), 22–3.

14. Rhodesia (today Zimbabwe) was a country that had separated from Great Britain under the leadership of Ian Smith in autumn 1965. The country had a race policy similar to South Africa and was not recognized by the UN or the African neighboring countries, but was part of the Internationella Tennisförbundet (International Tennis Organization). The match in Båstad was, after the demonstrations, moved to Bandol on the French Riviera. Interestingly, the attitudes and the strategies shifted drastically from 1968 to 1975 when a tennis match between Sweden and Chile was played at the same place in Båstad. The argument that sport and politics did not belong was absent, and the government stated "play and demonstrate" and encouraged demonstrations at the balconies as a way to reach out to the world. The new strategy was to use media to reach out, and September 20, 1975, calm demonstrations were organized in Båstad with 7 000 participants. Bjereld and Demker, *1968*, 115–16.

15. For a summary of a plenary debate on the "ASEA affair," see "Investering i Moçambique fördöms av regeringen," *Dagens Nyheter*, May 17, 1968, 14. On the radical left and Swedish policies on international development aid in the 1960s, see Annika Berg, Urban Lundberg, and Mattias Tydén, *En svindlande uppgift: Sverige och biståndet 1945–1975* (Stockholm: Ordfront, 2021), 319–25 and part 6.

16. "Partigränser sprängdes i aktion för u-länderna," *Dagens Nyheter*, May 27, 1968, 11.

17. Swedish Parliamentary Papers, Second Chamber Protocols, 1968, no. 24, 44 (for the debate in total, 5–57). After the demonstrations in Båstad a state investigation on the right to demonstrate was instigated, directed by the former head of the Social Democratic Youth League of Sweden Ingvar Carlsson, "Unga till attack mot Erlander: Demonstrationsrätten utreds," *Dagens Nyheter*, May 15, 1968, 1.

18. See for example, "Hermansson i Båstaddebatt 'Nej till våld,'" *Dagens Nyheter*, May 17, 1968, 1, 15; Ivar Lundgren, "Holmberg om regeringen: Oförmögen hejda våldet," *Dagens Nyheter*, June 17, 1968, 7. Also the editorial "Engagerande demokrati," *Dagens Nyheter*, May 17, 1968, 2.

19. Nylén, "Aktioner, alternativ."

20. The concept of an "aggressive consumer" was repeatedly used by Action Dialogue.

21. The origin of the Swedish Children's Day was a country-side summer camp for poor children living in the city organized by Agnes Lagerstedt in 1884. Later festivities were organized to collect money for the camps, and local associations were established all around Sweden. In 1967 the charity organization Barnens Dag (Children's Day) was established.

22. Thomas Wieslander and the organizers of Barnens Dag met at a conference at the Swedish Cooperative Union's conference center Vår Gård in Saltsjöbaden outside Stockholm in 1967. E-mail conversation between Kerstin Wickman and the author, March 26, 2020.

23. Anna Maria Roos, *Hem och hembygd: Sörgården* (Stockholm: Albert Bonniers förlag, 1912).

24. "Lång kö till hölass," *Dagens Nyheter*, August 22, 1968, 19.

25. Thomas Wieslander in "Barnens Dag delvis för barn," *Dagens Nyheter*, August 29, 1968, 24.

26. Inger Wennerlund, "Stora barn ville också ha lekplats," *Dagens Nyheter*, August 28, 1968, 24.

27. Wennerlund, "Stora barn ville också ha lekplats," 24.

Notes

28 The pedagogy as a form of capitalist critique involving children's "play" with reality was popular in certain (often left-wing) spheres in the 1960s, for example AG Spielumwelt at New Society for Fine Arts (nGbK) 1969–72. In 1970 an apartment in Berlin-Schöneberg was turned into a Spielklub where children built a "model city." Claudia Hummel, "Spielklub (Lekklubb) 1970/2020" (lecture, Konsthall C, Hökarängen/Stockholm, August 13, 2021.

29 Wennerlund, "Stora barn ville också ha lekplats," 24.

30 "Här bygger barnen höghus i Vasaparken," *Aftonbladet*, August 28, 1968, 9.

31 "Grattis alla barn 'Kåkstaden' får bli kvar i Vasaparken," *Expressen*, August 30, 1968, 20.

32 "Skräpbacken kvar Byalag i Vasaparken," *Dagens Nyheter*, September 2, 1968, 35. The group met Tuesday September 3, 1968.

33 Johan Huizinga, *Homo Ludens: A Study of the Play-Element in Culture*, (Boston: Beacon Press [1938], 1955); Herbert Marcuse, *One-Dimensional Man: Studies in the Ideology of Advanced Industrial Society* (Boston: Beacon Press, 1964).

34 Marjory Allen, "Why not use our Bomb Sites like this?," *Picture Post*, November 16, 1946, 26–7. For more on the British Adventure Playgrounds see Krista Cowman, "'The Atmosphere Is Permissive and Free': The Gendering of Activism in the British Adventure Playgrounds Movement, ca 1948–70," *Journal of Social History* 53, no. 1 (2019): 218–41; Francis Strauven, *Aldo van Eyck: The Shape of Relativity*, (Amsterdam: Architectura & Natura, 1998), 218–41; Lucie Glasheen, "Bombsites, Adventure Playgrounds and Reconstruction of London," *The London Journal* 44, no. 1 (2019): 54–74; Roy Kozlovsky, *The Architectures of Childhood: Children, Modern Architecture and the Reconstruction in Postwar England* (London: Routledge, 2016).

35 Isabelle Doucet, Tahl Kaminer, Simon Sadler, and Timothy Stott, "The Anarchist Child: Four Readings of The Child in the City" (paper presentation, EAHN Sixth International Meeting, June 2–5, 2021, Edinburgh, online). Cf. Kozlovsky, "Adventure Playgrounds and Post-war Reconstruction."

36 "Kidzania Dubai: An Interactive City, Run by Kids," accessed February 27, 2022, https://dubai.kidzania.com/en-ae/pages/what-is-kidzania. Cf. Priscila Fernandes film "For a Better World" (2012).

37 Sofie Berg et al., "Bygglekplatsen: En möjlighet idag," *Movium Fakta*, no. 2 (2020), accessed June 17, 2021, https://www.movium.slu.se/system/files/news/14473/files/movium_fakta_2_2020-bygglek-final-web.pdf.

38 Cf. Kozlovski, *The Architectures of Childhood*. The anarchist Colin Ward did also see the adventure playgrounds as a political experiment that could show "how subjects are to govern themselves"; see Isabelle Doucet, "Environmental Learning Revisited: Cities, Issues, Bodies," in *Architectural Education Through Materiality: Pedagogies of the 20th-Century Design*, eds. Elke Couchez and Rajesh Heynickx (London: Routledge, 2021).

39 "Forum" (TV-show), Sveriges Television, TV 1, October 1, 1968, 21.40–22.10, Svensk Mediedatabas, Kungliga Biblioteket (Royal Library), Stockholm.

40 The flyer cited in "Aktion Samtal fortsätter," *Dagens Nyheter*, September 23, 1968, 35.

41 Rebecka Tarschys, "Fredlig revolt på Söderbakgård. Staketen revs," *Dagens Nyheter*, September 22, 1968, 42.

42 Tarschys, "Fredlig revolt på Söderbakgård," 42.

43 Sabelle, "Aktion Samtal lovordas—och blir polisanmäld," *Svenska Dagbladet*, September 29, 1968, 29.

Notes

44 *Byggleken* was back at the museum in the end of March 1969, now organized by the museum together with Arkiv Samtal as part of the exhibition "Förbättra din skolgård" (Improve your school yard): "Stadsmuseet bygglekplats," *Dagens Nyheter*, March 29, 1969, 24; Margareta Klingberg, "Först fick barnen bygga det här huset—nu ska de vuxna riva ner det!" *Aftonbladet*, April 8, 1969.

45 The banner appeared at Valla torg in Årsta.

46 *Parklek*, a playground that started as a charity by kindergarten pioneers Maria Moberg and Ellen Moberg in the 1910s. The modern *Parklek* with educated staff started by the City Gardener Osvald Almqvist in 1936. In 1980 Stockholm had 200 staffed *Parklekar*.

47 Rebecka Tarschy, "Miljörevolt på lekplats," *Dagens Nyheter*, September 24, 1968, 32.

48 Tarschy, "Miljörevolt på lekplats."

49 Tarschy, "Miljörevolt på lekplats."

50 Anna-Lena Wik-Thorsell, "Daghemmet—en sluten värld? Fem fick följa med ut i den roliga vuxenvärlden," *Svenska Dagbladet*, September 25, 1968, 18.

51 Wik-Thorsell, "Daghemmet—en sluten värld?," 18.

52 "Upp till miljökamp med Aktion Samtal," *Dagens Nyheter*, September 28, 1968, 27.

53 Sabelle, "Aktion Samtal lovordas—och blir polisanmäld," 29.

54 Lundahl and Nielsen met at the Scandinavian Design Student Organization (SDO) and arranged seminars at Konstfack (University of Arts, Craft and Design) to update the study plans to address current topics such as "the third world," "handicap," "environment," and "communication" with participants such as Victor Papenek and Andrzej Pawlowski. Gunilla Lundahl, "Konsten är aktion. Att göra motstånd i Stockholm i slutet av 1960-talet," in *Konsthantverk i Sverige*, eds. Christina Zetterlund et al. (Tumba: Mångkulturellt centrum, 2015), 107–13.

55 Cf. references in note 3 above.

56 Moderna Museet, *Modellen: En modell för ett kvalitativt samhälle* (Stockholm: Moderna Museet & Bonnier, 1968), 2.

57 Moderna Museet, *Modellen*, 2.

58 See Site 3: The Collective House.

59 Moderna Museet, *Modellen*, 2.

60 Moderna Museet, *Modellen*, 2.

61 André Gorz, *Stratégie ouvrière et néocapitalisme* (Paris: Éd. du Seuil, 1964). Quote from the exhibition catalogue, trans. Lars Bang Larsen, in Larsen, "True Rulers of their Own Realm: Political Subjectivations in Palle Nielsen's The Model—A Model for a Qualitative Society," *Afterall. A Journal of Art, Context and Enquiry*, 16, no. 16 (Autumn/Winter 2007): 123 (120–6).

62 Bjereld and Demker, *1968*, 203.

63 Marianne Kärre, "Lär barn opponera, reagera, inte bara anpassas i grupp," *Dagens Nyheter*, October 14, 1968, 34.

64 Kärre, "Lär barn opponera, reagera, inte bara anpassas i grupp," 34.

65 Åsa Wall, "Lekfull debatt om *Modellen*," *Svenska Dagbladet*, October 16, 1968, 15.

66 Wall, "Lekfull debatt om *Modellen*," 15.

67 Later the organizers managed to exchange the foam-rubber sea with specially designed helter-skelters that allowed the kids to ride together.

Notes

68 It was the research project who financed the exhibition and money was raised from the Ministry of Education, the Swedish Co-operative Union's council for play (KFs lekråd), the local child welfare authority (Barnavårdsnämnden), and the Swedish Council for Building Research (Statens råd för byggnadsforskning). See documentation in The Moderna Museet archives.

69 As I have shown elsewhere the architectural environment as a site for constructing personal experiences counteracting desirable consumerism of commodities can be traced back to earlier exhibitions and architects, such as Sune Lindström. See Helena Mattsson, "Designing the Reasonable Consumer," in *Swedish Modernism: Architecture, Consumption and the Welfare State*, eds. Helena Mattsson and Sven-Olov Wallenstein (London: Black Dog, 2010); Helena Mattsson, "Life as a Full Scale Demonstration: Konsument i oändligheten, 1971," in *Place and Displacement: Exhibiting Architecture*, ed. Thordis Arrhenius (Zürich: Lars Müller, 2014).

70 "Moderna Museet 30 september till 20 oktober 1968: En modell för ett kvalitativt samhälle" (information leaflet), The Moderna Museet archives. For a report from the Modellen see Inger William-Olsson and Stina Sandels, *Fri lek i förskolan* (Stockholm: Lärarhögskolan, 1968). The psychology students Sören Järtby, Suzanne Kaplan, Kerstin Sandqvist, and Ellke Zürcher documented the observations, Marianne Kärre, "Västerås fick Modellen. 'Pyssologer' summerar," *Dagens Nyheter*, October 25, 1968, 39.

71 The psychologists made a summary of the results in the article by Kärre, "Västerås fick Modellen," 39.

72 Hjördis Nilsson, "Om att kräva ansvar och ge förtroende," in *Modellen*, 10.

73 Hans Evert René, "Så gammaldags!" *Expressen*, October 9, 1968, 4.

74 Mats G. Bengtsson, "Alla vuxna är papperstigrar," in *Modellen*, 16.

75 Anette Göthlund, "Arbete i verkstad och zon: Konstpedagogik för barn på Moderna Museet," in *Historieboken: Om Moderna Museet 1958–2008*, eds. Anna Tellgren, Martin Sundberg, and Johan Rosell (Stockholm: Moderna Museet, 2008).

76 Kärre, "Västerås fick *Modellen*," 59.

77 In the beginning of 1969 Action Dialogue changed their working methods from organizing direct actions to setting up an infrastructure supporting others to become activists in their local environments. They constructed an archive with materials from the earlier urban actions, and other activities, and changed the name to Archive Dialogue.

78 Agneta Pleijel and Lars Sjögren, "Arkiv Samtal: Intervju med Anders Svensson mars 1969," *Zenit. Nordisk socialistisk tidskrift*, no. 13 (1969): 36.

79 Pleijel and Sjögren, "Arkiv Samtal," 40.

80 "New York. Stort och vräkigt. Ja. Men billigare än ni tror (Läs vad New York-borna säger!)" [ad by United States Travel Service], *Dagens Nyheter*, March 21, 1969, 14.

81 Nylén, "Aktioner, alternativ," 12.

82 James H. Gilmore and B. Joseph Pine II, "Satisfaction, Sacrifice, Surprise: Three Small Steps Create One Giant Leap into the Experience Economy," *Strategy & Leadership* 28, no. 1 (2000): 18 (18–23). See also James H. Gilmore and B. Joseph Pine II, "Beyond Goods and Services," *Strategy & Leadership* 25, no. 3 (1997): 10–17.

83 Quoted from Stephen V. "Ward's review of Klingmann's Brandscapes: Architecture in the Experience Economy," *Urban Design International* 13, no. 1 (2008): 53.

84 Jacques Rancière quoted in Kristin Ross, *May 68 and Its Afterlives* (Chicago: University of Chicago Press, 2002), 22.

Notes

85 Rancière elaborates about aesthetics as potentially emancipatory when it opposes the old practice of political, not pointing toward what is wrong but affirming what is right. Mark Foster Gage, ed., *Aesthetics Equals Politics: New Discourses Across Art, Architecture, and Philosophy* (Cambridge, Mass.: MIT Press, 2019), 22–3.

86 Philippe Le Goff, "Capitalism, Crisis and Critique: Reassessing Régis Debray's 'Modest Contribution' to Understanding May 1968 in Light of Luc Boltanski and Eve Chiapello's Le nouvel esprit du capitalisme," *Modern & Contemporary France* 22, no. 2 (2014): 232.

87 Sarkozy quoted in Christian Laval, "May '68: Paving the Way for the Triumph of Neoliberalism? Rereading the Event with Foucault and Bourdieu,"*La Deleuziana. Online Journal of Philosophy*, no. 8(2018): 12.

88 Laval, "May '68", 11.

89 Ross, *May 68 and Its Afterlives*, 6.

90 Laval, "May '68", 14.

91 Laval, "May '68", 15–16.

92 Laval, "May '68", 19–20.

93 Luc Boltanski and Eve Chiapello, *The New Spirit of Capitalism* (London: Verso, 2005).

94 Luc Boltanski and Eve Chiapello, "The New Spirit of Capitalism," *International Journal of Politics, Culture, and Society* 18, nos. 3–4, 175–6.

95 Ross, *May 68 and Its Afterlives*, 11–12.

96 Melinda Cooper, Family Values: Between Neoliberalism and the New Conservatism (New York: Zone Books, 2017), 20–21.

97 Rebecka Tarschys, "Kämpa för bättre miljö," *Dagens Nyheter*, November 10, 1968, Sunday supplement, 4–5.

98 Cf. Footnote 11.

99 For a discussion on criticism and criticality in relation to architecture, see Doucet, *The Practice Turn in Architecture*, 21–3.

100 Walter Benjamin, *Illuminations: Essays and Reflections*, trans. Harry Zohn (New York: Schocken Books, 1969), 240.

101 Investigations into systems and structures to be found in nature and in "un-planned" situations were executed by many postwar architects and planners, such as Team X, Cedric Price, and Christopher Alexander. Mark Francis and Ray Lorenzo talk about a "romantic realm" of children participation: children as planners. See Mark Francis and Ray Lorenzo, "Seven Realms of Children's Participation," *Journal of Environmental Psychology* 22, nos. 1–2 (2002): 160.

102 Kozlovsky, "Adventure Playgrounds and Postwar Reconstruction."

103 Priscila Fernandes, "For a Better World."

104 Cf. Foucault, *The Birth of Biopolitics*, chap. 9.

Site 2

*   "The Suburb" is a rewritten version of "Where The Motorways Meet: Architecture and Corporatism in Sweden 1968," in *Architecture and The Welfare State*, eds. M. Swanerton, T. Avermaete and D. van den Heuvel (London: Routledge, 2014).

1 Robert Hartman, "Stopp för mjölken i Skärholmen!," *Aftonbladet*, February 21, 1972, 8.

Notes

2 Aino Karlsson and Anita Sundin, "Ja, det är vi som kallas 'Sveriges negrer,'" *Aftonbladet*, October 27, 1968, Sunday suppl., 2.

3 Lars-Olof Franzén, "Riv Skärholmen," *Dagens Nyheter*, September 10, 1968, 5.

4 Cf. the chapter "Corporatism" in this book.

5 Today in Sweden *utsatta områden* (vulnerable areas) are used by the police to categorize areas that are considered as parallel societies and therefore are treated in ways different from other areas, which is contrary to the earlier idea of a universal welfare. Denmark has drawn the policy around *utdsatte områder*, exposed areas (earlier called "ghettos" in Denmark), even further, and established laws that apply only in these areas. For a contemporary history demonstrating how the residents strikes back, see Mia Arp Fallov and Rasmus Hoffman Birk, "The 'Ghetto' Strikes Back: Resisting Welfare Sanctions and Stigmatizing Categorizations in Marginalized Residential Areas in Denmark," *Nordic Social Work Research*, published online, June 7, 2021, accessed January 21, 2022, https://doi.org/10.1080/2156857X.2021.1937289.

6 See for example research done by Jennifer Mack, Erik Stenberg, Nazeed Lisa Kings. The standard narrative of modernist architects as builders of the Swedish welfare state is to be found in, for example, Claes Caldenby, Jöran Lindwall, and Wilfried Wang, eds., *20th Century Architecture, 4: Sweden* (München: Prestel, 1998). For critical discussions of the narratives of the Swedish Welfare state see "Special Issue: Images of Sweden and the Nordic Countries," *Scandinavian Journal of History* 34, no. 3 (2009); and Urban Lundberg and Mattias Tydén, "In Search of the Swedish Model: Contested Historiography," in *Swedish Modernism: Architecture, Consumption, and the Welfare State*, eds. Helena Mattsson and Sven-Olov Wallenstein (London: Black Dog, 2010).

7 One of the most well-known researchers on modern corporatism is Phillippe Schmitter. See for example Philippe C. Schmitter, "Still in the Century of Corporatism," *The Review of Politics* 36, no. 1 (1974): 85–131; Philippe C. Schmitter, "Reflections on Where the Theory of Neo-Corporatism Has Gone and Where the Praxis of Neo-Corporatism May be Going," in *Patterns of Corporatist Policy-Making*, eds. Gerhard Lehmbruch and Philippe C. Schmitter (London: Sage, 1982).

8 As pointed out by Tom Avermaete and Dirk van der Heuvel the architects "were considered trailblazers of the welfare state that was too bureaucratic, too much one-size-fits-all, and too reformist." om Avermaete and Dirk van der Heuvel, "Obama, Please Tax Me! Architecture and the Politics of Redistribution," *Footprint* 5, no. 2 (2011): 2 (1–4).

9 The Investigation on Industrialisation of Building (Byggnadsindustrialiseringsutredningen) published three committee reports: SOU 1968:3, *Upphandling av stora bostadsprojekt: Delbetänkande avlämnat av Byggindustrialiseringsutredningen* (Stockholm: Inrikesdepartementet, 1968) [Purchasing of Large Housing Projects]; SOU 1969:63, *Rationellt småhusbyggande: Betänkande av Byggindustrialiseringsutredningen* (Stockholm: Inrikesdepartementet, 1969) [Rational Building of One Family Houses]; SOU 1971:52, *Byggandets industrialisering: Betänkande avgivet av Byggindustrialiseringsutredningen* (Stockholm: Inrikesdepartementet, 1971) [Industrialisation of Building].

10 William J. Reilly's planning algorithm from 1931 states that larger centers, cities, or places will have larger spheres of influence than smaller. The law was questioned in the 1960s, by, for example, Melvin Webber's theory of a Non-Place Urban Realm. See Miodrag Mitrašinovic, *Total Landscape, Theme Parks, Public Space* (Aldershot: Ashgate, 2006), 53–4. The quote comes from *Skärholmen* (Stockholm: Svenska Bostäder, 1968), 8.

11 Aina Andersson interviewed by Anders Hedve. Anders Hedve, "Jag älskar Skärholmen," in *Skärholmens Centrum 25 år* (Stockholm: Skärholmens hembygdsförening, 1993), 34.

12 *Skärholmen*, 7.

Notes

13 *Skärholmen*, 5. In 1969 Svenska Bostäder and the architects Boijsen & Efvergren published a catalogue as a proposal for a community center: Wilhelm Boijsen and Dag Efvergren, *Allaktivitetshus i Skärholmen? En debattinledning* (Vällingby: Svenska Bostäder, 1969).

14 Cf, Site 6: The Renewal.

15 "Förslag till Generalplan för Sätra Egendom" (Proposal to General Plan for Sätra Egendom), September 2, 1960, PL 5009, Byggnadsnämndens arkiv, Stockholms stadsbyggnadskontor (The Archive of the Building Committee, The Stockholm Town-Building Office, hereafter BA/SBK).

16 One of its signatories was Gösta Bohman, later to be leader for the Swedish Conservatives (1970-84).

17 Stockholms stads och läns köpmannaförbund, Remissvar till Stockholms stads stadsbyggnadskontor (Submission to Stockholm City Planning Office by Stockholm Retailer's Association), October 3, 1960, 1–6/27-32 PL 5009, BA/SBK.

18 Stockholms handelskammare, Skrivelse till Stockholms stads stadsbyggnadskontor (Submission to Stockholm City Planning Office by Stockholm Chamber of Commerce), October 7, 1960, 4/4. PL 5009, BA/SBK.

19 N.S. Lagerstedt et al., "Angående Generalplan för Sätra" (Regarding the General Plan for Sätra), September 24, 1960, PL 5009, BA/SBK.

20 L. Rydén, I. Lindberg, and L. Person, Stockholm School of Economics, "Skärholmens Centrum," 1963, 370–406, PL 5010, BA/SBK.

21 Cf. Pär Blomkvist, *Den goda vägens vänner. Väg- och billobbyn och framväxten av det svenska bilsamhället 1914-1959* (diss., Stockholms universitet, Stockholm: Symposion, 2001), 18–19; Eva Lindgren, *Samhällsförändring på väg: Perspektiv på den svenska bilismens utveckling mellan 1950 och 1970* (diss. Umeå universitet, Umeå: Umeå universitet, 2010), 19.

22 *Principles for Urban Planning with Respect to Road Safety: The Scaft Guidelines 1968* (Stockholm: The National Road Administration and the National Board of Urban Planning, 1968).

23 Per Lundin, *Bilsamhället: Ideologi, expertis och regelskapande i efterkrigstidens Sverige* (diss., Kungliga tekniska högskolan, Stockholm: Stockholmia förlag, 2008), 33.

24 Blomkvist, *Den goda vägens vänner*, 19.

25 Blomkvist, *Den goda vägens vänner*, 238.

26 This tendency is, of course, not a specific Swedish phenomenon; see for example Alison Smithson and Peter Smithson, "Mobility: Road Systems," *Architectural Design* 28, no. 10 (1958): 385–8; Alison Smithson, ed., *Team 10 Primer* (London: Studio Vista, 1968).

27 Even Smith Wergeland investigates the aesthetic aspects of infrastructure in a Norwegian context; see Wergeland, *From Utopia to Reality: Motorways as a Work of Art* (diss., Arkitektur- og designhøgskolen, Oslo: AHO, 2013).

28 Nationalization has never been an issue in Swedish social democracy, and in practice the Social Democrats have been reluctant to socializations of private companies. Jenny Andersson and Kjell Östberg, *Sveriges historia: 1965–2012* (Stockholm: Norstedts, 2013), 31–2.

29 In fact, the large-scale production of housing had already started before the Million Program. In 1965 90,000 apartments were produced. But the program was a way to secure the production and the large economical subvention over a longer period. Lisbeth Söderqvist has argued that the Million Program is a myth that never existed, because it was a development that started much earlier. Lisbeth Söderqvist, "Programmet som inte finns," *Arkitekten*, September (2008).

30 Kristina Grange, *Arkitekterna och byggbranschen: Om vikten av att upprätta ett kollektivt självförtroende* (diss. Chalmers tekniska högskola, Göteborg: Chalmers, 2005), 53–79.

Notes

31 As cited by Grange, *Arkitekterna och byggbranschen*, 65.
32 Grange, *Arkitekterna och byggbranschen*, 66.
33 Martin Hedenmo and Fredrik von Platen, *Bostadspolitiken: Svensk politik för boende, planering och byggande under 130 år* (Karlskrona: Boverket, 2007), 65–6.
34 Hedenmo and von Platen, *Bostadspolitiken*, 69.
35 As pointed out by Tom Avermaete and Dirk van der Heuvel the architects "were considered trailblazers of the welfare state that was too bureaucratic, too much one-size-fits-all, and too reformist." Avermaete and van der Heuvel, "Obama, Please Tax Me!," 2.
36 Lars Gyllensten, "Riv Skärholmen: Eller rösta bort stadsbyggarna?" *Dagens Nyheter*, September 12, 1968. Gyllensten published two additional articles in *Dagens Nyheter*: September 24, 1968, and October 10, 1968.

Corporatism

1 Philippe C. Schmitter, "Still the Century of Corporatism?," *The Review of Politics* 36, no. 1 (1974): 85–131.
2 Mihaïl Manoïlesco, *Le Siècle du Corporatisme: Doctrine du corporatisme intégral et pur* (Paris: Alcan, 1936). The original edition was published in 1934. Manoïlesco argued that "the ineluctable course of fate involves the transformation of all social and political institutions of our times in a corporatist direction" (quote from Schmitter, "Still the Century of Corporatism?," 85).
3 Schmitter, "Still the Century of Corporatism?," 86.
4 SOU 1990:44, *Demokrati och makt i Sverige: Maktutredningens huvudrapport* (Stockholm: Statsrådsberedningen, 1990).
5 Wolfgang Streeck and Philippe C. Schmitter, "From National Corporatism to Transnational Pluralism," *Politics & Society* 19, no. 2 (1991): 133–64. For a review on the history of corporatism see Oscar Molina and Martin Rhodes, "Corporatism: The Past, Present, and Future of a Concept," *Annual Review of Political Science* 5 no. 1 (2002): 305–31.
6 See for example Leif Lewin, "The Rise and Decline of Corporatism: The Case of Sweden," *European Journal of Political Research* 26, no. 1 (1994): 59–79; Bo Rothstein and Jonas Bergström, *Korporatismens fall och den svenska modellens kris* (Stockholm: SNS Förlag, 1999); SOU 1999:121, Jörgen Hermansson et al., *Avkorporativisering och lobbyism: Konturerna till en ny politisk modell: Demokratiutredningens forskarvolym XIII* (Stockholm: Fakta info direkt, 1999). Erik Lundberg, "Det postkorporativa deltagandet: Intresseorganisationerna i den nationella politiken," in SOU 2015:96, *Låt fler forma framtiden! Forskarantologi: Bilaga till betänkande av 2014 års Demokratiutredning* (Stockholm: Erlanders, 2015), 293–356.
7 Howard J. Wiarda, *Corporatism and Comparative Politics: The Other Great "Ism"* (Armonk: M.E. Sharpe, 1997).
8 Lewin, "The Rise and Decline of Corporatism," 60–1.
9 One of the most well-known researchers on modern corporatism is Philippe C. Schmitter. See for example Schmitter, "Still in the Century of Corporatism?"; Philippe C. Schmitter, "Reflections on Where the Theory of Neo-Corporatism has Gone and Where the Praxis of Neo-Corporatism May be Going," in *Patterns of Corporatist Policy-Making*, eds. Gerhard Lehmbruch and Philippe C. Schmitter (London: Sage, 1982).

Notes

10. SOU 1999:121.
11. SOU 1999:121, 11.
12. This is demonstrated more in detail in other chapters of this book, especially regarding the Million Program but also in relation to housing and domestic work.
13. See more about the Collective Housing Committee on page 72–4, 93.
14. Women's Building Forum's (KBF) response to the interim report by the Governmental Commission on the Plan- and Building ordinance was submitted to the Housing Minister Birgit Friggebo May 25, 1981, and November 8, 1982. WBF handed over the response to the proposal for Hansta. This can be compared with the situation in Holland where women in the 1980s (not specifically in relation to the built environment) achieved formalized arrangements in the Dutch corporatist system, but lost their influence in the 1990s while the gay/lesbian movement had the opposite development, being weak in the 1980s and gaining power in the 1990s. See Robert J. Davidson, "After Accommodation? Inclusion and Exclusion of Emancipation Interests in Dutch 'Democratic Corporatism'," *Acta Politica* 56, no. 1 (2021): 163–80.
15. Lewin, "The Rise and Decline of Corporatism"; on the "intensity problem" Lewin refers to Robert A. Dahl, *A Preface to Democratic Theory* (Chicago: The University of Chicago Press, 1956).
16. SOU 1999:121, 242.
17. For a discussion of this development see Site 4. The Globe, page 108–9.
18. SOU 1999:121,187–238.
19. Maiju Wuokko, "The Curious Compatibility of Consensus, Corporatism, and Neoliberalism: The Finnish Business Community and the Retasking of a Corporatist Welfare State," *Business History* 63, no. 4 (2021): 668–85.

Site 3

1. Dolores Hayden, "What would a Non-Sexist City Be Like? Speculations on Housing, Urban Design, and Human Work," *Signs* 5, no. 3, Suppl. (1980), S170-87.
2. Four years earlier a collective house was exhibited as a doll's house by Helga Henschen and Veronica Nygren at *Det handlar om vårt liv*, Kulturhuset, Stockholm, 1976.
3. For more on *barnrikehus* see for example Ulla Alm, *Cooperative Housing in Sweden* (Stockholm: H.W. Tullberg, 1939), 29–32, published by the Royal Swedish commission for the New York world's fair 1939; Alexander Davidson, *A Home of One's Own: Housing Policy in Sweden and New Zeeland from the 1940s to the 1990s* (Stockholm: Almqvist & Wiksell International, 1994), 76, 91, 96; Eva Rudberg, "Den tidiga funktionalismen: 1930–1940," in *Att bygga ett land: 1900-talets svenska arkitektur*, eds. Thorbjörn Andersson and Claes Caldenby (Stockholm: Byggforskningsrådet, 1998), 94.
4. On the third National Women's Liberation Conference in Manchester 1972 writer and feminist Selma James presented the demand for wages for housewives, and in the mid-1970s the Wages for Housework Campaign took form in different cities in the UK, Italy, and the United States. See also, Louise Toupin, Wages *For Housework: A History of International Feminist Movement 1972–77* (London Pluto Press, 2018); Silvia Federici, *Revolution at Point Zero: Housework, Reproduction, and Feminist Struggle* (Oakland: PM Press, 2020).

5   Gunnar Asplund, Wolter Gahn, Sven Markelius, Gregor Paulsson, Eskil Sundahl, and Uno Åhrén, *acceptera* (Stockholm: Tiden, 1931), 58. For an English translation see Lucy Creagh, Helena Kåberg, and Barbara Miller Lane, eds., *Modern Swedish Design: Three Founding Texts* (New York: Museum of Modern Art, 2008). The other two forms of housing being rental apartments and private houses.

6   See for example Dick Urban Vestbro, *Kollektivhus från enkökshus till bogemenskap* (Stockholm: Statens råd för byggnadsforskning, 1982).

7   I am grateful for the challenging investigations and discussions on intentional communities and collective living provided by the Master students at KTH School of Architecture 2021. I also want to thank Jenny Richards for inspiring and critical discussions on outsourcing, social reproduction, and care as part of her ongoing PhD-project "Outsourcing the Body" at Konstfack/KTH School of Architecture.

8   Nancy Fraser, "Behind Marx's Hidden Abode," *New Left Review*, no. 86 (March/April 2014): 69.

9   Co-housing was popularized by Kathryn McCamant and Charles Durett in McCamant and Durett, *Co-housing. A Contemporary Approach to Housing Ourselves* (Berkeley: Ten Speed Press, 1988). For the use of collaborative house see for example Dorit Fromm, *Collaborative Communities: Cohousing, Central Living, and Other New Forms of Housing with Shared Facilities* (New York: Van Nostrand Reinhold, 1991). For more on the use of terminology see Inga-Lisa Sangregorio, *Collaborative Housing in Sweden* (Stockholm & Borås: The Swedish Council for Building Research, 2000) and Dick Urban Vestbro and Liisa Horelli, "Design for Gender Equality: The History of Co-Housing Ideas and Realities," *Built Environment* 38, no. 3 (2012): 315–35.

10 The leader of the Social Democratic Party, Per Albin Hansson, introduced the concept *folkhemmet* (the People's Home). Swedish Parliamentary Papers, Second Chamber protocol, 1928 no. 3 (January 18, 1928): 9–21.

11 Cf. Dolores Hayden, *The Grand Domestic Revolution: A History of Feminist Design for American Homes, Neighborhoods, and Cities* (Cambridge, Mass.: MIT Press, 1981).

12 For the relation between utopian socialism and Swedish democracy see Yvonne Hirdman, *Att lägga livet tillrätta: Studier i svensk folkhemspolitik* (Stockholm: Carlsson, 1989), 25–62; Yvonne Hirdman, "The Happy 30s: A Short Story on Social Engineering and Gender Order in Sweden," in *Swedish Modernism: Architecture, Consumption and the Welfare State*, eds. Helena Mattsson and Sven-Olov Wallenstein (London: Black Dog, 2010), 69.

13 The awareness of the living environment's impact on the worker's character was spatially articulated in, for example, New Lanark (by Owen in collaboration with Jeremy Bentham). Welfare reforms such as eight hours' labor, eight hours' recreation, and eight hours' rest together with fostering elements such as the Institute for the Formation of Character would create the new society. Owen imagined creating unified social body made of "living machines," similar to the welfare state body smoothly connecting the individual to the larger unity of society. See Cornelia Lambert, "'Living Machines': Performance and Pedagogy at Robert Owen's Institute for the Formation of Character, New Lanark, 1816–1828," *The Journal of History of Childhood and Youth* 4, no. 3: 420 (419–33).

14 Visitors could enter New Lanark after paying tickets, which turned the institution into a lucrative business securing Owen's fortune. Owen has often been understood as a theorist and communistic social reformer, but, as argued by Trincidado and Santos-Redondo, his

Notes

main merit before 1813 was as an entrepreneur. Estrella Trincidado and Manuel Santos-Redondo, "Bentham and Owen on Entrepreneurship and Social Reform," *The European Journal of the History of Economic Thought* 21, no. 2 (2014): 252–77.

15 The first *folkhem* was "Adolf Fredriks folkhem" in Stockholm that opened in October 1898. The first application for a Peoples Home in an apartment on Karlsbergsvägen 16 was rejected in 1897. See *Dagens Nyheter*, November 11, 1897, 2; May 16, 1898, 1. For "The People's Home's Speech" see Swedish Parliamentary Papers, Second Chamber protocol, 1928 no. 3 (January 18, 1928), 9–21.

16 Johan Pries, Erik Jönsson, and Don Mitchell, "Parks and Houses for the People," *Places Journal*, May 2020, accessed April 11, 2021, https://doi.org/10.22269/200512.

17 Pries, Jönsson, and Mitchell argue that when the Social Democrats consolidated their parliamentary power across Scandinavian People's Houses' and People's Parks' functions were absorbed by the agencies of state and local authority planning. Pries, Jönsson and Mitchell, "Parks and Houses for the People," 1.

18 Alva and Gunnar Myrdal, *Kris i befolkningsfrågan* (Stockholm: Bonnier, 1934).

19 Sven-Olov Wallenstein, "A Family Affair: Swedish Modernism and the Administering of Life," *Swedish Modernism: Architecture, Consumption and the Welfare State*, eds. Helena Mattsson and Sven-Olov Wallenstein (London: Black Dog, 2010), 197.

20 Another important aspect of the housing policy was "an integrated market," meaning that private and public rental apartments should be treated the same (after 1974 it also included tenant-owner apartments) and a corporatist system with lease negotiations based on a strong and central tenant's association. Bo Bengtsson, "Sverige: Kommunal allmännytta och korporativa särintressen," in *Varför så olika? Nordisk bostadspolitik i jämförande historiskt ljus*, ed. Bo Bengtsson (Malmö: Égalité, 2006), 101–5.

21 Paula Blomqvist and Joakim Palme, "Universalism in Welfare Policy: The Swedish Case 1990," *Social Inclusion* 8, no. 1 (2020): 114; cf. Bo Rothstein, *Just Institutions Matter: The Moral and Political Logic of the Universal Welfare State* (Cambridge, Mass.: Cambridge University Press, 1998), 18–21; Gøsta Esping-Andersen, *The Three Worlds of Welfare Capitalism* (Cambridge, Mass.: Polity, 1990).

22 Referring to the commons, not as a space with open access, but held and conducted in common by a community. Cf. Elinor Ostrom, *Governing the Commons: The Evolution of Institutions for Collective Action* (Cambridge, Mass.: Cambridge University Press, 1990). See also the research project by Tom Avermaete and Irina Davidovici at ETH Zürich/gta, "Building the Commons: An Alternative Architectural History of the European City," accessed February 1, 2022, https://www.gta.arch.ethz.ch/researchprojects/building-the-commons-an-alternative-architectural-history-of-the-european-city.

23 Claes Caldenby, Pernilla Hagbert, and Cathrin Wasshede, "The Social Logic of Space: Community and Detachment," in *Contemporary Co-Housing in Europe. Towards Sustainable Cities?* (London & New York: Routledge, 2020).

24 Agnes Lagerstedt was influenced by the philanthropist Octavia Hill, who developed housing areas for workers in London. She was the founder of Stockholms Arbetarehem (Stockholm Workers Home) in 1892, which laid the ground for the housing cooperatives at the beginning of the twentieth century: HSB and SKB. Hemgården Centralkök (Hemgården Communal Kitchen) in Stockholm was a rational one-kitchen house with modern technology which had 60 two- to five-room apartments, central heating, central laundry, central bakery, central telephone, and elevator. It was inspired by the German Social Democrat Lily Braun's Haushaltsgenossenschaft consisting of 50–60 households

which was criticized by Clara Zetkin for being reformistic and hindering the revolution. See *Lily Braun, Frauenarbeit und Hauswirtschaft* (Berlin: Buchhandlung Vorwärts, 1901).

25 Vestbro and Horelli, "Design for Gender Equality," 321.

26 It was founded in 1923 by the architect Sven Wallander together with the Swedish Tenants' Organization as a response to the housing crises. The Swedish Tenants' Organization was the most powerful in Europe. Bengtsson, "Sverige," 101–57.

27 Claes Caldenby, *Kollektivhus: Sovjet och Sverige omkring 1930* (Stockholm: Statens råd för byggnadsforskning, 1979); Asplund et al., *acceptera*, 72–4.

28 Alexandra Kollontay (1872–1952) was an ambassador in Stockholm between 1930 and 1945, and before the revolution she resided in Stockholm in 1912 and 1914. Maria Lind, Michele Masucci, and Joanna Warsza, eds., *Red Love: A Reader on Alexandra Kollontai* (Stockholm & Berlin: Konstfack Collection & Sternberg Press, 2020).

29 "Kollektiva huset ökar nativiteten," *Dagens Nyheter*, December 6, 1932, 28.

30 Asplund et al., *acceptera*, 74.

31 Sven Markelius designed a huge collective house site in Stockholm (Alvik) with ten levels of building blocks that was never realized. The architect Hillevi Svedberg designed *Yrkeskvinnors hus*, YK-huset (Professional women's house) together with the architect Albin Stark (realized in 1939).

32 Jacques Donzelot, *The Policing of Families*, trans Robert Hurley (Baltimore: The Johns Hopkins University Press, 1997). First published as *La Police des familles* (Paris: Les Éditions de Minuit, 1977).

33 For example *Yrkeskvinnors klubb* (Professional Women's Club) and *Kvinnliga kontoristers förening* (Women Clerk's Organization). Cf. BiG-gruppen (Elly Berg et al.), *Det lilla kollektivhuset: En modell för praktisk tillämpning* (Stockholm: Byggforskningsrådet, 1982), 17–18.

34 Olle Engqvist was a progressive developer educated both as a building engineer and as an architect and part of Bostadssociala utredningen (The Social Housing Investigation, 1933–47) that started developing the company under another name in 1919. Engqvist was the developer for Kvinnornas hus (1938), Smaragden och Elfvinggården (1940), Lundagård (1941), Mariebergs kollektivhus (1944), Nockeby Familjehotell (1952), Kollektivhuset Blackeberg (1952), Hässelby Familjehotell (1955). These houses were designed by skilled architects such as Backström and Reinius, Erik and Tore Ahlsén, and Sven Ivar Lind.

35 As pointed out by Dolores Hayden, the Swedish model did not sufficiently challenge the exclusion of men from domestic work. Dolores Hayden, *The Grand Domestic Revolution*; Dolores Hayden, "What Would a Non-Sexist City Be Like? Speculations on Housing, Urban Design, and Human Work," *Signs* 5, no. 3, Suppl (1980): S170–87.

36 Bostadskollektiva kommittén (The Collective Housing Committee) consisted of Brita Åkerman, an important opinion leader and initiator of *Hemmens forskningsinstitut* (The Home's Research Institute) in 1944; the liberal politician Yngve Larsson; Rector Ester Arfwedson, Mrs. Rosa Dyring, Mayor August Johnson, Ombudsman Sven Kypengren, and the architect Göran Sidenbladh.

37 The directives to the committee from the Social Ministry quoted in SOU 1952:38, *Hemhjälp. Bostadskollektiva kommitténs betänkande 1* (Stockholm: Socialdepartementet, 1952), 5.

Notes

38　SOU 1952:38, *Hemhjälp* on domestic help; SOU 1954:3, *Kollektivhus*. *Bostadskollektiva kommitténs betänkande II* (Stockholm: Socialdepartementet, 1955) on collective houses; SOU 1955:8, *Tvätt*. *Bostadskollektiva kommitténs betänkande III* (Stockholm: Socialdepartementet, 1955) on laundry; SOU 1955:28, *Samlingslokaler*. *Bostadskollektiva kommitténs betänkande IV* (Stockholm: Socialdepartementet, 1955) on common premises; and SOU 1956:32, *Hemmen och samhällsplaneringen*. *Bostadskollektiva kommmitténs slutbetänkande* (Stockholm: Socialdepartementet, 1956) on home and urban planning.

39　The report *Kollektivhus* (1954) shows ambivalence to the collective house in a universal welfare state policy. SOU 1954:3, *Kollektivhus*, 87.

40　This had been the case since the regulation was instituted in 1942. According to the Collective Housing Committee the typology had successfully been incorporated into existing state policy and public housing companies that acquired or built a collective house could mortgage it to 100 percent, and cooperatives to 95 percent.

41　SOU 1954:3, *Kollektivhus*, 92. In the 1970s norms, recommendations, and regulations on financing were changed; see Bostadsstyrelsen, *God Bostad 5: Kollektivhus* (Stockholm: Bostadsstyrelsen, 1977). It was possible to get a state loan for 10 square meter common space/apartment in a collective house.

42　SOU 1965:32, *Höjd bostadsstandard*. *Betänkande avgivet av Bostadsbyggnadsutredningen* (Stockholm: Inrikesdepartementet, 1965), 502. *Höjd bostadsstandard* (increased housing standard) was the final report from the committee Bostadsbyggnadsutredningen (The House Building Committee), 1957–65, that laid the foundation for the Swedish government program to build one million apartments between 1965 and 1975 (the Million Program) with the architect and director of Statens Planverk (Swedish National Board of Urban Planning) Lennart Holm as the principal investigator.

43　Ingela Blomberg et al., *Levande kollektivhus: Att leva, bo och arbeta i Hässelby familjehotell* (Stockholm: Statens råd för byggnadsforskning, 1986), 147–8.

44　SOU 1968:38, *Boendeservice 1. Fakta och synpunkter sammanställda av den statliga servicekommittén* (Stockholm: Inrikesdepartementet, 1968), 17. Sven Thiberg (who became professor of *byggnadsfunktionslära* at KTH in 1970) was the secretary for the *Service committee* (1967–1973).

45　*Servicekommitténs utlåtande* (Stockholm: Konsum, 1969). The cooperation was inspired by Willy Maria Lundberg's proposal for a *betjäningsknut* (service knot) at Träslottet in Åbro.

46　Rebecka, "Amerikansk arkitekt: Service är en vara som kan bli lockbete," *Dagens Nyheter*, September 3, 1966, 14.

47　See for example SOU 1968:38, *Boendeservice 1*, 10; *Servicekommitténs utlåtande*, 40.

48　Cf. *Kvarteret Fältöversten* (Stockholm: Stockholms Stads Fastighetskontor, 1970).

49　See for example, Eva Eriksson, "Service och gemenskap kräver mycket mindre kollektivhus," *Dagens Nyheter*, March 4, 1976, 4.

50　Ingrid Sjöstrand, *Samhem: En bok om mänsklig miljö i mänsklig skala* (Stockholm: Aldus/Bonnier, 1973).

51　Sjöstrand, *Samhem*; Ingrid Sjöstrand, "Sorthem- eller samhem?" *Dagens Nyheter*, April 18, 1970, 4; Ingrid Sjöstrand, "Samhemmet på väg?" *Arkitekttidningen*, nos. 12–13 (1970): 9–10.

52　See Bostadsstyrelsen, *God Bostad: Förslag den15april1970* (Stockholm: Bostadsstyrelsens tekniska byrå, 1970). Cf. Sjöstrand, *Arkitekttidningen*, no. 12–13 (1970): 17.

Notes

53 Kommunstyrelsens kommitté för kvinnofrågor, *Service och gemenskap där vi bor i Stockholm* (Stockholm: Tiden, 1975); the exhibition *Det gäller vårt liv* that opened on Women's Day March 8, 1976, at Kulturhuset, Stockholm; the debate *Därför kollektivhus!* at Kulturhuset, Stockholm, November 18, 1976.

54 Ann Lindgren, "Alltfler vill bo i kollektivhus: Så här ska de åstadkommas," *Svenska Dagbladet*, May 3, 1976, 16.

55 The legally binding regulations in the Swedish Building Code *SBN 75* did not support collective living and it was not possible to reduce the size or standard of kitchens, hygiene areas, or storage. Instead *God Bostad 5* proposed to use flexible walls. *God Bostad* was a normative collection predating the Swedish Building Code (Svensk Byggnorm, SBN); see more, "The Code" in this book.

56 The Million Program resulted in a complete reversal of the housing situation, from the acute housing shortage in the 1930s, to an over production in the 1970s, and with 20,000 apartments not rented out in 1982.

57 Sten Gromark, *Boendegemenskap: En kritisk granskning av boendegemenskap som samhällsangelägenhet, av dess värden, villkor och förutsättningar samt exempel på praktisk tillämpning i ett västeuropeiskt sammanhang* (Diss., Chalmers tekniska högskola, Göteborg: Chalmers, 1983), 34.

58 "80-talets boendeformer" was a competition organized by Sveriges Arkitekters Riksförbund (Swedish Association of Architects) in collaboration with the municipality of Gävle. For the tendency to stress community building, see Gromark, *Boendegemenskap*, 35.

59 Cf. Gromark, *Boendegemenskap*, 36.

60 Lennart Schön, *An Economic History of Modern Sweden* (London/ New York: Routledge, 2012), 323.

61 Melinda Cooper, "The Blue-Collar Taxpayer - Trump and the Wages of White Men," lecture at the conference *Neoliberalism in the Nordics - Gathering Perspectives*, February 11, 2021.

62 Mario Tronti, "Factory and Society" [1963], trans. Guio Jacinto, *Operaismo in English*, accessed May 1, 2021, https://operaismoinenglish.wordpress.com/2013/06/13/factory-and-society. See also Tronti's, "Capital's Plan" (1963). *Operaismo in English*, accessed May 1, 2021, https://operaismoinenglish.wordpress.com/2010/09/30/social-capital/.

63 Manfredo Tafuri, *Architecture and Utopia: Design and Capitalist Development*, trans. Barbara Luigia La Penta (London: MIT Press, 1976).

64 See for example Mariarosa Dalla Costa, "Women and the Subversion of the Community" (1972), in *Women and the Subversion of the Community: A Mariarosa Dalla Costa Reader*, ed. Camille Barbagallo (Oakland: PM Press, 2019), 17–50: Silvia Federici, "Marx and Feminism," *tripleC* 16, no. 2 (2018): 472–3 (468–75).

65 Silvia Federici, *Revolution at Point Zero: Housework, Reproduction, and Feminist Struggle* (Oakland: PM Press, 2020), 19.

66 Mariarosa Dalla Costa, "Women and the Subversion of the Community."

67 The Swedish public housing system was built upon a public queuing system and the majority of apartments had to be distributed through the public system.

68 The history of Hässelby Familjehotell is based on the research project that followed, what was called "the nine yearlong tenants-experiment" to build up a collective living with shared domestic work. Ingela Blomberg, Irene Goodridge, Bertil Olsson, Gunilla Wiklund, and Pelle Wisten, *Levande kollektivhus. Att leva, bo och arbeta i Hässelby Familjehotell* (Stockholm: Statens råd for byggnadsforskning, 1986).

Notes

69 Aktionsgruppen för kollektivhus (Action Group for Collective Houses), formed in 1968, launched a discussion on collective houses relating to gender equality, collectivity, and community once raised by the collective house theoreticians of the 1930s. After Sandels joined the board it was a goal for the company to sublet the restaurant to external actors for profit.

70 When food service was written into the first-hand contract the resident had the legal right to the restaurant.

71 Vestbro, *Kollektivhus från enkökshus till bogemenskap*; Blomberg et al., *Levande kollektivhus*.

72 Pia Axelsson, "Polischock mot familjehotellet," *Dagens Nyheter*, July 21, 1979, 5.

73 Mullvaden was a housing block in Stockholm that was occupied in 1977 and was brutally taken over by the police in 1978. The occupation was widely discussed in the public press and contributed to a more intense criticism toward housing policy and increasing rents. Another important occupation in Stockholm took place at the housing block Järnet 1978–9. Both Mullvaden and Järnet were built in the end of the nineteenth century and were ultimately torn down.

74 Stockholm City Council Papers 1979, Private member's bill no. 15 (Motion av Gunnar Liedberg, c, angående kartläggning av hittills vunna erfarenheter av kollektivhusboende vid Hässelby familjehotell); Stockholm City Council Papers 1980, Reports and Memorandums no. 72 (Kommunstyrelsens utlåtande med anledning av motion av Gunnar Liedberg), 554.

75 Stockholm City Council Papers 1980, Reports and Memorandums no. 72, 550–1.

76 The 1974 "Women in Architecture" symposium at Washington University in St Louis, USA, was a key reference for the Swedish formation of architectural feminists: Kerstin Kärnekull "The Road to 'Living in Community' and the BIG-Model" (lecture, KTH School of Architecture, Stockholm, 24 February 2021). The Nordic context was important for the feminist movement, that is, Nordiska kvinnors bygg- och planforum (Nordic Women's Building and Planning Forum), that was formed in the late 1970s. In 1986 the women architects' association Athena was formed.

77 Wages for Housework (WfH) was founded by Mariarosa Della Costa and Silvia Federici in 1974. Federici started the New York group called "Wages for Housework Committee" in 1975. See, Silvia Federici, Wages Against Housework, (1975) reprinted in Federici, Revolution at point zero. See also, Louise Toupin, Wages for Housework: A History of an International Feminist Movement, 1972–77 (Vancouver: UBC Press, 2018).

78 Organized by the Swedish Association of Architects *Boplats 80* took place in a tent structure designed by Ralph Erskine in Kungsträdgården, a park in Stockholm city center.

79 Action Archive, "Witness seminar with BiG: Ingela Blomberg, Kerstin Kärnekull, Gunilla Lundahl, Ann Norrby, Inga-Lisa Sangregorio, Sonja Vidén" (seminar, ArkDes, Stockholm, April 12, 2019). See also Meike Schalk, Sara Brolund de Carvalho, and Helena Mattsson, "BiG Living and Working on Community," in *Architecture and Collective Life*, eds. Penny Lewis, Lorens Holm, and Sandra Costa Santos (London: Routledge, 2021).

80 In the early 1990s Sweden had the world's highest level of women in salaried employment. Nermo calls the 1950s and 1960s the housewife era, and he shows that less than 40 percent of all women had paid work between 1940 and 1960. Magnus Nermo, "Hundra år av könssegregering på den svenska arbetsmarknaden," *Sociologisk Forskning* 37, no. 2 (2000): 35–65.

81 Kerstin Kärnekull during, Action Archive, "Witness seminar with BiG."

82 Other important references for BiG were Rachel Carson's *Silent Spring* (Boston: Houghton Mifflin, 1962), which was translated into Swedish in 1963, and Margrit Kennedy's German eco-village Lebensgarten in Steyerberg. Important were furthermore the Longo Maï Co-operative in Limans that spread to Europe and Central America, local Swedish activist groups such as feminist Grupp 8, and the alternative environmental conference Pow Wow in Stockholm in 1972. The concept intermediary level was introduced by the sociologist Rita Liljeström (b. 1928), who published extensively, in English; see for example Rita Liljeström, Gunilla Fürst Mellström, and Gillan Liljeström Svensson, *Sex Roles in Transition: A Report on a Pilot Program in Sweden: International women's year 1975* (Stockholm: Svenska institutet, 1975).

83 Arbetsgruppen Bo i gemenskap (Elly Berg et al.), "Något genast: En lagom vardagsutopi" [competition proposal for HSB:s idétävling] 1979, AM 1995-23 (Lennart Holm's collection), Arkitektur- och designcentrum/ ARKDES (The Collections of The Swedish Centre for Architecture and Design), Stockholm.

84 Arbetsgruppen Bo i gemenskap, "Något genast," 2.

85 See for example Helen Jarvis, "Pragmatic Utopias: Intentional Gender-Democratic and Sustainable Communities," in *Routledge Handbook of Gender and Environment*, ed. Sherilyn MacGregor (London: Routledge, 2017), 447; BiG-gruppen, *Det lilla kollektivhuset*, 120.

86 Arbetsgruppen Bo i gemenskap, "Något genast," 4–5.

87 BiG-gruppen, *Det lilla kollektivhuset*.

88 Claes Caldenby and Åsa Walldén, *Kollektivhuset Stacken* (Göteborg: Korpen, 1984).

89 Social Democrat Mats Hulth was Social Welfare City Commissioner 1976–1982, and Real Estate City Commissioner (fastighetsborgarråd) 1982–1988. Vestbro, *Kollektivhus från enkökshus till bogemenskap*, 328.

90 Helen Jarvis, "Pragmatic Utopias: Intentional Gender-Democratic and Sustainable Communities," in *Routledge Handbook of Gender and Environment*, ed. Sherilyn MacGregor (London: Routledge, 2017), 433–46.

91 Public Housing Sweden, SABO, examined new forms of user influence in the tenancy, and the housing developer Riksbyggen developed "Värmdömodellen," a form of condominium which would be protected against rapid price increase. The cooperation Riksbyggen (still existing) was founded in 1940 by the builders' unions, and all profit goes back to the cooperation. It was owned by nonprofit interest organizations, local organizations (unions and people's movements'), and national organizations (unions and cooperative companies and organizations). For a discussion on collective living, tenures and land ownership, see Pier Vittoria Aureli, et al, "Promised Land: Housing from Commodification to Cooperation," *e-flux Architecture*, December 2019, accessed October 1, 2021. https://www.e-flux.com/architecture/collectivity/304772/promised-land-housing-from-commodification-to-cooperation/.

92 Stockholm City Council Papers 1982, Reports and Memorandums no. 231–41 (Utlåtande med anledning av förslag till avtal mellan kommunen och Svenska Riksbyggen angående anvisningsrätt—återköpsgaranti i enlighet med Riksbyggens modell för spekulationsfri bostadsrätt m. m.), 3607. At the beginning of the 1980s a family must have a yearly income of 200,000 Swedish kronor to afford a condominium in Stockholm City, which was 10 percent of the population. In 1969 the Swedish law against speculation on condominium, *Lagen den 19 juni 1942 (nr 430) om kontroll av upplåtelse och överlåtelse av bostadsrätt*, terminated, with the argument that it was not followed. Seventy percent of all sales of condominiums liable to tax was not declared in the declaration of income according to

Notes

Länsstyrelsen (the Stockholm County Administrative Board): Håkan Bergström, "Länsstyrelsen saknar 40 miljoner: 3 av 4 döljer vinst av såld bostadsrätt," *Svenska Dagbladet*, December 20, 1980, 10. Cf. Bengtsson, "Sverige," 127–8. Unfortunately, no statistics are to be found around the increase of condominium prices before 1996, but the speculation in housing has been an important obstacle for the development of collective housing. See for example the collective house Gebers outside Stockholm.

93 Stockholm City Council Papers 1982, Reports and Memorandums no. 231–41, 3607–8.

94 The research group included Birte Bech Jørgensen, Tarja Cronberg, Hedvig Vetergaard, Sigrun Kaul, Anne Saeterdal, Liisa Horelli, Kirsti Vespä, Ingela Blomberg (BiG), Birgit Krantz and Inga-Liisa Sangregorio (BIG). The subject Building Functional Analysis (BFA) focused on the interaction between humans and the built environment. It started as a research field in the 1950s connected to the need for better living conditions in Sweden and higher standard of housing. Carin Boalt became the first professor in BFA in 1964 and also the first female professor at a Swedish technical university. She initiated a "full-scale laboratory" for experimental research studies. See Ebba Högström, "Building Functional Analysis (BFA) (1964–1985)," in *Bloomsbury Global Encyclopedia of Women Architecture, 1960–2015*, eds. Lori Brown and Karen Burns (London: Bloomsbury, forthcoming).

95 Carson, *Silent Spring*. For models and strategies based on self-organization and decentralization Agnes Heller's and Rita Liljeström's work on everyday life as a process and an agent for change became important references. See Agnes Heller, *Everyday life*, trans. G.L. Campbell (London: Routledge & Kegan Paul, 1984); Rita Liljeström and Edmund Dahlström, *Arbetarkvinnor i hem- arbets- och samhällsliv* (Stockholm: Tiden, 1981).

96 Birgit Krantz, "Kvinnovisioner om ett nytt vardagsliv," *Kvinnovetenskaplig tidskrift* 12, no. 2 (1991): 43–53.

97 Krantz, "Kvinnovisioner om ett nytt vardagsliv," 49.

98 Birgit Krantz, "Sammanfattning," in *Bygga och bo på kvinnors villkor: Rapport fra konferense Rødhus Klit 27–30 august 1981*, eds. Ros-Mari Edström and Kerstin Kärnekull (Stockholm: Nordiska kvinnors bygg- och planforum, 1982).

99 Birte Bech Jørgensen, "Hvorfor gør det ikke noget?" and Charlotte Bloch, "Om forskel mellem det kendte og det endnu-ikke-kendte," in *Hverdagsliv, kultur og subjektivitet*, eds. Charlottee Bloch et al. (København: Akademisk Forlag, 1988).

100 Chris Booth and Rose Gilroy, "Gender-Aware Approaches to Local and Regional Development," *The Town Planning Review* 72, no 2 (2001): 217 (217–42). EuroFem was initially funded by Finland's Ministry of the Environment and was in 1996 rewarded under the European Union's fourth action framework "Equal Opportunities for Women and Men 1996-2000." The project compared a number of European experiments in enhancing citizen and women involvement, such as Frauen-Werk-Stadt in Vienna, Women's Design Service in London, Matrix' Planning For Real school in London, Women's House in Kokkola, and Northern Feminist University in Norway.

101 Booth and Gilroy, "Gender-Aware Approaches to Local and Regional Development," 229.

102 Minna Salmi and Riitta Kivimäki, cited in Booth and Gilroy, "Gender-Aware Approaches to Local and Regional Development," 219.

103 The quote is from an advertisement for the competition; see for example "Var med i kollektivhustävlingen!," *Svenska Dagbladet*, November 5, 1980, 8.

104 The competition was followed by an exhibition, with public debates and talks at Kulturhuset, gathering 20,000 visitors over 20 days. Stockholm City Council Papers

Notes

1983, Reports and Memorandums, Annex no. 57 (Kommunstyrelsens utlåtande och memorial, bihang nr 57: "Kollektivt boende i Stockholm: En slutrapport från kollektivhuskommittén"), 7.

105 Stockholm City Council Papers 1983, Reports and Memorandums, Annex no. 57, 10–11.

106 Vestbro and Horelli, "Design for Gender Equality," 328.

107 Färdknäppen (the Swedish expression for having a small drink before travel, or having sex to start a delivery) has lately reached international attention; see for example Michael LaFond ed., *Co-housing Cultures: Handbook for Self-Organized, Community-Oriented and Sustainable Housing* (Berlin: Jovis Verlag, 2012), discussing nine very different examples of co-housing cultures in practice, among them Färdknäppen in Stockholm. For more about Färdknäppen, see Schalk, Brolund de Carvalho and Mattsson, "BiG Living and Working on Community."

108 Gunilla Lundahl and Inga-Lisa Sangregorio, *Femton kollektivhus: En idé förverkligas* (Stockholm: Statens råd för byggnadsforskning, 1992).

109 Mats Egelius, "BiG prisar de små kollektivhusen," *Arkitektur*, no. 5 (1993): 60–1.

110 Michel Foucault, *History of Sexuality, vol. 1: An Introduction*, trans. Robert Hurley (New York: Pantheon Books, 1978); Donzelot, *The Policing of Families*.

111 Cf. Caldenby et al., "The Social Logic of Space."

112 For example, Inga-Lisa Sangregorio reflected on collective living as a threat toward our society after a debate on Kulturhuset in 1976. She referred to the military psychologist Jan Agrell, who argued that the future in Sweden looked bad when big-families and collective owning destroyed the will to carry weapon: Inga-Lisa Sangregorio, "Att bo kollektivt: Ett hot mot vårt samhälle?" *Dagens Nyheter*, November 27, 1976, 35.

113 Dick Urban Vestbro in "I välfärden. Är kollektivhus lösningen på det allt dyrare boendet?" (radio program), Swedish Radio, Channel 1, June 5, 1982, Svensk Mediedatabas, Kungliga Biblioteket (Royal Library), Stockholm.

114 Sidenbladh's statement was followed up by Brita Åkerman, who introduced the radical idea to collaborate around housework: "Would it be so unreasonable if the men in the collective houses undertook to invest some free time for common collective service (service in the restaurant, washing dishes, cleaning, going through all the floors of the house with floor cleaners and vacuum cleaners)?" Riksarkivet (The Swedish National Archives), Bostadskollektiva kommittén, SE/RA/321678, box 41, Minutes, March 3, 1949, 2–3.

115 Bostadsstyrelsen, *God Bostad* 5, 8.

116 Helena Ekstam, *Trångboddhet: Mellan bostadsstandard och boendemoral* (diss., Uppsala University, Uppsala: Acta Universitatis Upsaliensis, 2016), 22–3.

117 Helena Ekstam, "Om trångboddhet: Hur storleken på våra bostäder blev ett välfärdsproblem," *Sociologisk Forskning* 50, nos. 3–4 (2013): 217–18 (199–222).

118 Ekstam, *Trångboddhet*, 48–50.

119 Magnus Dahlstedt, "The Politics of Activation: Technologies of Mobilizing 'Multiethnic Suburbs' in Sweden," *Alternatives: Global, Local, Political* 33, no. 4 (2008): 481–504. For a discussion on the politics of activations and responsibilization, see Site 6: The Renewal.

120 The collective house is embedded in political inquiries, economic calculations, architectural layouts, emancipatory struggles, and urban planning by engaging all three poles of Fraser's triple movement—the market, social protection, and emancipation (cf. chapter Emancipations).

Notes

121 Premilla Nadasen, "How Capitalism Invented the Care Economy," *The Nation*, July 16, 2021, accessed October 3, 2021, https://www.thenation.com/article/society/care-workers-emotional-labor/.

122 Jenny Andersson, *The Library and the Workshop: Social Democracy and Capitalism in the Knowledge Age* (Stanford: Stanford University Press, 2010), 27.

123 Ronen Shamir, "The Age of Responsibilization: On Market-Embedded Morality," *Economy and Society* 37, no. 1 (2008): 1–19. For more on devolution and neoliberalization see Wendy Brown, *Undoing the Demos: Neoliberalism's Stealth Revolution* (New York: Zone Books, 2015), 132.

Human Capital

1 Gary Becker (1930–2014), a former student of Milton Friedman and professor at Chicago School of Economics. Gary Becker, *Human Capital: A Theoretical and Empirical Analysis, with Special Reference to Education* (New York: Columbia University Press, 1964). On the Third Way and "human capital" cr. Jenny Andersson, *The Library and the Workshop: Social Democracy and Capitalism in the Knowledge Age* (Stanford: Stanford University Press, 2010).

2 Theodore Schultz (1902–98), professor at Chicago School of Economics who received the Nobel Prize three years after the leader of the second-generation Chicago School of Economics, Milton Freedman (an award that was met by protests internationally). Theodore Schultz, *The Economic Value of Education* (New York: Columbia University Press, 1963); Theodore Schultz, *Investment in Human Capital: The Role of Education and of Research* (New York: New York Press, 1971).

3 Nils-Erik Sandberg, "Mänskligt beteende i ekonomisk analys," *Dagens Nyheter*, October 14, 1992, 2; Johan Schück, "Talar inte politik," *Dagens Nyheter*, December 8, 1992, C 2.

4 Adam Smith, *Wealth of Nations* (Chicago: University of Chicago Press, 1981 [1776]), 368 and 145 respectively. See also Joseph J. Spengler "The Invisible Hand and Other Matters. Adam Smith on Human Capital," *The American Economic Review* 67, no. 1 (1977): 32–6.

5 Gary Becker, *Human Capital: A Theoretical and Empirical Analysis, with Special Reference to Education*, 3rd ed. (Chicago: The University of Chicago Press, 1993), 16.

6 Foucault, *The Birth of Biopolitics: Lectures at the Collége de France, 1978–1979*, ed. Michel Senellart (Basingstoke: Palgrave Macmillan, 2008), 219–33.

7 Cf. Orsi Husz and Nikolas Glover, "Between Human Capital and Human Worth: Popular Valuations of Knowledge in 20th-Century Sweden," *Scandinavian Journal of History* 44, no. 4 (2019): 484–509.

8 According to Foucault, Theodore Schultz opened the field of research on human capital with, "The Emerging Economic Scene and its Relation to High School Education," in *The High School in a New Era. Papers Presented at the Conference on the American High School at the University of Chicago, October 28–30, 1957*, eds. Francis S. Chase and Harold A. Anderson (Chicago: University of Chicago press, 1958), see Foucault, *The Birth of Biopolitics*, 235, footnote 17. Other canonical texts on human capital are Jacob Mincer, "Investment in Human Capital and Personal Income Distribution," *Journal of Political Economy* 66, no. 4 (1958): 281–302; Gary Becker, "Investment in Human Capital: A Theoretical Analysis," *Journal of Political Economy* 70, no. 5, part 2 (1962): 9–49.

9 Foucault, *The Birth of Biopolitics*, 226.

Notes

10 Lennart Schön, *En modern svensk ekonomisk historia: Tillväxt och omvandling under två sekel* (Stockholm: SNS förlag, 2000), 508–17.

11 Joseph Schumpeter (1883–1950), political economist and professor at Harvard University influential in the field of innovation and entrepreneurship. Joseph Schumpeter, *Business Cycles: A Theoretical, Historical, and Statistical Analysis of the Capitalist Process* (New York: McGraw-Hill, 1939).

12 As part of branding Sweden as an IT nation the Swedish prime minister Carl Bildt sent the first e-mail between two Heads of Governments to Bill Clinton in 1994.

13 Andersson, *The Library and the Workshop*. See the chapter "The Political Economy of Knowledge," 24–43.

14 Andersson, *The Library and the Workshop*, 27.

15 *Löntagarfonder* (Wage Earner Funds) were invented by the labor movement's leading economist Rudolf Meidner in the 1970s.

16 For a history of the Knowledge Foundation, see Daniel Holmberg and Sverker Sörlin, *Förnyare i forskningslandskapet: KK-stiftelsen 1994–2019* (Stockholm: KK-Stiftelserna, 2019).

17 *God Bostad* (Good Housing) was a collection of regulations for domestic spaces published by the National Housing Board; it was valid 1954–67. See "The Code" in this book.

18 James S. Coleman, "Social Capital in the Creation of Human Capital," *American Journal of Sociology* 94 (Supplement 1988): S95–S120; James S. Coleman, *Foundations of Social Theory* (Cambridge Mass.: Harvard University Press, 1990). Pierre Bourdieu added the concept of cultural and social capital to human capital as a critique of the monetary view on human capital (by Schultz and Becker), but his theory of social capital is fundamentally different from Coleman's theory. If Coleman's social capital is a collective asset of a group (with the famous example of London/New York diamond merchants), for Bourdieu it is analyzed in relation to power, status, and inequality. Pierre Bourdieu, "The Forms of Capital," in *Handbook of Theory and Research for the Sociology of Education*, ed. John G. Richardson (Westport: Greenwood Press, 1986), 241–58. Robert Putnam popularized social capital in the early 1990s, and proposed social capital as a public good in his book *Bowling Alone: The Collapse and Revival of American Community* (New York: Simon & Schuster, 2000).

19 Coleman, *Foundations of Social Theory*, 304.

20 Andersson, *The Library and the Workshop*, 40–1.

21 Håkan Forsell, (ed.), *Den kalla och varma staden: Migration i stadsförändring i Stockholm efter 1970* (Stockholm: Stockholmia förlag, 2008), 9. Cf. David Harvey's discussions on entrepreneurial urban governance in "From Managerialism to Entrepreneurialism: The Transformation in Urban Governance in Late Capitalism," *Geografiska Annaler* 71, no. 1 (1989): 3–18. See also Neil Brenner, *New State Spaces: Urban Governance and the Rescaling of Statehood* (Oxford: Oxford University Press, 2004).

22 The committee's task was to investigate the dynamic role the city had on societal transformations: SOU 1989:68, *Storstadens partier och valdeltagande 1949–1988: Underlagsrapport från Storstadsutredningen* (Stockholm: Statsrådsberedningen, 1989), 11. Quoted in Forsell, *Den kalla och varma staden*, 9.

23 See chapter 4 "Urban Governance and the Nationalization of State Space: Political Geographies of Spatial Keynesianism" in Brenner, *New State Spaces*.

24 See Site 4: The Globe, and Site 5: The Postmodern Housing Area.

25 Cr. Andrea Muehlbach, *The Moral Neoliberal. Welfare and Citizenship in Italy* (Chicago: The University of Chicago Press, 2012). For more on the topic see Site 6: The Renewal.

Notes

26 For more on responsibilization, see Wendy Brown, *Undoing the Demos: Neoliberalism's Stealth Revolution* (New York: Zone Books, 2015), 133; Kelly Hannah-Moffat, *Punishment in Disguise: Penal Governance and Federal Imprisonment of Women in Canada* (Toronto: University of Toronto press, 2001); Ronen Shamir, "The Age of Responsibilization: On Market-Embedded Morality," *Economy and Society* 37, no. 1 (2008): 1–19. See also Site 6 in this book.

27 Andersson, *The Library and the Workshop*, 157.

Site 4

* "The Globe" is a version of "Third Way Architecture: Stockholm Globe City," *Journal of Architecture*, no. 7 (2016): 118–41. Reproduced by permission of Taylor & Francis Group.

1 Cartoon series "James Hund och den djävulska stadsplanen" (James the Dog and the city plan from hell) by Jonas Darnell and Patrik Norrman, *Dagens Nyheter*, August 18, 1991. A version of this chapter has been published in *Journal of Architecture*: "Third Way Architecture: Stockholm Globe City," *Journal of Architecture* 21, no. 1 (2016): 118–41.

2 Peter Celsing, who designed *Kulturhuset* in Stockholm, made this proposal for a cultural house in Sundsvall in the North of Sweden but it was never realized.

3 It was a dominant opinion in Swedish 1980s architectural discourse to resist international postmodernism and instead argue for leaving the rational functionalism behind through returning to its roots and starting all over again. See for example Christina Pech, "Arkitekturmuseets utställning Funktionalismens genombrott och kris: Ett bidrag till historieskrivningen om svensk 1900-tals arkitektur," in *Forskning i centrum*, ed., Monica Sand (Stockholm: Arkdes, 2014); Helena Mattsson, "Revisiting Swedish Postmodernism: Gendered Architecture and Other Stories," *Journal of Art History* 85, no. 1 (2016): 109–25.

4 Allan Pred, *Recognizing European Modernities: A Montage of the Present* (London: Routledge, 1995), 196.

5 Catharina Gabrielsson, "Through the Anxieties of Style: The Riggering of Neoliberalism and the New Vasa Museum in Stockholm," in *Neoliberalism on The Ground: Architecture and Transformation From the 1960s to the Present*, eds. Kenny Cupers, Catharina Gabrielsson and Helena Mattsson (Pittsburgh: University of Pittsburgh Press, 2020), 84.

6 Vällingby (1954) was the first ABC suburb to be completed, with similarities to the slightly earlier Stevenage New Town outside London. Sven Markelius drew up the plan for the area and Backström & Reinius designed the buildings.

7 "Official statement: City of Stockholm," February 14, 1985, 1, box F4f:3, Trafikkontoret och exploateringskontorets arkiv, Stockholms fastighetskontors arkiv, Stockholm (The Archive of the Stockholm Real Estate Department, The Archive of the Traffic Department, hereafter TEA/SFA) Site 5: The Postmodern Housing Area shows how postmodernism was a tool for the City to control private capital.

8 For more about the Swedish Third Way policy see "Introduction" in this book.

9 Scott Lash and Celia Lury, *Global Culture Industry: The Mediation of Things* (Cambridge: Polity, 2007), 7.

10 Jenny Andersson, *The Library and the Workshop: Social Democracy and Capitalism in the Knowledge Age* (Stanford: Stanford University Press, 2010), 27. Cf. the chapter "Human Capital" in this book.

11 See Valery Didelon, "Surfing the Wave of Neoliberalism: Rem Koolhaas in Lille," in *Neoliberalism on The Ground*, eds. Cupers et. al., 257–70; Rem Koolhaas, "Bigness

or the Problem of Large," in Rem Koolhaas, *Small Medium, Large, Extra-Large* (New York: Monacelli, 1995), 495–516; Brian Edwards, *London Docklands: Urban Design in an Age of Deregulation* (Oxford: Butterworth Architecture, 1992); Theresa Erin Enright, "Illuminating the Path to Grand Pari(s): Architecture and Urban Transformation in an Era of Neoliberalization," *Antipode* 46, no. 2 (2014): 382–403.; Maria Hellström Reimer, "Playing the Green Card — The Commodifying Fiction of a Derivative *Jardin-Forêt*," *Architecture and Culture* 5, no. 2: 279; Jesper Blomberg, *Ordning och kaos i projektsamarbete* (Stockholm: EFI, 1995), and Kerstin Sahlin, *Oklarhetens strategi: Organisering av projektsamarbete* (Lund: Studentlitteratur, 1989).

12   Cf. Ian Borden, "The Limehouse Link: The Architectural and Cultural History of a Monumental Road Tunnel in London's Docklands," *The Journal of Architecture* 21, no. 4 (2016): 651–75.

13   Kjell Nilsson, "Sverige missar VM i hockey," *Dagens Nyheter*, July 1, 1984, 33.

14   Kjell Nilsson, "Kommunen hämtar inspiration från Nordamerika: 'Hovet' får ansiktslyftning," *Dagens Nyheter*, September 11, 1984, 34.

15   Kjell Nilsson, "Stockholm får VM-om fyra år," *Dagens Nyheter*, April 27, 1985, 36.

16   Sverker Ottander, "Besluten kring Globen-projektet" (seminar paper, Dept. of Human Geography, Stockholm University, 1988), 2.

17   Randi Mossige-Norheim argues that the City officers and directors were able to satisfy both keen supporters of congress halls, inspired by the halls in Europe, and those of "city satellites" in the project. Randi Mossige-Norheim, "Globen: Storföretagens lekstuga," *Folket i bild/Kulturfront*, no. 23 (1988): 3.

18   "Official statement: City of Stockholm," February 14, 1985, 3, box F4f:3, Trafikkontoret och exploateringskontorets arkiv, Stockholms fastighetskontors arkiv, Stockholm (The Archive of the Stockholm Real Estate Department, The Archive of the Traffic Department, TEA/SFA). The City Council decided that the Local Planning Committee together with the Committee for Recreational Activities should investigate how *cityfilialerna* could be developed.

19   *Framtiden i folkets händer: Socialdemokratiskt program för medborgarskap och valfrihet* (Stockholm: Tiden, 1984).

20   "Kreativ finansiering: En förutsättning för Globen-projektet" [ad by Stadshypotek], *Dagens Nyheter*, September 10, 1988. Creative financing was a concept used by the state-owned PK Finans in ads for a campaign with the same name starting in 1979 and was running at least until 1986. In 1983 the governmental report *Creative Financing* was published and the government introduced measures to improve conditions for small and medium-sized enterprises in 1982 "[T]he measures have also attracted attention abroad and are considered to have made Sweden, together with France and the UK, a pioneering country in Europe as a promoter of venture capital investments and entrepreneurial spirit." SOU 1983:59, *Kreativ finansiering: Slutbetänkande av utredningen angående de små och medelstora företagens finansiella situation* (Stockholm: Finansdepartementet, 1983), 21.

21   "Official statement: City of Stockholm," February 14, 1985, 6, box F4f:3, TEA/SFA.

22   Blomberg, *Ordning och kaos i projektsamarbete;* Sahlin *Oklarhetens strategi*.

23   The architects working with the Globe project at Berg Arkitektkontor were Svante Berg, Lars Vretblad and Esbjörn Adamson. For an in-depth description of the process leading up to the first proposal by Berg Arkitektkontor see Blomberg, *Ordning och kaos i projektsamarbete*, 110–11. The final group consisted of Scandiaconsult AB (the leaders) and ABV as builder, Berg Arkitektkontor as architects, and EKF/Stockholms Badhus as financiers and property

Notes

managers. The other groups invited were: Skandia/JCC and the architects FFNS; Diös/Fabege/SPP and the architects Malmquist & Skoog Arkitektkontor AB together with Skidmore, Owing & Merill; SIAB and the architects Rosenberg & Ståhl together with Rocco Compagnone; Skanska and the architects VBB. "Official statement: City of Stockholm," February 14, 1985, 8, box F4f:3, TEA/SFA.

24 "Dokumentationen om vår grupps medverkan i Hovetprojektet," letter sent from G. Eklund and G. Ahlberg, Scandiaconsult AB, to the City of Stockholm, July 1, 1985, Files from Berg Arkitektkontor (currently in the authors possession).

25 Svante Berg (architect in charge), interview by the author, Stockholm, March 6, 2010.

26 Maria Kaika, "Autistic Architecture: The Fall of the Icon and the Rise of the Serial Object of Architecture," *Environment and Planning D: Society and Space* 29 (2011): 968–92.

27 Svante Berg, "Paper No.16 The Stockholm Globe Arena Project," [SB35-/rd], March 22, 1989, 16, Files from Berg Arkitektkontor (currently in the authors possession).

28 The new group took the name "Consortium Hovet" consisted of ABV and Berg Arkitektkontor from the old group; the building constructor ByggPaul AB the real estate developers Anders Nisses AB; SABA; SIAB; property manager Stancia Förvaltnings AB; the insurance company Valand Försäkringsbolaget. Blomberg, *Ordning och kaos i projektsamarbete*, 115–16.

29 Blomberg, *Ordning och kaos i projektsamarbete*, 120.

30 Blomberg, *Ordning och kaos i projektsamarbete*, 120.

31 "Projekttävling för Johanneshovs sport- och kulturcentrum: Tävlingsjuryns utlåtande," May 20, 1986, 6, box F4f:8, TEA/SFA.

32 *Johanneshovs sport- och kulturcentrum: Tävlingsprogram Stockholm 25 mars 1985* [Competition Brief] (Stockholm: Fritidsförvaltningen, Fastighetskontoret & Stadsbyggnadskontoret, 1985), 7, Files from Berg Arkitektkontor (currently in the authors possession); *Nya "Hovet": Sport och kulturcentrum* [pamphlet] (Stockholm: City of Stockholm, 1985), Files from Berg Arkitektkontor (currently in the authors possession).

33 Vänsterpartiet kommunisterna (The Communist Party) in the City council reacted strongly and had reservations against the proposal and the process: "Building facilities like this must first be a concern for the local authority, not profitable business for the building capital. The local authority must not lose its urban planning initiative." "Official statement 1986:90 RVIII," 6, box: F4f:3, TEA/SFA.

34 *Johanneshovs sport- och kulturcentrum* [Competition Brief], 17.

35 The economical transactions around the project are secret and no exact sums are public, neither from the city nor from the consortium. Even if it was forbidden for the city to trade with construction rights, that was what happened all through the project. After the contract was signed the City even ordered extra things that they later traded with more rights to build. Ottander, "Besluten kring Globen-projektet," 19.

36 The negotiations are documented in "the general agreements and sub agreements for the development of Johanneshov's sport and culture centre and the commercial buildings" from 1986, box F4f:14, TEA/SFA. The final founding principles are stated in the protocol from a meeting at SIAB with the consortium Hovet and representatives from Stockholm City, February 13, 1986, box: F4f:14, TEA/SFA.

37 Koolhaas, *Small, Medium, Large, Extra-Large*, 1208.

38 Svante Berg (architect in charge), interview by the author, Stockholm, 6 March 2010.

39 The Stockholm City Planning Office, "Beskrivning av utvärderingen av projekttävling för Johanneshovs sport- och kulturcentrum," January 1, 1986, Files from Berg Arkitektkontor (currently in the authors possession).

40 Helena Björkman and Martin Nauclér, eds., *Stockholm Globe Arena: A Document on its Conception and Creation* (Stockholm: Byggförlaget, 1989).

41 The workers completed the Globe in secret, ahead of schedule, and a surprised leadership could read in one of the largest evening papers the following morning: "Now the hat is on—Globen round as ball already yesterday." Eric Hörnfeldt, "Hatten är på: Globen rund som ett klot redan igår," *Expressen*, December 31, 1987, 24–5.

42 Blomberg, *Ordning och kaos*; Helen Runting and Fredrik Torisson, "Managing the Not-Yet: The Architectural Project under Semiocapitalism," *Architecture and Culture* 5, no. 2 (2017): 213–20.

43 See for example Philippe C. Schmitter, "Still in the Century of Corporatism," *The Review of Politics* 36, no. 1 (1974): 85–131; Philippe C. Schmitter, "Reflections on Where the Theory of Neo-Corporatism has Gone and Where the Praxis of Neo-Corporatism May be Going," in *Patterns of Corporatist Policy-Making*, eds. Gerhard Lehmbruch and Philippe C. Schmitter (London: Sage, 1982); Bo Rothstein, *Den korporativa staten: Intresseorganisationer och statsförvaltning i svensk politik* (Stockholm: Norstedts juridik, 1992). Cf. the chapter "Corporatism" in this book.

44 SOU 1999:121, Jörgen Hermansson et al., *Avkorporativisering och lobbyism: Konturerna till en ny politisk modell: Demokratiutredningens forskarvolym XIII* (Stockholm: Fakta info direkt, 1999), 11.

45 SOU 1999:121, 187–238.

46 *Offentlighetsprincipen: Kortfattat om lagstiftningen* (Stockholm: Justitiedepartementet, 2015), 4.

47 "The Globe is not a result of town planning worth its name, but of negotiations between a handful of local authority politicians and the businesses that are responsible for the constructions and the financing." Quote from Thomas Hall, "En rymdålderns Hattstuga," *Dagens Nyheter*, February 12, 1989. Eva Eriksson discusses the new planning methods marked by negotiations as something that limits the democratic processes in planning: Eva Eriksson, "Mot 1990-talet: Debatt vid Samfundet St Eriks höstmöte i Musikaliska akademin 18 november 1987," in *Stad i förvandling: Stockholms utveckling från 1930-tal till 1990-tal: Sankt Eriks årsbok*, ed. Björn Hallerdt (Stockholm: Samfundet S: tErik, 1988), 105–8. That the economical transactions and discussions were held behind locked doors was criticized by for example Thomas Paulsson in "Shakespeares teater inspirerade Globen," *Göteborgs-posten*, February 19, 1989, and Ottander, "Besluten kring Globen-projektet," 22–3.

48 "Official statement: City of Stockholm," February 14, 1985, 8, box F4f:3, TEA/SFA. The competition was open to everyone, but only the invited groups were paid a fee. Ingemar Josefsson argued that this was a way to secure serious proposals from the companies involved. Memorandum, November 29, 1984 (ibid. 7).

49 Minutes from the expert group meeting, no 3, August 27, 1985, 2, box F4f:8, TEA/SFA.

50 Minutes from the expert group meeting, no 3, August 27, 1985, 2, box F4f:8, TEA/SFA.

51 Time schedule for the competition, February–March, 1985; Approval of the competition brief, March 25 to October 31, 1985; competition, November–December, 1985; evaluation by the jury and a preliminary review of building permissions regarding chosen entries, January–February 1986; negotiations of agreements and decision on the

Notes

winner, March–April, 1986; building start. Official statement, February 14, 1985, box F4f:8, TEA/SFA.

52 Ingemar Josefsson, Memorandum, November 29, 1984, in Official statement: City of Stockholm, February 14, 1985, 6, box F4f:3, TEA/SFA.

53 City board statement 1986:190 RVIII, 1, box F4f:3, TEA/SFA.

54 "The green area around the pond (Slakthusdammen), the area's garden, is to be a high cultivated park. It should be designed as one of the central points in the area." Minutes from the jury meeting, no. 1, 3 March 1985, 3, box F4f:8, TEA/SFA.

55 The permission to start bulldozing was given by the City council in June, and they started on September 10 before any general or detailed agreement was made between the City and the consortium Hovet Centrum AB. Blomberg, *Ordning och kaos i projektsamarbete*, 142. The plan acquired legal force in December 1986; see Ottander, "Besluten kring Globen-projektet," 11. Already in the Official statements from the City, February 14, 1985, it is stated that the construction should be able to start in the spring 1986 and that the new plan would acquire legal force in the summer 1986. "Official statement: City of Stockholm," February 14, 1985, box F4f:3, TEA/SFA. First in 1991 Plan- och Bygglagen (the Planning and building law) was changed, so it was possible to get building permission before the plan had acquired legal force (but it could not be used until after the plan was legally recognized). *Svensk Författningssamling* (Swedish Code of Statues) 1987:10, "Plan och bygglag"; cf. *Svensk Författningssamling* 1991:604, "Lag om ändring i plan- och bygglagen."

56 According to Mossige-Norheim, "Globen: Storföretagens lekstuga," 3.

57 This process is documented in Blomberg, *Ordning och kaos i projektsamarbete*, 127–8.

58 Blomberg in *Ordning och kaos i projektsamarbete*, 127–8.

59 This was commented on in the press, for example Hall, "En rymdålderns Hattstuga"; Mats Edblom, "En boll är en boll är en boll," *Arkitektur*, no. 4 (1989), and Mossige-Norheim, "Globen: Storföretagens lekstuga."

60 City board statement 1986: 190 RVIII, Traffic Administration Office Archive, box F4f:3, 1.

61 Andersson, *The Library and the Workshop*, 40–2.

62 For a discussion on the disciplinary aspects of the event zone see Helena Mattsson, "Staging a Milieau: Surfaces and Event Zones," Jacob Nilsson and Sven-Olov Wallenstein (eds.) *Foucault, Biopolitics, and Governmentality* (Södertörn: Philosophical studies, 2013), 123–32.

63 For example in *Expressen*, January 29, 1989, 6–7; Mossige-Norheim, "Globen: Storföretagens lekstuga," 12; H. Hedberg and L. Claesson, "Samtidens spegelbild," *Arbetaren*, no. 26 (1989): 12.

64 It could be noted that the strategy to sell a "package" is also used in "planning by negotiation": "The initiative is most often taken by an exploiter who comes to the City with a package." Swedish Parliamentary Papers, Government Bill 1990/91:146, "Regeringens proposition om ändring i plan- och bygglagen (1987:19) m.m."

65 Scott Lash and Celia Lury, *Global Culture Industry: The Mediation of Things* (Cambridge, Mass.: Polity, 2007), 4.

66 Manuscript for a slide show, November 27, 1985, Files from Berg Arkitektkontor (currently in the author's possession).

67 Description of the competition project, October 31, 1985, [EA14–9], Files from Berg Arkitektkontor (currently in the authors possession).

68 Edblom, "En boll är en boll är en boll," 31.

69 Edblom, "En boll är en boll är en boll," 31.

70 Boltanski and Chiapello base their analysis on management texts. The study of architecture, on the other hand, broadens the notion of the "new spirit of capitalism" as architecture acts concomitant on different levels (e.g., the social and the artistic). Cf. Luc Boltanski and Eve Chiapello, *The New Spirit of Capitalism* (London: Verso, 2006).

The Code

1 Jamie Peck, Neil Brenner, and Nik Theodore, "Actually Existing Neoliberalism," in *The Sage Handbook of Neoliberalism*, ed. Damien Cahill et al. (New York: OUP, 2010), 3–15.

2 Operative performance-based codes were established in Boverkets byggregler (building codes issued by the National Board of Building) in 1994. The changes to the Swedish Building Code were made under pressure from the European Union, which Sweden joined in 1995. Marja Lundgren, *Performance in the Swedish Building Code* (lic. diss., Kungliga tekniska högskolan, Stockholm: KTH, 2019), 55–60.

3 There are many support structures that follow (and simplify) legal regulations, but also have an impact on the regulations, for example, the standards decided by private actors through SIS (Swedish Institute for Standards), part of ISO (International Organization for Standardization); AMA (Allmän material- och arbetsbeskrivning); and the SfB system, initiated by the national organization for architects SAR (Sveriges Arkitekters Riksförbund). SfB was the basis for the CIB (International Council for Building Research Studies and Documentation) founded in 1953, and later lay the foundations for the UK's first National Building Specifications in 1973. See Erik Sigge, *Architecture's Red Tape: Government Building Construction in Sweden, 1963–1973* (diss., Kungliga tekniska högskolan, Stockholm: KTH, 2017), 78–87.

4 Aggregate Architectural History Collaborative, *Governing by Design: Architecture, Economy, and Politics in the Twentieth Century* (Pittsburgh: PUP, 2012); Rob Imrie and Emma Street, *Architectural Design and Regulation* (Chichester: Wiley-Blackwell, 2011); Lundgren, *Performance*; Michael Osman, *Modernisms Visible Hand: Architecture and Regulation in America* (Minneapolis: University of Minnesota Press, 2018); Peg Rawes, "Housing Bipolitics and Care," in *Critical and Clinical Cartographies: Architecture, Robotics, Medicine, Philosophy*, eds. Andrej Radman and Heidi Sohn (Edinburgh: EUP, 2017); Liam Ross, *Pyrotechnic Cities: Architecture, Fire-Safety and Standardisation* (London: Routledge, 2022); Sigge, *Architecture's Red Tape*; Katie Lloyd Thomas, "Going into the Mould: Materials and Process in the Material Specification," *Radical Philosophy* 144 (2007): 16–25; Katie Lloyd Thomas, "'Of their Several Kinds': Forms of Clause in the Architectural Specification," *arq* 16, no. 3 (2012): 229–37.

5 Imrie and Street, *Architectural Design*, 72.

6 Bengt Larsson, Martin Letell, and Håkan Thörn, eds., *Transformations of the Swedish Welfare State* (Basingstoke: Palgrave Macmillan, 2012), 264.

7 Jamie Peck, *Constructions of Neoliberal Reason* (Oxford: OUP, 2010), 22–3.

8 John Braithwaite uses the term "regulated self-regulation" in *Regulation, Crime, Freedom* (Farnham: Ashgate, 2000) and *Regulatory Capitalism: How It Works, Ideas for Making It Work Better* (London: Edward Elgar, 2009). See also Finn Williams and David Knight, "The Rule of Regulation," public exhibition, Berlage Institute, Rotterdam, November 25–December 19, 2008. See also Imrie and Street, *Architectural Design*, ch. 3; Larsson, Letell and Thörn, *Transformations*, 264.

9 Larsson, Letell, and Thörn, *Transformations*, 264.

Notes

10 "A Triple Movement? Parsing the Politics of Crisis after Polanyi," *New Left Review*, no. 81 (2013), 210–32. Nancy Fraser, *Fortunes of Feminism: From State-Managed Capitalism to Neoliberal Crises* (London: Verso, 2013), 227–41.

11 Byggnads- och brandstadga för rikets städer (1874); Stadsplanelag (1931) and Byggnadsstadga för stad och landsbygd (1931); Byggnadsstadga (1947) and Byggnadslag (1947); Byggnadsstadga (1959); Plan- och bygglag (1987) and Plan- och byggförordning (1987).

12 The performance-based codes were issued in Boverkets byggregler, BBR, in 1994, later changed after Sweden joined the EU in 1995.

13 See Sigge, *Architecture's Red Tape*; Maria Perers, "Inside the Ideal Home: Changing Values in the Politics and Design of Apartment Living in Sweden *c.*1955–1995" (diss., Bard Graduate College, New York, 2019).

14 Lawrence Lessig, *Code: And Other Laws of Cyberspace* (New York: Basic, 1999).

15 *God Bostad* was instigated by Bostadsstyrelsen to regulate domestic space, published 1954 with revisions in 1956, 1960, and 1964. *God Bostad* was in force 1954–67 until *Swedish Building Code 1967* was published (Svensk byggnorm 1967, SBN 67).

16 The prominent architect Lennart Holm was general director of Statens Planverk (Swedish National Board of Urban Planning), 1967–89. Together with Bengt Edman of Villa Göth, he was mentioned by Reyner Banham, *The New Brutalism: Ethic or Aesthetic?* (New York: Reinhold, 1966) as the originator of a "new brutalism."

17 Deviations from the norm were tried out in the housing area Södra Station.

18 This was argued by the Näringslivets byggnadsdelegation (NBD, Business Building Delegation), see SOU 1982:9, *Ny plan- och bygglag: Remissammanställning utgiven av bostadsdepartementet* (Stockholm: Bostadsdepartementet, 1982), 37–8. Similar arguments were used against the older norms and *God Bostad* code; see Gun Sjödin, "Bostadsnormering: I morgon är idag i går," *Att Bo: Tidskrift för Bostadskooperation & Bostadspolitisk Debatt* 22, no. 6 (1972): 17–19; Lennart Holm, "50 år i bostadspolitiken: 40 bak och 10 fram," *SABO Utveckling* 11 (1989): 33–4; Perers, "Inside the Ideal Home," 450–6.

19 Gösta Blücher was one of the officials driving the revision of the building code in the late 1980s and went on to be the general director of the state authority, Boverket, 1988–97.

20 Gösta Blücher, interview by the author, Stockholm, February 18, 2016.

21 Helena Mattsson, "Revisiting Swedish Postmodernism: Gendered Architecture and Other Stories," *Journal of Art History* 85, no. 1 (2016): 109–25.

22 For a discussion of modernism in the Swedish regulations, see Monica Andersson, *Politik och stadsbyggande: Modernismen och byggnadslagstiftningen* (diss. Stockholms universitet, Stockholm: Stockholms universitet, 2009).

23 SOU 1979:66, *Ny plan- och bygglag, ii: Betänkande av PBL-utredningen: Markanvändning och byggande* (Stockholm: Bostadsdepartementet, 1979), 271; Lennart Holm et al., *Förslag till ändring av normerna för bostäder* (Stockholm: Statens Planverk, 1982), 2.

24 Greg C. Foliente, "Developments in Performance-based Building Codes and Standards," *Forest Products Journal* 50, no. 7/8 (2000): 12–21 at 12.

25 *BABS* (1946, 1950, 1960) and SBN (1967, 1975, 1980) were instigated by Kungliga Byggnadsstyrelsen and directed toward constructions and materials, while *God Bostad* (1954, 1956, 1960, 1964) was instigated by Bostadsstyrelsen.

26 "Introduction to Svensk Byggnorm 1967," in *Svensk byggnorm 67: Föreskrifter, råd och anvisningar för byggnadsväsendet utfärdade med stöd av 76 § byggnadsstadgan/BABS 1967*

(Stockholm: Statens Planverk, 1968), 519. *Svensk byggnorm 67* was published by the new authority, Statens Planverk (SPV, Swedish National Board of Urban Planning). When SPV was set up, the state loan system was changed and the two publications *BABS* and *God Bostad* were merged into the new Swedish Building Codes, SBN 67. For deciding on the Swedish "housing norm" presented in *God Bostad* and the proposed God Bostad 70 that was never realized because of the introduction of SBN 67, see Perers, "Inside the Ideal Home," 451.

27 Sigge, *Architecture's Red Tape*, 156.
28 Sigge, *Architecture's Red Tape*, 176–7.
29 Holm et al., *Förslag till ändring*, 12–13.
30 See Site 5, 138–43.
31 Lundgren, *Performance*, 13.
32 Lloyd Thomas, "Of their Several Kinds"; cf. Katie Lloyd Thomas, *Building Materials: Material Theory and the Architectural Specification* (London: Bloomsbury Visual Arts, 2021).
33 The National Board of Public Building clearly stated that the performance-based specification meant responsibility for the delivered design rested on producers and not on architects; see Sigge, *Architecture's Red Tape*, 176.
34 SOU 1974:21, *Markanvändning och byggande: Principer för lagstiftning: Betänkande avgivet av bygglagsutredningen* (Stockholm: Bostadsdepartementet, 1974), 203.
35 Nils Antoni, "Bygglådor: Mål medel och konsekvenser," in Olle Wåhlström, "Bygglådor-Byggsystem" (PhD course compendium, Planeringsmetodik, KTH, Stockholm, 1973), quoted in Sigge, *Architecture's Red Tape*, 182.
36 The National Board of Urban Planning in SOU 1982:9, 37 stressed how important it was that town planning committees, which had to implement the codes in the building permits they issued, recruited highly qualified staff with long experience to assess the new proposed performance-based codes.
37 A similar argument in relation to the British welfare state is made by Eleni A. Axioti, "Architecture as an Apparatus of Governance: (British) Architecture from the Welfare State to the State of Neoliberal Workfare" (diss., Open University, London, 2019).
38 Cf. Liam Ross, *Pyrotechnic Cities*. For Arup's innovative work with fire codes in a neoliberal regime, see Liam Ross, "Creative Uncertainty: Arup Associates: Fire Safety and the Metaengineering of Government," in *Neoliberalism on the Ground: Architecture and Transformation from the 1960s to the Present*, eds. Kenny Cupers, Catharina Gabrielsson, and Helena Mattsson (Pittsburgh: University of Pittsburgh, 2020), 270–93. For the Women's Building Forum, see the chapter "Emancipations" elsewhere this book.
39 Rawes, "Housing Biopolitics and Care," 80–100.
40 Rebecka Tarschys, "Kämpa för bättre miljö," *Dagens Nyheter*, November 10, 1968, Sunday supplement, 4–5.

Site 5

* "The Postmodern Housing Area" has been published as "From Norm to Form: Rethinking Swedish welfare state housing," in *Neoliberalism: An Architectural History*, eds. K. Cupers, C. Gabrielsson and H. Mattsson (Pittsburgh: University of Pittsburgh Press, 2019).
1 Léon Krier, "Sodermalm Not the Tavlingsomrade," *Architectural Design*, no. 54 (1984): 76.

Notes

2   Krier, "Sodermalm not the tavlingsomrade," 76–9. At first glance the competition entry had a very peculiar title, "Sodermalm Not the Tavlingsomrade" (Sodermalm not the Competion Site), but it referred to Krier's decision to work with a much larger area than the actual competition site. He proposed to turn the site, which had been allocated for housing, into an enormous park and change the urban character in the surrounding city by demolishing parts of the old city blocks to make them into "autonomous urban communities."

3   Krier, "Sodermalm not the tavlingsomrade," 79.

4   In six lectures between January 31 and March 21, 1979, Foucault discussed the emerging neoliberal state; see Michel Foucault, *The Birth of Biopolitics: Lectures at the Collége de France, 1978–1979*, ed. Michel Senellart (Basingstoke: Palgrave Macmillan, 2008). He talks about a "laxness" (190) that rests on two preconceptions: that the state tends to expand and take over what is external to it, that is, the civil society; and that it is a relationship, a genetic continuity, between all state forms, as administrative state, the welfare state, fascist state, the bureaucratic state, and so forth (see 187–90). For a discussion on the state phobia and crises of governmentality, see, for example, 76–7.

5   The fifty-year anniversary of the Stockholm Exhibition was in 1980, and a number of different exhibits and events commemorated it: *1930/80 Architecture Form Art* at Kulturhuset, Stockholm, *The Break-Through and Crises of Functionalism—Swedish Housing 1930–80* at the Museum of Architecture, Stockholm, and *The Uncompleted Functionalism* at the Rudolf Steiner Seminar in Järna. All these events could be seen as extensions of a long and much discussed criticism of Swedish functionalism in the 1970s, which opened the way for the development of new tracks in the functionalist program. But there were also other exhibits that were more distinctly related to the growing international postmodernist movement, such as *Manierismer* at the Swedish Art Academy and *The Eighty-Room Apartment* at Kulturhuset. See Christina Pech, *Arkitektur & motstånd. Om sökandet efter alternativ i svensk arkitektur 1970–1980* (diss. Kungliga Tekniska högskolan, Stockholm: Makadam förlag, 2011), 167–89; Catharina Gabrielsson, "Through the Anxieties of Style: The Riggering of Neoliberalism and the New Vasa Museum in Stockholm," in *Neoliberalism on The Ground: Architecture and Transformation From the 1960s to the Present*, eds. Kenny Cupers, Catharina Gabrielsson and Helena Mattsson (Pittsburgh: University of Pittsburgh Press, 2020), 68–71.

6   For an understanding of Third Way policy in a Swedish context, see Jenny Andersson, *The Library and the Workshop: Social Democracy and Capitalism in the Knowledge Age* (Stanford: Stanford University Press, 2010).

7   Bostadsstyrelsen, *God Bostad* (Stockholm: Bostadsstyrelsen, 1954–1967). For more on *God Bostad* see The Code in this book.

8   See, for example, Léon Krier, "The City within the City," *A+U*, Tokyo special issue (November 1977): 69–152, in which he expands on the idea of smaller units that work as independent units, integrating all functions.

9   For the general opinion that the area is perceived as a suburb, see Lars Brattberg, "Vi är förlamade av förträffliga styrsystem," *Dagens Nyheter*, July 31, 1983, 2.

10   The competition brief consisted of three different modules: habitation, the design of the area, and energy conservation.

11   Programgruppen för Södra Station, "Programsammanfattning," February 1983,6, box F4:3, Jan Inghes samling, Stockholms stadsarkiv (Stockholm City Archive, hereafter JIS/SA).

12   Lars Brattberg, "Södra Station—igen," *Stockholms-Tidningen*, July 23, 1983, 40.

13   Brattberg, "Vi är förlamade av förträffliga styrsystem," 2.

14   Brattberg, "Vi är förlamade av förträffliga styrsystem," 2.

Notes

15 "Stadsbyggnadsteori och gestaltning: Från kurser och seminarium hållna åren 1979–82," SBK-bulletinen 1984, box F5:1, JIS/SA.

16 For more on Swedish postmodernism, see Helena Mattsson, "Revisiting Swedish Postmodernism: Gendered Architecture and Other Stories," *Journal of Art History* 85, no. 1 (2016): 109–25; Gabrielsson, "Through the Anxieties of Style", in *Neoliberalism on The Ground*, 65–88; Pech, *Arkitektur och motstånd*, 167–206.

17 Bosse Bergman, "Stadens upplösta rum," *Arkitektur*, no. 1 (1980): 3–5; Fredric Bedoir, "Tillbaka till staden," *Arkitektur*, no. 7 (1991): 26.

18 Rebecka Gordan, "För en blandad befolkning," in *Den kalla och varma staden: Migration och stadsförändringar i Stockholm efter 170*, ed. Håkan Forsell (Stockholm: Stockholmia förlag, 2008), 145.

19 Sven Lorentzi, director for investigations at the City Planning Office, 1980–5, and director for the Planning Advisory Board (Planeringsberedningen), 1985–91, interview by the author, Stockholm, August 19, 2016.

20 Torsten Westman, "Gränser," *Arkitektur*, no. 1 (1983): 18.

21 For a similar conclusion about the function of postmodernism, see Felicity Scott, *Architecture or Techno-utopia: Politics After Modernism* (Cambridge, Mass.: MIT Press, 2007), 3.

22 For the role of the user and participatory urbanism as "politics beyond ideology" in French postwar planning, see "The Expertise of Participation," which is chapter 4 in Kenny Cupers, *The Social Project: Housing Postwar France* (Minneapolis: University of Minnesota Press, 2014), 137–82. The shift in the Swedish housing norms should be viewed in terms of the rising "better regulation" movement, being "part of a response by politicians and others to a perceived crisis relating to government, rule, and control." For "performance requirements" and building norms determined by what was then the Swedish National Board of Public Buildings (KBS), see Erik Sigge, *Architecture's Red Tape: Government Building Construction in Sweden, 1963–1973* (diss., KTH School of Architecture, Stockholm: KTH, 2017), 181–7. For building specifications in the UK, see Katie Lloyd Thomas and Tilo Amhoff, "Writing Work: Changing Practices of Architectural Specification," in *The Architect as Worker: Immaterial Labor, the Creative Class and the Politics of Design*, ed. Peggy Deamer (London: Bloomsbury, 2015), 121–43.

23 Birgit Friggebo became the minister of housing when the Liberals were back in power in the beginning of the 1990s, and her only mandate was to shut down the Housing Ministry.

24 Holm et al., *Förslag till ändring av normerna för bostäder*, 12–13.

25 Holm et al., *Förslag till ändring av normerna för bostäder*, 2–9.

26 SOU 1982:9, *Ny plan- och bygglag: Remissammanställning sammanställd av Bostadsdepartementet* (Stockholm: Bostadsdepartementet, 1982), 37. Here it is stressed how important it was for town planning committees, which had to implement the norms using the building permits they issued, to recruit highly qualified staff with considerable experience who were up to the complex task of evaluating "functional requirements."

27 Holm et al., *Förslag till ändring av normerna för bostäder*, 1.

28 Programgruppen för Södra Station, "Bebyggelseplan," 37, February 1983, box F4:3, JIS/SA.

29 It was controversial that some of the qualities guaranteed since the 1930s were on the brink of vanishing. See, for example, the statements of Mats Edblom, Bo Kjessel, Gunnar Matsson, and Inga Varg in the responses by Stockholms Arkitektförening to the City Planning Office's proposal for a Södra Station planning program, Stockholms arkitektförening, 'Yttrande over "Södra Stationsområdet—förslag till program," 1983, 3, box F4:3, JIS/SA.

30 Cf. Site 3: The Collective House and Emancipation in this book.

Notes

31 Programgruppen för Södra Station, "Södra Stationsområdet, 5. Boendeprogram," February 1983, 4, box F4:3, JIS/SA. The Planning Advisory Board (Planeringsberedningen) was a political body under the municipality's executive board; it prepared programs for larger planning projects (most often in the suburbs) in which they coordinated authorities and their claims for services—such as the need for schools, medical care, banks, post offices, and cultural houses. The programs laid the foundation for the City Planning Office in their work on the plans and more detailed programs. The Planning Advisory Board was closed down in the restructuring of the housing sector in 1991. Under the leadership of Sven Lorentzi, the Planning Advisory Board formulated five programs on the Södra Station area, and the "program for living/dwelling"—closely tied to the "plan for building" (bebyggelsplan) and the "program for premises" (lokalprogram)—stated the fundamental goals for demography, housing offices that signed up tenants for the apartments, sizes and design of apartments and groups of apartments, and common premises and citizen participation.

32 Programgruppen för Södra Station, "Lokalprogram," 15, box F4:3, JIS/SA.

33 Programgruppen för Södra Station, "Boendeprogram," 4. Among the five offices referenced in the main text were AB Svenska Bostäder and Svenska Riksbyggen.

34 Programgruppen för Södra Station, "Boendeprogram," 27.

35 Programgruppen för Södra Station, "Boendeprogram," 23.

36 Programgruppen för Södra Station, "Boendeprogram," 23.

37 Programgruppen för Södra Station, "Boendeprogram," 4.

38 Programgruppen för Södra Station, "Boendeprogram," 19.

39 Lars Brattberg, manuscript for the article "Resa mot oförenliga mål," 6, box F5:1, JIS/SA. A shortened version was published as "Vi är förlamade av förträffliga styrsystem," Dagens Nyheter, July 31, 1983, 2.

40 Christian Norberg-Schulz, *Genius Loci: Towards a Phenomenology of Architecture* (London: Academy, 1980), 42. The City Planning Office is explicitly referring to Norberg-Schulz's ideas of Nordic planning in the proposal for a plan. See Programgruppen för Södra Station, "Boendeprogram," 21.

41 Programgruppen för Södra Station, "Boendeprogram," 21.

42 For a discussion on the emergence of the interior in the nineteenth century as the inside (which expresses the individual subject and thus manifests "doubleness," that is, the interior works both as a concept, an image, or a fantasy, as well as a spatial and material reality), see Charles Rice, *The Emergence of the Interior: Architecture, Modernity, Domesticity* (London: Routledge, 2007).

43 Bedoir, "Tillbaka till staden," 26.

44 The two opposing agendas regarding norms and forms were spelled out in two lectures by Holm and Krier at the Royal Swedish Academy of Fine Arts in Stockholm and developed in an article by Krister Bjurström, "Form och form, Krier och Holm," *Arkitektur*, no. 4 (1981), 25–26.

45 Cf. the chapter Human capital. For a discussion of Gary Becker's human capital and Foucault's "ability machines" in relation to the city, see Reinhold Martin, *The Urban Apparatus: Mediapolitics and the City* (Minneapolis: University of Minnesota Press, 2016), 120–30.

46 Andersson, *The Library and the Workshop*, 27, 41.

47 Jan Inghe-Hagström, "Den nya staden vid Södra station," in *Söder 700: Sankt Eriks årsbok*, ed. Björn Hallerdt (Stockholm: Samfundet S: tErik, 1987), 76.

48 The quality programs were inspired by the "advanced programmes for coordination and design" that were used when planning and designing the IBA (Internationale Bauausstellung) in Berlin from 1984 to 1987. Jan Inghe-Hagström, "Södra Stationsområdet: Förebilder och gestaltning," *Plan*, no. 2–3 (1985): 115.

49 Jan Inghe-Hagström's private collection (Jan Inghes samling, JIS) was donated to the Stockholm City Archive.

50 Norberg-Schulz, *Genius Loci*, 18. A high-rise that was realized later and became part of this ensemble was designed by Henning Larsen Architects, but they withheld their firm's name when they saw that the final result was going to deviate too far from their design.

51 For a discussion on neoliberalization and Espaces d'Abraxas, see Anne Kockelkorn, "Palace of Mortgage: The Collapse of a Social Housing Monument in France," in *Neoliberalism on the Ground*, eds. Cupers et. al., 19–44.

52 The concept had also been in focus for the study circles held at the City Planning Office, and influences came from a wide range of theories, such as Rob Krier's "Stadtraum," Gordon Cullen's "townscape," and Kevin Lynch's "imageability." See, for example, "Att uppfatta staden: 3 metoder" [To register the city: 3 methods], where three studies were presented: "Measuring and Describing a City Space according to Rob Krier" (Jan Inghe-Hagström); "Experiencing the City according to Cullen" (Cristina Rådberg); and "Understanding the City and Its Design" (Dag Åberg), all in SBK-Bulletinen 1984, 38, box F5:1, JIS/SA.

53 See, for example: Lars Marcus, "Ett liv i parodi," *MAMA: Magasin for modern arkitektur*, no. 4 (1992): 52–7; David Zetterstad, "Stadsmässighetens tidevarv," *Valör: Konstvetenskapliga studier och forskning*, no. 5 (1992): 20–33; and Mona Jonsson-von Matern, "Låtsasstaden," *Plan: Tidskrift för planering av landsbygd och tätorter*, no. 3 (1994): 150–5.

54 Zetterstad, "Stadsmässighetens tidevarv," 32–3.

55 Marcus, "Ett liv i parodi," 52–7.

56 For an understanding of the "urban" as a way of seeing, arranging, and knowing the world, see Martin, *The Urban Apparatus*, 4.

57 Norberg-Schulz, *Genius Loci* (Inghe-Hagström's personal copy), 16, box F5:1, JIS/SA. For a discussion of Christian Norberg-Schulz, phenomenology, Gestalt psychology, and how "visual experience, being bounded or framed by the visual field, was paradigmatic of wholeness, synthesis, and closure," see Jorges Otero-Pailos, *Architecture's Historical Turn: Phenomenology and the Rise of the Postmodern* (Minneapolis: University of Minnesota Press, 2010), 156.

58 Kevin Lynch, *A Theory of Good City Form* (Cambridge, Mass.: MIT Press, 1981). Lynch outlines a normative theory of urban form and argues that one should use "performance dimensions"—vitality, sense, fit, access, and control—instead of rigid standards.

59 Kvalitetsprogram (Quality program), Kv Fatburen MM, DP 8454 A, 48, box F4:6, JIS/SA.

60 Norberg-Schulz, *Genius Loci*, 20–2. When one reads *Genius Loci* today, the cultural determinism is striking: the "Nordic man has to be friend with fog, ice and cold winds; he has to enjoy the creaking sound under the feet," while the "Arab, instead, has to be a friend of the infinitely extended, sandy desert and the burning sun" (21).

61 Inghe-Hagström made a marginal notation at Norberg-Schulz's discussion on dwelling, pointing out that "orientation is not that difficult but identification is." Although Norberg-Schulz seems to be the main influence for the planning process, Inghe-Hagström seems to struggle with the focus on the local character of place and the cultural determinism framing the theories of genius loci, and he writes in the margin, "[S]tay where you are,

Notes

do not protest = conservative." Norberg-Schulz, *Genius Loci*, 23 (Jan Inghe-Hagström's private copy, box F5:1, JIS/SA).

62 Norberg-Schulz, *Genius Loci*, 22.

63 See "Human Capital" in this book.

Emancipation

1 Nancy Fraser, *Fortunes of Feminism: From State-Managed Capitalism to Neoliberal Crises* (London: Verso, 2013).

2 Melinda Cooper, *Family Values: Between Neoliberalism and the new Social Conservatism* (New York: Zone Books, 2017), 12.

3 For a discussion on architecture's emancipatory possibilities, see Nadir Lahiji, ed., *Can Architecture be an Emancipatory Project? Dialogues on the Left* (Winchester: Zero Books, 2016).

4 Fraser, *Fortunes of Feminism*, 3.

5 Koselleck refers to Jeremy Bentham "who saw governments emerging that would have already emancipated themselves from established governments," Reinhardt Koselleck, *The Practice of Conceptual History: Timing History, Spacing Concepts*, trans. Todd Samuel Presner et al. (Stanford: Stanford University Press, 2002), 253.

6 Susanne Lettow argues that a focus on subjectivation reveals micro-physical power relations rather than dominating macro-structures, "whereas the study of dissent, rejection, and resistance has been largely marginalised." Susanne Lettow, "Editor's Introduction – Emancipation: Rethinking Subjectivity, Power, and Change," *Hypathia* 30, no. 3 (2015): 501–12.

7 Mary McLeod, "Architecture and Politics in the Reagan Era: From Postmodernism to Deconstructivism," *Assemblage*, 8, no. 8 (1989): 22–59.

8 McLeod, "Architecture and Politics in the Reagan Era," 54.

9 The Swedish feminist movement in architecture emerged in close collaboration with a large Scandinavian women network in architecture. See Lori Brown and Karen Burns, eds., *Bloomsbury Global Encyclopedia of Women Architecture, 1960–2015* (London: Bloomsbury, forthcoming).

10 Helena Mattsson, "Revisiting Swedish Postmodernism: Gendered Architecture and Other Stories," *Journal of Art History* 85, no. 1 (2016), 109–25; Helena Mattsson, "Shifting Gender and Acting Out History: Is There a Swedish Feminist-Postmodernist Architecture?," in *Feminist Futures of Spatial Practice: Materialism, Activism, Dialogues, Pedagogies, Projections*, eds. Meike Schalk et al. (Braunach: Spurbuchverlag, 2017).

11 Karl Polanyi, *The Great Transformation: The Political and Economic Origins of Our Time*, 2nd Beacon Paperback ed. (Boston: Beacon Press, 2001 [1944]). Polanyi demonstrated how struggles towards disembedded markets resulted in "fictitious commodities" such as land, labor, and money. He coined the concept of embeddedness, plausible inspired by the hands-on metaphor taken from his studies of coal mining; the extraction of the coal "embedded" in the rock walls. See Fred Block, "Introduction," in Polanyi, *The Great Transformation*, xxiv, footnote 10.

12 Fraser, *Fortunes of Feminism*, 230. Fraser outlines the theory of a triple movement in the chapter "Between Marketization and Social Protection: Resolving the Feminist Ambivalence." See also, "A Triple Movement: Parsing the Politics of Crises after Polanyi," *New Left Review*, no. 81 (2013), 210–32.

13 Fraser points out that emancipations are aligned neither with protection nor with marketization and can "diverge from both prongs of the double movement" when struggles, for example, do not tend to dismantle but transform existing modes of protection. Fraser, *Fortunes of Feminism*, 233. It is unclear what Fraser refers to as "aligning with" when she describes how emancipatory movements in the aftermath of the Second World War either aligned with marketization (e.g., New Leftists disempowered the social protection through criticizing the bureaucratically organized welfare state regime) or with social protection (second-wave feminists). For a critique of Fraser's framework see for example Jan Sparsam et. al., "The Renewal of a Critical Theory of capitalism and Crises: A Comment on Nancy Fraser's Interpretation of Polanyi's work," Working Paper 2014:17 der DFG-KollegforscherInnengruppe Postwachstumsgesellschaften, Friedrich-Schiller-Universität, Jena (2014), ResearchGate.net, accessed January 25, 2022, https://www.researchgate.net/publication/315701485_The_Renewal_of_a_Critical_Theory_of_Capitalism_and_Crisis_-_A_Comment_on_Nancy_Fraser%27s_Interpretation_of_Polanyi%27s_works; Chris O'Kane, "Critical Theory and the Criticism of Capitalism: An Immanent Criticism of Nancy Fraser's 'Systematic' 'crisis-Criticism' of Capitalism as an 'Institutionalized Social Order,'" *Science & Society* 85, no. 2 (2021): 207–35.

14 Melinda Cooper has criticized this position for leading "to the conclusion that resistance demands the restoration of family, albeit in a more progressive, egalitarian form." Implicit in this criticism is also a critique of Polanyi's paradoxical view on the social protection countermovements as external to capitalism, but also necessary for, and initiated by, the market itself, and Cooper suggests that the "double movement" instead should be understood as fully internal to the dynamic of capital; economic liberalism and political conservatism are both expressions of modern capital. Cooper, *Family Values*, 13–14. For a similar criticism of Polanyi see also Angela Mitropoulos, *Contract & Contagion: From Biopolitics to Oikonomia* (New York: Minor Compositions, 2012); Martijn Konings, *The Emotional Logic of Capitalism: What Progressives Have Missed* (Stanford: Stanford University Press, 2015).

15 See Site 3: The Collective House.

16 Erik Swyngedouw, "Illiberalism and the Democratic Paradox: The Infernal Dialectic of Neoliberal Emancipation," *European Journal of Social Theory*, published online, June 30, 2021, https://doi.org/10.1177%2F13684310211027079, 2.

17 For Scott's discussion on Foucault see Joan Scott, "The Vexed Relationship of Emancipation and Equality," *History of the Present* 2, no. 2 (2012): 157–8.

Site 6

1 Anita Snis, "Hyresgästerna bestämmer hur husen ska byggas om," *BoFast: Tidning för bostäder och fastighetsförvaltning*, no. 8 (1991): 18.

2 Ylva Larsson, "Tensta: Förändring under samverkan," *Plan: Tidskrift för planering av landsbygd och tätorten*, no. 3 (1993): 135–41.

3 Samuel Sandström, letter to Stockholm Traffic Department, June 1989, box 1980-89, F 43DC: 79, Stockholms gatukontor, Västra regionens diarieförda handlingar, Stockholms stadsarkiv (the Stockholm City Archives).

4 S.-G. Södergren and Bruno Jonsson, reply to private letter, June 12, 1988, box F3dc:79, Stockholms gatukontor (Stockholm Traffic Department, hereafter GK).

5 Hans Wilborg and & S.-G. Södergren, "Tjänsteutlåtande," box F3dc:79, GK.

Notes

6   The fact that the work to change the attitudes of the residents also made the City of Stockholm consider it reasonable that local schools and housing companies were involved in paying for the campaign. Sture Palmgren to Ulf Brynell, January 18, 1985, "Antiskräpkampanj i Tensta/Rinkeby våren 1985," box F3dc:79, GK.

7   A labor immigration began in the late 1940s in Sweden, and rose considerably in the mid-1960s. In 1967 the first immigration restrictions were introduced. In the 1970s and 1980s there was a shift toward refugee immigration and to relatives of immigrants already living in Sweden. See Dag Blanck and Mattias Tydén, "Becoming Multicultural? The Development of Swedish Immigrant Policy," in *Welfare States in Trouble: Historical Perspectives on Canada and Sweden*, eds. Sune Åkerman and Jack L. Granatstein (Umeå: Swedish Science Press, 1995), 57–70. For the built environment and ethnic segregation in Sweden, see for example Roger Andersson, Lena Magnusson Turner, and Emma Holmqvist, "Contextualizing Ethnic Residential Segregation in Sweden: Welfare, Housing and Migration-Related Policies," *Country Report for Sweden*, December 2010, Norface, accessed January 27, 2022, http://uu.diva-portal.org/smash/record.jsf?pid=diva2%3A472568&dswid=896. For a detailed study of Syriac immigration in Södertälje outside Stockholm and "urban design from below," see Jennifer Mack, *The Construction of Equality: Syriac Immigration and the Swedish City* (Minneapolis: University of Minnesota Press, 2017).

8   In the 1970s, Sweden, Canada, and Australia were the first countries in the West to introduce the notion of multiculturalism in political management. See Mats Wickström, "The Deifference White Ethnics Made: The Multiculturalist Turn of Sweden in Comparison to the Cases of Canada and Denmark", Heidi vad JØnsson, Elizabeth Onasch, Saara Pellander, and Mats Wickström (eds.) *Migration and Welfare States: Policies, Discourses and Institutions* (Helsinki: Nordic Center of Excellence NordWel, 2013), 25-58. See the Swedish Government Official Report SOU 1996:55, *Sverige, framtiden och mångfalden: Slutbetänkande från Invandrarpolitiska kommittén* (Stockholm: Arbetsmarknadsdepartmentet, 1996).

9   Irene Molina, *Stadens rasifiering: Etnisk boendesegregering i folkhemmet* (diss., Uppsala University, Uppsala: Uppsala University, 1997).

10 Rune Premfors, *Den starka demokratin* (Stockholm: Atlas, 2000), 175; Kristina Boréus, *Högervåg: Nyliberalismen och kampen om språket i offentlig debatt, 1969–1989* (Stockholm: Tiden, 1994).

11 Mack, *The Construction of Equality*, esp. Chapter 5, "Greetings from Hollywood! Enclaves and Participation."

12 Nazem Tahvilzadeh and Lisa Kings "Under Pressure: Invited Participation Amidst Planning Conflicts," in *Conflict in the City: Contested Urban Spaces and Local Democracy*, eds. Enrico Gualini, Marco Allegra, and João Morais Mourato (Berlin: Jovis Verlag GmbH, 2015); Heather M. Watkins, "Beyond Sweat Equity: Community Organizing Beyond the Third Way," *Urban Studies* 54, no. 7 (2017): 2139–54; Nicholas Rose, *Powers of Freedom: Reframing Political Thought* (Cambridge: Cambridge University Press, 1999). For a similar discussion on how participation became a "system-immanent criticism" in the planning of IBA 84/87, see Eva Maria Hierzer and Philipp Markus Schörkhuber, "Infrastructural Critique: The Upside Down of the Bottom-Up: A Case Study of the IBA Berlin 84/87," *Footprint*, no. 13 (Autumn 2013): 115–22.

13 Magnus Dahlstedt, "The Politics of Activation: Technologies of Mobilizing 'Multiethnic Suburbs' in Sweden," *Alternatives: Global, Local, Political* 33, no. 4 (2008): 483 (481–504).

14 See for example Paul Davidoff, "Advocacy and Pluralism in Planning," *Journal of the American Institute of Planners* 32, no. 4 (1965): 331–8; Norman Krumholz, "A Retrospective View of Equity Planning: Cleveland 1969–1979," *Journal of the American Planning*

Association 48, no. 2 (1982): 163–74. For a discussion about the participatory turn, see Maros Krivy and Tahl Kaminer "Introduction: Participatory Turn in Urbanism," *Footprint*, no. 13 (Autumn 2013): 1–6. See also Andrea Cornwall, "Introduction: New democratic Spaces? The Politics and Dynamics of Institutionalised Participation," *IDS Bulletin* 35, no. 2, (2004): 1–10.

15 Cf. Maria Lind, ed. *Tensta Museum: Reports from New Sweden* (London: Sternberg Press, 2021).

16 For a discussion on the role played by invited participation in the planning process of a marginalized urban area, Botkyrka, outside Stockholm, see Nazem Tahvilzadeh and Lisa Kings "Under Pressure: Invited Participation Amidst Planning Conflicts," in *Conflict in the City: Contested Urban Spaces and Local Democracy*, eds. Enrico Gualini, Marco Allegra, and João Morais Mourato (Berlin: Jovis Verlag GmbH, 2015), 94–111.

17 Olle Bengtzon, Jan Delden, and Jan Lundgren, *Rapport Tensta* (Stockholm: PAN/Norstedt, 1970).

18 Urban Ericsson, Irene Molina, and Per-Markku Ristilammi, *Miljonprogram och media: Föreställningar om människor och förorter* (Trelleborg: Integrationsverket & Riksantikvarieämbetet, 2002), 18.

19 A campaign—*Vi flytt' int'* (We Won't Move!)—was organized in the late 1960s protesting labor migration from Northern Sweden toward the more industrialized Southern parts.

20 The Danish Government, *Ét Danmark uden parallelsamfund: Ingen ghettoer i 2030* (København: Økonomi- og Indenrigsministeriet, 2018). Cf. Mette-Louise E. Johansen and Steffen B. Jensen, "'They want us out': Urban Regeneration and the Limits of Integration in the Danish Welfare State," *Critique of Anthropology* 37, no. 3 (2017): 297–316; Mia Arp Fallow and Rasmus Hoffman Birk, "The 'Ghetto' Strikes Back: Resisting Welfare Sanctions and Stigmatizing Categorizations in Marginalized Residential Areas in Denmark," *Nordic Social Work Research*, published online, June 7, 2021, https://doi.org/10.1080/2156857X.2021.1937289; Heidi Svenningsen Kajita, Jennifer Mack, Svava Riesto, and Meike Schalk, "Between Technologies of Power and Notions of Solidarity" (paper, International Conference: Spaces of Welfare, The Royal Danish Academy, online, May 6–7, 2021). The strategy used in Denmark to move people is based on numeric data that can be understood in relation to surveillance systems used to "solve" the "problem of migration." See Sabelo J. Ndlovu-Gatsheni, "Provisional Notes on Decolonizing Research Methodology and Undoing Its Dirty History," *Journal of Developing Societies* 35, no. 4 (2019): 481–92.

21 Cf. Jennifer Mack, "Renovation Year Zero: Swedish Welfare Landscapes of Anxiety, 1975 to the Present," *Bebyggelsehistorisk tidskrift*, no. 76 (2019): 63–79. Another major government housing program was ROT, *renovering—ombyggnad—tillbyggnad* (renovation—rebuilding—extension), 1983–93, mainly aimed at older buildings in the inner cities, but later also including the Million Program.

22 On the history of Swedish public housing companies, see "1976–1990: Bostadsbeståndet förbättras och förvaltningen utvecklas," accessed January 25, 2021, https://www.allmannyttan.se/historia/historiska-epoker/1976-1990-bostadsbestandet-forbattras-och-forvaltningen-utvecklas/.

23 Familjebostäder, "Boinflytandeverksamheten 1984" (in the author's possession).

24 Annika Sörman, "Vi känner att de lyssnar på oss," in Loggia Arkitekter AB, AB Familjebostäder Väster, and Hyresgästföreningen Södra Järva, *Tensta, förändring under samverkan,* (Stockholm: Arkitektkopia, 1993), 18, Action Archive.

Notes

25 According to statements at a seminar in 2014 by Sven Lorentzi, director of research in the Real Estate Department 1984–88, and Monica Andersson, the deputy mayor and real estate commissioner of the Real Estate Department (Stadsbyggnadsborgarråd) 1988–91: Action Archive, "Transcript: Witness Seminar March 5, 2014, 18.30–21.00 at Tensta konsthall (Tensta Art Hall) Concerning the Event of the International Housing Renewal Conference in Tensta 1989" (in the authors possession), 6, 12.

26 When there was no longer a need for new apartments, public housing companies entered a new phase focusing on management rather than production. Mats Hulth, "Miljonprogram för miljonprogrammet," August 13, 1985, box F1cf:7, Stockholms fastighetskontor, Stockholms stadsarkiv (Stockholm Real Estate Department, Stockholm City Archive, hereafter SFA/SA).

27 The representatives came from the city's administration, from social services, from the housing companies, from the police, from *bostadsförmedlingen* (the housing office), and from *Hyresgästföreningen* (The Resident's Association) and was led by the Stockholm Real Estate Department.

28 "Ett preliminärt utvecklingsprogram för södra Järva stadsdelarna Tensta Hjulsta Rinkeby," appendix 5, 4–5, in "Lägesrapport från arbetet med program för förbättringar i Stockholms miljonprogramområden," May 23, 1986, box F1cf:7, SFA/SA.

29 "Lägesrapport från arbetet med program för förbättringar i Stockholms miljonprogramområden," May 23, 1986, 18-22, box F1cf:7, SFA/SA. The "radical coordination" was partly based on the program proposal formulated by the Hansta Committee on coordinated municipal services, adopted in February 1984, and would also form the basis for other city districts. The Danish Tingbjerg model also stood as a model.

30 Philip Mirowski, *Never Let a Serious Crisis Go to Waste: How Neoliberalism Survived the Financial Meltdown* (London: Verso, 2013).

31 According to a parliamentary private bill, none of the areas in the Million Program met this requirement. Monica Andersson, "Att spränga igenom asfalten," *Aftonbladet*, June 21, 1989. Swedish Parliamentary Papers, Private Bill 1987/88:Bo220 (Lars Ulander et al.), "Motion om bidrag till förnyelseåtgärder inom miljonprogrammets bostadsområden." The renewal grant was later included in the Million Program areas but was removed in 1989. Between 1986 and 1992, a renewal grant existed for apartments and outdoor environments in areas with major social problems, and projects intended to create new meeting places in vulnerable areas were awarded. Of 155 million Swedish kronor, 86 went to metropolitan areas. In 1988, *Storstadsutredningen* (the Metropolitan Investigation) was appointed, which resulted in the government report *Storstadsliv: Rika möjligheter—hårda villkor* (Metropolitan Life: Rich Opportunities— Harsh Conditions), where different solutions were presented: e.g. decentralization of housing companies; increased opportunities for residents to take over management; and cooperative tenancy. Boverket, *Socialt hållbar stadsutveckling: En kunskapsöversikt* (Stockholm: Boverket, 2010), 27–8; SOU 1990:36, *Storstadsliv: Rika möjligheter—hårda villkor: Slutbetänkande av storstadsutredningen* (Stockholm: Statsrådsberedningen, 1990).

32 The decision to remove the renewal grant was criticized by the local reference groups in Tensta/Rinkeby in a letter to the Government. It was pointed out that the renewal work that started in 1987 was based on renewal support applied for by the public housing companies and that a larger budget also was linked to these projects. Juan Fonseca and Mats Linell, Letter to the government, January 25, 1989, Häfte 1, Action Archive.

33 Monica Andersson, "Miljonprogrammet allas ansvar," *Dagens Nyheter*, December 21, 1990, D3.

Notes

34 The housing seminar was a collaboration between Stockholm's Real Estate Department and the consulting company Närbo AB. Invited participants were architect Rod Hackney, project manager Florence Ostier, high school teacher Pierre Soler, professor of industrial organization Erol Sayin, architect Leena Laukasto, tenant representative Bertha Gilkey, architect Jörgen Andersen, and political scientist and city planner Eisse Kalk.

35 Inger Holmqvist, Marja Lång-Ericsson, Thomas Ney, Jarmo Riihinen, "Seminarium om förnyelse av bostadsområden," Tensta 1989, Stockholms Fastighetsnämnd/närbo, 1989, 1, Action Archive.

36 Holmqvist et al., "Seminarium om förnyelse av bostadsområden," 1.

37 Holmqvist et al., "Seminarium om förnyelse av bostadsområden," 1.

38 Most of the material is gone from the archives, but the conference, however, led to a publication and an exhibition that was displayed in the district council building and travelled to the Nordic-Baltic Architecture Triennal in Tallinn 1990.

39 A.L. Högberg and S. Österberg, "Kvalitet i bostadsförvaltning: Hyresgästernas bedömningar i löpande förvaltning och inför en förnyelsesituation," Stockholm: Tekniska högskolan, Institutet för bostadsförvaltning, 1987, Action Archive.

40 Larsson, "Tensta"; Familjebostäder, Head Office protocols, November 2, 1992, par. 23, Action Archive.

41 The project's management team consisted of representatives of the housing company (Annika Johansson, Familjebostäder), the architects (Ylva Larsson, Loggia Arkitekter), and the tenants (Raymond Sköld, Tenants' Association).

42 The architect was Archibald Frid, and the apartments were ready for occupancy in 1969.

43 Loggia Arkitekter AB, *Tensta, förändring under samverkan*, 54.

44 Economic conditions changed radically, state aid such as renewal grants had already been withdrawn several years earlier, and the "second million program" had also been terminated.

45 Larsson, "Tensta," 17.

46 Larsson, "Tensta," 141.

47 "Minnesanteckningar förda vid ett möte mellan Glömmingegränds lokala hyresgästförening, Familjebostäders distrikt och NCC samt Loggia arkitekter" (memory notes from a meeting with Glömmingegränd's local tenant association, the public housing company Familjebostäder, the construction company NCC and the architects Loggia), October 11, 1993, AB Familjebostäders arkiv, box E2b:3, SA.

48 "Minnesanteckningar förda vid ett möte mellan Glömmingegränds lokala hyresgästförening, Familjebostäders distrikt och NCC samt Loggia arkitekter."

49 Letter from Per-Olof Abrahamsson to Rolf Johansson, Familjebostäder, April 22, 1994, AB Familjebostäders arkiv, box E2b:3, SA.

50 Molina, *Stadens rasifiering*; Irene Molina, "Intersektionella rumsligheter," *Tidskrift för genusvetenskap*, no. 3 (2007): 7–21.

51 Molina, "Intersektionella rumsligheter," 16.

52 Swedish Parliamentary Papers, Private Bill 1987/88:Bo220 (Lars Ulander et al.), "Motion om bidrag till förnyelseåtgärder inom miljonprogrammets bostadsområden," 13.

53 City of Stockholm, Memorandum 1988:175 RI, 3109, SA.

Notes

54 Transcript: Witness Seminar March 5, 2014, 18.30 -21.00 at Tensta konsthall (Tensta Art Hall) Concerning the Event of the International Housing Renewal Conference in Tensta 1989," 31, Action Archive.

55 Karl-Olov Arnstberg, "Klichéer om förort: Tensta är inte bara ett betongghetto och social misär," *Svenska Dagbladet*, December 7, 1990, 2.

56 Cf. Annika Johansson in Sörman, "Vi känner att de lyssnar på oss." In connection with the new Planning and Building Act in 1987, a Housing Rehabilitation Act was introduced and the state conversion loans were to be tested against the tenants' opinions. The tenants' perception of the renewal could only be disregarded after having been tried in a court of law. In 1994, the Housing Rehabilitation Act was abolished and the tenants' statutory influence decreased.

57 Jennifer Mack, "Impossible Nostalgia: Green Affect in the Landscapes of the Swedish Million Programme," *Landscape Research*, published online January 16, 2021, accessed March 1, 2022, https://doi.org/10.1080/01426397.2020.1858248.

58 The seminar was organized by Action Archive and was part of the exhibition "Tensta Museum: Reports from New Sweden," October 2013 -May 2014 at Tensta Konsthall, curated by Maria Lind. Action Archive, "Transcript: Witness Seminar March 5, 2014, 18.30 -21.00 at Tensta konsthall (Tensta Art Hall) Concerning the Event of the International Housing Renewal Conference in Tensta 1989," Action Archive.

59 For more on the witness seminar see Meike Schalk, "Old News From a Contact Zone: Action Archive in Tensta," in *The Social (Re)Production of Architecture: Politics, Values and Actions in Contemporary Practice*, eds. Doina Petrescu and Kim Trogal (London: Routledge, 2017); Helena Mattsson and Meike Schalk, "Action Archive: Oral History as Performance," in *Speaking of Buildings: Oral History in Architectural Research*, eds., Janina Gosseye, Naomi Staed, and Deborah van der Plath (New York: Princeton Architectural Press, 2019).

60 Paul Goodman talks about an unfinished situation in relation to personal experiences but also of "unfinished revolutions" regarding greater historical movements. See Schalk, "Old News From a Contact Zone," 335.

61 Few records are left from the 1989 housing conference, see "Tensta-Stockholm-Sweden: Renewal action in suburban Stockholm," Stockholms Fastighetskontor/Närbo, 1989, Action Archive; Inger Holmqvist et al., "Seminarium om förnyelse av bostadsområden, Tensta 1989," box F3dc:79, GK.

62 Brown, *Undoing the Demos*, 131–2.

63 Brown, *Undoing the Demos*, 133. For more on responsibilization and moral, see Kelly Hannah-Moffat, *Punishment in Disguise: Penal Governance and Canadian Women's Imprisonment* (Toronto: University of Toronto Press, 2001); Richard V. Ericson and Aaron Doyle, eds., *Risk and Morality* (Toronto: University of Toronto Press, 2003); Ronen Shamir, "The Age of Responsibilization: On Market-Embedded Morality," *Economy and Society* 37, no. 1: 1–19; For a discussion on moral, neoliberalization and the welfare state, see Andrea Muehlebach, *The Moral Neoliberal. Welfare and Citizenship in Italy* (Chicago: University of Chicago Press, 2012).

64 Shamir, "The Age of Responsibilization," 7.

65 Sara Schindler, "Architectural Exclusion: Discrimination Through Physical Design of the Built Environment," *The Yale Law Journal* 124, no. 16 (2015): 1934–2024.

66 In a Swedish context "new patterns of responsibilization" has been described as a transformation from the citizen as the subject of welfare policies, to a consumer or *brukare* (user). The user must be "in commando of her/his desires and needs, and ready to articulate them as interests." The postwar *reasonable* consumer had turned into the *responsible*

consumer or user of the 1980s. For a discussion about new patterns of responsibilization in relation to the Swedish welfare state and neoliberalizations, see Bengt Larsson, Martin Letell, and Håkan Thörn, eds., *Transformations of the Swedish Welfare State: From Social Engineering to Governance?* (New York: Palgrave Macmillan, 2012), 265–6.

67 For a similar discussion in relation to the planning of churches and mosques, see Jennifer Mack, "An Awkward Technocracy: Mosques, Churches, and Urban Planners in Neoliberal Sweden," *American Ethnologist* 46, no. 1 (2019): 89–104. Mack shows how the aesthetic and social language used by architects and planners are seen as neutral, and are used as tools of mediation believing that these will help them to integrate (ibid., 102).

68 Dahlstedt, "The Politics of Activation," 483; for a similar example in the UK: Heather Watkins, "Beyond Sweat Equity: Community Organizing Beyond the Third Way," *Urban Studies* 54, no. 9 (2017): 2139–54; *Svensk Författningssamling* (Swedish Code of Statues) 1987:10, "Plan och bygglag"; *En uthållig demokrati! Sammanfattning av Demokratiutredningen: Politik för folkstyrelse på 2000-talet* (Stockholm: Landstingsförbundet, 2000).

69 As pointed out by Maros Krivy and Tahl Kaminer, projects based on participation may take paths that are difficult to predict, and they can support widely differing social and political agendas. Krivy and Kaminer, "Introduction," 2.

70 The concept of "social capital" is ambiguous, and may support xenophobic attitudes and notions that a multicultural environment reduces the social capital. Robert Putnam, *Making Democracy Work: Civic Tradition in Modern Italy* (Princeton: Princeton University Press, 1992); Paul Collier, *Exodus: How Migration Is Changing the World* (Oxford: Oxford University Press, 2013).

71 Cf. Sten Gromark, *Boendegemenskap: En kritisk granskning av boendegemenskap som samhällsangelägenhet, av dess värden, villkor och förutsättningar samt exempel på praktisk tillämpning i ett västeuropeiskt sammanhang* (Diss., Chalmers tekniska högskola, Göteborg: Chalmers, 1983), 34.

Epilogue

1 For more about the Swedish bank crises and economic history 1975–2010, see: Lennart Schön, *Economic History of Modern Sweden* (London: Taylor & Francis, 2012), 277–331.

2 Kjell-Olof Feldt, *Alla dessa dagar: I regeringen 1982–1990* (Stockholm: Norstedts, 1991), 260.

3 *Stadshypotek* was a fund that financed housing construction by lending money to property owners. In 1991, the government transformed the local *Stadshypoteksföreningarna* associations by pooling their funds into a single limited company, *Stadshypoteket AB* (Urban Mortgage Bank of Sweden), which later was bought by Handelsbanken.

4 Feldt, *Alla dessa dagar*, 281–3.

5 Beyond being educated as an architect, Backström received a PhD from KTH in real estate economics. In the 1970s, the moniker "real estate speculator" was derogatory and there were major discussions in the media about Backström's handling of homes and buildings as financial resources. Backström received extensive criticism for not reinvesting in buildings or taking care of maintenance. The law was repealed in 2010. *Svensk Författningssamling* (Swedish Code of Statues) 1975:1132 ("Lex Backström").

6 Jesper Blomberg, *Ordning och kaos i projektsamarbete* (Stockholm: EFI, 1995).

Notes

7   Cf. Mike Althorpe, "The Car and The Elephant: The Story of Reconstruction at The Elephant and Castle," accessed February 26, 2022, http://thecarandtheelephant.com.

8   The Swedish crisis in the 1990s started with the finance and real estate company Nyckeln suspending its payments in October 1990. At the time, the company had credit losses of three billion Swedish crowns.

9   The Million Program has gone from being heavily criticized to becoming a highly sought-after investment property. For a discussion on the impact of calculus and capital in the contemporary Swedish housing sector, see: Stig Westherdahl, *Det självspelande pianot: Kalkylerna och kapitalet som skapar Sveriges bostadskris* (Årsta: Dokument Press, 2021). I am grateful for inspiring discussions with the PhD student Anna Livia Voersel, which have enriched my view on this topic. Voersel is working on a dissertation that critically investigates and situates current housing policies.

10 Anthony Giddens, *The Third Way: The Renewal of Social Democracy* (Oxford: Polity Press, 1998), 74–5.

11 Foucault talks about "the ability-machine" producing human value that cannot be separated from the human individual. Michel Foucault, *The Birth of Biopolitics: Lectures at the Collège de France, 1978–1979*, ed. Michel Senellart, trans. Graham Burchell (Basingstoke: Palgrave Macmillan, 2008), 226–9.

12 How "culture as a resource" is enfolded into neoliberal economy policy is discussed by George Yúdice in *The Expendiency of Culture. The Use of Culture in the Global Era* (Durham and London: Duke University Press, 2003). See also Scott Lash and Celia Lury, *Global Culture Industry: The Mediation of Things* (Cambridge, UK and Malden, MA: Polity Press, 2007).

REFERENCES

Archives Consulted

Riksarkivet, Stockholm (The Swedish National Archives, abbrev. RA)
Stockholms stadsarkiv (Stockholm City Archive, abbrev. SA)
Jan Inghes samling/Stockholms stadsarkiv (abbrev. JIS/SA)
Kungliga Biblioteket, Stockholm (Royal Library/The National Library of Sweden, abbrev. KB)
Action Archive, Stockholm
ArkDes, Stockholm (Centre for Architecture and Design, abbrev. AD)
Berg Arkitektkontor (files currently in the authors possession)
Moderna Museet, Stockholm
Stockholms fastighetskontor (Stockholm Real Estate Department, abbrev. SFA)
Stockholms gatukontor (Stockholm Traffic Department, abbrev. GK)
Stockholms stadsbyggnadskontor (Stockholm Town-Building Office, abbrev. SBK)

Published Sources

Allen, Marjory, "Why not use our Bomb Sites like this?," *Picture Post*, November 16, 1946.
Alm, Ulla, *Cooperative Housing in Sweden* (Stockholm: H.W. Tullberg, 1939).
Asplund, Gunnar, Wolter Gahn, Sven Markelius, Gregor Paulsson, Eskil Sundahl and Uno Åhrén, *Acceptera* (Stockholm: Tiden, 1931).
Bedoir, Fredric, "Tillbaka till staden," *Arkitektur*, no. 7 (1991): 26.
Bengtsson, Mats G., "Alla vuxna är papperstigrar," in *Modellen: En modell för ett kvalitativt samhälle* (Stockholm: Moderna Museet & Bonnier, 1968).
Bergman, Bosse, "Stadens upplösta rum," *Arkitektur*, no. 1 (1980): 3–5.
BiG-gruppen (Elly Berg et al.), *Det lilla kollektivhuset: En modell för praktisk tillämpning* (Stockholm: Byggforskningsrådet, 1982).
Blomberg, Ingela et al., *Levande kollektivhus: Att leva, bo och arbeta i Hässelby familjehotell* (Stockholm: Statens råd för byggnadsforskning 1986).
Boijsen, Wilhelm and Dag Efvergren, *Allaktivitetshus i Skärholmen? En debattinledning* (Vällingby: Svenska Bostäder, 1969).
Bostadsstyrelsen, *God Bostad* (Stockholm: Bostadsstyrelsen, 1954–1967).
Bostadsstyrelsen, *God Bostad: Förslag den 15 april 1970* (Stockholm: Bostadsstyrelsens tekniska byrå, 1970).
Bostadsstyrelsen, *God Bostad 5: Kollektivhus* (Stockholm: Bostadsstyrelsen, 1977).
Boverket, *Socialt hållbar stadsutveckling: En kunskapsöversikt* (Stockholm: Boverket, 2010)
Caldenby, Claes, *Kollektivhus: Sovjet och Sverige omkring 1930* (Stockholm: Statens råd för byggnadsforskning, 1979).
Caldenby, Claes and Åsa Walldén, *Kollektivhuset Stacken* (Göteborg: Korpen, 1984).
Carson, Rachel, *Silent Spring* (Boston: Houghton Mifflin, 1962).
Chalmers tekniska högskola, *Principles for Urban Planning with Respect to Road Safety: The SCAFT Guidelines 1968* (Stockholm: The National Road Administration and the National Board of Urban Planning, 1968).

References

Danish Government, *Ét Danmark uden parallelsamfund: Ingen ghettoer i 2030* (København: Økonomi- og Indenrigsministeriet, 2018).

Demokratiutredningen, *En uthållig demokrati! Sammanfattning av Demokratiutredningen: Politik för folkstyrelse på 2000-talet* (Stockholm: Landstingsförbundet, 2000).

Edblom, Mats, "En boll är en boll är en boll," *Arkitektur*, no. 5 (1989): 30–1.

Egelius, Mats, "BiG prisar de små kollektivhusen," *Arkitektur*, no. 5 (1993): 60–1.

Eriksson, Eva, "Mot 1990-talet: Debatt vid Samfundet St Eriks höstmöte i Musikaliska akademin 18 november 1987," in *Stad i förvandling: Stockholms utveckling från 1930-tal till 1990-tal: Sankt Eriks årsbok*, ed. Björn Hallerdt (Stockholm: Samfundet S:t Erik, 1988).

Feldt, Kjell-Olof, *Den tredje vägen: En politik för Sverige* (Stockholm: Tiden, 1985).

Feldt, Kjell-Olof, *Alla dessa dagar: I regeringen 1982–1990* (Stockholm: Norstedts, 1991).

Franzen, Lars-Olof, "Riv Skärholmen," *Dagens Nyheter*, September 9, 1968.

Gilmore, James H. and B. Joseph Pine II, "Beyond Goods and Services," *Strategy & Leadership* 25, no. 3 (1997): 10–17.

Gilmore, James H. and B. Joseph Pine II, "Satisfaction, Sacrifice, Surprise: Three Small Steps Create One Giant Leap into the Experience Economy," *Strategy & Leadership* 28, no. 1 (2000): 18–23.

Göthlund, Anette, "Arbete i verkstad och zon: Konstpedagogik för barn på Moderna Museet," in *Historieboken: Om Moderna Museet 1958–2008*, eds. Anna Tellgren, Martin Sundberg and Johan Rosell (Stockholm: Moderna Museet, 2008).

Hall, "En rymdålderns Hattstuga," *Dagens Nyheter*, February 19, (1989): 2.

Hedve, Anders, "Jag älskar Skärholmen," in *Skärholmens Centrum 25 år* (Stockholm: Skärholmens hembygdsförening, 1993).

Holm, Lennart, *50 år i bostadspolitiken: 40 bak och 10 fram* (Stockholm: Sabo, 1989).

Holm, Lennart et al., *Förslag till ändring av normerna för bostäder, kapitel 71 Svensk byggnorm (SBN 1980)* (Stockholm: Statens planverk, 1982).

Inghe-Hagström, Jan, "Den nya staden vid Södra station," in *Söder 700: Sankt Eriks årsbok*, ed. Björn Hallerdt (Stockholm: Samfundet S: tErik, 1987).

Jonsson-von Matern, Mona, "Låtsasstaden," *Plan: Tidskrift för planering av landsbygd och tätorter*, no. 3 (1994): 150–5.

Justitiedepartementet, *Offentlighetsprincipen: Kortfattat om lagstiftningen* (Stockholm: Justitiedepartementet, 2015).

Kommunstyrelsens kommitté för kvinnofrågor, *Service och gemenskap där vi bor i Stockholm* (Stockholm: Tiden, 1975).

Konsum Stockholm, *Servicekommitténs utlåtande* (Stockholm: Konsum, 1969).

Krantz, Birgit, "Sammanfattning," in i *Bygga och bo på kvinnors villkor: Rapport fra konferense Rødhus Klit 27–30 august 1981*, eds. Ros-Mari Edström and Kerstin Kärnekull (Stockholm: Nordiska kvinnors bygg- och planforum, 1982).

Krier, Léon, "The City within the City," *A+U*, Tokyo special issue (November 1977): 69–152.

Krier, Léon, "Sodermalm Not the Tavlingsomrade," *Architectural Design*, 54, nos. 7–8 (1984): 77–9.

Krister, Bjurström, "Form and Form, Krier and Holm," *Arkitektur*, no. 4 (1981).

Larsson, Ylva, "Tensta: Förändring under samverkan," *Plan: Tidskrift för planering av landsbygd och tätorten*, no. 3 (1993): 135–41.

Lundahl, Gunilla and Inga-Lisa Sangregorio, *Femton kollektivhus: En idé förverkligas* (Stockholm: Statens råd för byggnadsforskning, 1992).

Lundahl, Gunilla, "Konsten är aktion," in *Konsthantverk i Sverige*, eds. Christina Zetterlund et al. (Tumba: Mångkulturellt centrum, 2015), 107–13.

Manoïlesco, Mihaïl, *Le Siècle du Corporatisme: Doctrine du corporatisme intégral et pur* (Paris: Alcan, 1936).

Marcus, Lars, "Ett liv i parodi," *MAMA: Magasin for modern arkitektur*, no. 4 (1992): 52–7.

Marcuse, Herbert, *Eros and Civilization: A Philosophical Inquiry into Freud* (New York: Vintage, 1955).

References

Marcuse, Herbert, *One-Dimensional Man: Studies in the Ideology of Advanced Industrial Society* (Boston: Beacon Press, 1964).
Moderna, Museet, *Modellen: En modell för ett kvalitativt samhälle* (Stockholm: Moderna Museet & Bonnier, 1968).
Mossige-Norheim, Randi, "Globen: Storföretagens lekstuga," *Folket i bild/Kulturfront*, no. 23 (1988): 3.
Myrdal, Alva and Gunnar Myrdal, *Kris i befolkningsfrågan* (Stockholm: Bonnier, 1934).
Nilsson, Hjördis, "Om att kräva ansvar och ge förtroende," in *Modellen: En modell för ett kvalitativt samhälle* (Stockholm: Moderna Museet & Bonnier, 1968).
Nylén, Leif, "Aktioner, alternativ," *Paletten* 29, no. 4 (1968): 12.
Ohlin, Bengt, "Some Notes on the Stockholm Theory of savings and Investment I," *Economic Journal* 47 (1937): 221–40.
Pleijel, Agneta and Lars Sjögren, "Arkiv Samtal: Intervju med Anders Svensson mars 1969," *Zenit. Nordisk socialistisk tidskrift*, no. 13 (1969): 36.
Reich, Wilhelm, *The Mass Psychology of Fascism* (New York: Orgone Institute Press, 1946).
Riksdagstrycket (Swedish Parliamentary Papers).
Roos, Anna Maria, *Hem och hembygd i Önnemo* (Stockholm: Bonnier, 1915).
Schultz, Theodore, "The Emerging Economic Scene and its Relation to High School Education," in *The High School in a New* Era. *Papers Presented at the Conference on the American High School at the University of Chicago, October 28–30,1957*, eds. Francis S. Chase and Harold A. Anderson (Chicago: University of Chicago press, 1958).
Schultz, Theodore, *The Economic Value of Education* (New York: Columbia University Press, 1963).
Schultz, Theodore, *Investment in Human Capital: The Role of Education and of Research* (New York: Free Press, 1971).
Schumpeter, Joseph, *Business cycles: A Theoretical, Historical, and Statistical Analysis of the Capitalist Process* (New York: McGraw-Hill, 1939).
Sveriges Socialdemokratiska Arbetareparti, *Framtiden i folkets händer: Socialdemokratiskt program för medborgarskap och valfrihet* (Stockholm: Tiden, 1984).
Sjödin, Gun, "Bostadsnormering: I morgon är idag i går," *Att bo: Tidskrift för bostadskooperation och bostadspolitisk debatt* 22, no. 6 (1972): 17–19.
Sjöstrand, Ingrid, "Samhemmet på väg?," *Arkitekttidningen*, no. 12–13 (1970): 9–10.
Smithson, Alison, ed., *Team 10 Primer* (London: Studio Vista, 1968).
Smithson, Alison and Peter Smithson, "Mobility: Road Systems," *Architectural Design* 28, no. 10 (1958): 385–8.
Snis, Anita, "Hyresgästerna bestämmer hur husen ska byggas om," *BoFast: Tidning för bostäder och fastighetsförvaltning*, no. 8 (1991): 18.
Söderqvist, Lisbeth, "Programmet som inte finns," *Arkitekten* (September, 2008).
Statens planverk "Introduction to Svensk Byggnorm 1967," in *Svensk byggnorm 67: Föreskrifter, råd och anvisningar för byggnadsväsendet utfärdade med stöd av 76 § byggnadsstadgan/BABS 1967* (Stockholm: Statens Planverk, 1968).
Stockholms stadsfullmäktiges handlingar (Stockholm City Council Papers).
Svensk Författningssamling (Swedish Code of Statues).
Svenska Bostäder, *Skärholmen* (Stockholm: Svenska Bostäder, 1968).
Vestbro, Dick Urban, *Kollektivhus från enkökshus till bogemenskap* (Stockholm: Statens råd för byggnadsforskning, 1982).
Westman, Torsten, "Gränser," *Arkitektur*, no. 1 (1983): 18.
Zetterstad, David, "Stadsmässighetens tidevarv," *Valör: Konstvetenskapliga studier och forskning*, no. 5 (1992): 20–33.

References

Newspapers

Aftonbladet (Stockholm)
Arbetaren (Stockholm)
Dagens Nyheter (Stockholm)
Expressen (Stockholm)
Göteborgs-Posten (Göteborg)
Hudiksvallstidningen (Hudiksvall)
Stockholms-Tidningen (Stockholm)
Svenska Dagbladet (Stockholm)
The Economist (London)

Swedish Government Official Reports (Statens Offentliga Utredningar, SOU)

SOU 1952:38, *Hemhjälp. Bostadskollektiva kommitténs betänkande 1* (Stockholm: Socialdepartementet, 1952).
SOU 1954:3, *Kollektivhus. Bostadskollektiva kommitténs betänkande II* (Stockholm: Socialdepartementet, 1955).
SOU 1955:28, *Samlingslokaler. Bostadskollektiva kommitténs betänkande IV* (Stockholm: Socialdepartementet, 1955).
SOU 1955:8, *Tvätt. Bostadskollektiva kommitténs betänkande III* (Stockholm: Socialdepartementet, 1955).
SOU 1956:32, *Hemmen och samhällsplaneringen. Bostadskollektiva kommmitténs slutbetänkande* (Stockholm: Socialdepartementet, 1956).
SOU 1965:32, *Höjd bostadsstandard. Betänkande avgivet av Bostadsbyggnadsutredningen* (Stockholm: Inrikesdepartementet, 1965).
SOU 1968:3, *Upphandling av stora bostadsprojekt: Delbetänkande avlämnat av Byggindustrialiseringsutredningen* (Stockholm: Inrikesdepartementet, 1968).
SOU 1968:38, *Boendeservice 1. Fakta och synpunkter sammanställda av den statliga servicekommittén* (Stockholm: Inrikesdepartementet, 1968).
SOU 1969:63, *Rationellt småhusbyggande: Betänkande av Byggindustrialiseringsutredningen* (Stockholm: Inrikesdepartementet, 1969).
SOU 1971:52, *Byggandets industrialisering: Betänkande avgivet av Byggindustrialiseringsutredningen* (Stockholm: Inrikesdepartementet, 1971).
SOU 1974:21, *Markanvändning och byggande: Principer för lagstiftning: Betänkande avgivet av bygglagsutredningen* (Stockholm: Bostadsdepartementet, 1974).
SOU 1975:17, *Markanvändning och byggande. Remissammanställning* (Stockholm: Bostadsdepartementet, 1975).
SOU 1979:66, *Ny plan- och bygglag, del 2: Betänkande av PBL-utredningen: Markanvändning och byggande* (Stockholm: Bostadsdepartementet, 1979).
SOU 1982:9, *Ny plan- och bygglag: Remissammanställning sammanställd av Bostadsdepartementet* (Stockholm: Bostadsdepartementet, 1982).
SOU 1983:59, *Kreativ finansiering: Slutbetänkande av utredningen angående de små och medelstora företagens finansiella situation* (Stockholm: Finansdepartementet, 1983), 21.
SOU 1989:68, *Storstadens partier och valdeltagande 1949–1988: Underlagsrapport från Storstadsutredningen* (Stockholm: Statsrådsberedningen, 1989).
SOU 1990:36, *Storstadsliv: Rika möjligheter—hårda villkor: Slutbetänkande av storstadsutredningen* (Stockholm: Statsrådsberedningen, 1990).
SOU 1990:44, *Demokrati och makt i Sverige: Maktutredningens huvudrapport* (Stockholm: Statsrådsberedningen, 1990).

References

SOU 1992:24, *Avreglerad bostadsmarknad. Delbetänkande av utredningen om statens stöd för bostadsfinansieringen* (Stockholm: Finansdepartementet, 1992).
SOU 1992:47, *Avreglerad bostadsmarknad, Del II: Slutbetänkande av utredningen om statens stöd för bostadsfinansieringen* (Stockholm: Finansdepartementet, 1992).
SOU 1996:55, *Sverige, framtiden och mångfalden: Slutbetänkande från Invandrarpolitiska kommittén* (Stockholm: Arbetsmarknadsdepartmentet, 1996).
SOU 1999:121, Jörgen Hermansson et al., *Avkorporativisering och lobbyism: Konturerna till en ny politisk modell: Demokratiutredningens forskarvolym XIII* (Stockholm: Fakta info direkt, 1999).

Interviews etc

Ahlqvist, Bengt, interview by the author, February 1, 2013.
Alenius, Stefan, interview by the author, October 28, 2014.
Berg, Svante, interview by the author, Stockholm, March 6, 2010.
Bergman, Bosse, interview by the author, October 23, 2015.
Blücher, Gösta, interview by the author, Stockholm, February 18, 2016.
Lorentzi, Sven, interview by the author, Stockholm, August 19, 2016.
Lundahl, Gunilla, interview by the author, October 10, 2014.
Wickman, Kerstin, e-mail conversation with the author, March 26, 2020.

Seminars and Lectures

Action Archive, "Witness seminar with BiG: Ingela Blomberg, Kerstin Kärnekull, Gunilla Lundahl, Ann Norrby, Inga-Lisa Sangregorio, Sonja Vidén," Arkitektur- och designcentrum/ ARKDES, Stockholm, April 12, 2019 (transcript in the authors possession).
Action Archive, "Witness Seminar Concerning the Event of the International Housing Renewal Conference in Tensta 1989," Tensta konsthall (Tensta Art Hall), Stockholm, March 5, 2014 (transcript in the authors possession).
Doucet, Isabelle, Tahl Kaminer, Simon Sadler and Timothy Stott, "The Anarchist Child: Four Readings of The Child in the City" (paper presentation, EAHN Sixth International Meeting, June 2–5, 2021, Edinburgh, online).
Hummel, Claudia, "Spielklub (Lekklubb) 1970/2020," lecture, Konsthall C, Hökarängen/ Stockholm, August 13, 2021.
Kajita, Heidi Svenningsen, Jennifer Mack, Svava Riesto and Meike Schalk, "Between Technologies of Power and Notions of Solidarity" (paper, International Conference: Spaces of Welfare, The Royal Danish Academy, May 6–7, 2021, online).

Film, Radio, and TV

"For a Better World" (film), by Priscila Fernandes, 2012.
"Forum" (TV-show), Sveriges Television, TV 1, October 1, 1968, Svensk Mediedatabas, Kungliga Biblioteket (Royal Library), Stockholm.
"Kidzania Dubai: An Interactive City, Run by Kids" (film), accessed February 27, 2022, https:// dubai.kidzania.com/en-ae/pages/what-is-kidzania
"I välfärden: Är kollektivhus lösningen på det allt dyrare boendet?" (radio program), Sveriges Radio, P1, June 5, 1982, Svensk Mediedatabas, Kungliga Biblioteket (Royal Library), Stockholm.

References

Digital Sources

Althorpe, Mike, "The Car and The Elephant: The Story of Reconstruction at The Elephant and Castle," accessed February 26, 2022, http://thecarandtheelephant.com.

Andersson, Roger, Lena Magnusson Turner and Emma Holmqvist, "Contextualizing Ethnic Residential Segregation in Sweden: Welfare, Housing and Migration-Related Policies," Country report for Sweden, December 2010, Norface, accessed January 27, 2022, http://uu.diva-portal.org/smash/record.jsf?pid=diva2%3A472568&dswid=896.

Aureli, Pier Vittoria et al., "Promised Land: Housing from Commodification to Cooperation," e-flux Architecture, December 2019, accessed October 1, 2021, https://www.e-flux.com/architecture/collectivity/304772/promised-land-housing-from-commodification-to-cooperation/.

Avermaete, Tom and Davidovici at ETH Zürich/gta, "Building the Commons: An Alternative Architectural History of the European City," accessed February 1, 2022, https://www.gta.arch.ethz.ch/researchprojects/building-the-commons-an-alternative-architectural-history-of-the-european-city.

Berg, Sofie et al., "Bygglekplatsen: En möjlighet idag," *Movium Fakta*, no. 2 (2020), accessed June 17, 2021, https://www.movium.slu.se/system/files/news/14473/files/movium_fakta_2_2020-bygglek-final-web.pdf.

Fallov, Mia Arp and Rasmus Hoffman Birk, "The 'Ghetto' Strikes Back: Resisting Welfare Sanctions and Stigmatizing Categorizations in Marginalized Residential Areas in Denmark," *Nordic Social Work Research*, published online, June 7, 2021, accessed January 21, 2022, https://doi.org/10.1080/2156857X.2021.1937289.

Fernandes, Priscila, "For a Better World," 2012, accessed March 1, 2022, https://priscilafernandes.net/projects/for-a-better-world.

Kidzania Dubai: An Interactive City, Run by Kids, accessed February 27, 2022, https://dubai.kidzania.com/en-ae/pages/what-is-kidzania.

Laval, Christian, "May '68: Paving the Way for the Triumph of Neoliberalism? Rereading the Event with Foucault and Bourdieu', *La Deleuziana. Online Journal of Philosophy*, no. 8 (2018), http://www.ladeleuziana.org/2018/12/31/8-la-pensee-dix-huit/.

Mack, Jennifer, "Impossible Nostalgia: Green Affect in the Landscapes of the Swedish Million Programme," *Landscape Research*, published online, January 16, 2021, accessed March 1, 2022, https://doi.org/10.1080/01426397.2020.1858248.

"1976–1990: Bostadsbeståndet förbättras och förvaltningen utvecklas," accessed January 25, 2021, https://www.allmannyttan.se/historia/historiska-epoker/1976-1990-bostadsbestandet-forbattras-och-forvaltningen-utvecklas/.

Pries, Johan, Erik Jönsson and Don Mitchell, "Parks and Houses for the People," *Places Journal*, May 2020, accessed April 11, 2021, https://doi.org/10.22269/200512.

Nadasen, Premilla, "How Capitalism Invented the Care Economy," *The Nation*, July 16, 2021, accessed October 3, 2021, https://www.thenation.com/article/society/care-workers-emotional-labor/.

Sparsam, Jan, et. al., "The Renewal of a Critical Theory of capitalism and Crises: A Comment on Nancy Fraser's Interpretation of Polanyi's work," Working Paper 2014:17 der DFG-KollegforscherInnengruppe Postwachstumsgesellschaften, Friedrich-Schiller-Universität, Jena (2014), ResearchGate.net, accessed January 25, 2022, https://www.researchgate.net/publication/315701485_The_Renewal_of_a_Critical_Theory_of_Capitalism_and_Crisis_-_A_Comment_on_Nancy_Fraser%27s_Interpretation_of_Polanyi%27s_works.

Swyngedouw, Erik, "Illiberalism and the Democratic Paradox: The Infernal Dialectic of Neoliberal Emancipation," *European Journal of Social Theory*, published online, June 30, 2021, https://doi.org/10.1177%2F13684310211027079, 2.

References

Tronti, Mario, "Factory and Society" [1963], trans. Guio Jacinto, *Operaismo in English*, accessed May 1, 2021, https://operaismoinenglish.wordpress.com/2013/06/13/factory-and-society.

Literature

Adkins, Lisa, Melinda Cooper and Martijn Konings, *The Asset Economy: Property Ownership and the New Logic of Inequality* (Cambridge: Polity Press, 2020).
Aggregate, eds., *Governing by Design: Architecture, Economy, and Politics in the Twentieth Century* (Pittsburgh: Pittsburgh university Press, 2012).
Akcan, Esra, *Open Architecture: Migration, Citizenship, and the Urban Renewal of Berlin-Kreuzberg by IBA—1984/87* (Basel: Birkhauser Verlag GmbH, 2018).
Almqvist, Roland, *New Public Management: NPM om konkurrensutsättning, kontrakt och kontroll* (Malmö: Liber, 2006).
Åmark, Klas, *Hundra år av välfärdspolitik: Välfärdsstatens framväxt i Norge och Sverige* (Umeå: Boréa, 2005).
Andersson, Jenny (ed.), "Special Issue: Images of Sweden and the Nordic Countries," *Scandinavian Journal of History* 34, no. 3 (2009).
Andersson, Jenny, *The Library and the Workshop: Social Democracy and Capitalism in the Knowledge Age* (Stanford: Stanford University Press, 2010).
Andersson, Jenny, "Drivkrafterna bakom nyliberaliseringen kom från många olika håll," *Tidskriften Respons*, no. 1 (2020): 19–23.
Andersson, Jenny and Kjell Östberg, *Sveriges historia: 1965–2012* (Stockholm: Norstedts, 2013).
Andersson, Monica, *Politik och stadsbyggande: Modernismen och byggnadslagstiftningen* (diss. Stockholms universitet, Stockholm: Stockholms universitet, 2009).
Arestis, Philip and Malcolm Sawyer, "Economics of the 'Third Way': Introduction," in *The Economics of the Third Way*, eds. Philip Arestis and Malcolm Sawyer (Cheltenham: Edward Elgar Publishing), 6–7.
Avermaete, Tom and Dirk van der Heuvel, "Obama, please tax me! Architecture and the politics of redistribution," *Footprint* 5, no. 2 (2011): 1–4.
Axioti, Eleni A., "Architecture as an Apparatus of Governance: (British) Architecture from the Welfare State to the State of Neoliberal Workfare" (unpublished diss. Architectural Association/ The Open University, London, 2019).
Bang Larsen, Lars, "True Rulers of their Own Realm: Political Subjectivations in Palle Nielsen's The Model—A Model for a Qualitative Society," *Afterall. A Journal of Art, Context and Enquiry* 16, no. 16 (Autumn/Winter, 2007): 120–6.
Bang Larsen, Lars, *The Model: A Model for a Qualitative Society* (Barcelona: Museu d'Art Contemporani Barcelona, 2010).
Becker, Gary, "Investment in Human Capital: A Theoretical Analysis," *Journal of Political Economy* 70, no. 5, part 2 (1962): 9–49.
Becker, Gary, *Human Capital: A Theoretical and Empirical Analysis, With Special Reference to Education* (New York: Columbia University Press, 1964).
Becker, Gary, *Human Capital: A Theoretical and Empirical Analysis, With Special Reference to Education*, 3rd ed. (Chicago: The University of Chicago Press, 1993).
Bengtsson, Bo, "Sverige: Kommunal allmännytta och korporativa särintressen," in *Varför så olika? Nordisk bostadspolitik i jämförande historiskt ljus*, ed. Bo Bengtsson (Malmö: Égalité, 2006).
Bengtsson, Erik, "The Swedish *Sonderweg* in Question: Democratization and Inequality in Comparative Perspective, c. 1750–1920," *Past and Present* 244, no. 1, (2019): 123–61.
Bengtsson, Erik, *Världens jämlikaste land?* (Lund: Arkiv förlag, 2020).

References

Benjamin, Walter, *Illuminations: Essays and Reflections*, trans. Harry Zohn (New York: Schocken Books: 1969).
Berg, Annika, Urban Lundberg and Mattias Tydén, *En svindlande uppgift: Sverige och biståndet 1945–1975* (Stockholm: Ordfront, 2021).
Bjereld, Ulf and Marie Demker, *1968: När allt började*, paperback ed. (Stockholm: Hjalmarson & Högberg, 2018).
Björkman, Helena and Martin Nauclér, eds., *Stockholm Globe Arena: A Document on its Conception and Creation* (Stockholm: Byggförlaget, 1989).
Blanck, Dag and Mattias Tydén, "Becoming Multicultural? The Development of Swedish Immigrant Policy," in *Welfare States in Trouble: Historical Perspectives on Canada and Sweden*, eds. Sune Åkerman and Jack L. Granatstein (Umeå: Swedish Science Press, 1995).
Bloch, Charlotte, "Om forskel mellem det kendte og det endnu-ikke-kendte," in *Hverdagsliv, kultur og subjektivitet*, eds. Charlottee Bloch et al. (København: Akademisk Forlag, 1988).
Block, Fred, "Introduction," in Karl Polanyi, *The Great Transformation: The Political and Economic Origins of Our Time*, 2nd Beacon Paperback ed. (Boston: Beacon Press, 2001).
Blomberg, Jesper, *Ordning och kaos i projektsamarbete* (Stockholm: EFI, 1995).
Blomkvist, Pär, *Den goda vägens vänner. Väg- och billobbyn och framväxten av det svenska bilsamhället 1914–1959* (diss., Stockholms universitet, Stockholm: Symposion, 2001).
Blomqvist, Paula and Joakim Palme, "Universalism in Welfare Policy: The Swedish Case 1990," *Social Inclusion* 8, no. 1 (2020): 114.
Booth, Chris and Rose Gilroy, "Gender-Aware Approaches to Local and Regional Development", *The Town Planning Review* 72, no. 2 (2001): 217–42.
Boréus, Kristina, *Högervåg: Nyliberalismen och kampen om språket i offentlig debatt, 1969–1989* (Stockholm: Tiden, 1994).
Boltanski, Luc and Eve Chiapello, *The New Spirit of Capitalism* (London: Verso, 2006).
Bourdieu, Pierre, "The Forms of capital," in *Handbook of Theory and Research for the Sociology of Education*, ed. John G. Richardson (Westport: Greenwood Press, 1986).
Braithwaite, John, *Regulation, Crime, Freedom* (Farnham: Ashgate, 2000).
Braithwaite, John, *Regulatory Capitalism: How it Works, ideas for Making it Work Better* (London: Edward Elgar, 2009).
Braun, Lily, *Frauenarbeit und Hauswirtschaft* (Berlin: Buchhandlung Vorwärts, 1901).
Brenner, Neil, *New State Spaces: Urban Governance and the Rescaling of Statehood* (Oxford: Oxford University Press, 2004).
Brenner, Neil, Jamie Peck and Nik Theodore, "Variegated Neoliberalization: Geographies, Modalities Pathways," *Global Networks* 10, no. 2 (2010): 1–4.
Brown, Lori and Karen Burns, eds., *Bloomsbury Global Encyclopedia of Women Architecture, 1960–2015* (London: Bloomsbury, forthcoming).
Brown, Michael K., ed., *Remaking the Welfare State: Retrenchment and Social Policy in America and Europe* (Philadelphia: Temple University Press, 1988).
Brown, Wendy, *Undoing the Demos: Neoliberalism's Stealth Revolution* (New York: Zone Books, 2015).
Caldenby, Claes, Jöran Lindwall and Wilfried Wang, eds., *20th Century Architecture, 4: Sweden* (München: Prestel, 1998).
Caldenby, Claes, Pernilla Hagbert and Cathrin Wasshede, "The Social Logic of Space: Community and Detachment," in *Contemporary Co-Housing in Europe. Towards Sustainable Cities?* (London & New York: Routledge, 2020).
Carlsson, Ingvar, *Så tänkte jag: Politik & dramatik* (Stockholm: Hjalmarson & Högberg, 2003).
Childs, Marquis W., *Sweden: The Middle Way* (New Haven: Yale University, 1936).
Christiansen, Niels Finn et al., eds., *The Nordic Model of Welfare: A Historical Reappraisal* (Copenhagen: University of Copenhagen & Museum Tusculanum Press, 2006).

References

Coleman, James S., "Social Capital in the Creation of Human Capital," *American Journal of Sociology* 94, Supplement (1988): S95–S120.
Coleman, James S., *Foundations of Social Theory* (Cambridge Mass.: Harvard University Press, 1990).
Collier, Paul, *Exodus: How Migration is Changing the World* (Oxford: Oxford University Press, 2013).
Cooper, Melinda, *Family Values: Between Neoliberalism and the New Social Conservatism* (New York: Zone Books, 2017).
Cornwall, Andrea, "Introduction: New democratic Spaces? The Politics and Dynamics of Institutionalised Participation," *IDS Bulletin* 35, no. 2 (2004): 1–10.
Cowman, Krista, "'The Atmosphere is Permissive and Free': The Gendering of Activism in the British Adventure Playgrounds Movement, ca 1948–70," *Journal of Social History* 53, no. 1 (2019): 218–41.
Creagh, Lucy, "From *acceptera* to Vällingby: The Discourse of Individuality and Community in Sweden (1931–54)," *Footprint* 5, no. 2 (2011): 5–24.
Creagh, Lucy, Helena Kåberg and Barbara Miller Lane, eds., *Modern Swedish Design: Three Founding Texts* (New York: Museum of Modern Art, 2008).
Cupers, Kenny, *The Social Project: Housing Postwar France* (Minneapolis: University of Minnesota Press, 2014).
Cupers, Kenny, Catharina Gabrielsson and Helena Mattsson, eds., *Neoliberalism on the Ground: Architecture and Transformations From the 1960s to the Present* (Pittsburgh: University of Pittsburgh Press, 2020).
Dahl, Robert A., *A Preface to Democratic Theory* (Chicago: The University of Chicago Press, 1956).
Dahlstedt, Magnus, "The Politics of Activation: Technologies of Mobilizing 'Multiethnic Suburbs' in Sweden," *Alternatives: Global, Local, Political* 33, no. 4 (2008): 481–504.
Dalla Costa, Mariarosa, "Women and the Subversion of the Community" (1972), in *Women and the Subversion of the Community: A Mariarosa Dalla Costa Reader*, ed. Camille Barbagallo (Oakland: PM Press, 2019).
Davidoff, Paul, "Advocacy and Pluralism in Planning," *Journal of the American Institute of Planners* 32, no. 4 (1965): 331–8.
Davidson, Alexander, *A Home of One's Own: Housing Policy in Sweden and New Zeeland from the 1940s to the 1990s* (Stockholm: Almqvist & Wiksell International, 1994).
Davidson, Robert J., "After Accommodation? Inclusion and Exclusion of Emancipation Interests in Dutch 'Democratic Corporatism,'" *Acta Politica* 56, no. 1 (2021): 163–80.
Deamer, Peggy, ed., *Architecture and Capitalism: 1845 to the Present* (London: Routledge, 2013).
Deeming, Christopher, "The Lost and New 'Liberal World' of Welfare Capitalism: A Critical Assessment of Gøsta Esping-Andersen, *The Three Worlds of Welfare Capitalism* a Quarter Century Later," *Social Policy & Society* 16, no. 3 (2017): 405–22.
Deleuze, Gilles and Felix Guattari, *A Thousand Plateaus: Capitalism and Schizophrenia* (Minneapolis: University of Minnesota Press, 1987).
Deleuze, Gilles and Félix Guattari, *Anti-Oedipus: Capitalism and Schizophrenia*, trans. Robert Hurley et al. (Minneapolis: University of Minnesota Press, 1996 [1972]).
Dennis, Bengt, *500%* (Stockholm: DN, 1998).
Didelon, Valery, "Surfing the Wave of Neoliberalism: Rem Koolhaas in Lille" in *Neoliberalism on The Ground: Architecture and Transformation From the 1960s to the Present*, eds. Kenny Cupers, Catharina Gabrielsson and Helena Mattsson (Pittsburgh: University of Pittsburgh Press, 2020).
Donzelot, Jacques, *The Policing of Families*, trans. Robert Hurley (Baltimore: The Johns Hopkins University Press, 1997).

References

Doucet, Isabelle, *The Practice Turn in Architecture: Brussels after 1968* (Farnham: Ashgate, 2015).

Doucet, Isabelle, "Environmental Learning Revisited: Cities, Issues, Bodies," in *Architectural Education Through Materiality: Pedagogies of the 20th-Century Design*, eds. Elke Couchez and Rajesh Heynickx (London: Routledge, 2021).

Edling, Nils, "The primacy of Welfare Politics: Note on the Language of the Swedish Social Democrats and their Adversaries in the 1930s," in *Multi-layered Historicity of the Present: Approaches to Social Science History*, eds. Heidi Haggren, Johanna Rainio Niemi and Jussi Vauhkonen (Helsinki: University of Helsinki, 2013), 125–50.

Edling, Nils (ed.), *The Changing Meanings of the Welfare State: Histories of a Key Concept in the Nordic Countries* (New York: Berghan, 2019).

Ekstam, Helena, "Om trångboddhet: Hur storleken på våra bostäder blev ett välfärdsproblem," *Sociologisk Forskning* 50, no. 3/4 (2013): 199–222.

Ekstam, Helena, *Trångboddhet: Mellan bostadsstandard och boendemoral* (diss., Uppsala University, Uppsala: Acta Universitatis Upsaliensis, 2016).

Ericson, Richard V. and Aaron Doyle, eds., *Risk and Morality* (Toronto: University of Toronto Press, 2003).

Ericsson, Urban, Irene Molina and Per-Markku Ristilammi, *Miljonprogram och media: Föreställningar om människor och förorter* (Trelleborg: Integrationsverket & Riksantikvarieämbetet, 2002).

Esping-Andersen, Gøsta, *The Three Worlds of Welfare Capitalism* (Cambridge: Polity Press, 1990).

Federici, Silvia, "Marx and Feminism," *tripleC* 16, no. 2 (2018): 468–75.

Federici, Silvia, *Revolution at Point Zero: Housework, Reproduction, and Feminist Struggle* (Oakland: PM Press, 2020).

Foliente, Greg C., "Developments in Performance-based Building Codes and Standards," *Forest Products Journal* 50, no. 7/8 (2000): 12–21.

Forsell, Håkan, ed., *Den kalla och varma staden: Migration i stadsförändring i Stockholm efter 1970* (Stockholm: Stockholmia förlag, 2008).

Foucault, Michel, *History of sexuality, vol. 1: An Introduction*, trans. Robert Hurley (New York: Pantheon Books, 1978).

Foucault, Michel, *The Birth of Biopolitics: Lectures at the Collège de France, 1978–1979*, ed. Michel Senellart, trans. Graham Burchell (Basingstoke: Palgrave Macmillan, 2008).

Foster Gage, Mark, ed., *Aesthetics Equals Politics: New Discourses across Art, Architecture, and Philosophy* (Cambridge, Mass.: MIT Press, 2019).

Francis, Mark and Ray Lorenzo, "Seven Realms of Children's Participation," *Journal of Environmental Psychology* 22, nos. 1–2 (2002): 160.

Fraser, Nancy, "After the Family Wage: A Postindustrial Thought Experiment," in Fraser, *Fortunes of Feminism: From State-Managed Capitalism to Neoliberal Crisis* (London: Verso, 2013).

Fraser, Nancy, *Fortunes of Feminism: From State-Managed Capitalism to Neoliberal Crises* (London/New York: Verso, 2013).

Fraser, Nancy, "Behind Marx's Hidden Abode," *New Left Review*, no. 86 (March/April, 2014): 55–72.

Fromm, Dorit, *Collaborative Communities: Cohousing, Central Living, and Other New Forms of Housing with Shared Facilities* (New York: Van Nostrand Reinhold, 1991).

Fromm, Erich, *Marx's Concept of Man* (New York: F. Ungar Pub. Co., 1961).

Gabrielsson, Catharina, "Through the Anxieties of Style: The Riggering of Neoliberalism and the New Vasa Museum in Stockholm," in *Neoliberalism on The Ground: Architecture and Transformation From the 1960s to the Present*, eds. Kenny Cupers, Catharina Gabrielsson and Helena Mattsson (Pittsburgh: University of Pittsburgh Press, 2020).

Gabrielsson, Catharina and Helena Mattsson, guest, eds., "Special Issue: Solids and Flows— Architecture and Capitalism," *Architecture and Culture* 5, no. 2 (2017): 157–341.

References

Gane, Nicholas, "The Governmentalities of Neoliberalism: Panopticism, Post-Panopticism and Beyond," *The Sociological Review* 60 (2012): 611–34.

Giddens, Anthony, *The Third Way: The Renewal of Social Democracy* (Oxford: Polity Press, 1998).

Gilmore, James H. and B. Joseph Pine II, "Satisfaction, Sacrifice, Surprise: Three Small Steps Create One Giant Leap into the Experience Economy," *Strategy & Leadership* 28, no. 1 (2000): 18–23.

Gordan, Rebecka, "För en blandad befolkning," in *Den kalla och varma staden: migration och stadsförändringar i Stockholm efter 170*, ed. Håkan Forsell (Stockholm: Stockholmia förlag, 2008).

Gorz, André, *Stratégie ouvrière et néocapitalisme* (Paris: Éd. du Seuil, 1964).

Grange, Kristina, *Arkitekterna och byggbranschen: Om vikten att upprätta ett kollektivt självförtroende* (diss. Chalmers tekniska högskola, Göteborg: Chalmers, 2005).

Gromark, Sten, *Boendegemenskap: En kritisk granskning av boendegemenskap som samhällsangelägenhet, av dess värden, villkor och förutsättningar samt exempel på praktisk tillämpning i ett västeuropeiskt sammanhang* (Diss., Chalmers tekniska högskola, Göteborg: Chalmers, 1983).

Hannah-Moffat, Kelly, *Punishment in Disguise: Penal Governance and Federal Imprisonment of Women in Canada* (Toronto: University of Toronto press, 2001).

Harvey, David, *A Brief History of Neoliberalism* (Oxford: Oxford University Press, 2005).

Hayden, Dolores, "What Would a Non-Sexist City Be Like? Speculations on Housing, Urban Design, and Human Work," *Signs* 5, no. 3, Supplement (1980): S170–S187.

Hayden, Dolores, *The Grand Domestic Revolution: A History of Feminist Design for American Homes, Neighborhoods, and Cities* (Cambridge, Mass.: MIT Press, 1981).

Hedenmo, Martin and Fredrik von Platen, *Bostadspolitiken: Svensk politik för boende, planering och byggande under 130 år* (Karlskrona: Boverket, 2007).

Heller, Agnes, *Everyday life*, trans. G.L. Campbell (London: Routledge & Kegan Paul, 1984).

Hermansson, Jörgen et al., *Avkorporativisering och lobbyism: Konturerna till en ny politisk modell: Demokratiutredningens forskarvolym XIII* (Stockholm: Fakta info direkt, 1999).

Hierzer, Eva Maria and Philipp Markus Schörkhuber, "Infrastructural Critique: The Upside Down of the Bottom-Up: A case Study of the IBA Berlin 84/87," *Footprint*, no. 13 (Autumn, 2013): 115–22.

Hiller, Christian et al., eds., *Housing After the Neoliberal Turn: International Case Studies* (Leipzig: Spector Books, 2016).

Hirdman, Yvonne, *Att lägga livet tillrätta: Studier i svensk folkhemspolitik* (Stockholm: Carlsson, 1989).

Hirdman, Yvonne, "The Happy 30s: A Short Story on Social Engineering and Gender Order in Sweden," in *Swedish Modernism: Architecture, Consumption and the Welfare State*, eds. Helena Mattsson and Sven-Olov Wallenstein (London: Black Dog, 2010).

Högström, Ebba, "Building Functional Analysis (BFA) (1964–1985)," in *Bloomsbury Global Encyclopedia of Women Architecture, 1960–2015*, eds. Lori Brown and Karen Burns (London: Bloomsbury, forthcoming).

Holmberg, Daniel and Sverker Sörlin, *Förnyare i forskningslandskapet: KK-stiftelsen 1994–2019* (Stockholm: KK-Stiftelserna, 2019).

Hood, Christopher, "A Public management for all Seasons?," *Public Administration* 69, no. 1 (1991): 3–19

Hood, Christopher, "The 'New Public Management' in the 1980s: Variation on a Theme," *Accounting Organizations & Society* 20, no. 2/3 (1995): 93–109.

Huizinga, Johan, *Homo Ludens: A Study of the Play-Element in Culture* (Boston: Beacon Press, 1955 [1938]).

References

Husz, Orsi and Nikolas Glover, "Between Human Capital and Human Worth: Popular Valuations of Knowledge in 20th-Century Sweden," *Scandinavian Journal of History* 44, no. 4 (2019): 484–509.

Imrie, Rob and Emma Street, *Architectural Design and Regulation* (Chichester: Wiley-Blackwell, 2011).

Jarvis, Helen, "Pragmatic Utopias: Intentional Gender-Democratic and Sustainable Communities," in *Routledge Handbook of Gender and Environment*, ed. Sherilyn MacGregor (London: Routledge, 2017).

Johansen, Mette-Louise E. and Steffen B. Jensen, "'They want us out': Urban Regeneration and the Limits of Integration in the Danish Welfare State', *Critique of Anthropology* 37, no. 3 (2017): 297–316.

Jørgensen, Birte Bech, "Hvorfor gør det ikke noget?," in *Hverdagsliv, kultur og subjektivitet*, eds. Charlottee Bloch et al. (København: Akademisk Forlag, 1988).

Kaika, Maria, "Autistic Architecture: The Fall of the Icon and the Rise of the Serial Object of Architecture," *Environment and Planning D: Society and Space* 29 (2011): 968–92.

Kaminer, Tahl, Miguel Robles-Dúran and Heidi Sohn, eds., *Urban Assymmetries: Studies and Projects on Neoliberal Urbanization* (Rotterdam: nai 010 publishers, 2011).

Kaminer, Tahl, *The Efficacy of Architecture: Political Contestation and Agency* (London: Routledge, 2017).

Klingman, Anna, *Brandscapes: Architecture in the Experience Economy* (Cambridge, Mass.: MIT Press, 2007).

Kockelkorn, Anne, "Palace of Mortgage: The Collapse of a Social Housing Monument in France," in *Neoliberalism on The Ground: Architecture and Transformation From the 1960s to the Present*, eds. Kenny Cupers, Catharina Gabrielsson and Helena Mattsson (Pittsburgh: University of Pittsburgh Press, 2020).

Konings, Martijn, *The Emotional Logic of Capitalism: What Progressives Have Missed* (Stanford: Stanford University Press, 2015).

Koolhaas, Rem, *Small Medium, Large, Extra-Large* (New York: Monacelli cop., 1995).

Koselleck, Reinhardt, *The Practice of Conceptual History: Timing History, Spacing Concepts*, trans. Todd Samuel Presner et al. (Stanford: Stanford University Press, 2002).

Kozlovsky, Roy, "Adventure Playgrounds and Post-war Reconstruction," in *Designing Modern Childhoods: History, Space, and the Material Culture of Children*, eds. Marta Gutman and Ning de Coninck-Smith (New Brunswick: Rutgers University Press, 2008).

Kozlovski, Roy, *The Architectures of Childhood: Children, Modern Architecture and Reconstruction in Postwar England* (London: Ashgate, 2013).

Kragh, Martin, "The 'Wigforss Connection': The Stockholm School vs. Keynes Debate Revisited," *The European Journal of the History of Economic Thought* 21, no. 4 (2014): 635–63.

Krantz, Birgit, "Kvinnovisioner om ett nytt vardagsliv," *Kvinnovetenskaplig tidskrift* 12, no. 2 (1991): 43–53.

Krivy, Maros and Tahl Kaminer "Introduction: Participatory Turn in Urbanism," *Footprint*, no. 13 (Autumn, 2013): 1–6.

Krumholz, Norman, "A Retrospective View of Equity Planning: Cleveland 1969-1979," *Journal of the American Planning Association* 48, no. 2 (1982): 163–74.

LaFond, Michael, ed., *Co-housing Cultures: Handbook for Self-Organized, Community-Oriented and Sustainable Housing* (Berlin: Jovis Verlag, 2012).

Lahiji, Nadir, ed., *Can Architecture be an Emancipatory Project? Dialogues on the Left* (Winchester: Zero Books, 2016).

Lambert, Cornelia, "'Living Machines': Performance and Pedagogy at Robert Owen's Institute for the Formation of Character, New Lanark, 1816-1828," *The Journal of History of Childhood and Youth* 4, no. 3: 419–33.

References

Larsson, Bengt, Martin Letell and Håkan Thörn, eds., *Transformations of the Swedish Welfare State: From Social Engineering to Governance?* (New York: Palgrave Macmillan, 2012).

Lash, Scott and Celia Lury, *Global Culture Industry: The Mediation of Things* (Cambridge: Polity, 2007).

Laval, Christian, "Foucault and Bourdieu: To Each His Own Neoliberalism?," *Sociologia & Antropologia* 7, no. 1 (2017): 63–75.

Lessig, Lawrence, *Code and Other Laws of Cyberspace* (New York: Basic Books, 1999).

Lewin, Leif, "The Rise and Decline of Corporatism: The Case of Sweden," *European Journal of Political Research* 26, no. 1 (1994): 59–79.

Liljeström, Rita, Gunilla Fürst Mellström and Gillan Liljeström Svensson, *Sex Roles in Transition: A Report on a Pilot Program in Sweden: International Women's Year 1975* (Stockholm: Svenska institutet, 1975).

Liljeström, Rita and Edmund Dahlström, *Arbetarkvinnor i hem- arbets- och samhällsliv* (Stockholm: Tiden, 1981).

Lind, Maria and Lars Bang Larsen, eds., *The New Model: An Inquiry* (Berlin: Sternberg press, 2020).

Lind, Maria, Michele Masucci and Joanna Warsza, eds., *Red Love: A Reader on Alexandra Kollontai* (Stockholm & Berlin: Konstfack Collection & Sternberg Press, 2020).

Lindgren, Eva, *Samhällsförändring på väg: Perspektiv på den svenska bilismens utveckling mellan 1950 och 1970* (diss. Umeå universitet, Umeå: Umeå universitet, 2010).

Lloyd, Thomas Katie, "Going into the Mould: Materials and Process in the Material Specification," *Radical Philosophy* 144 (July/August, 2007): 16–25.

Lloyd, Thomas Katie, "'Of their Several Kinds': Forms of Clause in the Architectural Specification," *arq* 16, no. 3 (2012): 229–37.

Lloyd, Thomas Katie, *Building Materials: Material Theory and the Architectural Specification* (London: Bloomsbury Visual Arts, 2021).

Lloyd, Thomas Katie and Tilo Amhoff, "Writing Work: Changing Practices of Architectural Specification," in *The Architect as Worker: Immaterial Labor, the Creative Class and the Politics of Design*, ed. Peggy Deamer (London: Bloomsbury, 2015).

Löschke, Sandra Karina, ed., *Non-Standard Architectural Production: Between Aesthetic Experience and Social Action* (London: Routledge, 2019).

Lucie, Glasheen, "Bombsites, Adventure Playgrounds and Reconstruction of London," *The London Journal* 44, no. 1 (2019): 54–74.

Lundberg, Erik, "Det postkorporativa deltagandet: Intresseorganisationerna i den nationella politiken," in SOU 2015:96, *Låt fler forma framtiden! Forskarantologi: Bilaga till betänkande av 2014 års Demokratiutredning* (Stockholm: Erlanders, 2015).

Lundberg, Urban and Mattias Tydén, "In Search of the Swedish Model: Contested Historiography," in *Swedish Modernism: Architecture, Consumption, and the Welfare State*, eds. Helena Mattsson and Sven-Olov Wallenstein (London: Black Dog, 2010).

Lundgren, Marja, *Performance in the Swedish Building Code* (licentiate thesis, Kungliga tekniska högskolan, Stockholm: KTH, 2019).

Lundin, Per, *Bilsamhället: Ideologi, expertis och regelskapande i efterkrigstidens Sverige* (diss., Kungliga tekniska högskolan, Stockholm: Stockholmia förlag, 2008).

Lynch, Kevin, *A Theory of Good City Form* (Cambridge, Mass.: MIT Press, 1981).

Lyotard, Jean-François, *Libidinal Economy*, trans. Ian Hamilton Grant (Bloomington: Indiana University Press, 1993 [1974]).

Löschke, Sandra Karina, ed., *Non-Standard Architectural Production: Between Aesthetic Experience and Social Action* (London: Routledge, 2019)

Mack, Jennifer, "Hello Consumer! Skärholmen centre from the Million Program to the mall," in *Shopping Towns Europe: Commercial Collectivity and the Architecture of the Shopping Centre, 1945–1975*, eds. Janina Gosseye and Tom Avermaete (London: Bloomsbury Academic, 2017).

References

Mack, Jennifer, *The Construction of Equality: Syriac Immigration and the Swedish City* (Minneapolis: University of Minnesota Press, 2017).

Mack, Jennifer, "An Awkward Technocracy: Mosques, Churches, and Urban Planners in Neoliberal Sweden," *American Ethnologist* 46, no. 1 (2019): 89–104.

Mack, Jennifer, "Renovation Year Zero: Swedish Welfare Landscapes of Anxiety, 1975 to the Present," *Bebyggelsehistorisk tidskrift* 76 (2019): 63–79.

Martin, Reinhold, *Utopia's Ghost: Architecture and Postmodernism, Again* (Minneapolis: University of Minnesota Press, 2010).

Martin, Reinhold, "Epilogue: Neoliberalism and Architecture, Backward" in *Neoliberalism on The Ground: Architecture and Transformation From the 1960s to the Present*, eds. Kenny Cupers, Catharina Gabrielsson and Helena Mattsson (Pittsburgh: University of Pittsburgh Press, 2020).

Martin, Reinhold, *The Urban Apparatus: Mediapolitics and the City* (Minneapolis: University of Minnesota Press, 2016).

Mattsson, Helena, "Designing the Reasonable Consumer: Standardisation and Personalisation in Swedish Functionalism," in *Swedish Modernism: Architecture, Consumption, and the Welfare State*, eds. Helena Mattsson and Sven-Olov Wallenstein (London: Black Dog, 2010).

Mattsson, Helena, "Demonstrations as a Curatorial Practice: The Swedish Exhibition Scene from She to ARARAT, 1966–1977," in *Exhibiting Architecture: A Paradox?*, eds. Eeva-Liisa Pelkonen, Carson Chan and David Andrew Tasman (New Haven: Yale School of Architecture, 2015).

Mattsson, Helena, "Life as a Full Scale Demonstration: Konsument i oändligheten, 1971," in *Place and Displacement: Exhibiting Architecture*, ed. Thordis Arrhenius (Zürich: Lars Müller, 2014).

Mattsson, Helena, "Revisiting Swedish Postmodernism: Gendered Architecture and Other Stories," *Journal of Art History* 85, no. 1 (2016): 109–25.

Mattsson, Helena, "Third Way Architecture: Stockholm Globe City," *Journal of Architecture* 21, no. 1 (2016): 118–41.

Mattsson, Helena, "Shifting Gender and Acting Out History: Is There a Swedish Feminist-Postmodernist Architecture?," in *Feminist Futures of Spatial Practice: Materialism, Activism, Dialogues, Pedagogies, Projections*, eds. Meike Schalk et al. (Braunach: Spurbuchverlag, 2017).

Mattsson, Helena, "1968 Modellen: En modell för ett kvalitativt samhälle" and "1976 ARARAT," in *Exhibit A. Exhibitions That Transformed Architecture 1948–2000*, ed. Eeva-Liisa Pelkonen (New York: Phaidon Press Ltd, 2018).

Mattsson, Helena and Meike Schalk, "Action Archive: Oral History as Performance," in *Speaking of Buildings: Oral history in Architectural Research*, eds. Janina Gosseye, Naomi Stead and Deborah van der Plaat (New York: Princeton Architectural Press, 2019).

McCamant, Kathryn and Charles Durett, *Co-housing. A Contemporary Approach to Housing Ourselves* (Berkeley: Ten Speed Press, 1988).

McLeod, Mary, "Architecture and Politics in the Reagan Era: From Postmodernism to Deconstructivism," *Assemblage* 8, no. 8 (1989): 22–59.

Mincer, Jacob, "Investment in human capital and personal income distribution," *Journal of Political Economy* 66, no. 4 (1958): 281–302.

Mirowski, Philip, *Never Let a Serious Crisis Go to Waste: How Neoliberalism Survived the Financial Meltdown* (London: Verso, 2013).

Mitrašinovic, Miodrag, *Total Landscape, Theme Parks, Public Space* (Aldershot: Ashgate, 2006).

Mitropoulos, Angela, *Contract & Contagion: From Biopolitics to Oikonomia* (New York: Minor Compositions, 2012).

References

Molina, Irene, *Stadens rasifiering: Etnisk boendesegregering i folkhemmet* (diss., Uppsala University, Uppsala: Uppsala University, 1997).
Molina, Irene, "Intersektionella rumsligheter," *Tidskrift för genusvetenskap*, no. 3 (2007): 7–21.
Molina, Oscar and Martin Rhodes, "Corporatism: The Past, Present, and Future of a Concept," *Annual Review of Political Science* 5, no. 1 (2002): 305–31.
Montin, Stig, *Moderna kommuner*, 3rd ed. (Malmö: Liber, 2007).
Moody, Kim, *From Welfare State to Real State: Regime Change in New York City, 1974 to the Present* (New York & London: The New Press, 2007).
Muehlebach, Andrea, *The Moral Neoliberal: Welfare and Citizenship in Italy* (Chicago: University of Chicago Press, 2012).
Ndlovu-Gatsheni, Sabelo J., "Provisional Notes on Decolonizing Research Methodology and Undoing Its Dirty History," *Journal of Developing Societies* 35, no. 4 (2019): 481–92.
Nermo, Magnus, "Hundra år av könssegregering på den svenska arbetsmarknaden," *Sociologisk Forskning* 37, no. 2 (2000): 35–65.
Norberg-Schulz, Christian, *Genius Loci: Towards a Phenomenology of Architecture* (London: Academy, 1980).
O'Kane, Chris, "Critical Theory and the Criticism of Capitalism: An Immanent Criticism of Nancy Fraser's 'Systematic' 'crisis-Criticism' of Capitalism as an 'Institutionalized Social Order,'" *Science & Society* 85, no. 2 (2021): 207–35.
Osman, Michael, *Modernisms Visible Hand: Architecture and Regulation in America* (Minneapolis: University of Minnesota Press, 2018).
Östberg, Kjell, *När allt var i rörelse: Sextiotalsradikaliseringen och de sociala rörelserna* (Stockholm: Prisma/Södertörns högskola, 2002).
Ostrom, Elinor, *Governing the Commons: The Evolution of Institutions for Collective Action* (Cambridge: Cambridge University Press, 1990).
Otero-Pailos, Jorges, *Architecture's Historical Turn: Phenomenology and the Rise of the Postmodern* (Minneapolis: University of Minnesota Press, 2010).
Ottander, Sverker, "Besluten kring Globen-projektet" (seminar paper, Dept. of Human Geography, Stockholm University, 1988).
Patinkin, Don, "On the Relation Between Keynesian Economics and the 'Stockholm School,'" *Scandinavian Journal of Economics* 80, no. 2 (1978): 135–43.
Pech, Christina, *Arkitektur och motstånd: Om sökandet efter alternative i svensk arkitektur 1970–1980* (diss. Kungliga Tekniska högskolan, Stockholm: Makadam förlag, 2011).
Pech, Christina, "Arkitekturmuseets utställning Funktionalismens genombrott och kris: Ett bidrag till historieskrivningen om svensk 1900-tals arkitektur," in *Forskning i centrum*, ed., Monica Sand (Stockholm: Arkdes, 2014).
Peck, Jamie, *Constructions of Neoliberal Reason* (Oxford: Oxford University Press, 2010).
Peck, Jamie, Neil Brenner and Nik Theodore, "Actually Existing Neoliberalism," in *The Sage Handbook of Neoliberalism*, eds. Damien Cahill et al. (New York: Oxford University Press, 2010).
Perers, Maria, "Inside the Ideal Home: Changing Values in the Politics and Design of Apartment Living in Sweden c. 1955–1995" (unpublished diss. Bard Graduate College, New York, 2019).
Pierson, Paul, *Dismantling the Welfare State? Reagan, Thatcher and the Politics of Retrenchment* (Cambridge: Cambridge University Press, 1994).
Piketty, Thomas, *Capital in the Twenty-First Century* (Cambridge, Mass.: Belknap Press, 2014)
Piketty, Thomas, *Capital and Ideology*, trans. Arthur Goldhammer (Cambridge, Mass.: Belknap Press, 2020).
Pimpare, Stephen, "Toward a new Welfare History," *Journal of Policy History* 19, no. 2 (2007): 234–52.
Pine, Joseph B. and James H. Gilmore, *The Experience Economy: Work is Theatre and Every Business a Stage* (Boston: Harvard Business School, 1999).

References

Polanyi, Karl, *The Great Transformation: The Political and Economic Origins of Our Time*, 2nd Beacon Paperback ed. (Boston: Beacon Press, 2001 [1944]).
Pred, Allan, *Recognizing European Modernities: A Montage of the Present* (London: Routledge, 1995).
Premfors, Rune, *Den starka demokratin* (Stockholm: Atlas, 2000).
Pries, Johan, *Social Neoliberalism through Urban Planning: Bureaucratic Formations and Contradictions in Malmö since 1986* (diss. Lund University, Lund: Lund University, 2017).
Psarra, Sophia, ed., *The Production Sites of Architecture* (London: Routledge, 2019).
Putnam, Robert, *Making Democracy Work: Civic tradition in Modern Italy* (Princeton: Princeton University Press, 1992).
Putnam, Robert, *Bowling Alone: The Collapse and Revival of American Community* (New York: Simon & Schuster, 2000).
Rancièr, Jacques and Mark Foster Gage, "Politics Equals Aesthetics: A Conversation Between Jacques Rancièr and Mark Foster Gage," in *Aesthetics Equals Politics: New Discourses Across Art, Architecture, and Philosophy*, ed. Mark Foster Gage (Cambridge, Mass.: The MIT Press, 2019).
Rawes, Peg, "Housing Bipolitics and Care," in *Critical and Clinical Cartographies: Architecture, Robotics, Medicine, Philosophy*, eds. Andrej Radman and Heidi Sohn (Edinburgh: Edinburgh University Press, 2017).
Rice, Charles, *The Emergence of the Interior: Architecture, Modernity, Domesticity* (London: Routledge, 2007).
Rose, Nicholas, *Powers of Freedom: Reframing Political Thought* (Cambridge: Cambridge University Press 1999).
Rosenberg, Frida, *The Construction of Construction: The Wenner-Gren Center and the Possibility of Steel Building in Postwar Sweden* (diss. Kungliga tekniska högskolan, Stockholm: KTH, 2018).
Ross, Kristin, *May 68 and Its Afterlives* (Chicago: University of Chicago Press, 2002).
Ross, Liam, "'Creative Uncertainty: Arup Associates; Fire Safety and the Metaengineering of Government," in *Neoliberalism on the Ground. Architecture and Transformation from the 1960s to the Present*, eds. Kenny Cupers, Catharina Gabrielsson and Helena Mattsson (Pittsburgh: University of Pittsburgh, 2020).
Ross, Liam, *Pyrotechnic Cities: Architecture, Fire-Safety and Standardisation* (London: Routledge, 2022).
Rothstein, Bo, *Den korporativa staten: Intresseorganisationer och statsförvaltning i svensk politik* (Stockholm: Norstedts juridik, 1992).
Rothstein, Bo, *Just Institutions Matter: The Moral and Political Logic of the Universal Welfare State* (Cambridge: Cambridge University Press, 1998).
Rothstein, Bo and Jonas Bergström, *Korporatismens fall och den svenska modellens kris* (Stockholm: SNS Förlag, 1999).
Rudberg, Eva, "Den tidiga funktionalismen: 1930–1940," in *Att bygga ett land: 1900-talets svenska arkitektur*, eds. Thorbjörn Andersson and Claes Caldenby (Stockholm: Byggforskningsrådet, 1998).
Runting, Helen, *Architectures of the Unbuilt Environment* (diss. Kungliga tekniska högskolan, Stockholm: KTH, 2018).
Runting, Helen and Fredrik Torisson, "Managing the Not-Yet: The Architectural Project under Semiocapitalism," *Architecture and Culture* 5, no. 2 (2017): 213–20.
Ruud, Guttorm, *Sites of Crises: Histories of Satellite Town* (diss. The Oslo School of Architecture and Design, Oslo, 2021).
Sadri, Hossein, eds., *Neo-liberalism and the Architecture of the Post-Professional Era* (Cham: Springer, 2018).
Sahlin, Kerstin, *Oklarhetens strategi: Organisering av projektsamarbete* (Lund: Studentlitteratur, 1989).
Salomon, Kim, *Rebeller i takt med tiden: FNL-rörelsen och 60-talets politiska ritualer* (Stockholm: Rabén Prisma, 1996).

References

Sangregorio, Inga-Lisa, *Collaborative Housing in Sweden* (Stockholm & Borås: The Swedish Council for Building Research, 2000).

Schalk, Meike, "Old News from a Contact Zone: Action Archive in Tensta," in *The Social (Re)Production of Architecture: Politics, Values and Actions in Contemporary Practice*, eds. Doina Petrescu and Kim Trogal (London: Routledge, 2017).

Schalk, Meike, Sara Brolund de Carvalho and Helena Mattsson, "BiG Living and Working on Community," in *Architecture and Collective Life*, eds. Penny Lewis, Lorens Holm and Sandra Costa Santos (London: Routledge, 2021).

Schindler, Sara, "Architectural Exclusion: Discrimination Through Physical Design of the Built Environment," *The Yale Law Journal* 124, no. 16 (2015): 1934–2024.

Schmitter, Philippe C., "Still the Century of Corporatism?," *The Review of Politics* 36, no. 1 (1974): 85–131.

Schmitter, Philippe C., "Reflections on Where the Theory of Neo-Corporatism has Gone and Where the Praxis of Neo-Corporatism May be Going," in *Patterns of Corporatist Policy-Making*, eds. Gerhard Lehmbruch and Philippe C. Schmitter (London: Sage, 1982).

Schön, Lennart, *En modern svensk ekonomisk historia: Tillväxt och omvandling under två sekel* (Stockholm: SNS förlag, 2000).

Scott, Felicity, *Architecture or Techno-utopia: Politics after Modernism* (Cambridge, Mass.: MIT Press, 2007).

Scott, Joan, "The Vexed Relationship of Emancipation and Equality," *History of the Present* 2, no. 2 (2012): 157–8.

Shamir, Ronen, "The Age of Responsibilization: On Market-Embedded Morality," *Economy and Society* 37, no. 1 (2008): 1–19.

Sigge, Erik, *Architecture's Red Tape: Government Building Construction in Sweden, 1963–1973* (diss. Kungliga tekniska högskolan, Stockholm: KTH, 2017).

Sjöstrand, Ingrid, *Samhem: En bok om mänsklig miljö i mänsklig skala* (Stockholm: Aldus/Bonnier, 1973).

Smith, Adam, *Wealth of Nations* (Chicago: University of Chicago Press, 1981 [1776]).

Smith, Wergeland Even, *From Utopia to Reality: Motorways as a Work of Art* (diss., Arkitektur- og designhøgskolen, Oslo: AHO, 2013).

Spencer, Douglas, *The Architecture of Neoliberalism: How Contemporary Architecture became an Instrument of Control and Compliance* (New York: Bloomsbury Academic, 2016).

Spencer, Douglas, *Critique of Architecture: Essays on Theory, Autonomy, and Political Economy* (Basel: Birkhäuser, 2021).

Spengler, Joseph J., "The invisible Hand and Other Matters. Adam Smith on Human Capital," *The American Economic Review* 67, no. 1 (1977): 32–6.

Starke, Peter, "The Politics of Welfare State Retrenchment: A Literature Review," *Social Policy & Administration* 40, no. 1 (2006): 104–20.

Strauven, Francis, *Aldo van Eyck: The Shape of Relativity*, rev. ed. (Amsterdam: Architectura & Natura, 1998).

Streeck, Wolfgang and Philippe C. Schmitter, "From National Corporatism to Transnational Pluralism," *Politics & Society* 19, no. 2 (1991): 133–64.

Susanne, Lettow, "Editor's Introduction – Emancipation: Rethinking Subjectivity, Power, and Change," *Hypathia* 30, no. 3 (2015): 501–12.

Tafuri, Manfredo, *Architecture and Utopia: Design and Capitalist Development*, trans. Barbara Luigia La Penta (London: MIT Press, 1976).

Tahvilzadeh, Nazem and Lisa Kings "Under Pressure: Invited Participation Amidst Planning Conflicts," in *Conflict in the City: Contested Urban Spaces and Local Democracy*, eds. Enrico Gualini, Marco Allegra and João Morais Mourato (Berlin: Jovis Verlag GmbH, 2015).

References

Trincidado, Estrella and Manuel Santos-Redondo, "Bentham and Owen on Entrepreneurship and Social Reform," *The European Journal of the History of Economic Thought* 21, no. 2 (2014): 252–77.

Urban, Florian, *Neo-historical East Berlin: Architecture and Urban Design in the German Democratic Republic 1970–1990* (Farnham: Ashgate, 2009).

Vestbro, Dick Urban and Liisa Horelli, "Design for Gender Equality: The History of Co-Housing ideas and Realities," *Built Environment* 38, no. 3 (2012): 315–35.

Wallenstein, Sven-Olov, *Biopolitics and the Emergence of Modern Architecture* (New York: Princeton Architectural, 2009).

Wallenstein, Sven-Olov, "A Family Affair: Swedish Modernism and the Administering of Life," in *Swedish Modernism: Architecture, Consumption and the Welfare State*, eds. Helena Mattsson and Sven-Olov Wallenstein (London: Black Dog, 2010).

Ward, Stephen V., Review of Anna Klingmann's "Brandscapes: Architecture in the Experience economy," *Urban Design International* 13, no. 1 (2008): 53.

Watkins, Heather M., "Beyond Sweat Equity: Community Organizing Beyond the Third Way," *Urban Studies* 54, no. 7 (2017): 2139–54.

Westherdahl, Stig, *Det självspelande pianot: Kalkylerna och kapitalet som skapar Sveriges bostadskris* (Årsta: Dokument Press, 2021).

Wiarda, Howard J., *Corporatism and Comparative Politics: The Other Great "Ism"* (Armonk: M.E. Sharpe, 1997).

Wickström, Martin, "The Difference White Ethnics Made: The Multiculturalist Turn of Sweden in Comparison to the Cases of Canada and Denmark", Heidi vad JØnsson, Elizabeth Onasch, Saara Pellander, and Mats Wickström (eds.) *Migration and Welfare States: Policies, Discourses and Institutions* (Helsinki: Nordic Center of Excellence NordWel, 2013), 25–58.

William-Olsson, Inger and Stina Sandels, *Fri lek i förskolan* (Stockholm: Lärarhögskolan, 1968).

Wuokko, Maiju, "The Curious Compatibility of Consensus, Corporatism, and Neoliberalism: The Finnish Business Community and the Retasking of a Corporatist Welfare State," *Business History* 63, no. 4 (2021): 668–85.

Yúdice, George, *The Expendiency of Culture. The Use of Culture in the Global Era* (Durham and London: Duke University Press, 2003).

Åström, Gertrud and Yvonne Hirdman, eds., *Kontrakt i kris* (Helsingborg: Carlssons, 1992).

INDEX

acceptera (1931, "Accept") 63, 66
Acking, C.-A. 81
Action Dialogue 19–22, 26–33, 37–9, 42–3, 45, 53, 56, 195 n.77
Adkins, L. 2
Agrell, J. 93
Aktionsgruppen för kollektivhus (Action Group for Collective Houses) 206 n.69
Allen, M. 27
allmännyttan (public housing) 67
Alvik project 68, 203 n.31
Åmark, K. 188 n.34
Andersson, J. 11, 98
arbetsboksmodellen (the logbook model) 167, 169
architecture 5–6
    feminist emancipation 153–5
    historiography 183–4
    human capital theory and 99–100
    and postwar neocorporatism 59–60
    as resource 183
    role 1–3, 42–3, 55, 183
    women's movements in 90
assemblage 5–6, 11–12, 21, 182, 186 n.20
Avermaete, T. 3, 197 n.8, 199 n.35, 202 n.22

Backström, A. 180, 231 n.5
Backström & Reinius 71
Backström, S. 180
Baietto, J.-P. 110
barnrikehus (large-family homes) 63
Båstad demonstration 21–2, 192 n.14, 192 n.17
Bech-Jørgensen, B. 89
Becker, G. 97–8, 210 n.1
Bengtsson, A. 27
Benjamin, W. 42
Berg Arkitektkontor 105, 108, 111, 117, 213 n.23
Berg, S. 104–5, 108, 110
Bildt, C. 15, 190 n.65
Bjereld, U. 191 n.6
Blair, T. 15
Blomberg, J. 108
Blücher, G. 125–6, 218 n.19
Boendeservice report (housing services) 74
Bofill, R. 136, 139, 144, 146, 148
Bofill's Arc project 146–7
bogemenskap (living-community) 87
Bo i gemenskap (Live in Community or BiG) 63, 84, 86–9, 90–1, 95, 100, 153, 207 n.82

Boijsen, W. 47, 49, 51, 197 n.13
Boltanski, L. 40–1
Boplats 80 (Habitat 80) 62–3, 85, 95, 135, 139
Bostadsförmedlingen (Public Housing Agency) 91
Bostadskollektiva kommittén (The Collective Housing Committee) 203 n.36
Bostadsociala utredningen (The Report on the Social Condition of Housing) 7
Bourdieu, P. 40, 211 n.18
Boverket's Building Regulations (BBR) 138
Braithwaite, J. 217 n.8
Brandscape (Klingmann) 38
Brattberg, L. 136–7, 141, 222 n.39
Brenner, N. 123
Brown, W. 176
Building Charter 124, 126
building industry 47, 52–3, 55, 107, 125–7
Byalagen 26, 32, 78
Bygglagutredning (BLU) 128
bygglek (building play) 26–30, 35–7

Capital and Ideology (Piketty) 187 n.27
Carlsson, I. 10
Carson, R. 89
Celsing, P. 104, 212 n.2
Chiapello, E. 41, 217 n.70
Children's Day 22–6, 28, 192 n.21
Childs, M. 7
cityfilialer 106–7, 213 n.18
city-likeness 14, 101, 136, 144
Clayford, P. 181
co-housing 64–5, 81, 87, 88, 91, 94, 100–1, 154–5, 201 n.9
Coleman, J. S. 99–100, 211 n.18
collective house 63–4, 209 n.120
    large-scale 65–7
    small-scale 67–73, 95
Collective Housing Committee 59–60, 72–4, 90–1, 95, 204 n.40
Conservative government 9, 15, 171
Cooper, M. 2, 80, 225 n.14
corporatism 6, 16, 45–6, 57–61, 152
countermovement 2, 6, 15, 20–1, 41, 53, 76–81, 85, 95, 152, 181, 225 n.14
creative financing 108, 213 n.20

Index

Dahlstedt, M. 159
Dahlström, M. 177
Dalla Costa, M. 81, 84
Debray, R. 40
decommodification 8
Demker, M. 191 n.6
deregulation 1, 9–10, 12–14, 16, 42, 65, 95, 97, 123, 125–6, 133, 137, 144, 149, 179–81
derivative trade/market 1, 181
Derkert, C. 32, 35
Dismantling the Welfare State? (Pierson) 11
doll's house model 62–3
Donzelot, J. 68, 92–3
Doucet, I. 21
dynamique d'enfer (Baietto) 110

Efvergren, D. 47, 49, 51, 197 n.13
Ekdahl, B. 107
Ekstam, H. 94
Elephant & Castle 179–84
Engqvist, O. 70, 82–3, 203 n.34
environmental guerrillas 19
Erlander, T. 22
Esping-Andersen, G. 8
EuroFem 90, 208 n.100

Fahlström, Ö. 33
Fältöversten 76–7
Familjebostäder (Family Housing) 4, 91, 157, 162–3, 167–8, 171–2, 174, 186 n.18
familjeservice (family service) 74
Färdknäppen 91–2, 209 n.107
Feldt, K.-O. 9–10, 45, 179–80
feminist emancipation 153–5
Fernandes, P. 43
Foliente, G. C. 126
folkhemmet (the People's Home) 7, 33, 65, 187 n.24, 201 n.10, 202 n.15
Forsell, H. 100
Fortunes of Feminism (Fraser) 151, 225 n.13
Foucault, M. 11, 40, 92, 98, 123, 131, 150, 189 n.50, 189 n.54, 210 n.8, 232 n.11
Framtidsformer 183, 190 n.66
Fraser, N. 17, 64, 91, 124, 126, 151, 153–5, 182, 224 n.12, 225 n.13
Freud, S. 42, 164, 191 n.11
Friggebo, B. 138, 221 n.23
frikommuntänkandet (the autonomous approach) 163, 166

Gabrielsson, C. 105, 189 n.56
Giddens, A. 15, 183
Gilmore, J. 38
Globe Arena 16–17, 97, 103, 106, 109, 115, 117–20
Globe City project 57, 61, 98, 100–1, 103–6, 108, 110–13, 115–17, 121–2

God Bostad 5 (Good Housing) 78–80, 93–4, 99, 124–6, 133, 205 n.55, 211 n.17, 218 n.15, 219 n.26
Goodman, P. 175
Gorz, A. 33, 37
Grange, K. 52
Great Transformation, The (Polanyi) 154, 224 n.11
Gyllenhammar, P. G. 51
Gyllensten, L. 53–4

Hackney, R. 166
Hansson, P. A. 66, 187 n.24, 201 n.10
Harpsunddemokratin 8
Harvey, D. 10, 211 n.21
Hässelby Familjehotell (Hässelby Family Hotel) 81–4, 87, 90, 205 n.68
Hayden, D. 63, 203 n.35
Hemgården Centralkök (communal kitchen) 67, 202 n.24
Hirdman, Y. 188 n.36
Höjd bostadsstandard (Improved housing standard) 74, 204 n.42
Höjer-Ljungqvist 79
Holm, L. 127, 138, 218 n.16
Homo Ludens (Huizinga) 26–7
Hovet 109–10, 113–15
HSB Service Center 76, 140–1
Huizinga, J. 26–7
Hultén, P. 32
Hulth, M. 87, 162, 207 n.89
human capital 6, 16, 43, 97–9, 106–7, 115, 143, 150, 211 n.18
economic 100–1
theory and architecture 99–100
Human Capital (Becker) 98

implementation phase 171–2
Improved housing standards 74, 204 n.42
Imrie, R. 123
Inghe-Hagström, J. 131–2, 137, 143–5, 148, 223 n.49, 223 n.61
intensity problem 60
intermediary level 58, 86–7, 90, 95, 100, 207 n.82
Internationella Tennisförbundet (International Tennis Organization) 192 n.14

James, S. 200 n.4
Johansson, A. 172
Johansson, I. 115
John Ericssonsgatan 33, 68–71
Josefsson, I. 107

Kahn, H. 34
Kaminer, T. 231 n.68
Kärnekull, K. 89
Keynes, J. M. 8

Index

Kids Visiting Society 30, 43
KidZania 27, 43
kindergarten 30, 32–3, 35, 37, 66–8, 71, 78–9, 82, 89, 172, 183, 194 n.46
Klingmann, A. 38
kollektivhus (collective house) 65, 93, 182, 204 n.39
Kollektivhuskommittén (Collective Housing Committee) 90
Kollontay, A. 67–8, 203 n.28
Konings, M. 2
Koselleck, R. 152, 224 n.5
Kozlovsky, R. 27
Krantz, B. 89
Krier, L. 131–2, 134, 136, 143, 219 n.1, 220 n.2
Krivy, M. 227 n.14, 231 n.68
Kvarteret Glömmingegränd 157, 162, 167–71
kvartersvärdar (building wardens) 172
Kvinnors Byggforum (Women's Building Forum or KBF) 60, 84, 153, 200 n.14

Lagerstedt, A. 67, 192 n.21, 202 n.24
Låginkomstutredningen (the official inquiry into low incomes) 20
Laing, R. D. 37
Landsorganisationen (LO, the Swedish Trade Union Confederation) 52
Larsson, Y. 157, 168, 172–3
Laval, C. 40
Lessig, L. 124
Lettow, S. 224 n.6
Lex Pysslingen law 89
Library and the Workshop, The (Andersson) 11
Liljeroth, H. 113
Lindroos, B. 141
Lind, S. I. 71
Lloyd Thomas, K. 127
lobbying/lobbyism 39, 57–8, 61, 112
Loggia Arkitekter 157, 167–72, 177
Lundahl, G. 32, 194 n.54
Lundgren, M. 127
Lynch, K. 147, 223 n.58

Mack, J. 158, 161
McLeod, M. 4, 153
Maktutredningen (the Power and Democracy Commission) 58
Manoïlesco, M. 57, 199 n.2
Marieberg Collective House 71
Markelius, S. 66, 68–9, 203 n.31
marketization 2, 38, 65, 91, 94, 124, 128, 137, 151, 154, 182, 189 n.57, 225 n.13
Martin, R. 6, 13, 146
Marx, K. 42, 191 n.11
Million Program 10, 45–6, 52–3, 55, 57, 59, 74, 99, 131, 153, 155, 157–61, 173–4, 181, 198 n.29, 205 n.56, 228 n.31, 232 n.9

Millions for the Million Program 158–9, 162–4, 166
Mincer, J. 98, 210 n.8
Modellen (exhibition) 16, 18–20, 32–7, 42–3, 68, 100
modernism 13–14, 43, 126
Molina, I. 161, 173
Mullvaden 84, 206 n.73
Mussolini, B. 58
Myrdal, A. 60, 66, 68
Myrdal, G. 66, 68

Nadasen, P. 94
National Board of Public Building 124, 219 n.33
neocorporatism 57–60
neoliberalism/neoliberalization 2–6, 9–13, 15–16, 37, 43, 48, 64, 91, 94–5, 106, 123–6, 128–9, 133, 138, 151, 153–5, 159, 161, 172, 174–7, 126, 182–3
  corporatism as 6, 16, 45–6, 57–61, 152
  definition of 11
  effects of 176
  emancipation movements and 39–41, 94, 155
  pre-history of 20–1
  Third Way 126, 151, 154
  trauma of 175
New Everyday Life project 88–90, 100
New Lanark 66, 201 nn.13–14
new public management (NPM) 12–13, 17, 95, 133, 139, 143, 155
Nielsen, P. 19, 27, 32, 35, 37, 194 n.54
Norberg-Schulz, C. 14, 136, 141, 144–6, 148, 223–4 n.61
Nordqvist, L. 179–81
Norman, A.-M. 44
November Revolution 179
Nyckeln 181, 232 n.8
Nylén, L. 38, 45, 105

Ostier, F. 166
Owen, R. 66, 201 n.13, 201–2 n.14

Palme, O. 19–20, 34–5, 45, 56, 179
Parkleken playground 29–30, 194 n.46
Peck, J. 4, 123
performance-based codes 17, 126–8, 132–3, 138–43, 217 n.2, 219 n.36
Pettersson, C.-G. 113
phalanstères 66
Pierson, P. 11
Piketty, T. 2, 7, 187 n.27
Pine, J. 38
Planning Advisory Board (Planeringsberedningen) 222 n.31
Planning and Building Act 4, 158, 177, 183, 230 n.55
Pleijel, A. 38
Polanyi, K. 154, 224 n.11, 225 n.14

Index

postmodernism 6, 13–14, 17
   deregulation and 148–50
   and planning process 134–8
Pred, A. 105
privatization 10, 14, 65, 91, 93, 95, 161–2
progressive public administration (PPA) 13

radikal samordning (radical coordination) 48, 163
Rancière, J. 38–9, 196 n.85
Rawes, P. 128
Reagan, R. 11, 106, 179
Regeneration Area 181
Reilly, W. J. 47, 50, 197 n.10
renewal project 157–9, 161–7, 170–1, 173–7, 182
reregulations 12, 17, 42
resident participation 158–9, 161–4, 167–72, 174, 176
responsibilization 95, 101, 155, 176–7, 230–1 n.66
retrenchment 6, 11–12, 16, 58, 91, 95, 100–1, 143, 155, 159
Rhodesia (Zimbabwe) 21, 192 n.14
Riksbyggen 207 n.91
Röda Söder (Red South) 140–1
Rosengren, B. 141
Ross, K. 40
Ross, L. 128

Saltsjöbadsavtalet (Saltsjöbaden agreement) 8, 188 n.30
samhem (co-home) 76–8, 87
Sangregorio, I.-L. 89, 209 n.112
Sarkozy, N. 40
SBN 80 137–8
Schalk, M. 175
Schindler, S. 176
Schmitter, P. C. 57–8
Schröder, G. 15
Schultz, T. 97–8, 210 n.2, 210 n.8
Schumpeter, J. 98, 101, 211 n.11
Scott, J. 155
Scott, T. 27
Second World War 7, 24, 58, 123–4, 225 n.13
service center 72, 74–6, 95
servicecentraler (service centers) 74
serviceknutar (service points) 74
Servicekommitténs utlåtande 204 n.45
Sherry, J. 38
Sidenbladh, G. 93, 209 n.114
Sigge, E. 126
Silent Spring (Carson) 89
Sjögren, L. 38
Sjöstrand, I. 76, 78, 87
Skärholmen 45–6
   blueprint 46–8
   Centrum 48–9, 51–2, 54–5
   consumer organizations 48–50

housewives of 44–5, 56, 60
Smith, A. 97
Smith, I. 192 n.14
social capital 63, 95, 99–101, 143, 177, 183, 211 n.18, 231 n.70
Social Democrats 7–9, 22, 33, 46, 52, 66, 84, 95, 110, 138, 151, 164, 175, 187 n.24, 198 n.28, 202 n.17
social privatization (social isolation) 91, 93, 95
social reproduction 16, 63–7, 72–6, 81, 84–8, 91, 94–5, 99, 101, 182
Socialtjänstlagen (the Social Services Act) 79
social worker 68
Södra Station 17, 96, 97, 100–1, 106, 126–7, 130–9, 141–50, 183
Sollentuna service house 76–8
Sørensen, C. T. 27
Sörgården 23–5
Stadshypotek 108, 179, 231 n.3
Stark, A. 70
Statens Planverk (the Swedish National Board of Urban Planning) 125, 219 n.26
stealth revolution 172–4, 176
Stockholm
   Chamber of Commerce 46, 49–50
   City of 10, 12–13, 17, 25, 48, 107–8, 110–11, 122, 134, 159, 162, 164
   City Planning Office 14, 48, 50, 106, 113, 131, 136–7, 139, 141, 143, 148, 150, 215 n.39, 221 n.29, 222 n.31, 222 n.40, 223 n.52
   Globe City 10, 57, 61, 98, 100–1, 103, 106, 113, 115, 121, 152
Stockholm Exhibition, The (1930) 7, 63, 131, 220 n.5
Stockholmshem 141
Stolplyckan 79–80, 89
Storstadsutredningen (the Commission on Metropolitan Problems) 100, 228 n.31
Streeck, W. 58
Street, E. 123
supermodel 1, 4, 179
Svedberg, H. 70, 203 n.31
Sveriges Allmännyttiga Bostadsföretag (SABO) 162, 207 n.91
Swedish Association of Architects (SAR) 113
Swedish Building Code (SBN, *Svensk byggnorm*) 123–8, 132, 190 n.60, 205 n.55, 217 n.2, 218–19 n.26
Swedish Central Bank 9–10
Swedish Cooperative Union 74
Swedish Roads Association, The 50–2, 60, 152
Swyngedouw, E. 155

Tafuri, M. 20, 81
80-talets boendeformer (1980s housing forms) 79, 205 n.58

Index

Tarschys, R. 29
Tensta 5, 17, 101, 155, 157–68, 172–8, 182–3
Thatcher, M. 11, 106, 179, 181
Theodore, N. 123
Third Way policy 9–12, 15–16, 40, 43, 95, 97–8, 100–1, 106, 113, 126, 132, 137, 148, 151, 153–5, 176
Third Way, The (Giddens) 15
triple movement (Fraser) 17, 124, 126, 154, 209 n.120, 224 n.12
Tronti, M. 81
Turner, J. 74

utsatta områden (vulnerable areas) 161, 197 n.5

Vägplan för Sverige (Road Plan for Sweden) 51
Vällingby 48, 212 n.6
van den Heuvel, D. 3, 197 n.8, 199 n.35
Vänsterpartiet kommunisterna (The Communist Party) 214 n.33

Värmdömodellen 207 n.91
Vestbro, D. U. 64, 93

Wages for Housework (WfH) 85, 200 n.4, 206 n.77
Wallander, S. 203 n.26
Wallenstein, S.-O. 66
Wealth of Nations (Smith) 97
Westman, T. 137
Wieslander, T. 22, 24–5, 192 n.22
Wigforss, E. 8, 188 n.32
Wiklander, J. 168
Women's Building Forum (WBF) 200 n.14
World Trade Center (Vasaterminalen) 180
Wuokko, M. 61

Yrkeskvinnors Klubb (Professional Women's Club) 70

Zabetski, G. 107

www.ingramcontent.com/pod-product-compliance
Lightning Source LLC
Chambersburg PA
CBHW050348230426
43663CB00010B/2033